CLARETTA

CLARETTA
MUSSOLINI'S LAST LOVER

R. J. B. BOSWORTH

YALE UNIVERSITY PRESS
NEW HAVEN AND LONDON

Copyright © 2017 R.J.B. Bosworth

All rights reserved. This book may not be reproduced in whole or in part, in any form (beyond that copying permitted by Sections 107 and 108 of the U.S. Copyright Law and except by reviewers for the public press) without written permission from the publishers.

For information about this and other Yale University Press publications, please contact:
U.S. Office: sales.press@yale.edu   yalebooks.com
Europe Office: sales@yaleup.co.uk   yalebooks.co.uk

Typeset in Adobe Garamond Pro by IDSUK (DataConnection) Ltd
Printed in Great Britain by TJ International Ltd, Padstow, Cornwall

Library of Congress Cataloging-in-Publication Data

Names: Bosworth, R. J. B., author.
Title: Claretta : Mussolini's last lover / R.J.B. Bosworth.
Description: New Haven : Yale University Press, 2017. | Includes
   bibliographical references and index.
Identifiers: LCCN 2016044930 | ISBN 9780300214277 (cloth : alkaline paper)
Subjects: LCSH: Petacci, Clara, 1912–1945. | Petacci, Clara,
   1912–1945—Diaries. | Mussolini, Benito, 1883–1945—Relations with women. |
   Mistresses—Italy—Biography. | Women fascists—Italy—Biography. |
   Italy—History—1922–1945—Biography. | BISAC: BIOGRAPHY & AUTOBIOGRAPHY /
   Women. | HISTORY / Europe / Italy. | HISTORY / Modern / 20th Century. |
   BIOGRAPHY & AUTOBIOGRAPHY / Presidents & Heads of State.
Classification: LCC DG575.P455 B78 2017 | DDC 945.091092 [B]—dc23
LC record available at https://lccn.loc.gov/2016044930

A catalogue record for this book is available from the British Library.

10 9 8 7 6 5 4 3 2 1

MIX
Paper from
responsible sources
FSC
www.fsc.org   FSC® C013056

For Mimmo Franzinelli

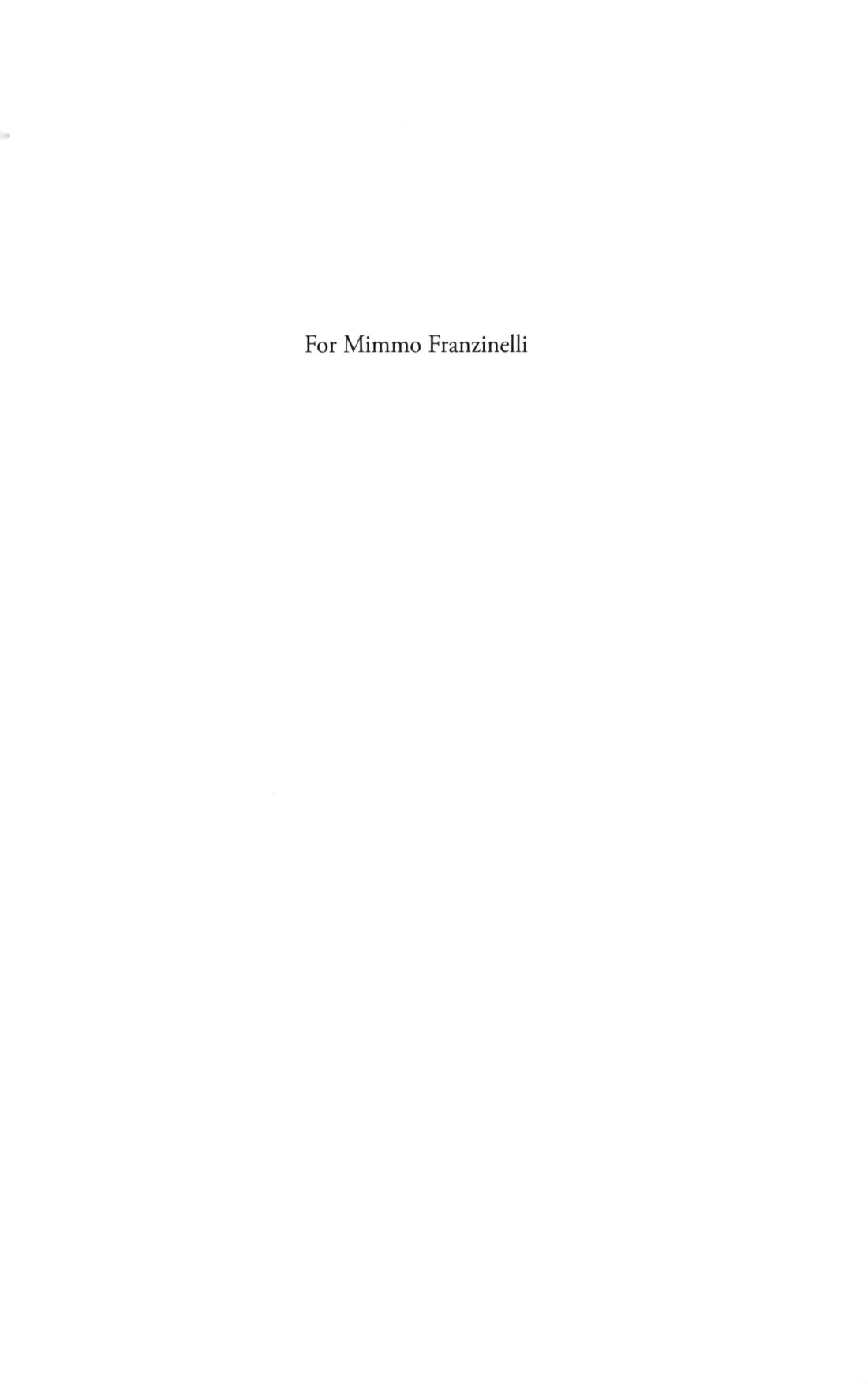

Then there are her relatives, who are usually poisonous. They need jobs, recommendations, subsidies, expensive operations or interminable cures for incurable diseases, and embarrassing interventions to get them out of various spots of trouble. To part with an old mistress can be one of the most difficult, delicate, and expensive operations in a man's life, often much more troublesome than a church annulment. It is such a formidable task, at times, that many timid men go without a mistress for fear of not being able to get rid of her when the time should come.

    Luigi Barzini, *Memories of mistresses: reflections from a life*

CONTENTS

	Introduction: Ghosts, diaries and a dictator's lover	1
1	Sex and the coming dictator	29
2	A dictator's distractions: His Muse and other bedfellows	56
3	And so . . . pause . . . to bed: Predatory Dictator meets Catholic Girl	84
4	Sex, love and jealousy: Politics and the family	111
5	Warring in public and private life	141
6	The winter of a patriarch and his *Ducessa*	172
7	Death in the afternoon	204
	Conclusion: A diarist's tale	235
	Acknowledgements	*247*
	Endnotes	*250*
	Bibliography	*283*
	Index	*301*
	Illustration credits	*312*

INTRODUCTION
Ghosts, diaries and a dictator's lover

In the memory of the wide world, Claretta Petacci occupies a single, visual, niche.[1] It is the macabre image of her hanging upside down at Piazzale Loreto in Milan on 29 April 1945, her skirts chastely pinned but her upper chest bloodied and bullet-holed. Diminutive in contrast with those Fascist bosses who shared her fate, she swung dead beside her lover and *Duce*, Benito Mussolini, while a vengeful crowd bayed its hatred and derision. Her naturally curly dark hair was now tangled; for one classically aware observer, its dishevelled state reminded him of the Medusa, even though, he added, her pretty face remained unblemished.[2] The expensive black kid shoes (size 33), which she had worn the previous day on her small and delicate feet, were lost. But, as would be revealed by a later exhumation, there lay meticulously sewn into the shoulder pads of her camisole 'an antique diamond ring, a gold locket studded with 17 small diamonds spelling out the letters C and B. Inside was preserved a tiny note with the motto "Clara, I am you and you are me. Ben 24 April 1932–24 April 1941" and a miniature gold box containing a rosary acquired at the sanctuary of Santa Rita at Cascia in Umbria'.[3]

Such detail may endlessly fascinate Italians, but the rest of the world has scarcely shown more than a passing interest in Petacci's fate. To be sure, some mutterings were immediately voiced about the 'barbarity' of the scene at Piazzale Loreto, with pious assertion that the innocent lover had not deserved the cruel dictator's fate. On 3 May 1945 Lord Birkenhead wrote to the London *Daily Telegraph* in execration of 'the horrendous Saturnalia' of Piazzale Loreto, where Claretta had been hung 'like a hen, beaten, bound and put on sale'; her fate had amounted to 'the most savage and cruel exhibition of the century'.[4] The American poet, Ezra Pound, during the war an unapologetic propagandist of Fascism, and in 1945 locked up in a US military prison before being incarcerated for a decade at a lunatic asylum in Washington, mourned the sacrificial deaths of 'Ben and la Clara' in his *Pisan cantos*.[5] In the 1960s the world-wandering, New Zealand-born 'Count' Geoffrey Wladislaw Vaile Potocki de Montalk (he claimed Polish aristocratic descent), effusively hymned a 'dear heroine', who had bravely sacrificed herself for love.[6] Sardonically driven by the expectation that Fascist sex could swell audience numbers, in 1975 the BBC sponsored a play archly entitled *Private affairs: Caesar and Claretta*. In its presentation, the young Helen Mirren enhanced her career playing Claretta as she followed her road to Piazzale Loreto. According to a review in *The Times*, Mirren was notably convincing when, portraying the events of 27 April 1945, 'layer after silk layer slithered to the floor as she prepared for bed' or when, the next morning, 'she left for what she believed to be liberation she was so excited she had no time to fetch her knickers from the bed and gave a hideous little giggle of hope as she went out of the farmhouse'.[7]

Shortly afterwards, the Scottish dramatist Robert David MacDonald brought Claretta and Hitler's partner, Eva Braun, together in a work entitled *Summit conference*. Dedicated to Rolf Hochhuth and saluting *The representative*, with its bitter critique of Pope Pius XII's attitude to the Holocaust, as 'the most important European play since the war', *Summit conference* explored the Holocaust with greater attention than it did Italian Fascism. 'Clara'[8] was represented as the female version of a timeless Italian Machiavel: 'I am the Duce's whore, and that is what they call me,' she was portrayed as saying. 'I am a scandal but at least I am a public scandal. Every month, I give 200,000 lire to the poor, and they look at my clothes and smell my scent and they spit – and take the money.'[9] The play was revived at the Lyric in London in 1982, on this occasion with another distinguished actor, Glenda Jackson, playing Claretta, but met with poor reviews. An acerbic critic wrote that 'it suggests something Giraudoux might have written on a bad day'.[10] Still less successful was a racehorse called Petacci – it may be wondered how the callers pronounced the filly's name – which ran unplaced a few times in 1977–8 and was then sent to stud.[11]

Such were mere flickerings of posthumous international interest. No doubt, then and later, further fleeting attention was aroused when a film or a book or a scandal was reported from Italy. In 1974–5 Carlo Lizzani's romanticised *Mussolini: ultimo atto* ('The last days of Mussolini') targeted a global market through the deployment of international stars, with Rod Steiger as the *Duce*[12] and Henry Fonda as Cardinal Alfredo Ildefonso Schuster, archbishop of Milan. However, the role of Claretta fell to the less well-known Lisa Gastoni and not, as was originally rumoured, to Liz Taylor (with Richard Burton and not Steiger to play Mussolini).[13] Ten years later, the Neapolitan director Pasquale Squitieri directly (and sympathetically) portrayed Petacci's life in a film called *Claretta*, with a semi-documentary beginning. He employed his partner, Claudia Cardinale, in the title role, her performance winning a silver medal at the Venice Biennale of 1985.[14] Squitieri, a cinematographer with many contacts on the Italian political right, readily persuaded Claretta's surviving younger sibling, Myriam,[15] to be interviewed. But no international stars joined them and the film caused few ripples outside Italy.

Popular historical accounts in languages other than Italian remain sparse, with the most recent, Roberto Olla's translated *Il Duce and his women* (2011), dwindling to the end of its narrative around 1936 and therefore, despite some description of Claretta, scarcely focusing on her.[16] In his avowedly revisionist biography of Mussolini, the journalist Nicholas Farrell, who took residence in the *Duce*'s home town of Predappio and regularly writes for the *Spectator* in critique of the Italian left, preferred brevity to detail. 'Italian women,' he maintained, '. . . queued up – literally – to make love' to Mussolini. Claretta, Farrell added, possessed the requisite qualities of 'big breasts' and 'powerful hips' and, in his opinion, little more needed to be known about her.[17]

As such remarks demonstrate, Claretta's story has frequently aroused foreign stereotypes about Latin lovers, with the assumption that every Italian male, and certainly any in power, aimed to live in a perpetual 'bunga bunga' party. Typical was the leaked report published in the *Guardian* that, when preparing for a state dinner with Italian Prime Minister Silvio Berlusconi, the British premier David Cameron joked that the main agenda in Rome was 'jacuzzis and whores'.[18] Cameron's apparent assumptions were little different from those of American ambassador Joseph Kennedy (himself no model of uxorious care) three generations earlier, when, in March 1939, he counselled that the quickest way to keep Italy onside in the deteriorating international situation would be to despatch 'six American chorus girls' to Rome to divert Mussolini and Galeazzo Ciano, his son-in-law, minister of foreign affairs and alleged competitor as a sexual athlete.[19]

But, if the world has largely forgotten Claretta, Italy remembers. Scarcely a week passes without some further reference to her on the web or in the news. In 2015, for example, fans learned that a 1939 Alfa Romeo Sport Berlina, the very car that Claretta and her brother Marcello had driven to their deaths in April 1945, had been auctioned in Paris for $2.1 million.[20] A few months later, a (clunky) 1936 Bianchi bicycle, allegedly a February 1943 present from 'Ben' to his lover, was put on eBay by a Foligno-based seller for a cheaper but still pricey €250,000.[21] More melodramatic was a set of reports in 2011–12 that Petacci's ghost had appeared four times on the lakeside at Salò, 'capital' of the Repubblica Sociale Italiana (RSI; Italian Social Republic), the puny regime of a puppet dictator between 1943 and 1945. Dressed in a flowing 1930s-style gown, 'tall and beautiful', the apparition, perhaps seeking sweetness still, had become visible just outside the elegant Vassalli *gelateria* looking out over Lago di Garda. In April 2012, at a delicate moment in national political history, with the Berlusconi era coming to an end, the spectre spoke up to condemn rightist infighting and leftist temptations. Two Sicilians and two Lombards, it was reported, heard the ghost whisper to perpetually bickering Italians: 'Ben said, do stop it now!' Massimo Merendi, chief of the Associazione National Ghost Uncover [*sic*], was engaged to examine the case further, it was promised, but the truth of Petacci's presence could not be doubted.[22]

Memory flourishes at other sites along Lago di Garda, where at Salò in June 2015 a museum and 'study centre' for the RSI opened, amid controversy, for visits and seminars.[23] There and elsewhere in the neighbourhood, maps advise how to find 'twenty places important in the RSI'. The most beauteous is the Villa Fiordaliso, where Petacci, her parents, Japanese diplomatic staff and an SS guard lived in 1943–4 in what must have been a crowded house. The villa was initially built for its German owner, Otto Vèzi, in 1907 in full 'Liberty' (Art Nouveau) style, thereby forming a small part of those developments that led Italian nationalists to bewail the fate of the *Gardasee*, as they bitterly rechristened the area around the lake. After German defeat in the war, in 1928 it was bought and enlarged by the wealthy Lombard Botturi-Polenghi family. In recent decades it has been lovingly restored by its owner, Max Tosetti, as has the adjacent Renaissance Torre San Marco.

Each is set on the lakeside just below the Vittoriale degli Italiani, the extensive palace where the poet Gabriele D'Annunzio indulged himself and his syncretic tastes through his declining years.[24] Today the Villa Fiordaliso is a centre for lavish weddings and dinners, while overnight guests are offered the opportunity 'to sleep in Claretta's bed', still furnished as it was in 1944.[25] (A sceptic might note tartly, however, that she and the *Duce* rarely passed a night there; whatever quick coitus they managed between 1943 and 1945 usually occurred in the Torre San Marco.) Nonetheless, among those said to have enjoyed the contemporary lavish facilities at the villa and/or to have been emotionally moved by their historical resonance are Laurence Olivier, Monica Vitti, Claudia Cardinale and 'Stormin' Norman' Schwarzkopf. Silvio Berlusconi has also relaxed 'in this room of sighs', a popular historian has confided with a nudge and a wink. 'And of just one thing we can be sure. He was not alone.'[26]

A hardcover copy of the romantic popular biography, Roberto Gervaso's *Claretta: la donna che morì per Mussolini* ('Claretta: the woman who died for Mussolini'), is made available by the management of the hotel for contemplation and written commentary.[27] Sadly, the more celebrated guests seem to have forgone this opportunity, although visitors who have reflected on their meeting with Claretta's spirit have arrived from as far afield as Australia, New Zealand, Kazakhstan and Venezuela. They have kept their opinions for the most part apolitical and sentimental (with possible national differences): 'Our unforgetable [*sic*] day. The Italians really know how to live' (a couple from Dallas, September 2002); or the more ecstatic French couple 'E et G, une nuit torride, inoubliable, et pleine de sentiments, faits partagées à deux. Peut-être avons-nous ravivé l'idylle magnifique entre Claretta et Il Duce' (July 2004). Another French pair were briefer one month later, recording: 'Calme, douceur et volupté.' Other sentiments were prosaic: 'We did sleep in a very historical room but I was here with my wife lovely Margie and not with a lover like Claretta' (a couple, perhaps German, perhaps not, from Munich, September 2007). More directly connected with the Mussolini–Petacci story were two Italians who recalled lyrically: 'I am yours . . . You are mine . . . for ever if God wants it . . . so Ben and Claretta wrote . . . so you and I write.'

Thirty kilometres north along the lake, the Villa Feltrinelli has been converted into a larger and still more up-market hotel whose staff acknowledge that Mussolini's bedroom is always the first to be booked. There, the *Duce* and quite a few of his extended family lived in 1943–5. But the presence of his wife, Rachele, ensured that Claretta never stretched languorously on this bed. Quite a bit further north at Obermais/Maia Alta above Merano in the German-speaking sector of the Trentino-Alto Adige, locals still readily identify a 'castle' as the 'Villa Petacci' (actually called the Villa Schildhof and erected in 1911), and are sure there was regular sexual congress there. They are deluded. The villa was acquired in April 1943 from two Hungarian noblemen by Claretta's brother Marcello, and acted as a redoubt for the whole family at a difficult moment later that year and in 1944–5 (then minus Claretta).[28]

The Petacci family's most vaunted dwelling place, however, was the stridently modernist Villa Camilluccia, a massive – 700-square-metre, 32-room, 2-storey – residence in the northern suburbs of Rome beneath Monte Mario. At first appearance it might suggest a full conversion of the Petaccis to the taste and philosophy of Fascism. However, much about it belied its apparent commitment to revolution, rather confirming the family's determination to climb socially by any means. Occupying a large block of land at Via della Camilluccia 355–7, it was equipped with a swimming pool, tennis court (according to gossip, the court was never prepared for play and the pool's drainage system did not work),[29] terraces replete with gymnastic equipment, orchard, flower garden, chicken run and two separate guard posts, while boasting a huge *salone* with crystal doors (the servants' quarters doubled as an air raid shelter). Claretta's own bedroom, equipped with large mirrors, exuded female sentiment of a cloying kind, displaying a fondness for silk fabric conforming to her taste in plunging negligees, and a devotion to the colour pink in its furnishings and even its telephone.

After the fall of the dictatorship the Villa Camilluccia experienced an uneven fate. It was sacked by an aggrieved populace in July 1943 and then handed over to the Istituto del Santissimo Crocifisso, a Catholic charitable organisation – founded under Fascism – committed to children's welfare.[30] Following the establishment of the Italian postwar republic, those members of the Petacci family who had escaped Claretta's and Marcello's fate in 1945 sued for the Villa's return with tardy success: in 1960 the Italian state paid out an ordered 22.5 million lire (of a requested 104 million) in compensation.[31] But Myriam and the Petacci parents lacked sufficient will or capital to restore it, with the Villa lingering for a time as the 'Palazzi restaurant' before being bulldozed in 1975. The site, somewhat incongruously, now houses the Iraqi embassy. However, its story still attracts naive celebration by cultural historians lauding 'a courageous example of modern architecture, spare and essential, with an intense and complex use of space' and hailing it as an effective marriage of Le Corbusier and Palladio.[32]

Less remarked upon but worth a tourist visit in Rome is the Petacci family tomb in the Campo Verano, the city's cemetery, spreading behind the Basilica of San Lorenzo towards the Tiburtina railway yards, and subject to vicious Allied bombing on 19 July 1943, an attack which triggered the *Duce*'s first fall. Claretta's corpse was interred there one spring day on 16 March 1956. Her remains had travelled a complex course from the Piazzale Loreto, even if, unlike those of her partner Mussolini, they had not suffered the bathetic fate of being purloined by nostalgic admirers.[33] The final burial in Rome had been allowed by the Italian state after Ugo De Pilato, the lawyer of Claretta's still living parents, Dr Francesco Saverio Petacci and Giuseppina Persichetti, petitioned the government in January 1954 for charity. 'Two elderly parents, severely struck by fate,' De Pilato wrote in lachrymose vein, could thereby find some closure, a mandatory concession when 'the memory of this unhappy creature inspires throughout Italy and outside the country merely sentiments of sorrowing sympathy and reverence' and neither criticism nor disdain.[34]

In the present day, few of the tourists who throng Rome find their way to the mausoleum. Yet to bask in this small corner of the city's history does have its attractions for a visitor. The web offers two pathways to the Petacci tomb. In the romantic evocation of the Rome daily *Il Messaggero* – which under the regime employed her doctor-father as a medical commentator – Claretta is recalled as 'Mussolini's woman', it being stressed that she 'died tragically'. Nonetheless, it is quickly admitted that the tomb of the comic film star Alberto Sordi has more appeal, with many other actors resting nearby awaiting veneration.[35] A local news-sheet counsels a rival track. Its 'third itinerary' directs pilgrims past the Jewish sector of the cemetery and on to the nearby tomb of the comic dramatist, Eduardo De Filippo. Up a rise to the right rest the remains of his brother, Peppino, buried in a pyramid-shaped edifice. Opposite stands the tomb of the Petaccis and just a little further on, we are told, that of Attilio Ferraris, a celebrated footballer in the Fascist years, who in 1934 was a member of the first Italy squad to win the World Cup.[36]

It is plain, therefore, that a host of ideas and memories whisper across the contemporary Campo Verano.[37] But the Petacci tomb deserves inspection. It is built, as was expected in the 1950s, of pre-stressed concrete, now blackening and crumbling with age and carbonation, and is reached via a short stairway. From this elevated site, the tomb rises some 30 feet farther into the skies, being surmounted by a slightly curved roof. A long glass shield, broken into rectangles, protects the inhumations. At the bottom, Francesco Saverio and his wife lie united in death, as they were in life. On the side, Claretta's younger sister, the sometime starlet Myriam, rests alone. But these family members are as subordinate to Claretta here as they were in history. It is she who commands the tomb.

Above the first layer of interments and pushed back a little lies a solid black marble coffin. It is labelled CLARETTA 28-II-1912 – 28-IV-45. Strikingly set above it is a white marble statue, larger than life-size, of the dead woman. She is wrapped in what might be a sheet or toga (and not her favoured negligee, often worn late into the afternoon).[38] Her shoulders, upper arms, hands and feet are bare, with her upper leg revealed beneath a diaphanous layer. Her right knee is slightly raised, suggesting motion, although her legs are placed primly together. She has her chin up, with her breasts thrust forward (perhaps to the pleasure of Mussolini's passing ghost). Her hair is a little unkempt. Her smile is contained. But the most expressive feature of the statue is the large hands, which are turned outwards, presenting her arms and shoulders, bashfully offering herself and her soul to a chosen partner. In death, Claretta remains young and austerely beautiful. The lines of her body may be exposed but not in a sensual manner; her sculptor has left her decorously promising eternal love, not lust.[39] It may be, nonetheless, that the tomb's history is passing. On 28 October 2015, ninety-third anniversary of the Fascist takeover in Rome, the tomb was reported to be in serious decay and of potential danger to onlookers; no surviving member of the Petacci family had then offered to repair it.[40] In August 2016 it was officially declared to be in 'a state of abandon' and therefore a possible object of removal, with the authorities complaining that all attempts to contact the family heirs in the USA had failed. But, shortly after, another report indicated that Ferdinando Petacci had been actively trying to preserve the family tomb and blamed the cemetery authorities for their failure to assist him.[41]

After all, Campo Verano is not the only site of Claretta's physical commemoration. Inevitably the centres near Lake Como, where lover and dictator were executed, have also from time to time sought to record suffering and death (and to attract visitors). In 2010 the Berlusconian mayor of Giulino di Mezzegra caused some consternation by urging in an online article the erection of a statue of Claretta on the left side of the Villa Belmonte, at the gates of which it was generally agreed Mussolini and his partner met their end.[42] Controversy lingers to this day, with rival fascists and neofascists contesting the wording that should accompany a small surviving memorial there, and continuing to debate whether Claretta's death can in any way be justified.[43] Fifty years earlier, similar controversy arose after the family erected an 80cm by 40cm cross on a white marble base in memory of their dead daughter, 'innocent victim of a horrible crime' – government toleration being granted with the cautious request that the memorial not intrude onto public land or constitute a traffic hazard.[44] Soon, however, other phantasms gave more troubling meaning to the site with neofascists adding a plaque to Mussolini and the Fascist cause, an appendage that prompted police intervention and the transfer of the commemorative material to the town cemetery.[45]

Sites of memory carry power. But Claretta's story also retains its spark in written version. Indeed, in a neoliberal age which glories in the individual and celebrity, Claretta and her fate loom ever larger in popular histories of Mussolini and his Italian dictatorship. Their implications deserve analysis. An extensive literature, much of it foreign, has been regularly alarmed since 1945 whenever fascist political groupings have surfaced in Italy.[46] The country did, after all, unlike Germany, allow the existence of an avowedly neofascist party, the Movimento Sociale Italiano (MSI; Italian Social Movement), the title invoking the radical-sounding ideology of the RSI or, more subtly, the message that '*Mussolini [è] sempre immortale*' ('Mussolini lives for ever').[47] Following the collapse of the Soviet Union, the MSI became an acceptable partner of Berlusconian government, before, like its communist enemy, abandoning its past identity (and name) during the change from First to Second Republic and swearing itself now 'post-fascist'. Yet the MSI was not the only home of admirers of the interwar dictatorship. With or without the approval of the MSI's leadership, more extreme fascist grouplets have existed and still exist, with Casa [Ezra] Pound being the most active current example.[48]

The allure of neofascism, however defined, retains a fascination to some, although the main ideological inheritance is transferred less by the ghost of Mussolini, despite regular pictorial representation of a dominating *Duce*,[49] and more by that of Hitler or, for example, Corneliu Zelea Codreanu, the poetic and mystical leader of the Romanian Legion of the Archangel Michael. In any case, when surveying the anti-democratic right in Italy, it is important to underline that, across the postwar generations, it was not so much Mussolini's mind as his body (and, often enough, if with some hesitations, its mingling with Claretta's) that entranced some Italians. Hardly was the dictator dead and his regime destroyed than the Mussolini family re-emerged at the centre of memory reconstruction. Each of Mussolini's legitimate offspring, except for Anna Maria, a sufferer since childhood of polio, published accounts of their childhoods. The eldest son, Vittorio, provided a model of buoyant description in 1957 through the celebrated firm of Mondadori in Milan.[50] That same year, Mussolini's younger sister Edvige also sketched a sanguine recollection of her brother, a memoir published in Florence by La Fenice ('The Phoenix', meant to be

INTRODUCTION

a telling name), a business that was assembling what became forty-four volumes of Mussolini's *Opera omnia* (they omit all but the skimpiest and most formal reference to Claretta).[51] Edda, Mussolini's eldest child, had been estranged from her father by his failure to prevent the execution of her husband, Galeazzo Ciano, in January 1944, and, as early as 1952, a short work recounting that 'tragedy' or 'betrayal' appeared under the authorship of an adaptable ex-Fascist intellectual, Emilio Settimelli.[52] Other, more forgiving autobiographical works followed, even after Edda's death in 1995.[53] Prize for the best title should, however, go to a study by Fabrizio, Edda's eldest child, born in Shanghai in 1931. It is entitled *Quando il nonno fece fucilare papà* ('When Grandpa had Daddy shot').[54]

By then, it was the *Duce*'s youngest son, Romano, born in 1927 and a globally applauded jazz pianist, who was assuming the lead in representing the family,[55] perhaps in part stimulated by the political career of his daughter, Alessandra, in and beyond the MSI.[56] After an initial career in modelling and risqué film, Alessandra Mussolini kept the family name in the headlines through campaigning that has combined her grandfather's political and sexual appeal.[57] Romano died in 2006 but his name survives in the Centro Studi Romano Mussolini and the attached Museo Mussolini, which today can be visited at the Villa Carpena, the Romagna estate purchased under the dictatorship.[58] In 2013–14, Mussolini's birthplace in the *paese* of Predappio, near Forlì, housed an extensive exhibition on the young *Duce*'s life, illustrated by a lavish guide edited by Franco Moschi, a more distant member of the clan.[59] Rumours continue of the establishment of another museum in the surviving and aesthetically attractive Casa del Fascio (the former Fascist Party headquarters) at Predappio. Others of the extensive new generation of the family have engaged in well-publicised historical reflection[60] and legal process,[61] while one entrepreneurial relative was reported to have moved from offering private lessons in seduction to launch a 'Seduction School' at Cervia on the Romagnol Adriatic.[62]

Back in the first decades after 1945, each family member had produced his or her book with the assistance of an eager journalist and, in its pages, there were few attempts to do more than portray a happy surface of family life. Pride of place in this insertion of the Mussolinis into memory and nostalgia went to Mussolini's widow, Rachele, who had led the way for the entire family with a memoir published by Mondadori in 1948; its two accompanying postwar photographs illustrated Rachele either virtuously knitting or hand-making *fettuccine*.[63] Serialised first in sixteen issues by the illustrated magazine, *Oggi*, and then much translated, Rachele's words reached a remarkable claimed total circulation of more than 104 million readers.[64] Her account made only passing reference to Claretta, until a brief admission of Rachele's public confrontation with her in October 1944. The younger woman's conjunction with the *Duce* in death was blamed on unknown forces, who 'at the last minute wanted to put her near Benito in order to heighten the scandal involved'.[65]

Until her death in October 1979, sudden enough to forestall a planned audience with Pope John Paul II,[66] Rachele stayed in the news, whether through autobiographical writings or interviews (journalists were needed for both).[67] The image that resulted was of an ever-loyal wife and mother, expert at cooking pasta and the other dishes of her region, a generous but demanding and by no means stupid head of her family's domestic hearth.[68] Certainly regime propaganda and perhaps reality had long represented Rachele this way.[69] But, under the postwar republic, her embodiment of a 'timeless' *sposa e madre esemplare* ('ideal wife and mother') was confirmed.

The real heartland of what has been brilliantly defined as a popular 'nostalgia ... without knowing well, in truth, for what precisely'[70] was located less in books than in the photographic weeklies and monthlies, which, almost immediately after 1945, became the preferred reading of middle Italy. *Oggi*, the most successful of these ventures, soon had a circulation of well over a million copies, and its nearest competitor, *Gente*, 300,000.[71] By 1974 *Oggi*'s run had grown to more than 4 million.[72] The preferred subject matter of such weeklies was 'an infinite quantity' of written or photographic memory. When Mussolini appeared in its pages, he tended to be 'in intimate, familial dress', the *Duce*, it was averred, having instituted a 'special sort of dictatorship'.[73] Readers might also agree that he headed a special sort of family, although the term was not used, where, as a 'typical Italian male', he could range unhindered from Rachele's bed. (Actually, the two slept in separate wings of the Villa Torlonia, their estate in Rome, given all but rent-free to the family from 1929.) Even while they expatiated on Mussolini's human (and humane) normality, the weeklies

INTRODUCTION

did not forget the 'tragic love story' of 'Ben and Clara'.[74] As a piece in *Oggi* in 1952 underlined, in her death, Claretta had above all shown herself 'a faithful and courageous woman'.[75]

Prompting the memory of this part of Mussolini's life were the surviving members of the Petacci family. They were led by Claretta's little sister Myriam, who may have had a faltering career in cinema but who knew something about publicity and was committed to resuscitating the honour of her family at least as fervently as were the Mussolinis theirs. In 1950 Myriam came back from sanctuary in Franco's Spain to launch legal proceedings to claim her sister's recently discovered diaries and other papers. Defeat followed initial victory in that case but, during 1955, Myriam won space in four successive issues of *Oggi* to tell her and her sister's story.[76] In time, not long before her death on 24 May 1991, she published a fuller memoir and self-defence with the assistance of the journalist Santi Corvaja.[77]

In the photo-magazines, Myriam was joined by Zita Ritossa ('Zizi'), the partner of her brother, Marcello, and mother of his two sons, Benvenuto Edgar (born in 1939) and Ferdinando, two years his junior. Unlike Myriam, by then in Spain, Zita, her husband and children were, like Claretta, members of the final convoy that was blocked by partisans near Dongo on 27 April 1945, with fatal results for Marcello. Ritossa, who had given an extensive interview to a journalist, Luigi Saolini, as early as October 1945,[78] bolstered no fewer than fourteen issues of *Tempo*, another of the illustrated magazines, in 1957 giving her account of this event, her own family life and the stony reception which she had received from the Petaccis when introduced to them as Marcello's partner; the two did not marry. In 1975 Ritossa added a shorter account in *Oggi*, focusing on Claretta.[79] In between, she tried to fob off Myriam and her parents in their attempts to sue her for 'an unacceptable disclosure of matters pertaining to private life'; legal judgment on the case swung backwards and forwards in 1958, 1960 and 1961, before the Cassazione supreme court ruled in the Petaccis' favour on 20 April 1963.[80] The postwar history of the Petaccis has been studded with – usually newsworthy – litigation. It still is.

Nonetheless, during the first decades after the war, the Petaccis did not prevail over the Mussolini family in their struggle to attract public approval of their past. Indeed, in 1956 an editorialist in *Tempo* declared that, for all the romance in Claretta's life and death, she should be viewed as merely a 'minor figure in the history that we are living'.[81] Such a dismissive conclusion must have appealed to the Mussolinis: Rachele had continued to refuse to talk about her husband's last affair or at best pronounced patronisingly that she was sorry for how Claretta had died and now took pious pains to remember her in her recitations of the *Ave Maria*.[82]

In highlighting this primacy of the legitimate family, the key document was 'Mussolini's last letter to his wife', where he affirmed that 'you know that you have been for me the only woman I have really loved. I swear it before God and our Bruno at this supreme moment.' It was first published in Rachele's initial memoirs and its authenticity was later approved in Mussolini's *Opera Omnia*.[83] However, no original survives. Some historians have therefore concluded that there was no such correspondence and the invention sprang from the unsparing struggle that Rachele was prosecuting posthumously against Claretta. Before her death Rachele is said to have admitted the forgery to a biographer, Anita Pensotti.[84] Yet Pensotti had elsewhere commented on Rachele's limited literacy compensated by her iron memory, even for exact phrases.[85] In any case, as a more recent biographer of Rachele has urged, the epistolary sentiments were by no means contrary to Mussolini's conflicted attitude to his wife and family on the one hand and to his young lover on the other, or a reverse of his marked tendency to appease the chivvying woman who was then nearest to him.[86] It may be that no last tearful letter was scribbled by a repentant *Duce*; and yet its attitudes (and its hypocrisy) may well have expressed Mussolini's mind late in April 1945.

As the postwar decades passed, the popular pull of memory of dictatorship did to some extent lessen, even if Red Brigade terrorists thought that, by kidnapping and murdering the loquacious Christian Democrat party secretary Aldo Moro in 1978, they could thereby expose the fascism lurking beneath the mask of the Italian version of liberal democracy. Academic historians were by then using the massive if unevenly preserved archives of the dictatorship to examine it, with Renzo De Felice composing a biography of Mussolini that ran past 6,000 pages. De Felice disclosed the shadows and, more controversially, some lights in the regime and its dictator. But he remained a rigorously neo-Rankean political historian, eschewing serious commentary on the *Duce*'s private life and personal emotions. Claretta he dismissed in a short ten pages as apolitical by most definitions;[87] her major mention in his volumes was primly confined to a documentary appendix. There, De Felice recounted a jaundiced description by a secret agent, General Giacomo Carboni, of a visit to the Villa Camilluccia in July 1943, just before the dictator's overthrow by his colleagues in the Fascist Grand Council and at which time, as shall be seen below, the lovers' relationship was in some crisis. Carboni described Claretta as 'an insignificant little person', while her bedroom, into which he claimed to have peeked, reminded him, with its ceiling and wall mirrors (allegedly installed at the wish of Claretta's mother), a double bed with a rare silk coverlet, adjoined by a black marble bathroom equipped with large central bath set on paving decorated with mosaics in the 'Roman manner', of the tasteless pseudo-grandeur of 'the set of an American film'.[88]

De Felice was by no means the only historian of Fascism. A vivid democratic debate flourished, and still flourishes, inside and outside Italy about the nature of the dictatorship and its proclaimed totalitarianism (it was the pioneer of this term).[89] Mostly, however, neither Claretta nor the complications of family life under the regime has stimulated much serious review,[90] with Italian academic historians frequently professing an austere deprecation of biography and 'scandal'.

In regard to the national reckoning with history, the fall of the Soviet Union and the global triumph of neoliberalism shifted the scene in Italy, where the cultural division into a (largely latent) popular sympathy or nostalgia for Fascism countered by a high cultural commitment to anti-Fascism now withered away along with the nomenclature and apparent ideological base of the country's political parties. With this drastic change, at least in appearance, sentimental readings of Mussolini and his regime and family revived, being expressed most vividly by Berlusconi, the pre-eminent politician of the new era (if scarcely an orthodox neoliberal). Mussolini, Berlusconi pronounced, 'never killed anyone', while the places where he confined his political enemies were, in reality, *villeggiature*, 'holiday camps'.[91] He compared his own travails in ruling to those of the *Duce*, in his mind another Italian leader prevented from doing good by the intractability of the national population.[92]

Such pronouncements from on high fitted into a revival of affection for the regime, with the damnation of Fascism as the partner of Hitlerian Nazism now obscured by an emphasis on the private, the personal and the emotional (and the sexual). In such circumstances, it is no surprise to find that Claretta's ghost is not confined to sporadic appearance outside a *gelateria*. Instead she has become ever more significant as a symbol and 'heroine' of the regime and, many now accept, her 'personal tragedy' carries more important messages and lessons into the present than does the fall of the regime. It is true that Mussolinis of the younger generation still sometimes fill the news. But Rachele, the 'peasant housewife', now looks an old-fashioned figure from an Italy that has been lost, whereas Claretta can be portrayed as a feisty modern woman and even a proto-feminist.

Striking in this regard is Roberto Festorazzi's 2012 popular biography, emphatic that Claretta 'died for love of Mussolini'.[93] Festorazzi is a historian ready to purvey some of the more outrageous conspiracy theories that circle over 'the last days of Mussolini' and has been happy to acknowledge his admiration for a Fascist grandfather.[94] But, privileging the personal over the ideological, he elevated Claretta to a higher historical plain than she had earlier achieved. Especially after 1943, she was, Festorazzi has contended, a 'sort of *Ducessa*', 'queen' of the RSI–Nazi alliance, a 'fervent Fascist' new woman, and 'pro-German in her innermost marrow'. All in all, she acted as Mussolini's 'lover, friend, secretary, confidante, faithful disciple and goad'.[95] Such a record renders her 'a contemporary heroine', 'a universal symbol of the deepest oaths of love'. By her behaviour in April 1945, Claretta riveted onto the 'act of dying a symbolic force, a profound drama, a visceral pathos, in a word, a dignity which the execution of the *Duce* alone could not have had'.[96] Her sacrifice had absolved Mussolini of many of his sins. Yet such saintly qualities did not entail a diminution of her sensual power. Claretta, Festorazzi concluded, is a myth, largely because she is 'the type of woman that every male dreams of and desires, even while knowing he cannot deserve her'.[97]

If this interpretation is to be believed, it might almost be thought that Claretta was a more significant Fascist than Mussolini. Yet in composing his book, Festorazzi made only minor use of the massive documentation,

INTRODUCTION

which, over the last decade, has significantly elevated Claretta's importance in modern Italian history, and disclosed evidence that carried implications well beyond national borders. No historian of the regime can now fail to consult the diaries that Claretta scrawled almost every day into a succession of notebooks after she first met the *Duce* in April 1932. To the revelations in that source – many older and powerful men have had sex with younger women but an account from the female partner is highly unusual – can be added an extensive correspondence. During the nineteen months of the RSI's existence, Mussolini wrote no fewer than 318 letters to his lover. An edition of these, including in footnotes many of Claretta's responses, appeared in 2011, with decidedly forgiving academic commentary.[98] Claretta wrote back to her lover, often at greater length, and other members of her family – father, mother and sister – also found reason to send extended epistles to the dictator.

Claretta's record may be an indispensable source for the comprehension of Mussolini's regime but another of the many ironies in the history and historiography of Fascism is the controversial place of diaries in the dictatorship's telling. Long pre-eminent was that composed by Mussolini's son-in-law Ciano, born in 1903 and from 1936 to 1943 the youngest foreign minister in Europe. By 1943 Ciano, in his heart a young conservative, Fascist-style, had transmuted his early callow enthusiasm for the Axis into a bitter dislike of his German allies. On the evening of 24/25 July he duly voted to remove his father-in-law from power. Amid the confusion that followed, Ciano was foolish enough to seek sanctuary in Germany, defying Edda's advice to go to what would have been a more accommodating Spain.[99] He was soon arrested and confined in Verona, with both the Nazis and radical Fascists determined on his execution in retribution for the July 'betrayal', and – everyone, including Mussolini, knew – for the more general failings and equivocations of the Italian dictatorship. While the RSI was establishing itself and Mussolini was trying to work out what his life meant as a puppet dictator at Gardone, Ciano went to his death on 11 January 1944. Both Rachele and Claretta vengefully approved his punishment.[100] Mussolini, who acknowledged that he was the person really responsible for the faults attributed to Ciano, accepted it much more uneasily, with a typical mixture of unhappiness and self-pity.

Urgent in Ciano's defence had been his wife, Edda, Mussolini's eldest and favourite child. Then and later, she might have been willing to admit that 'marriage was not my most authentic vocation'. But, at the death, she stood by her man as purposefully as both Rachele and Claretta had done in July 1943 and would do, or seek to do, in 1945. When it was plain that Ciano was to die, Edda fled with her children and an accommodating partner to Switzerland, carrying with her the extensive diaries, often anti-German in their import, that had been kept by her husband. According to Edda, they weighed no less than 48 kilos, six more than she herself when she reached Ischia in 1945. Concealed with difficulty beneath her winter clothes as she crossed the border, they occasioned scurrilous rumours that she was pregnant.[101] In such flight, she broke with her father to his frequent lament. On publication after 1945, the Ciano diaries became the most basic source of all serious accounts of the regime, with their exposure of not so much German arrogance and perfidy as Fascist levity and bellicosity.[102]

As has already been noted, the immediate postwar years unleashed a flood of memoir-writing in Italy as in other combatant states, almost all of it exculpatory, much military or diplomatic, and little of major significance. Over the next generations, the major addition to such literature was the diary of Giuseppe Bottai, the most self-consciously intellectual of Fascist ministers, if a man who nurtured something like a crush on his leader. It appeared in 1982. Bottai survived the war and died in 1959, while his son, Bruno, made a highly successful diplomatic career, rising to be bureaucratic head of the Ministry of Foreign Affairs (and honorary president of the Federazione Italiana del Cricket). In retirement, Bruno Bottai published his own family story, which, however, lacked the glamour of the Petaccis and Mussolinis.[103]

Shadowing such publication and any understanding of the regime was another diary, Mussolini's own. Quite a few survivors from the regime, including his sister, claimed to have seen the *Duce* regularly jotting down notes and opinions.[104] The fate of such alleged writings soon became a rich part of the vivid conspiracy theories which were circling, and continue to circle, over Mussolini's last days and which, as will be noticed later in this book, include claims about the treasure that he, the Petaccis

INTRODUCTION

and others who went to their doom may have been carrying, as well as a 'lost' packet of letters, which the *Duce* and Winston Churchill had allegedly exchanged over the years. There is also the issue of how exactly the dictator and his lover died and why she did so, with Churchill again starring as the one who, it is claimed, wanted most to be rid of her. (For more detail, see chapter 7.) Yet the simple truth remains that the correspondence has never emerged, and the case for it ever having existed is slight to non-existent.

In regard to the general history of the regime, central place in arguments about missing evidence should be assigned to the 'Mussolini diaries', the false Mussolini diaries that is. The fine contemporary historian Mimmo Franzinelli has trenchantly narrated how they appeared, reappeared and then appeared again and, despite frequent exposure of forgery, stubbornly failed to die.[105] Their composition began at Vercelli in the early 1950s at the hands of Giulio Panvini Rosati, a pensioner who had once worked for the local police under the RSI, his wife Rosetta Prelli (still in awe of Mussolini's and Gabriele D'Annunzio's charisma) and their daughter Amalia ('Mimi'). The women made themselves into experts in mimicking Mussolini's handwriting, and were soon adroitly penning a version of the regime's past. They finished their labour in 1955. They then tried to sell their handiwork for millions of lire, soon assisted by intermediaries from the world of neofascism, and persuaded Mondadori to assess the diaries. However, when consulted, Rachele and other members of the family denied their authenticity, although a sale did go ahead with *Time-Life*. Just as a fortune beckoned, however, suspicious journalists from *Il Corriere della Sera* asked for police evaluation and the sham was exposed.

In April 1959 Amalia was arrested and put on trial for forgery and fraud, soon to be found guilty; she and Rosa Panvini were sentenced to brief terms in gaol from which they were quickly released.[106] The first act of the history of the Mussolini diaries was thereby over, except for a brief epilogue in 1967, when mother and daughter (despite Amalia having had brief further trouble over forging a cheque to a local butcher) again sold their labour, this time to *The Sunday Times*. However, the renewed falsehood was quickly apparent, and there were further arrests, with De Felice signalling his authoritative disapproval of the pages given to him for inspection. Rosa Panvini died in 1968 and, although Amalia lived on to 1986, she failed to convince with an imaginative new claim to have acted as a medium of the *Duce* when doing her writing.[107]

But the diaries had not lost their charge. A bizarre struggle over them continued among 'expert' academic historians, both Italian and foreign, who were regularly asked their opinion of the texts. The Englishman Denis Mack Smith, from his base at All Souls Oxford often in battle with De Felice, announced that the calligraphy was definitely Mussolini's, adding in sphinx-like words that this 'was the diary that Mussolini would have wanted to write'.[108] Brian R. Sullivan, a North American expert in the tenebrous world of the secret services, declared the material genuine but then recanted in 1987, after hostile graphological analysis at Sotheby's. Soon he changed tack once more, now taking up existing Italian suggestions that Mussolini had copied his own diaries some time at Salò (or had them copied by a third party) and that revision explained their variation from what he had written in the 1930s.[109]

The diaries, it was becoming evident, were impossible to kill off in a turbid world of masked owners and special agents seeking scoops for their press barons on either side of the Atlantic, as well as in that Italian arena where memory and popular history promiscuously mingled. Academic historians did not help much. Before his death, De Felice in 1995 made a U-turn of his own to suggest that the material 'could have preserved the echo of the originals'. Nicholas Farrell also plumped for authenticity.[110] Emilio Gentile, De Felice's successor at Rome University, demurred, as later did Giordano Bruno Guerri, Bottai's biographer. But Romano Mussolini reversed his own and his family's longstanding dismissal of the diaries and in 2005 proclaimed their trustworthiness.[111] Act three of the diaries' drama was about to begin.

Marcello Dell'Utri, a Sicilian senator who had for decades worked closely with Berlusconi in financial, cultural, press and political matters, emerged as the new protagonist of the diaries, even if he found much other work on his plate. He had held a key role in the foundation of Forza Italia (1993), the initial Berlusconian 'party'. From 1997 to 2013 Dell'Utri was also fighting a sustained battle in the courts against claims that he nourished close ties with the Mafia. Eventually, in 2014, after Berlusconi had

INTRODUCTION

fallen from office, Dell'Utri was condemned to seven years' confinement, with numerous other misdemeanours on his record or still under trial. After fleeing to Lebanon, he was arrested there, returned to Italy and gaoled.

It was this man who, in 2007, announced that the diaries had been purchased from Swiss owners by a local company, seemingly under his aegis, and would now be made available through the well-known publishers, Bompiani. Ignoring the reiterated doubts of Gentile, Guerri and other leading Italian historians of Fascism, between 2010 and 2012 Bompiani put onto the market four volumes of what it called 'the diaries of Mussolini, real or conjectured' (*presunti*). Covering the years from 1935 to 1939, they were given further exposure by the ultra-neoliberal and anti-leftist daily paper *Libero*, which in March–April 2011 serialised the writings in thirty parts. Its editor, Maurizio Belpietro, took pains to 'honour' Dell'Utri for their discovery and, it was said, sales of the paper increased markedly.[112] Displaying his own anti-anti-Fascism or more, Dell'Utri did not forbear to speak in September 2010 at a conference in Rome arranged by the Associazione di promozione sociale Casa Pound Italia ('The Society for Promoting Casa Pound to the Italian People') in celebration of 'the diaries re-found', while Pasquale Squitieri, whose career in cinema had been enlarged by a term as a Berlusconian member of parliament, took rhetoric to new and empyrean flights when he told another Rome conference in November: 'We must cut the word false from the documents. Are the Gospels false? Jesus left nothing written down.'[113]

The first volume of the diaries to be published, that covering the year of 1939, was bolstered with a lengthy, if anonymous, introduction. There, some of the worries about the veracity of the material were conceded but always with the claim that there was an equal, and probably more convincing, view that they were genuine. Helpfully, Emilio Gentile's once authoritative rejection was now conditioned by a note saying, despite his grave doubts, that he could not fully judge the diaries' authenticity. Similarly, readers learned that Eugenio Di Rienzo, an editor of *Nuova Rivista Storica*, a leading academic journal, had qualified his repudiation with the Delphic remark that, 'if we are dealing with a falsehood, it is, like all falsehood, based on an element of truth'.[114] The introduction ended with what was stated to be a wholly objective 'scientific' analysis positively adjudging the writing style, and the chemical composition of the paper and ink used.[115] Sales rocketed past 10,000.[116]

Bompiani's publication was not complete before Mario Monti replaced Berlusconi as prime minister in November 2011, while in the background Dell'Utri's troubles in court multiplied. Moreover, in April 2011 Franzinelli published his devastating (and courageous) exposure of the long history of the diaries' faking. His denunciation did earn a brief acknowledgement at the back of reprints of the 1939 diary.[117] When the entries allegedly covering the years between 1935 and 1937 followed, the introduction was again included but eventually accompanied by the admission that Franzinelli had indeed picked up 'mistakes', while it was also now announced that a trial was proceeding in Switzerland over who actually owned the diaries.[118]

To be sure, the farcical tale of the Hitler diaries, with its own pattern of business corruption and levity and academic vanity, offset with occasional honesty and scholarship, is better known than the Mussolini story.[119] In historical celebrity, the *Führer* always trumps the *Duce*. Yet the fraudulent Fascist writings have been harder to kill. Italians have shown themselves more readily won over than their sometime German allies by dulcified accounts of dictatorship and by the idea that conspiracies obscure the truth with the same inevitability of winter fogs in the Val Padana. As one popular historian stated in 2014, history was a synonym for lying, in practice never more than victors' accounts.[120] In such circumstances, it would be rash to conclude that, in the long-playing melodrama of the Mussolini diaries, Italians will not eventually be persuaded to watch act four.

In this Italian predilection for mysteriously hidden evidence lurks another deep irony. One major reason why anyone who flicks through the content of the *Diari veri o presunti* might conclude that they are forged is that they contain no mention of Claretta Petacci.[121] Rather, and presumably fitting the life assumptions of a mother and daughter from Vercelli, Mussolini's private life appears conventional, with him not forgetting to expatiate on his deep respect for Rachele and his love for his (legitimate) children. 'The family is everything for me,' he was made to write in November 1939, 'the squeak of the door, the special smell, a well-known object come back into my attention, the sound of the voices of

INTRODUCTION

those who are mine, restore me and fill me with comfort . . . Rachele has known how to give our house the simple and healthy, patriarchal, nature of our Romagna.'[122]

Yet while Dell'Utri, Bompiani and *Libero* were pressing on regardless with selling the fake diaries, it was already becoming widely known that Mussolini's last lover had left behind a hefty record of their affair and of many other aspects of the last decade of the dictatorship. A genuinely intimate account of the *Duce* could now oust the forged version. In November 2009 the journalist Mauro Suttora, a senior editor of *Oggi* among other attainments, had edited a valuable selection of Claretta's flood of entries (her scribblings in 1938 alone covered 1,810 pages, although many of these contained fewer than one hundred words). Suttora's edition covered the years from 1932 to 1938.[123] In his introduction, the journalist briefly described the diaries' provenance, underlining the comment of Emilio Re, the inspector general of the state archives who presided over their discovery in 1950, that 'people search for Mussolini's diaries. But the real and important Mussolini diaries are these ones by Petacci, where the dictator becomes a man and is revealed without make-up or artifice. In the diaries and letters there can be found not merely the dictator's romantic life but also high politics and, on crucial occasions, the life of the entire country.'[124]

Claretta's diaries may have long been shrouded by the Italian state. But their pathway into the archives was clear enough. Just before her final flight to Milan on 18 April 1945, Claretta had packed her personal records into crates and passed them into the hands of her friend, Countess Caterina Cervis, who worked for D'Annunzio's widow, owner of the Vittoriale complex, which included the Villa Mirabella, Petacci's last sanctuary by Lago di Garda. Cervis and her husband buried the trove and, after 1945, began to realise that it might bring them financial gain.

The surviving Petaccis either had similar ideas or were moved by familial piety. In October 1949 Giuseppina Persichetti was the first of their number to return from Spain. When she arrived at Gardone, however, the Cervises received her frostily, refusing her requests to hand over what Claretta had entrusted to them. In February 1950 a leak to *Il Corriere della Sera* made public what had been done in 1945, with the effect that Italian government officials recovered the Petacci papers. They carried them off to the archives in Rome where Emilio Re prepared a full catalogue.[125] With Myriam now also back in Italy, in July 1951 the Petacci family sued for the return of their property, seeking 394,935 lire in additional compensation. The favourable judgement in January 1952 was reversed on appeal, with the state's lawyers emphasising that the documentation had 'genuine political import' and was not merely private, for it demonstrated that Claretta's influence on the *Duce* had steadily grown. 'Petacci', the court heard, 'may have lacked the highest degree of education. But she was not deprived of natural ingenuity and sometimes, when not blinded by jealousy, was possessed of penetrative understanding.' Moreover, given the way that she recorded what Mussolini said over the phone 'almost stenographically', the diaries could be viewed as much Mussolini's as hers.[126] They belonged therefore to national and not just Petacci family history.

Legal activity continued over the return of the Villa Camilluccia, the possible prosecution of those partisans who had killed Mussolini and his lover, and the dispute with Zita Ritossa. However, the Petacci papers remained securely in the vaults of the Archivio Centrale dello Stato, a grand Fascist building in the model regime suburb of EUR (Esposizione Universale Romana), planned under the dictatorship and, perhaps paradoxically, completed after 1945.[127] Hopes that the papers would fall back into family hands evaporated. Claretta's mother, Giuseppina, died in March 1962; her father Francesco Saverio in 1970. Ever since the war, Myriam had acted as the real head of the family and custodian of Claretta's positive memory. Her life ended in May 1991 amid further controversy and talk of new litigation.

The spur was the emergence in the family of Ferdinando Petacci, the second son of Claretta's elder brother, Marcello. Ferdinando had worked in a range of business activity in the Americas, from 1983 residing in various parts of the USA. His main address is now in Tempe, Arizona. Over her last years, Myriam lived in a flat in EUR in declining economic circumstances. She was nursed by Rita D'Agostini, once a maid in the Mussolini family house and a staunch supporter of the MSI. But, when Ferdinando arrived for his aunt's funeral, he charged D'Agostini with purloining jewels that Myriam had conserved, with stealing 23 million lire from her accounts and even with hastening her death. Prime among the lost property was,

INTRODUCTION

allegedly, a 'testament' that Claretta had written down before her death and, presumably, not passed on to the Cervises.[128] In response, D'Agostini came out fighting, telling journalists that she was the real Fascist. Myriam, she reported, 'could not bear' her nephew who, in return, had ignored her and done nothing to alleviate her 'squalid, solitary, final agony'. Nothing that he claimed was true, she concluded firmly.[129]

No concrete results of this spat have been recorded and, since then, no further talk of any mysterious last writings by Claretta has recurred. But Ferdinando has very much become the new head of the family and ever-active conservator of (a version of) Claretta's memory, as well as that of his parents and grandparents.

In regard to its trove of Petacci papers, the Archivio Centrale rigorously observed a seventy-year rule. But such a fiat meant that, from the first decade of the new millennium, the diaries could be read and assessed by journalists and scholars and made available for public reckoning. As was noted above, a first selection from the material, covering the years from 1932 to 1938, was published by Suttora in 2009. Two years later, with Franzinelli now editing, another extensive selection appeared with entries from 1939 to 1940. A further volume, again edited by Franzinelli and covering the tumultuous times from 1941 to 1945, has, for obscure reasons, not been published at my time of writing.[130]

For Ferdinando, issues involving his aunt and parents have become imbricated with the vast theorising about Churchill's dealings with Mussolini that has involved many Italian historians and commentators. Its origin may well have lain in Fascist wartime propaganda depicting 'the English' as the prime national enemy and was certainly cherished by neofascists after 1945; one grew almost apoplectic in expressing his dislike of Churchill's fat pink face, which he compared to 'that of an over-fed eunuch'.[131] This associated story of forgery, political manipulation, naive or wilful misreading and/or invention of evidence has recently been recounted by Franzinelli, with the same immense critical skill that he displayed in unravelling the faking of the Mussolini diaries.[132] Ferdinando Petacci, who must reject such findings, had already made plain his views in a preface attached to Suttora's collection,[133] and took them further in a coda published with the volume about 1939–40.[134] In this latter case,

CLARETTA

Ferdinando began with the assertion that his aunt had actually been an 'anti-Fascist' arguing that, right from the first meeting in 1932 with the *Duce*, she had been motivated not by passion but the desire to spy. It was that devotion which kept her attached to the *Duce*, even when he began to mistreat her. Whatever her sex life, she remained in her soul a Catholic, and her profound religious belief eliminated any temptation to indulge in that anti-Semitism legislated by the regime after 1938. In Ferdinando's reading, the diaries were therefore not 'real', since they did not really convey his aunt's actual thoughts and personality (and covert actions), but only Mussolini's. For example they did not hint at the possibility that, given his contacts in the Vatican, Francesco Saverio Petacci could have acted as a conduit to pass Claretta's secrets to the British.

After such remarkable claims, Ferdinando switched his attention to Churchill and to the 'lost' Mussolini letters, reiterating the views of the numerous paladins of this conspiracy theory that, in 1945, the ruthless British prime minister needed to dispose of embarrassing papers and agents who had served their use. Ferdinando gave a new twist to the conspiracies, suggesting that the diaries had probably been interfered with somehow and by somebody. They had, for example, been manipulated to accuse Mussolini of responsibility for the Holocaust, when he was not really a sincere anti-Semite. So, Petacci concluded with a bleak refusal of the merit of any historiography, 'in so far as Italy is concerned, only archaeologists in some far-off future perhaps will be able to reconstruct the history of our country, if technological advances allow them to distinguish between false and authentic documentation'.[135]

Failing any evidence to sustain Ferdinando Petacci's spirited comprehension of his national and family history, an analyst has every reason to rejoice in the amplitude of the Petacci papers and in the bright light that they throw on the Italian dictatorship and many of the interpretative disputes that mark it (as they should do while democratic history can thrive or survive as 'an argument without end').[136] For anybody wanting to probe the nature of Mussolini's dictatorship, in sum, diaries – real and conjectured – are the beginning of wisdom.

What Ciano reported in his version, published quickly in the postwar period, was largely political and diplomatic, although the fact that he was

INTRODUCTION

a brilliant young man ensured that his unspoken assumptions revealed much about how a natural young conservative coped with chat about Fascist revolution and its totalitarian realignment, in theory, of all Italian hearts and minds. Predictably, the fake Mussolini diaries tie simplistically with the historiographical assumptions of 1950, privileging high politics and the making of peace and war. They naturally connect with the old-fashioned, neo-Rankean approach to history, sustained to his death in 1996 by De Felice as the doyen of Fascist studies, and by no means yet abandoned in many Italian and foreign academic studies of the regime.

By contrast, the Petacci diaries and letters, and the other material, doubtless on occasion fragile and scandalous, need to be read between the lines, just as all historical sources do. Claretta was undoubtedly 'telling her own story' as she obsessively scribbled down every remark her lover directed at her, either over the phone or when they were in more intimate contact, whether to do with their latest squabble or with politics and ideology. She was also endeavouring to tell the *Duce*'s story as a man of sublime grandeur (and occasional personal weakness). Claretta may have been starstruck. But she never lost a sense of self nor a kind of self-importance. The haste of her writing demonstrates an urgency that drove her as a diarist, stark proof that her subjectivity was engrained into her pages. As time went on and she matured in her own fashion, she became ever more resolute in a self-defined task to stiffen the *Duce* against his sea of troubles.

It would be naive to ask whether Claretta was telling the truth in her pages, and there must have been occasions when she misunderstood or slanted material in her own favour. Diarists, by definition, like to think that they matter and are given to exaggeration on that score. Yet the verisimilitude of Claretta's account is unchallengeable and it and the other sources that can be brought to bear on the Petacci family story open new avenues of understanding of the Mussolini dictatorship and its curious medley of avowedly 'totalitarian' social engineering and practical compromise with existing Italian histories. In so doing, Claretta's extensive papers fit neatly into the new preoccupation of historians with emotions and psychology and what may be the deep springs of human actions. Their pages record orgasm, the extrusion of most bodily fluids, hysteria, fainting fits, illness, anger, jealousy, possessiveness, love and hate, music, poetry, reading and art, as well as politics. They illuminate the 'private' at least as much as they do the 'public'. They draw attention to the Catholic, the familial, the local and Roman, the bourgeois, the personal, while displaying – despite the deep hostility that Claretta and her family provoked among those most committed to the RSI – the Fascist, even the radical fascist. In entering the world of Claretta Petacci and her family, readers will confront a 'real' Italy, one that was not merely 'legal' or ideological. Claretta's story may lack the depth of tragedy. But, in its human texture, commitment and contradiction, as well as its female representation of 'love' and sex in high places, it is worth deep and detailed reflection.

1

SEX AND THE COMING DICTATOR

One per day through his adult life. Five thousand. Four hundred. One hundred and sixty-two. About twenty (by Rachele's reckoning). The number of women with whom Mussolini is said to have had sex varies wildly.[1] In a conversation with a (male) admirer in 1937, Mussolini deprecated too elevated an estimate of his sexual prowess. 'As far as women are concerned,' he declared, 'my experience is the same as all healthy men, neither more nor less than others. If I, Mussolini, had had truck with all the women they claim for me, I would have to have been a stallion rather than a man.' A Don Giovanni or a 'ladies' man' must be despised, he added.[2] By contrast, when indulging in bed-chat with Claretta, Mussolini boasted on one occasion that he simply could not remember the tally of women whom he had penetrated. Then he liked to savour how, some time not long after his installation as prime minister, he had kept fourteen different lovers on the go at the same time, satisfying four of them every day. In May 1938 he boasted to the wide-eyed Claretta that he had sex with one at 8 p.m., another at 9, another at 10 . . . before climaxing with 'a terrible Brazilian' whose name he had forgotten (leaving open the distinct possibility that he was fantasising to his credulous young partner).[3] On another occasion, he complained to Claretta that, in 1923–4, he had been lonely, with only Margherita Sarfatti, Bianca Ceccato and another woman showing up in his bed from time to time.[4]

Any sexual pleasure for him or them may have been brief. Quinto Navarra, major-domo at Palazzo Venezia, in his graphic but controversial memoirs, allegedly written after the war by two journalists on the make, reckoned the *Duce* took two or three minutes over each copulation,[5] with the implication picked up by the biographer Denis Mack Smith that sex with this dictator was rape or something similar to it – 'sadism' not love.[6]

Whatever the case – and all the literature on the subject, marked as it is by scandal, innuendo or sentiment, needs sceptical scrutiny – by most accounts sex and Mussolini went together as automatically as a horse and carriage. To use a cruder parallel from the animal world adopted by the sometime Fascist and later radical conservative and celebrity journalist Indro Montanelli the dictator dealt with women as 'a cock does his hens'.[7] A contemporary journalist-historian, Roberto Olla, has a more circumspect metaphor: 'sex . . . was at the centre of the myth of Mussolini: all the rest turned upon this, like a wheel around a hub'.[8] The most extreme representation of the *Duce* in this regard came in a tract written in 1945 by Carlo Emilio Gadda, another intellectual with a Fascist past by then renounced. It was entitled *Eros e Priapo*. Long held to be obscene, the work was published in expurgated version in 1967 when Gadda labelled his old leader 'the leading Harvester, Fantasist and Ejaculator' of Italy. Under this dictator's rule, he declared, all that women had to do for the *patria* was 'to let themselves be fucked'. In his opinion, the *Duce*'s governance was less revolutionary or tyrannical than priapic.[9]

It is therefore surprising to find Alexander Geppert, a German cultural historian, maintaining that Adolf Hitler was 'an adored object of desire, a powerful sex symbol and a pined-for lover', stimulating in his fans carnality of greater intensity than that aroused by Mussolini. The Italian dictator, by contrast, Geppert argues, 'appears as a different type of leader – less sexualised and more avuncular – who was to be contacted for direct advice and uncomplicated assistance' by women of the people.[10] Geppert's sample of Germans is meagre and he seems to have done no serious research on Italy. He has not noticed, for example, a letter reeking with childish passion that Mussolini received from a Florentine first communicant in May 1936. 'I, so little, with so many defects, so distracted and sometimes disobedient to Mamma and Papà, so negligent with my school work, such an egoist', she wrote with pre-teenage angst to a master on high. 'If only I could receive you together with Jesus! To be on my tongue, to lie on my chest, to rest on my poor heart! How good that would be!' she concluded in innocent intermingling of fleshly fellatio and holy sacrament.[11]

Nonetheless, Geppert may have a point worth noting: much of the development of Mussolini's image as a Latin lover run wild actually occurred after the war, where stories of his rampages became a natural partner to the sentimentalising of the dictatorship in the illustrated weeklies. Before 1945 ordinary Italians, if it is possible to use the term, in the great majority of cases lived their daily lives far from the centres of power, and Geppert is correct in arguing that Fascist welfare policies, despite what now can be comprehended as their corruption and confusion,[12] were marketed by an active and adroit propaganda as gushing like a fountain from the dictator himself. The Archivio Centrale preserves tens of thousands of letters, written by Italians to their dictator, the majority of which seek implicit or explicit gain through Mussolini's personal intervention and are more interested in property, employment and improved living conditions than sex.[13]

Moreover, there are other reasons to doubt the common implication that Mussolini was unusual in his sexual reach and performance. After all, the literature hostile to autocratic power is filled with sex scandals and regularly insists that dictators display their ruthlessness in bed as unrestrainedly as they do in public policy. The behaviour of such Julio-Claudian emperors as Caligula and Nero (or, with a different gender cast, Tiberius), as slyly described by Suetonius and Tacitus, has been a lasting model. In more recent times, especially, and perhaps in Mussolini's wake (however transmuted by local factors), pen portraits of the copulative habits of dictators have remained conspicuous. Muammar Gaddafi, a French journalist declared, was 'a tyrant who ruled through sex, obsessed with the idea of one day possessing the wives or daughters of the rich and powerful, of his ministers and generals, of chiefs of state and monarchs'. On a daily basis, Gaddafi made do with raping and enslaving 'hundreds of young girls', the charge runs. Only in brutal and rapid sexual congress could he be truly satiated in his rise from poor Bedouin to 'Brotherly Leader' of his people.[14]

More flamboyant was Jean-Bédel Bokassa in the Central African Republic, an admirer of Napoleon who, in 1976, elevated himself to emperor. Bokassa tallied seventeen legitimate wives and thirty recognised progeny, of whom one bore the euphonious name Charlemagne. An expert on his regime has suggested that Bokassa's children numbered 'in the hundreds';[15] with this quiverful, Bokassa eclipsed his imperial model. In regard to the romance of power, however, Napoleon is still an eminent figure and one from whom it is hard to separate politics and sex. The Frenchman is especially remembered for his frank expression of love. As he wrote to Josephine Beauharnais, he longed to 'kiss her heart and then lower on her body, much, *much* lower'.[16] Not for nothing was Mussolini the (co-)author of a play about Napoleon, being given to muse uneasily with Claretta whether he yet had come up to the Corsican's heroic ideal.[17] Petacci was, however, no Josephine, being far too prudish to allow her diary to record their physicality over-frankly; she coyly wrote 'c..o' for *culo* ('bum'), 'p . . .' for *puttana* ('whore') and could not spell pederast or haemorrhoid,[18] while Mussolini's own youthful bodice-ripper, *The cardinal's mistress* (1910), was scarcely explicit in its depiction of sex.[19]

If dictators (and they are always male) are often assumed to have been rampant in their lust, other prominent men of the Fascist era scarcely confined themselves to the marriage bed. The Futurist poet Filippo Tommaso Marinetti assured his diary in 1917 that he needed a new woman every day. 'I am always a man of rapid and violent coitus,' he ruminated complacently, 'then comes sleep and detachment' (although, in possible retribution for such sexism, in 1923 he married Benedetta Cappa, twenty-one years his junior; she proved at least as thrusting a personality as he).[20] Before that, Marinetti's self-consciously wicked denunciation of the family as 'an inferior sentiment, almost animal, created by fear' was wildly inaccurate as a presage of the behaviour of actual families, like the Petaccis and Mussolinis, under Fascism.[21]

Gabriele D'Annunzio, another poet whose political appeal made him a serious rival to Mussolini as a post-First World War *Duce*, judged himself immodestly to be 'the world's greatest lover'. According to his most recent biographer, D'Annunzio possessed special flair in cunnilingus (a sceptical historian might wonder whether Claretta could imagine that version of intimacy).[22] On the other side of the gender divide lay Doris Duranti, early cinema star and sometime lover of Alessandro Pavolini, the secretary of the revived Partito Fascista Repubblicano (PFR; Republican Fascist

Party) under the Repubblica Sociale Italiana, who claimed in her memoirs to have bedded at least one hundred men.[23] She was also demanding: early in their relationship, Pavolini was reported to have given her five expensive furs just as a token of love.[24]

Taking lovers was standard practice among Fascist Party hierarchs. As was noted, Ciano was thought a competitor with his father-in-law in his array of sexual partners. Italo Balbo, the most serious potential rival to Mussolini within the Fascist Party, while remaining solicitous towards his wife (she was the daughter of a rich banker) and family, found time for numerous affairs. There were even rumours of intercourse with Crown Princess Maria José, who was locked in a loveless marriage with Umberto, the heir to the throne. When Balbo was rusticated in 1933 to be governor of Libya, he took with him his young lover, the actor Laura Adami, and patronised her appearances there as Ophelia, Juliet and in other celebrated roles.[25] Adami, born in 1913, was a year younger than Claretta. Michele Bianchi, Roberto Farinacci, Ettore Muti, Arturo Bocchini and many other Fascist bosses behaved similarly.[26] Mussolini's private secretariat kept extensive, and presumably useful, files on the sexual peccadilloes of the regime's ruling elite; there, charges of adultery were at least as common as complaints about peculation.[27]

But too inflated emphasis on dictators and Italians may be mistaken. After all, American president John F. Kennedy assured the gentlemanly British prime minister Harold Macmillan (who had the courtesy to put up with his wife's longstanding affair with his bisexual friend, Robert Boothby), that he needed a woman every three days or else would be rent by a terrible headache.[28] Another biographer reckons it was one per day but adds that Kennedy declared that his 'passion' was 'spent quickly' and readily 'disposed of like an itch'.[29] An aide computed knowingly that, in so far as the administration of the American empire was concerned, sex demanded 'less time than tennis'.[30] In our own era, Dominique Strauss-Kahn sounds as though he was at least as ruthless as Kennedy in his mating habits,[31] while Berlusconi retailed a myth of himself as a great lover as enthusiastically as did Mussolini.[32]

Nor was patriarchal behaviour very different in that generation which made Italy during the Risorgimento. Giuseppe Garibaldi, for one, broke immediately with a second wife thirty-four years his junior when he heard allegations of her infidelity. His next wife, married in 1880 just before his death, was forty years younger than he and the wet nurse of his grandchildren. Earlier, as Lucy Riall has described, Garibaldi 'had a series of passionate, overlapping relationships with several women', some of them foreign.[33]

Patriarchal attitudes and actions may flourish wherever men gather. But, of modern ideologies, Fascism is the most extreme in putting men on top in its imagined ideal society. In that regard, Victoria De Grazia began her study *How Fascism ruled women*: 'Mussolini's regime stood for returning women to home and hearth, restoring patriarchal authority, and confining female destiny to bearing babies.'[34] Often enough, Mussolini was crass in expressing his contempt for women. As he assured his celebrated interviewer, Emil Ludwig, in 1932, with himself in mind, 'women exert no influence upon strong men'. After all, he added, they were 'analytical, not synthetical' and could only 'play a passive part' in the great world. 'During all the centuries of civilisation', they had followed and not led men, he concluded sententiously.[35]

Quite a few historians have accepted that Mussolini's Ascension Day speech in 1927 was the crucial guide to his regime's purpose with its pledge to 'dictate demography' and thereby police and animate the bedrooms of the masses.[36] Yet the most recent study of the fate of the Italian family under the dictatorship has concluded that Fascism failed to decide 'the exact contours of the family discourse that it wanted to propagate', with the result being that, throughout the era, Catholicism, not the dictatorship, 'offered the dominant model of family life in Italy'. The regime failed to alter either the law or Italians' 'long-standing beliefs, habits and customs' in regard to their family loyalty.[37] Similarly De Grazia wryly deployed the cliché in her book's title in order to expose the actual variation and confusion of policy and practice, especially where there was radical chat about the marshalling of the 'new Fascist woman'.

In examining Claretta Petacci and her world, it is important therefore to underline that Mussolini's behaviour towards his sexual partners was more nuanced than sensational accounts of the 'Great Ejaculator' have allowed. It may be that evidence about his other relationships is less reliable and extensive than that revealed so rapturously about Claretta's ties with the *Duce* in her papers. Yet a full comprehension of their affair in turn demands knowledge of the dictator's other dealings with women and a portrayal of how Mussolini behaved sexually during his socialist youth, his Fascist rise to power and once installed as dictator.

By his own account, his first intercourse occurred while a teenager in a local brothel, as it must have done for many boys of his class. The woman, he recalled, was older than he was and much more experienced. It was not his only meeting with a prostitute. When serving his term of military conscription in 1905–6, he informed Claretta in 1938, 'I often went to the brothel where the women were rather knowing and dirty. But they initiated me into the mysteries and vices of sex.' Before that 'a romantic', afterwards, he explained coldly, 'I have regarded all the women whom I have taken as if they were in a brothel. For my carnal satisfaction.'[38]

The chronology of Mussolini's memory was as vague as his sentiments were crude and peremptory. But there are accounts, more or less credible, of fleeting affairs with women, often the wives of other men, who crossed his path while he was a primary school teacher in the provinces or a questing socialist emigrant in Switzerland and the Austrian Trentino. When he was teaching at Tolmezzo, for example, he disclosed to Claretta, 'the girls were wild for me', but the name of only one of them – Graziosa – had stuck in his memory.[39] The use of force was often a key part of Mussolini's recollection, and a method to be applauded. Whether events happened exactly as he described and whether male aggression was unusual in his world at the time remains imponderable. More established is the claim that, at Trento in 1909, he fathered a boy child on a socialist comrade called Fernanda Oss Facchinelli. But the baby did not survive infancy and the relationship soon ended.[40]

Apart from his 'sainted mother', Rosa Maltoni, who died, aged only forty-six, in 1904 – Mussolini never ceased to invoke this reverent or clichéd image of her maternal love for him in his waywardness[41] – the most impressive woman whom he met in these years as an aspirant revolutionary was the Russian Marxist Angelica Balabanoff. Five years his senior, she assumed a major part in his life as a teacher of elementary dialectics, a legacy that remained with him as dictator when he had frequent need to appear knowing, without having the time or will to master the subject involved.[42] A recent biographer of Balabanoff has contended that she and Mussolini were lovers from when they met in Switzerland for almost a decade until 1913, but the contention seems based on the fancy, common in that era, and certainly held by Mussolini, that a man and a woman could not be alone together without sexual congress.[43] If there was once a fondness between them, Balabanoff had radically changed her mind in a work first published in New York in 1942, where her character study of the dictator was devastatingly hostile. 'Naturally diffident, a misanthrope, always worried about looking a fool, envious of those who knew anything ... Mussolini saw in every intellectual an enemy and competitor.' For all loyal socialists, she concluded, he was nothing more than 'A *Man bought and sold*, a *Judas*, a *murderous Cain*.'[44] Mussolini, by contrast, was surprisingly generous in his recollection of her, telling a young male admirer that she had indeed taught him how to think.[45]

Speculation about a period when many wild oats were sown does not end but takes a new course after the commencement of the *Duce*'s partnership with his eventual wife and the mother of his five legitimate children, Rachele Guidi, late in 1909. The two were joined in a socialist small-town romance, with Mussolini soon carrying off his young lover (born in April 1890, she was almost seven years his junior) from his father's home through the rain so they could live together in a tiny flat at Forlì, where Mussolini was the editor and sole serious journalist on the staff of the earnestly entitled local socialist paper, *La Lotta di Classe* ('The Class Struggle'). As he later drooled in his rough manner to Claretta, Rachele was then 'in flower, buxom, with magnificent breasts, beautiful'. 'A peasant', he added in evident sop to his bourgeois lover's readily aroused jealousy, 'but a beautiful one'. One day, he ran on, 'I threw her on an armchair and took her virginity ... with my accustomed violence.' Soon thereafter she fell pregnant and, accepting her plea that he not abandon her, they agreed to pursue a life together, with the result that he abandoned a half-idea he was treasuring of immigrating to the USA.[46]

The first child of this relationship was a daughter, Edda, born on 1 September 1910. Until just before they set up house together, Rachele had been residing with her mother, Anna Guidi, who herself was the lover of Mussolini's father, Alessandro, prompting unsubstantiated claims that Rachele may have been Benito's half-sister.[47] Scandalmongers on occasion have similarly asserted that Edda was 'really' Balabanoff's child,[48] and even contended that, after she had grown up, Mussolini committed incest with her.[49]

In 1912 a momentous change occurred in Mussolini's life when his revolutionary faction triumphed at the Socialist Party congress at Reggio Emilia. In reward for this victory, Mussolini, still only twenty-nine, was promoted to editor of the main party newspaper, *Avanti!*, which had just moved its office from Rome to Italy's business capital, Milan. Now Edda, her father and mother rented a flat in a bustling modern city; for Benito Mussolini confinement in the dull and politically flaccid provinces was over. This new world proffered fresh sexual opportunity: Mussolini was scarcely confined by comradeship with his partner, Rachele, (*'la mia compagna'*, as he called her),[50] even though they took out a civil marriage certificate in December 1915, before Rachele gave birth to two further children, sons Vittorio and Bruno, in September 1916 and April 1918.

While his legitimate family was expanding, Mussolini's political life was subject to momentous change. From 1911 to 1914 he assumed a leading Party role as a socialist revolutionary, as well as proving a capable journalist and business manager on *Avanti!* The outbreak of European war brought a radical shift when, in October, following the guidance of many of his country's leading intellectuals, Mussolini swung round to demand national entry into the conflict and did so at the cost of expulsion from the Socialist Party and the loss of his editorship of its daily paper. He quickly returned to the fray as editor of his own newspaper, *Il Popolo d'Italia* ('The People of Italy'), its Mazzinian or warmongering populism announcing that he now spoke for the nation above class. Italy finally did enter battle against Austria in May 1915, and five months later Mussolini accepted conscription into the national armed forces, serving at the front along the Isonzo valley until wounded by shrapnel on 24 February 1917 in an accidental explosion behind the lines.[51] But words and guns did not entirely fill his life. Through these hectic times, Mussolini, despite his union with Rachele, formed continuing relationships with three other women, Leda Rafanelli, Margherita Grassini Sarfatti and Ida Dalser, as his actual or hoped for sexual partners.

CLARETTA

It was before the war that, on 28 February 1912, Clara ('Claretta') Petacci was born into a respectable, ambitious and deeply Catholic Roman bourgeois family (utterly antithetical to Mussolini's then-imagined destiny as the leader of socialist and universal revolution). She owed her name to their devotion to Santa Chiara, an early follower of St Francis of Assisi. The *pater familias* was Francesco Saverio (Francis Xavier) Petacci, the piety of his name evoking the family's longstanding and continuing links with the Vatican. Francesco Saverio had, however, been born in Constantinople in 1883, making him the same age as Mussolini. In the Turkish capital, his father, Edoardo, worked as a senior official in the Ottoman postal service, allegedly pioneering its use of stamps. Edoardo Petacci was one of those not uncommon Italian professionals who had for centuries been scattered around the Mediterranean basin, in an experts' imperialism still lacking overt ties with that of the modern nation state. It was a background that Francesco Saverio shared with the Futurist chief Marinetti, born in Alexandria in 1876 to a lawyer and businessman who gave counsel to the khedive of Egypt.

In 1902 F.S. Petacci returned to Italy to complete medical training, rejoicing in the recommendations and patronage of his doctor uncle, Giuseppe, who held a prestigious post in the pope's medical service. There, in 1915, he found space for his nephew. Francesco Saverio's practice as a doctor was better rewarded financially in successive clinics that he operated, one being in the flourishing new Roman suburb of Monteverde. By the 1930s F.S. Petacci directed another medical practice, purposefully situated at Via Nazionale 69 in the city centre.

In 1909 Francesco Saverio had married his cousin, Giuseppina Persichetti, born in 1888 into a fertile Catholic family; she had seven siblings. Her father, Augusto, at least according to his granddaughter, Myriam, had been a leader of the Italian Catholic Youth Society soon after that body came into existence in 1867.[52] The Petaccis and the Mussolinis may have been a class apart but, similar to Benito and Rachele, there was no delay in the arrival of children to Giuseppina and Francesco Saverio. A son was born on 1 May 1910, May Day. The Petaccis utterly rejected that date's coincidence with the socialist workers' festival by christening their son Marcello Cesare Augusto, thereby arming him with that *romanità* (spirit of classical Rome) which would become a major theme in Fascist propaganda but which had already before 1914 beguiled the minds of respectable Romans.

During the next year of *Cinquantennio* (fiftieth anniversary celebrations of national unity), the grandiose Victor Emmanuel monument was opened athwart the ancient Capitol and the nation embarked on aggressive and brutal imperial conquest of the Ottoman provinces of Tripolitania and Cyrenaica, which the Italians called Libya, drawing on the Latin word for North Africa.[53] Rhetoricians hailed the augmented power of the 'Third Italy' and exulted in its modern 'legionaries' 'reclaiming an empire'. By contrast, the revolutionary socialist, Mussolini, at the time of Edda's birth deeply and ostentatiously anti-national and anti-clerical, lambasted Rome as 'a parasitic city, full of landladies, shoeshine boys, prostitutes, priests and bureaucrats'.[54] Mussolini's soul, unlike those of the Petaccis, was certainly not yet Roman.

Dreams of empire among the bourgeoisie did not necessarily convert into action. When Marcello grew to manhood, as will be seen below, he proved less Caesar Augustus than princeling, assiduously seeking promotion and financial gain through his sister's influence. Meanwhile, for more than a decade, with Giuseppina somehow controlling her fertility, he and Claretta were the Petaccis' only children, before Myriam completed the new generation on 31 May 1923. All were proud to be Petaccis; parents and offspring were deeply bonded as a family, with a commitment that neither Claretta's entry into Mussolini's bed nor the 'tragedy' of 1945 weakened for an instant.

Such developments in the lives of Roman bourgeois occurred well beyond Mussolini's ken. In Milan, however, there was plenty to do for the new editor of *Avanti!* and aspirant leader of a socialist movement seemingly fixed on revolution, even if he never renounced his own social and intellectual ambitions. Advances in his public life could readily be matched by fresh excitement in his private. Now among his widening contacts was Leda Rafanelli, a new woman of the belle époque, primed to open Mussolini's mind to a rich and world-girdling span of culture and politics. An anarchist of independent cast, Rafanelli flirted with what was called 'Arabism' and 'the spirit of the East', read books, presided over a salon and enthused about gender and racial equality. An observer might add that, if photos are to be believed, she looked her age and, with a large nose, slim figure and her dark eyes fixed on the camera, she was anything but a conventional 'Italian' beauty. But, for a questing Mussolini, it was easy to conjoin physical and intellectual appeal.

Indeed, Rafanelli's range and unconventionality stunned the young man from Forlì. Her endorsement of 'free love' seemed enticingly to offer him a more earthy consummation of their friendship, although it is doubtful whether coitus between the two ever occurred. Nonetheless, hard at work in his editorial position, and writing furiously there and elsewhere, Mussolini eagerly found time for penning frequent epistles to Rafanelli and for plotting meetings with her in his spare time, either in the afternoon when others might take siesta or late at night, trysts that might entail sex. In pressing himself upon her, Mussolini often adopted a flamboyance that, in retrospect, sounds more hers than his: 'With you I feel miles from Milan, politics, journalism, Italy, the West, Europe . . . Let's read Nietzsche and the Quran together.' 'Let's talk unrestrainedly of the past, of the present, of the future: of everything and nothing.' Yet the practical could creep in: 'Listen. I am free every afternoon. Write to me when I can come, and I shall be there punctual and discreet', he wrote, coyly signing himself off 'B'.[55]

Sadly for Mussolini's hopes that Leda's feminine magnetism could pull him away from his humdrum life with what he told her deprecatingly was his 'domestic tribe',[56] their politics were not to prove compatible. With the outbreak of the First World War in August 1914, and the debate it at once unleashed over how the 'least of the Great Powers' could most benefit from it, his and Rafanelli's paths separated for ever. By October 1914 Mussolini had succumbed to the idea that Italian participation in battle must accelerate social revolution (and his own advancement), while she kept an anarchist's hatred of the war-making state, its militarism and imperialism. Correspondence between the two ceased. In later years Rafanelli kept to her faith, never regretting her loss of contact with the 'class traitor', Mussolini. She endured Fascism, for a time still able to publish but eventually reduced to poverty. By the 1930s she was getting by as a fortune-teller and teacher of Arabic. However, she outlived the *Duce*, after 1945 publishing some of their letters. With typical sangfroid, she greeted the imposition of Christian Democrat rule in Italy by republishing an early polemic she had written against priestly chastity.[57] She died at a good age in 1971. A memoir came out four years later.[58]

In any case, during much the same months that Mussolini was being uncharacteristically starry-eyed about matters of the soul in communion with Rafanelli, another older woman, also born in 1880, entered his life, offering sex as well as social, cultural and political instruction. Her name was Margherita Grassini Sarfatti, sprung from a wealthy Venetian Jewish family and married at eighteen to the socialist lawyer Cesare Sarfatti, fourteen years her elder. They had two sons and a daughter, born respectively in 1900, 1902 and 1909. A photo from 1912 shows that, by then, Sarfatti had begun to put on the weight of encroaching middle age, with a figure that was matriarchal not lissom. It displays her as having possessed a round face, regular features, curly hair, rich jewels, and an elegant and expensive gown. She certainly was not as idiosyncratic-looking as Rafanelli but she, too, was not classically beautiful.

Sarfatti's English-language biographers, Philip Cannistraro and Brian Sullivan, have labelled her 'Mussolini's other woman', although this claim for exclusivity will be seen, through the following pages, to be undeserved.[59] Cannistraro and Sullivan state that the two had become lovers by 1913. At that time, Sarfatti presided over a more orthodox and worldly salon than Rafanelli's. Wealthy, confident and independent, Sarfatti rendered herself an important figure in Milan's artistic life, while also being a socialist activist. She belonged many rungs up the class ladder from Benito and Rachele, who still lived in a small flat on the edge of the city and were troubled by household bills; Rachele frequently lamented that her partner spent too much money on books, objects that were not for her.[60] However, Sarfatti met Mussolini at a gathering of the city's intellectual elites and decided immediately that he was another 'Napoleon', adding, with what might be read as a combination of sexual attraction and effortless superiority, that he, too, like the French hero, was a parvenu anxious to rise, equipped with burning eyes and irresistible physicality.[61]

Rafanelli was thought to have had an affair with the Futurist painter Carlo Carrà when they both for a while lived in Egypt. But Sarfatti was in contact with all of Italy's 'generation of 1914', among them Marinetti, D'Annunzio and Giuseppe Prezzolini, the editor of the intellectually independent journal *La Voce*, where Mussolini had assiduously endeavoured to establish a presence. To these three could be added a slew of painters, philosophers and poets who ranged a long way from the Sarfattis' commitment to socialism (they were equally alive to current developments in feminism and Zionism). Although Cesare and Margherita's marriage was drifting apart, the two lived in a large and elegant apartment among the best people of the city and could afford to run a country house near Lake Como and the Swiss border, eloquently depicted by Cannistraro and Sullivan as 'a rustic two-story structure decorated with green shutters and a red stucco exterior. Perched on the edge of a hillside . . . [it] commanded a magnificent view of the valley below and the Alpine foothills beyond.'[62]

Her wealth and self-confidence allowed Sarfatti to talk glibly, then and later, about achieving a revolution in national consciousness[63] and ideas (and, behind them, a savoir-faire) that attracted Mussolini, still aspiring to make his own intellectual mark and hopeful of giving his personal imprint to socialist thought. Holding almost painful intellectual aspirations, Mussolini had zealously improved his qualifications to teach middle school French through an exam at Bologna University in November 1907.[64] At home, where he could command his own status, Rachele, at least according to her postwar memoirs, was expected respectfully to address him as *professore* until after the birth of their fourth child in 1927.[65] No wonder, in 1912, he was ready to accept any invitation from Sarfatti. Here then was another older woman, like Rafanelli (and Balabanoff) at least as much in control of her relationship with the young socialist editor as he was. In their initial contact, she did most of the teaching and he the learning.

In contrast to the war's impact on Mussolini's relationship with Rafanelli, battle strengthened rather than shattered this tie. The death of Sarfatti's eldest son, Roberto, not yet eighteen, in January 1918, on one of his first forays to the front as a lieutenant, reinforced his mother's firming commitment to the nation of Italy and her renunciation of cosmopolitan socialism for what was becoming Fascism. As will be seen in the next chapter, through the 1920s Sarfatti for a time cemented a place as the most important woman in Mussolini's (and Italy's) life. She became a major intellectual force in the dictatorship, even if, by the late 1930s and with the regime drifting ever more into anti-Semitism, Mussolini assured Claretta that his sexual congress with the Venetian had only lasted two years, by implication from 1918 to 1920, and that he had always resented in a manly fashion Sarfatti's arrogant interference in high politics and seen through her cultural pretensions.[66]

Today Sarfatti remains a figure of debate, a situation enhanced by the fact that her unpublished archive apparently preserves 1,272 letters sent by Mussolini to her over the decades, a tally which, if correct, surpasses his correspondence with Claretta. In the Sarfatti letters, a rich source may await historians of Mussolini's sexual congress, although a recent republication of a disorganised tract, edited with recurrent interventions by Sullivan, scribbled down by Sarfatti in 1947, is of meagre value. It is full of ire against the *Duce* and emphatic that he was indeed a mad dictator, a victim of incurable syphilis, presumably caught in his youth.[67] The charge about his venereal infection cannot entirely be written off and has been given some support in a detailed analysis of Mussolini's recuperation in 1917 after his wounding at the front in a military hospital.[68] However, the presence of syphilis was not endorsed either by Mussolini's Nazi doctor, Georg Zachariae, in tests conducted in 1943–4,[69] nor by the American medical team who, in 1945, detached brain slivers from the dictator's corpse for autopsy.[70] Moreover, no sign of damaging inheritance of the disease by the legitimate and illegitimate children whom Mussolini fathered has been detected (with the dubious exception of Benito Albino, son of Ida Dalser, whose life and death are described below). An Italian observer with some medical training has concluded that Mussolini may well have caught gonorrhoea from one of his early brothel visits but denied that there is any evidence of the much more serious disease.[71] In sum, the allegations about syphilis must be treated as unproven, and be viewed with all the greater suspicion given the recurrent temptation to pronounce that political 'bad guys' are also very likely mad.

In Ida Irene Dalser (born – like Sarfatti and Rafanelli – in 1880), Mussolini was to form a relationship with someone who was not his social and intellectual superior. Sarfatti and Rafanelli, in their different ways, exploited their lover in as energetic a fashion as he did them. By contrast, Dalser was Mussolini's financial and social victim.

Dalser had been born at Sopramonte, a village in the hills above the city of Trento, then ruled by Austria and to become one of Italy's major territorial gains from the First World War. Her father was the mayor of the *paese* and relatively well off, if scarcely the class equal of the Sarfattis.[72] Nearby lay the small town of Pergine, equipped with an ample asylum for the mentally unstable that would eventually number Dalser among its patients; it is set evocatively below the medieval castle that once guarded the town and its valley. In her twenties, she trained as a nurse at Innsbruck and then, more adventurously, in massage and orthopaedics in Paris. Enriched by a modest inheritance, in February 1913 Dalser opened in Milan the Salone Orientale d'Igiene e Bellezza Mademoiselle Ida ('Mademoiselle Ida's Eastern Salon of Health and Beauty'), enticing customers through a joint evocation of the fascinating East and French romance. By then a photo shows a dark, plumpish woman with heavy tresses, wide lips and a long cleft or dimpled chin.

At around this time Dalser met Mussolini, it is said on an occasion when she had entered the office of *Avanti!* in order to place an advertisement for her business.[73] The two could reminisce over the fact that each had lived for a while at Trento but not met there, and 'Professor' Mussolini may have been tantalised by her French accent and familiarity with Paris, always the city of his dreams. Sex began soon afterwards, perhaps initially aroused by a massage that Ida gave Benito at her salon. By 1914 the two were indeed close, Mussolini writing kindly to her in August after her brother died in the Habsburg armies in Galicia, and while Mussolini was still a vociferous socialist opponent of 'the atrocious and bestial war that is covering the whole of Europe with blood'.[74]

One month later, Mussolini, in the way that he had, dashed off a letter during a visit to Rome to 'My little Ida', assuring her: 'I embrace you with all the passion of our moments of intimacy and love. I am your savage friend and lover, Benito.'[75] 'I have you in my blood and you have me in your blood',[76] he added, with a sentiment destined to recur in more decorous phrasing during his relationship with Claretta. But Mussolini's private dealings with Dalser now rubbed up against his public life when he renounced the editorship of *Avanti!* and set up at *Il Popolo d'Italia*. It has long been established that the heavy cost of this venture was borne by pro-war Italian capitalists and the French, and later British, secret services.[77] But another contributor to Mussolini's swift re-emergence as a journalist was Ida Dalser, who, perhaps thinking of herself as his 'wife', sold her beauty salon in his cause, resulting in her moving to cheap lodgings on Milan's periphery. She also switched her own politics from the socialist to the patriotic, anxious – as so many others of Mussolini's women were – to follow where her man led. Soon after, Dalser fell pregnant and on 11 November 1915 bore the son whom she named Benito Albino and whom she asserted was Mussolini's.[78]

Some commentators claim that, late in 1914, Dalser and Mussolini went through a church wedding ceremony, a year before the civil marriage that formally united the *Duce* and Rachele in what may have been bigamy. But allegations about the other matrimony depend on 'stolen' or non-existent documents. Mimmo Franzinelli, for one, is unconvinced that Mussolini could then have been dragged into church for whatever purpose.[79] Unsurprisingly, Marco Bellocchio's prize-winning 2009 film version of the story, entitled ironically *Vincere* ('Conquest'), takes the bigamy for granted. With that move up-market and up-class which is so often part of cinematic representation, the film portrays a world that was much lusher than the one Benito and Ida (and Rachele) actually occupied. The more clear-eyed critics concede that *Vincere* scarcely aspired to narrow historical accuracy, however much Bellocchio did expose to his audiences Dalser's victimhood and Mussolini's tyranny.[80]

One month after the birth of Dalser's son, Mussolini, by then a corporal in the army, in marrying Rachele produced official confusion over his personal details, which the military did not at first plumb. When they wanted to inform his wife of an attack of typhus, they approached Ida, not Rachele. In April 1916 there was a violent physical confrontation between Ida and Rachele beside their man's hospital bed, where the (pregnant) Rachele proved the stouter fighter, driving her rival off amid tears and imprecations.[81] Whatever doubts Mussolini may have had about the choice between these women, later that year, with the birth of a new legitimate son – named Vittorio as a sign of coming victory – the *Duce*, as he was already being called by his admirers, tried to pay Dalser a de facto alimony of 200 lire per month. This act implied her dismissal from his bed, although he did acknowledge his paternity of 'Benittino', as his mother called him.

But Dalser was not happy to be shrugged off and, for quite a few years, hauled her one-time partner from court to court. Moreover, she took every possible opportunity, preferably public, to castigate Mussolini for deserting her and their son, even if, two decades later, Mussolini assured Claretta complacently that 'Ida' had been utterly forgotten, just as Sarfatti and other old lovers had been.[82] 'Coward, pig, assassin, traitor', Dalser would yell beneath his flat or office window, while informing any who wanted to listen that she had been 'seduced and abandoned', as had her son, by her perfidious sometime comrade and lover.[83] Mussolini's then close associate Cesare Rossi recalled her 'neurotic and intransigent temperament', while also noting how Mussolini threatened her with a revolver in 1920 when he endeavoured in Fascist manner violently to frighten her off.[84] Rachele, Rossi added, carefully watched over these continuing ramifications of the affair and, in manly conversation, Mussolini allowed that he should be grateful for his legitimate wife's care and willingness to forgive his carnal sins. In her plain good sense, she resembled Napoleon's mother, he murmured with a parallel that would often spring to his mind.[85]

Much later, at a pause in his lovemaking with Claretta, Mussolini revealed a little more of his memory of the matter when he affirmed that Dalser had gone mad, and swore that Benito Albino had not been his son. 'Too many', he grouched, 'are attributed to me.'[86] There is little doubt, however, that he was lying, perhaps trying to deny to himself responsibility for Dalser and her son's sad fate. Painful their later lives were. Once Mussolini had achieved political power, he delegated the embarrassment of Dalser to be sorted out by his younger (more respectable and Catholic) brother Arnaldo, so often what Italians call a *portaborsa* ('bagman', or personal agent).[87] From June 1926 Dalser, on the orders of the prefect of Trento accepting intimations from on high, was confined to the asylum at Pergine, where she remained for years, when possible talking or writing furiously to inveigh against her fate, and, according to recent analysis, sane.[88] Her destiny in this regard has been newly emphasised over the last years,[89] all the more because of the parallels that may exist between her case and the habits of the post-Stalin USSR in using allegations of mental infirmity as a way of silencing its opponents.

To her utter dismay, Dalser was now separated from her son, who was rusticated to a distant college in the Piedmontese hills and subject to surveillance lest he try to leave. His surname was now officially not Mussolini, but Bernardi, after a local Fascist chief in the Trentino who had been persuaded it was wise to be his protector (of a kind). Benito Albino grew towards an uneasy manhood, still every now and again insisting that he was 'Benito Mussolini, son of the other Benito Mussolini'.[90]

On the night of 15/16 July 1935, with a far-off *Duce* busy planning the invasion of Ethiopia, Dalser managed to escape from her de facto prison at Pergine, using the classic method of tying her sheets together and clambering down them from her bedroom window. She reached Trento by 3 a.m. As dawn broke, however, the police picked her up. In punishment for her infraction of officialdom's rules, she was now transferred to another asylum on the island of San Clemente in the Venetian lagoon that was restricted to women patients. It was an institution governed with the severest discipline and secure against flight. Perhaps abandoning hope, she died there on 3 December 1937 of a cerebral haemorrhage, reduced at last to a helpless victim of the *Duce*'s unremitting harshness.

Their son's fate was little better. When, in 1932, he began to form a relationship with a local female worker – a pleasant and buxom woman – the two were separated and Benittino was sent to La Spezia under instruction in the navy. A cruise to the Far East followed. However, when he returned to Italy in June 1935 he too was diagnosed as mentally unstable and confined to the vast mental hospital in the Villa Crivelli Pusterla at Monbello in Lombardy.[91] He stayed there, failing in one attempt at escape in January 1936 and getting nowhere in an appeal he tried to send to his father two years later. Benito Albino died on 26 August 1942 in poverty, his father not answering pleas to expand on basic funeral costs of 331.50 lire.[92] Here perished the last surviving member of the unhappiest of Mussolini's 'other families'.

* * *

Yet there were quite a few such families and their histories are not all as sad nor as replete with melodrama as that of Ida and Benittino. After his months at the front and his wounding, in June 1917 Mussolini resumed his editorship of *Il Popolo d'Italia* and was soon purposefully dragging it out of threatened financial failure. His stance in favour of the war and a revolution to be led by 'the men of the trenches' – to his mind a natural aristocracy of will and achievement best represented by himself – grew steadily more intransigent. By the end of 1917 the military defeat at Caporetto and the near-collapse of Italian participation in the war made him seem far-sighted, since now even orthodox liberal politicians took up the cry that the nation must conquer at all and any cost. In December 1917 more than 150 deputies and 90 senators formed themselves into the Fascio Parlamentare di Difesa Nazionale (Parliamentary Union for National Defence), without yet knowing the meaning that 'Fascism' was soon to acquire.[93] The still loosely organised Fasci di combattimento were to be founded in Milan on 23 March 1919, while the Partito Nazionale Fascista (PNF; National Fascist Party) emerged on 9 November 1921 in order to suture divisions that had begun to damage Fascist growth especially across the northern regions of the country. Now Mussolini lacked further serious challenge as his movement's *Duce*. It was less than a year before he became prime minister, following the paramilitary half-coup known as the March on Rome (celebrated thereafter on 28 October). Open dictatorship began after a speech on 3 January 1925 where he brazenly endorsed all Fascist violence. Italy fell to the rule of a 'totalitarian' regime (the adjective was now invented).

Busy times for a political chieftain, it might seem, and also for a man with three young children to look after 'at home' (Rachele was seriously afflicted by the influenza epidemic of 1918 that took many lives and, the following year, Bruno's survival was imperilled by an attack of diphtheria).[94] Nonetheless Mussolini found space for another affair, one that also produced a son, this time with a young, slim woman with naturally curly, fair hair whom he met after she won employment in the office of *Il Popolo d'Italia*. Her name was Bianca Ceccato. Her talented son was to call himself Glauco Di Salle, after his stepfather. Following the Second World War and until his death in 2000, De Salle had a distinguished career as a playwright and cultural administrator. For some years up to 1976 he worked in the management of the great publishing house Mondadori, an enterprise, as has already been seen above, much interested in selling the memory of Fascism.

It was during this time that his mother was persuaded to 'tell all' about what she called her 'love story' (the celebrated American film, based on the vastly popular novel by Eric Segal, came out in 1970). In 1977, after some revelations in the weekly *Panorama*, under the pseudonym 'Bianca Veneziana' (Ceccato's mother was born in Venice), a memoir of her affair with Mussolini was published under the title *Storia italiana d'amore* ('An Italian love story'). It did not equal Segal in sales. Nor can its accuracy be guaranteed. A historian may report its evidence but always with suspicion that what it says was contaminated by the long gap between its writing and the events it described. It may be as useful for understanding memory in the 1970s as it is for what happened in 1917 and after.

Nonetheless, the tale it tells of office grooming and seduction by an older, more sexually experienced and worldly-wise man, is credible. Like Ida Dalser, Ceccato was born in the Austrian-owned Alto Adige/Süd Tirol, but was a generation younger, her date of birth being 18 January 1900. During her childhood her parents changed lodgings frequently and her father, a seaman, was often away. At one time or another Bianca went to school in Venice, Treviso and Sondrio, moving to Milan to live with an uncle soon after the start of the war, after her mother's florist business had failed owing to the departure of tourists from Venice. In 1917 Ceccato was pleased to obtain a secretarial position on *Il Popolo d'Italia*, without, she claimed, having any idea of its political orientation. Mussolini now appeared, limping due to the wound on his ankle (in 1945 he still needed orthopaedic help to his lower left leg). 'He spoke in rapid phrases,' she remembered, 'and in a dry tone'.[95]

He noticed her, with what was likely predatory intent, and quickly promoted her to be his secretary at double her existing pay. Matters proceeded thereafter with predictable steps. First he caressed her hands one day when she brought him something; next he bought her a coffee. Then there was 'another, less paternal, touch' and he kissed her hand. One cold windy night they met outside office hours. He quizzed her about her life (and possible sexual experience) and then sent her grandly home in a carriage, a poor girl given a glimpse of the great life. The pattern recurred as spring 1918 began to unfold.

A young girl's fancy might turn to love and Bianca was flattered to be taken out by a soldier friend of hers. At news of that flirtation, Mussolini exploded with jealousy and sacked her out of hand. However, others on the office staff intervened and 'an elderly journalist' offered to write a letter of apology for her, with the counsel that it be sent to Naples, where Mussolini had gone on some political deal or other.[96] The trick worked and Bianca got her job back. But now Mussolini became more pressing, writing her three letters in reply to her ghosted effort. In them he spoke of love and desire, expressing the hope that he could 'dress her in silk and hear the rustle, . . . put a diadem on her head' or, in heartily male imagining, 'drive her across Italy in my high-octane automobile'.[97]

For a few weeks she resisted, despite her innocence not yet seduced by his clichés. But he stepped up his campaign, telling her that the tapping of her typewriter was distracting him from his daily labours into contemplation of her 'white hands'.[98] By May 1918 there were lavish gifts deposited on her desk; a bunch of red roses, a perfumed personal notebook, and, with a flash of authorial vanity, a copy of his *War diary*, which had been serialised in the paper since 1915. One day, Mussolini fondled her hands and kissed her fingers one by one.

Now it was 21 May and Mussolini melodramatically mumbled that he would kill himself unless they could satisfy their love, sounding like a sex-struck boy when he was twice her age. They met outside the Teatro Lirico, where once Donizetti's *L'elisir d'amore* ('The elixir of love') had premiered and where Mussolini was destined to make his last public speech in December 1944. Around the corner lay a small hotel. Mussolini pushed her through the entrance and soon they were in a 'cold, inhospitable, almost bare room', furnished with two iron beds and little else. She took off her hat; he laid his stick aside. They pushed the beds together. A maid arrived bearing 'a dish of *prosciutto crudo*, some bread rolls, a bottle of *spumante*'; 'it was my wedding banquet', she recalled ruefully, while Mussolini expatiated again of suicide, his and hers.[99] After this lovemaking finished and they separated, Mussolini wrote her another letter of intense romance: 'Today, my love, I drank the sweetest cup of your virginity . . . It is midnight and now you are asleep. I shall pass by your window and waft you a kiss from the tips of my fingers. In the blinding clarity of a spring moon. Your devil adores you.'[100]

SEX AND THE COMING DICTATOR

The affair continued tumultuously, at least according to Bianca's memory. Mussolini presented her with a pistol so she could defend herself 'against all those who will want to bring you harm'.[101] Perhaps more winningly, there was money to buy herself a stylish hat and new shoes, and then, later, after he had a financial coup on the stock market, a new suit. Her mother learned of the affair and threatened the married man, 'Signor Mussolini', with retribution, prompting him to talk vaguely of divorce from Rachele some time in the future; Signora Ceccato drew back when Mussolini extracted his own revolver and, at the same time, magnanimously promised financial support for her daughter.[102] There was a trip to the beach, which resulted in another violent copulation resembling rape.[103] When Bianca fell pregnant, Mussolini organised and paid for an abortion, buying her a gold box where she could place their mutual photos as a talisman of love. In 1919 the sex continued. In their bed-chat, Mussolini grew sentimental about his mother, 'who had loved him so very much'; he was also given to reciting the details of earlier affairs.[104] He took her to see *Aida* from a box at La Scala, but fell asleep and snored (he had been drinking). They had a weekend together in romantic Venice and were rowed about in a gondola. Earlier, she had prayed for him at Mass when she knew he was about to fight a duel. He confided to her that Rachele only wanted to be a peasant and did not read books as she did.

With the arrival of summer, she told her partner that she now wanted to bear his child. But it took her prayers to the Madonna at the Cappella del Sacro Cuore in what was about to become the city's Catholic University before, in February 1920, she again found herself with child. Glauco was born on 30 October. Mussolini had fussed over Bianca during her pregnancy and after the birth was, for a while, tender towards her and their infant. Separation only came after Mussolini moved to Rome to become prime minister and, even then, he made sure Bianca received 2,000 lire per month in living expenses. He did, however, offer the cynical advice that 'all men, my dear, should dedicate at least ten minutes per day to their own wives. If a wife feels betrayed by her husband, she will end by betraying him.'[105] The relationship between Bianca and Benito only finished after she fell in love with another man, presumably her future husband, Giuseppe Di Salle, six years her junior; they eventually had two children of their own. In 1927 the police raided their flat, seizing the love letters that Mussolini had written to her. Ruminating over past conquests, as he liked to do with Claretta (and as he had done with Bianca), Mussolini remembered that it was Bianca who told him, whether truthfully or not, that Rachele was having an affair. Then he did admit that Bianca's son was probably his. 'But nothing needed doing', he told his new lover. 'She does not interest me a jot any more.'[106]

In Claretta's record of her affair with Mussolini there are quite a few parallels with Bianca's story, enough to arouse suspicion that Glauco Di Salle, embellishing his elderly mother's memory, added details that owed something to what, by the mid-1970s, had already been revealed about 'Ben and Clara'. Claretta, too, recorded a complaisant (and greedy) mother, a somewhat paradoxical female religiosity, a countering claim of devilry by Mussolini, his golden recollection of Rosa Maltoni's maternal love, exchanged threats of death and suicide, and rapid and violent coitus. Yet the Petacci diaries had not yet become available and at least some of the love story there narrated between Mussolini and 'Bianca Veneziana' may be true. Mussolini certainly recorded her name in his listing of past conquests to Claretta. Nonetheless, Bianca Ceccato was unusual in her youth, virginity and body shape compared with other women who bore, or claimed to have borne, Mussolini's children.

On 19 October 1922, with the March on Rome in early preparation, Mussolini became the father of another illegitimate child, Elena Curti. This daughter, unlike Glauco Di Salle, was destined to accompany her father in that convoy which took him and Claretta to their deaths in April 1945. During the *Duce*'s last days, she was a member of one of the five families or sub-families who clung to him, in a *reductio ad absurdum* of Italian familism (actions which will be narrated in detail in chapter 7). Again, quite a lot of the information available on Curti's life is post facto, recorded in even more recent times than that concerning Ceccato, the key source being the publication in 2003 of the memoirs of the eighty-year-old Elena, who had only just come back to live in Italy from self-imposed political exile in Spain.[107] Over the next years, she became something of a celebrity in the world of Berlusconian 'anti-anti-Fascist' revisionism, all the more because in 1943 she had opted to back the RSI. According to her interviewers, she is a sassy old lady, still alive in 2016, and happy to confirm rightist conspiracy theories about the reality of a Mussolini diary and a florid correspondence between the *Duce* and Churchill.[108] With what may be regarded in some circles as charming idiosyncrasy, she believed that astrology provides a fine explanation of historical actions and, like Claretta, at an earlier time she enjoyed painting.

In her memoirs and interviews, there is only thin evidence of Elena Curti's begetting. It seems that her father, Bruno, a member of a Fascist paramilitary squad, was gaoled late in 1921 for a violent attack on his party's socialist enemies. While he was locked away, his boss, with little sense of honour, slept with Angela Cucciati, his twenty-two-year-old wife (already the mother of a two-year-old child). Angela had been born at Lodi into a small business family, who soon transferred their work to Milan; she lived until 1978. Pregnancy resulted from her affair with Mussolini, which was over by February or March 1922 (when Bruno Curti left prison). Roberto Festorazzi describes Angela unkindly as 'a seamstress with large breasts who worked in a fashion shop'.[109] A surviving photo more fetchingly shows a pretty young woman with dark curly hair, a generous mouth and a wistful look.

According to Elena, the love between her mother and the *Duce* did not die but rather was rekindled in visits that she made often enough to Rome, notably after her marriage broke down in 1929. Again in Elena's memory, Mussolini would ring to summon Angela to his side and did not mind having to do so four or five times before he could reach her and make their assignation, which could also be in Milan, should Mussolini be visiting there.[110] Other proof of such trysts is lacking, however, and the state archives show Mussolini rejecting a request for an interview from Angela Cucciati in March 1933. Another file that year recorded rumours from a tapped telephone of a new affair in her life.[111] At around the same time, Cucciati's passport was taken from her.[112] Perhaps to escape this imbroglio, in 1930 Elena had been carried off by her legal father, who was reportedly dismayed by continuing police surveillance of the family, and placed in a boarding school.[113] She grew up slowly thereafter, having limited contact with either of her legal parents or grandparents. Eventual release from college was, she recalled, 'traumatic'.[114]

What does seem to be true is that, in 1941, her mother took her to the Italian capital, after telling her who her real father was, and arranged a meeting with the *Duce*. The dictator, Elena claimed, was 'indulgent and understanding' of her nineteen-year-old self. When she and her mother returned to Milan, he rang to talk philosophy, which she wanted to study. Soon he sent her an introductory history of Greek philosophy, the attraction of which was augmented by the banknotes stuffed into it. The archives contain her letter of thanks, not for the money, but merely hoping that Mussolini would approve of her decision to take her study of philosophy further.[115] Thereafter she and her father became and remained friends; she moved back to Rome and the two met regularly throughout the *Duce*'s last years, much (as will be seen) to Claretta's disgust – she assumed Benito had found a new, younger, lover, and was not disabused of her fears until April 1945. In her diaries, however, Claretta confirmed that Mussolini had bedded Angela Cucciati and acknowledged his daughter.[116]

Here, then, is another curious tale, one that cannot be wholly verified but does ring true, at least in regard to Elena Curti's place in Mussolini's life from 1942 to 1945. Back in 1922 Mussolini was meanwhile wrestling with the complications of government, which became greater on 10 June 1924 when a band of squadrists, whose chief had received training in Chicago, kidnapped the moderate socialist parliamentarian Giacomo Matteotti from beside the Tiber in Rome, before beating and murdering him. For six months Fascism and its *Duce* tumbled into crisis while the old national elites – monarchy, papacy, business, industry, agriculture and intellectuals – worked out whether violence so near the prime minister could be tolerated.[117] It was. Italy was indeed to fall under the yoke of Mussolini's dictatorship.

Safely installed as his nation's *Duce* (but one adroitly seeking a deal with the Vatican), on 28 December 1925 Benito and Rachele were finally united in religious ceremony. Their three children (Edda, Vittorio and Bruno) had been baptised two years earlier, with matters kept in the family, since the officiating priest was Don Colombo Bondanini, Arnaldo Mussolini's brother-in-law.[118] Whatever had been happening to Benito and Rachele over the last years in their bedtime behaviour, they now produced two more children, another son, Romano (born 26 September 1927, his name once more expressing *romanità*, if not so grandly as that of

Marcello Cesare Augusto Petacci) and a second daughter, Anna Maria (born 3 September 1929). In such fecundity, Rachele and Benito were doing their well-publicised best to enhance national demographic growth. The *Duce*, however, was still tied to Margherita Sarfatti and to a number of other women, at least three more of whom would bear his children. In both his public and private life he had come a long way, but he had not yet reached his climax.

2

A DICTATOR'S DISTRACTIONS
His Muse and other bedfellows

Violet Gibson was another woman in Mussolini's life. He did not go to bed with her. Rather, just before 11 a.m. on the morning of 7 April 1926, this genteel Irish lady of aristocratic background shot at the dictator as he emerged from an official appointment at the Campidoglio in Rome. (He had just launched an international surgeons' conference.) The bullet Gibson fired winged him where his nose met his forehead. After a moment of panic in the crowd, Mussolini had a bandage stuck across the shallow wound. With considerable courage, that afternoon he allowed himself to be photographed as he fulfilled other speaking duties, first to party officials and then to city crowds in the evening. He eventually rang his brother, Arnaldo, in Milan, as he was accustomed to do late each night. Arnaldo gave thanks to God for protecting the *Duce*. Pope Pius XI, whom Gibson had also half thought of killing, agreed. In gratitude for the dictator's survival, *Te Deum* services were sung across the country.[1]

The next morning, Mussolini departed on a naval vessel on a mission to Libya; a photograph taken at the time shows him striding along the deck with a plaster covering most of his nose. Gibson sat in gaol awaiting the sluggish process of Italian justice. Judges and diplomats debated her case with care and attention. More than a year later, on 12 May 1927, she was expelled from the country to spend the rest of her days confined in St Andrews Hospital for Mental Diseases at Northampton.[2] Conditions there were less harsh than the ones Ida Dalser was experiencing at Pergine, although Gibson's sympathetic biographer is doubtful whether she should have been pent up for life. Violet Gibson long outlived the *Duce*, dying on 2 May 1956.

Among the many who reacted to Mussolini's seemingly miraculous escape from assassination was a fourteen-year-old bourgeois Roman girl, Claretta Petacci. Not a great success at school (she did not enter one of Rome's celebrated *licei*, where the ambitious children of the city's elite, soon to include Vittorio and Bruno Mussolini, were educated), Petacci was thought by her parents to be somewhat delicate. It was her brother Marcello who, it was planned, would follow the family tradition and go into medicine. If a fulsome posthumous publication, edited by his father, is to be believed, Marcello Cesare Augusto was by 1926 already making his mark. Two years earlier, when only fourteen, he had published a written piece about 'Africa', and was soon giving public talks on St Francis, Dante and other writers. After attending middle school at the private Istituto cattolico di Sant'Apollinare in Rome, he did not complete *liceo* in the Italian capital, instead moving to Brussels before entering university at Pisa.

Throughout these years, his admiring father recalled, Marcello had eagerly served the Fascist and patriotic cause, founding a youth group at the Sant'Apollinare, where he enrolled 'his school friends and even some engaged in priestly training'.[3] Marcello had been precocious in his political awakening, joining Associazione Nazionalista Italiana (ANI; Italian Nationalist Association) before his tenth birthday in 1920, and quickly becoming a 'centurion' in their youth group. 'That year and the following ones, he engaged in frequent battles with subversives, especially in the Monteverde area', F.S. Petacci reported proudly. 'His temperament meant that he gave no allowance to the fact that his adversaries were often numerically superior' when they engaged in their suburban skirmishes. Sternly he resisted their deviant plots and stood alert beside his flag, 'on one occasion with rather grave medical results'.[4] When the ANI, which was much more respectable in class terms than the PNF, dissolved itself early in 1923, Marcello rapidly became a card-carrying Fascist and, still only thirteen, 'participated in all the meetings and [punitive] expeditions' of his branch in Rome.[5]

If Marcello was preparing himself for an active and rewarding masculine life under Italy's new regime, Claretta, like the great majority of girls of her class background, was readied for Catholic marriage. Formal education began with the nuns in elementary school and was completed before the end of middle school in the tripartite Italian system. Her training entailed some familiarity with music (she took lessons on the harp, the violin and the piano, without advancing too far in her playing) and art. In this latter case, she displayed in adulthood an ability for depicting country scenes and a more surprising skill in caricature.[6] Her mother, then and later, was rarely without her rosary beads, and the Petaccis saw no contradiction between their Catholic and Fascist (and class and family) beliefs. However, in her choice of fandom, and covering her schoolbooks with images of her peerless hero, Mussolini, young Claretta displayed a hint of teenage rebellion against the many images of the Madonna and the innumerable saints that sustained the church's presence in Italian lives.[7] Perhaps, given her father's vocation, she had been especially aware of her leader's speech on 7 April to surgeons from across the world.

Certainly, that very afternoon, Gibson's assault provoked Claretta, from her comfortable apartment on the wide avenue running beside the Tiber about halfway between the Victor Emmanuel monument and St Peter's, to pen the national leader a long, passionate letter. Renouncing female mildness, it thirsted for vengeance. How dreadful it was that a woman had been involved, Claretta exclaimed. 'What ignominy, what cowardice, what opprobrium' (can her vocabulary have been spruced up by mother?). 'But, then, she is a foreigner and that explains everything!' Claretta maintained with ready xenophobia. How appalling that there had been this and other attempted attacks on one who was 'my super great *Duce*, our life, our hope, our glory'. 'O, *Duce*, why was I not with you?' she added with teenage rage and self-obsession. 'Could I not have strangled that murderous woman who wounded you [Te], a divine being? Could I not have cut her out for ever from Italian soil, stained with your blood, your grand, good, sincere, Romagnol blood?' Then, she mused with a shift back to more intimate emotion, might she not have lain her 'head on your chest so I could still hear the beats of your great heart?' But it was not the time for too many girlish dreams. Rather she must stand up for discipline. As a 'small but ardent Fascist', her letter ended, she, like all Blackshirts, was ready fervently to swear, 'in the motto that expresses all the love that my young heart feels for you! *Duce*, my life is for you! The *Duce* is safe! *Viva il Duce*' and signed 'Clara Petacci, (fourteen years old), Lungo Tevere Cenci, number 10'.[8]

* * *

Claretta never forgot the ardour that in 1926 had aroused her to such heights but rather remembered it with advantages. Not long after her sex life with Mussolini began, her lover's flicking over old photos turned up an image of Violet Gibson. 'How overwhelming it is!' she recorded herself as muttering in reaction. 'To see that old ugly black [dame] with glasses who is pointing a gun a few steps from your face . . . In this photo,' she reflected, 'you can see and understand that inexplicable instant that kept you safe.' He had turned his head and 'that unconscious move saved him. God saved him for our *patria*.' Moralising done, Claretta trembled at the thought and clung to her lover with renewed passion. The old man did not seem to share the fierceness of her sentiments, however, instead complacently patting himself on the back about how lucky he had always been.[9]

After all, he may have reflected, when Gibson fired on the dictator, Claretta was just another biddably loyal teenager. At that time, apart from Rachele, the leading woman in the *Duce*'s life was still Margherita Sarfatti. Indeed it was in that year of 1926 that Sarfatti published a book entitled *Dux*, which many observers have viewed as the key work in cementing an image of the dictator in Italian hearts and so establishing a personality cult. Actually the biography was first published in English in September of the previous year under the less aggressive sounding title *The life of Benito Mussolini*, and sought to combine a reading of the *Duce* that could attract both Italians and foreigners.[10] Yet, an analyst of the story of Mussolini's representation has argued that, from 1926, the dictator became an ever more exalted being,[11] one translated into the divine essence that Claretta had worshipped in her letter.

Sarfatti, whose husband had died in January 1924, had been persuaded to write *Dux* not long afterwards, receiving approval and assistance from

Mussolini and ignoring the fears that beset the *Duce* that the Matteotti crisis would end his career. Her own biographers provide an extensive analysis of the text or texts, given that there were variations between the English and Italian editions. They note how she could not resist inserting herself into the book's pages, explaining that she viewed it 'as a kind of dual biography. She wove her presence subtly into the narrative at every important phase, and recorded her presence at all major events'.[12] Yet, rather than saluting her, readers were more likely to absorb the image of a grand and popular leader who had risen 'by sheer force of will above his squalid environment' in the provincial Romagna.[13] Sarfatti exaggerated Mussolini's poverty all the more plausibly since his modest origins in Predappio were so different from her family's Venetian opulence. In so far as the installation of the dictatorship was concerned, Sarfatti asserted, other Fascists scarcely mattered. Mussolini dominated all as 'a vigorous and courageous man of action, the master of horses, airplanes, sports cars, and speedboats', naturally and inevitably elevated to his proper role as 'prime minister and world statesman'.[14] Her nation was now indeed 'Mussolini's Italy'.

In her narration Sarfatti did not hide the dictator's sex life, justifying to him her choice in that regard with the comment that the biography was 'taken up largely with details which you, perhaps, will dismiss as gossip'. But, she added knowingly, 'I have read too much of history to disdain gossip.'[15] So she acknowledged the wild oats that he had broadcast in his youth and even made coded reference to Dalser. Rachele, by contrast, she ignored completely (in return, the *Duce*'s legal wife nourished a lifelong hatred of Sarfatti).[16] In a way that was well tailored to Mussolini's autobiographical musings, warmest mention of a woman was given to his mother, Rosa Maltoni. Only a mother's 'female tenderness', Sarfatti declared in amiable phrases, 'can teach and keep alive in the warrior that gentleness which is simultaneously pure force. It recalls that dream-like image of maternal tenderness in the heart of a boy growing to be a man. It is thus the greatest, most profound and precious, the unique, live point of contact which the Leader can retain with ordinary men.'[17] A Fascist boy, it seemed, owed much to his Mamma. With less than feminist sentiment, Sarfatti announced that she was happy to write what she called 'a woman's book' that did not refrain from intimacy, yet approved her sometime partner's misogyny and the increasingly patriarchal Fascist intention aggressively to deny any prospect of suffrage or other form of enhanced female equality.[18]

Perhaps somewhere between the lines of the biography, evidence could be detected of the withering of Sarfatti's physical ties with Mussolini. At the end of the book she noted that, during the war, Mussolini had told her that he was ready to die, since he now had children. They ensured, he stated, that '*I am continued*'.[19] Sarfatti was one partner whom the *Duce* had not impregnated. Nonetheless, for quite a few more years, she could rejoice in being what her sentimental biographers call the *Duce*'s 'Muse'.[20] For a decade following its foundation in 1922, she occupied a major editorial role in the party's theoretical journal, *Gerarchia*, and, in her salon and in the regime's cultural politics, she strenuously sponsored the cause of what she called the *Novecento italiano* ('Italian twentieth century'). This movement, composed of intellectuals happy to accept her patronage, was to express the Fascist version of modernism, 'preparing our forces and militarising our spirit' against the nation's competitors and foes.[21] It was to make Milan, and perhaps Rome, surpass Paris as the city of the modern mind, art, architecture and all cultural form. It was to confirm Sarfatti, in the metaphor of Cannistraro and Sullivan, as 'the uncrowned [cultural] queen of Italy'.[22] In acceptance of this status and her national identity, in December 1929 Sarfatti was baptised in a private ceremony by Pietro Tacchi Venturi, the Jesuit who regularly acted as the middleman between pope and *Duce*.[23] From 1931 Sarfatti moved into a commodious eighteen-room flat in the Via dei Villini, only a few hundred metres from the Villa Torlonia.[24] In most senses, other than the physical, she clung to her role as 'Mussolini's other woman'.

Now Sarfatti's ambitious daughter, Fiammetta, also opted for the Christian over the Jewish faith, while Amedeo, the banker son of the family, became a Catholic in 1932. For quite some time, Fiammetta had been her mother's public companion until married into the upper echelons of the aristocracy in October 1933 (her husband was Livio Gaetani d'Aragona, of an ancient Neapolitan family that had once sired Pope Boniface VIII, born Benedetto Caetani). Almost a decade later, the Petaccis would also delight in joining themselves to the nobility, although Myriam's husband, the 'Marchese' Armando Boggiano, was scarcely the equal in social caché or ancient bloodlines to the Gaetanis. Nonetheless, historians over-ready to locate a social and cultural revolution in Mussolini's Italy plainly underestimate this *tendresse* for affiliation into the aristocracy among the movement's female elites. Within the Mussolini family itself, Galeazzo Ciano in 1939 could rejoice in being the 2nd count of Cortelazzo, a title, doubtless *nouveau*, that had been granted to his father, the admiral and Fascist minister, Costanzo Ciano. It was one of the many signs of her son-in-law's elevated class stature that Rachele held against him.

Sarfatti may have sought to entrench her family as well as her intellectual clients into the most distinguished sectors of Italian life. But she also acted for a time as a sort of personal assistant to Mussolini. Once established in Rome as prime minister, Mussolini did not automatically bring his wife and growing legitimate family to share his life there, instead leaving them in Milan under the supervision of his brother, Arnaldo, after 28 October 1922 editor of *Il Popolo d'Italia,* and his portly sister, Edvige. In 1925 the family purchased the estate called the Villa Carpena near Forlì (raising the Mussolinis to landowners, if not aristocrats).[25] Rachele, preferring the country to the city, was always happiest there. Two years later, the family holdings in the Romagna – *la provincia del Duce* ('the *Duce*'s territory', in regime propaganda) – were augmented when the Mussolinis graciously accepted the donation 'by the people' of the Rocca delle Caminate, a heavily restored castle in the region. The family also had use of a beach house at Riccione on the Adriatic. It was only on 15 November 1929 that the Villa Torlonia, with its large park on the Via Nomentana not far beyond Rome's Aurelian Walls, became the regular urban residence of Rachele and the children, the reuniting of the family spurred by the entry of Vittorio and Bruno into the Torquato Tasso *liceo*, which stood less than half a kilometre away.[26]

Until this transfer, Mussolini led the de facto bachelor existence that is not unknown in other politicians' lives. Sarfatti had found him a flat on the top floor of Via Rasella 155 in central Rome, down the hill from the royal Quirinal Palace. There the household was run by a capable woman from Gubbio called Cesira Carocci (born 1884). Sarfatti had chosen this housekeeper too, as well as selecting a dentist, an optician and a gynaecologist for the Mussolinis. She similarly arranged the eventual deal whereby the aristocratic Torlonia family (who had Jewish origins) offered their villa to the nation's leader at a peppercorn rent; Mussolini took over rooms there in July 1925, although he did not yet abandon his flat in the Via Rasella.[27] Carocci, who is said to have readily performed such basic tasks as cooking and washing for the *Duce* (and even purchasing his underwear), lasted in her role until 1934 when Rachele, jealous of Carocci's past clientelistic relationship with Sarfatti, belatedly sacked her.[28] Then and later, Mussolini, in this case certainly a good master and perhaps with gilded memories of his rumbustious freedom in the Via Rasella, went out of his way to subsidise Carocci's retirement, taking time even in 1944 to send her 5,000 lire from his personal funds.[29]

* * *

It has already been noted how Mussolini loved to go back over his past affairs in his conversations with Petacci, such half-pornographic historical recollection presumably aimed at arousing them both. In their chats Mussolini often returned to his time in the Via Rasella and his happy bedding of very many women there. He also remembered his physical collapse in February 1925, when he had vomited blood, in what was probably the first manifestation of the ulcer that would trouble him throughout the rest of his life. He was grateful that Carocci had rushed to his aid and brought in the doctors, well before the news reached Rachele in Milan.

In his sexual encounters during these years, Mussolini ranged widely. He even reached into the aristocracy in an affair apparently commencing in 1923 with the Sicilian Giulia Alliata di Monreale, principessa di Gangi (born 1888).[30] A photo shows her dark, soulful and sultry, wearing elegant pearls. The two met after she petitioned him for special aid to her family estates and they remained in contact, notably much later during the war, when Claretta, at least according to the postwar memoirs of Ercole Boratto, Mussolini's chauffeur, was neurotically jealous of her and her ostentatious sensuality, and equally put off by her aristocratic demeanour.[31]

Noble in title but little else was another lover, Countess Giulia Carminati di Brambilla. She was the partner but not the wife of the count of that title, a landowner near Rovigo. She had been born Giulia Matavelli in the province of Como in 1892, the daughter of a postman, and so, like the other, more genuinely noble Giulia, was about the same age as Rachele Mussolini.[32] Neither was in any sense an ingénue. It seems likely that Brambilla and the *Duce* had sex for the first time in 1921.[33] Not long afterwards, two other Fascist bosses, Francesco Giunta and Cesare Forni, fought a duel over her favours.[34] Despite what many deemed her promiscuity, she kept a tie alive with the *Duce* over the next two decades. If not often his bed partner, the countess acted as a secret agent for her sometime lover, deeply irritating Claretta by being a fertile source of malicious rumour about her young rival.[35] By the late 1930s photos show a sturdy, even mannish, woman whom Claretta claimed was a bottle blonde, very much looking her years.[36] A forgiving popular historian has described her more courteously as 'not very tall, but attractive, plump according to the tastes of the time and of extraordinary sensuality'.[37]

Apart from deprecating Brambilla as a gossip, in February 1938 Claretta was not wholly convinced that her physical relationship with the *Duce* was dead. A month later, Mussolini was driven to assure her that the countess was the last of his old lovers to be sent away; actually, he joked, it was she who had removed herself from his bed some time ago.[38] Nonetheless Brambilla kept up correspondence with the dictator, now intimating to him that Claretta had been 'disloyal', a charge that disgusted the younger woman, all the more given what she viewed as Mussolini's insouciant reaction to such allegation.[39] Moreover, Brambilla kept appearing at social events where the *Duce* was obliged to be, forcing Mussolini to find new words to deny that Brambilla mattered. In April 1938 he informed Claretta that, actually, the woman was 'mad' but, he added, perhaps summoning memories of Dalser and her public insults to him, she should be feared for her spite and unpredictability. In any case, he 'detested' her.[40]

Despite such venom, no action to banish the countess from his world resulted. Rather, Mussolini seems to have decided weakly that Brambilla was part of the static that blurred the background of his private life. It was only at Christmas 1944 that another of her tirades against Claretta, on this occasion running to eighteen pages, drove Mussolini to outright expostulation: 'Dear countess and comrade, I beg you not to dim my already exhausted vision with letters that are simply too long, and I also beg you not to make judgements about people who do not matter to you. I beg you to inform yourself better if you think it is worthwhile entering into the private affairs of others and collecting, as you do, the insults and gossip of idiots and the malicious.'[41] Whether as a result or because the war was now so desperate, no further letters from her seem to have reached Mussolini's desk.

* * *

A third lover from the 1920s, but one who was sufficiently provocative to be sent into an earlier exile, was Cornelia Tanzi, a poet and dancer born in 1908. Tanzi was a sexually experienced woman who happily embraced Roman high society during these decades. She earned her greatest notoriety, when, after the liberation of Rome, she was one of the first to be condemned for collaborationism, which may have been polite code for her promiscuous dealings with Mussolini, other party chiefs and, after 1943, the German military. Certainly by the 1990s her activity was portrayed, and forgiven, as such,[42] although in 1944 there had also been complaints about her greedy search for financial reward; her salon in the Via Margutta was said to have become a springboard for intellectuals on the make.[43] In 1938 Tanzi was the object of further nattering between the dictator and Claretta, with Mussolini dismissing her as a 'whore', whom he had never loved at all.[44]

In more cavalier fashion than with Brambilla, Tanzi paid no attention to Fascist decorum, with phone taps revealing her devil-may-care boasts about imprinting her lipstick deep onto the *Duce*'s lips during their sexual congress. As Mussolini remarked to the ingenuous Claretta, he was worried and irritated that her forthrightness was demeaning of him. He had therefore rung Tanzi to tell her to desist, ordering her to get out of Rome 'for two or three years'. She did so.[45] When she returned to the capital, she remained under police surveillance, despite suffering from breast cancer.[46] As Mussolini repeated on more than one occasion, what he really disliked was the way that Tanzi and Brambilla went around the country boasting that they had bedded him. For the patriarchal dictator, it scarcely needed noting, male promiscuity was all to the good but open female sexuality was not.⁴⁷ Any close contact between Tanzi and the *Duce* now ceased, although, following Italy's entry into the war on the side of the Nazis in June 1940, Mussolini did moralise about her arrest for breaking petrol rationing and misusing a government-owned car.⁴⁸

Two years earlier, Mussolini had gone into detail with Claretta about what it had been like to have sex with Cornelia Tanzi: 'She wasn't ugly', he muttered. 'Really she was neither beautiful nor ugly. She had long, long legs, and was slender, soft, tall, dark. But she was frigid, coldness personified . . . Reckon with the fact that she never felt anything at all even with me. She would arrive, strip, let her slip fall, so you could see her two long legs. Then she would lie down and be ready to go without any particular sign of anything. Always indifferent, [afterwards] she would get dressed again and leave. All in less than half an hour. To tell you the truth, the last time for me was a dreadful struggle', Mussolini admitted, because he could not arouse himself to an erection. 'Then, I don't know, that day she had on a perfume, with a really disgusting smell. Sorry, but you know I am really very aware of such things.' He had never loved her and their coitus had been a terrible effort for him; but then he was an 'animal', he concluded complacently.⁴⁹

Another brief bed partner of these years, but one about whom only a little is known, was Ines De Spuches, the wife of a squadrist from Brescia who, by 1927, was reinforcing imperial rule in Libya. A son called Benito, who was probably the dictator's, was born that year. Young Benito was destined to be killed, little more than a boy, by partisans in February 1944 after he had enrolled in the RSI's Guardia Nazionale Repubblicana (GNR; National Republican Guard), an event solemnly recorded by Claretta with her indefatigable registration of her rivals' history.⁵⁰ In April 1940 the dictator mentioned to his lover that he had noticed De Spuches' name as attending a ceremony over which he had presided in the Foro Mussolini (now the Foro Italico). 'I didn't even look at her,' he assured his Claretta briefly. 'She makes me sick.'⁵¹

* * *

Of those women with whom he no longer consorted the one who lived on in his memory was Margherita Sarfatti, with his frequent bleak recollection to Claretta of their deeds together. Sarfatti's recollections were similarly bitter: in the tract that she wrote in 1947, but which remained unpublished, she was insistent on the subject of his drift into tertiary syphilis (Mussolini had already been deeply perturbed at the news in 1939 that she was contemplating another study of his life).[52] Eventually she would insist that, after he removed her from her cultural leadership, Mussolini 'increasingly surrounded himself with poorly educated, even ignorant, individuals', people – whether male or female – who were just not of her class.[53] Once she had been dropped from the regime's decision-makers, she contended in exculpation, 'behind the mask of Fascism lay an abyss of corruption, nepotism, favouritism and arbitrary lawlessness'.[54]

But Mussolini's rancour has left a more detailed record, if only because Claretta so eagerly recorded her partner's splenetic rejection of the claim that it was Sarfatti who had made him. Not long into her diary, Claretta noted in November 1937 Mussolini's irritation when he remembered that 'Margheritaccia' ('Yucky Margherita', the suffix expressing eloquently his current aversion) had ill-naturedly told him that his ugly short legs wrecked his otherwise grand male beauty (which, naturally, Claretta hailed). Then, he ran on to the reminiscence that the active sexual relations of Benito and Margherita had only lasted through 1918–20, during which period, he would later add, he was not having sex with his wife. To kindle the affair, Sarfatti had propositioned him, he contended, while they were sharing a taxi, once they alighted dragging him off to a hotel room. There, he narrated, 'it was ghastly, terrible . . . I could not do anything. I thought it might be the position we had adopted, I changed various times, nothing, impossible. Nothing happened. It was the stench of her flesh.' However, he continued, eventually he 'got used to it'. 'But, the first time nothing.' He might have gone further in such description but Claretta noted primly: 'I interrupted him from his over-intimate description of the meeting because it was annoying me too much.'[55]

Thereafter Sarfatti retained a prominent place in their conversations, all the more since Mussolini was increasingly given to a crass anti-Semitism that underscored the regime's more studiously intellectual *Manifesto della Razza* ('Race Manifesto'), issued on 14 July 1938 to emphasise Fascism's opposition to the principles of the French Revolution of 1789.[56] Sarfatti, Mussolini retorted on another occasion, was 'an ugly witch', resembling a badly restored painting. In fact she, like Brambilla, was one of those women who, he charged, once they reached a certain age, 'give themselves to the chauffeur, the waiter, the portiere (caretaker). And are ready to pay them', desperately and despairingly promiscuous. She was no longer Sarfatti, he and his new lover joked, but *Rifatti* ('the done-over one').[57] Her intelligence was 'Jewish' and that meant he had been able to have sex with other women in front of her, for example Ester Lombardo (1895–1982), a writer and feminist, in some dissent from the regime; she was also of Jewish extraction.[58]

Contrary to his contention that their sexual relationship had ended in 1920, in his memory he still numbered Sarfatti as one of his horde of bed partners in 1924.[59] But, by August 1938, he had decided that allowing Sarfatti to write *Dux* had been the greatest mistake of his life, since it had contaminated his story with hers. Inevitably she had written what he now knew was a 'Jewish' book; like all of her race, she was a 'fanatic', scorning himself and all other Italians, the entire Gentile race, as *goyim*: this word Mussolini was sure should be translated as 'dogs', perceiving it to express an ageless Jewish contempt and antipathy towards anyone not of their blood and religion.[60] Now he had decided that the smell, which had disgusted him during their first sexual meeting, was 'Jewish'; she and all her people composed the 'cursed race, the killers of God'.[61] In reality, he told Claretta, he had been a convinced racist since 1921; in that regard he had no need to mimic Hitler. Certainly he had cut all ties with Sarfatti since 1934, when she left *Gerarchia*.[62]

In January 1940 his memory became still more brutal, although its accuracy was doubtful. 'No, I never loved her,' he told Claretta. 'Rather she trapped me with that Jewish insistence and impudence that they use to sniff out the man of the moment. Imagine that she had the courage to turn up at the hospital where I lay with my war wound and where my wife was present.' On that occasion she fled, but 'from then on, she never left me in peace for a moment . . . I told you that it didn't work the first time. We never really were in harness; there was always something dividing us. There was a tremendous argument we had from 10 in the evening till 5 in the morning. It was then that I realised that I was deeply anti-Semitic.' He and Sarfatti squabbled over the meaning of an ivory crucifix that stood on his table. She claimed that it was really a Jewish symbol that the Christians had stolen. 'That was the death of our relationship,' Mussolini avowed with a version of virtue that might appeal to the daughter of a papal physician. 'It was then that the chasm of race opened between us.'[63]

Despite such dictatorial ranting and the grossness of his anti-Semitic prejudice, Mussolini did not condemn Sarfatti to death or imprison her in a concentration camp (he complained to Claretta that Sarfatti had not thanked him for such generosity, and again blamed her Jewishness for the ingratitude).[64] Rather in December 1938 she was allowed to depart to Paris where she flirted with the established anti-Fascist exile community, while telling anyone who wanted to listen of her 'boundless hatred' of Mussolini. In March 1939 she was joined by her son Amedeo, en route to a refreshed banking career in Montevideo, who relieved her complaints about 'pauperism' by passing over thirty-six diamonds that he had brought from his mother's stock at home. Despite the ever-toughening legislation against Jewish businesses and properties in Italy, the regime also permitted the export of quite a few of her valuable collection of paintings and sculptures.[65]

When, in September, the Germans invaded Poland, sparking the Second World War (with Italy for nine months adopting a policy of 'non-belligerence'), Margherita Sarfatti fled across Spain to Portugal. At that perilous moment, Mussolini personally intervened to allow her an Italian passport that ensured her passage. By mid-September Sarfatti had joined her son in Uruguay.[66] Her daughter, Fiammetta, lived out the war in Italy, where she died in 1989, celebrated in the press for her aristocratic taste and her vast and beautiful art collection.[67] Following time in Argentina and the USA, Margherita Sarfatti returned to Italy in 1947, dying in her villa near Lake Como in October 1961.

Countess Fiammetta did well to ignore the scandalous gossip, retailed by Mussolini's chauffeur after the war, and given some credence by popular historians of the *Duce*'s sex life, that she, while a teenager as young as fourteen, had joined her mother in romps with the dictator.[68] Certainly the Petacci diaries have no report of any such events. Rather Mussolini briefly named Fiammetta when he was expatiating on the pretentiousness of aristocratic salons: 'the human collection that evening was revolting, disastrous. I've never seen uglier men and women. Of the two hundred women perhaps ten were passable,' he remarked disparagingly. 'Sarfatti's daughter was there but she kept turning her back on me.'[69]

Still greater scandal was stirred by Mussolini's telling Petacci that no less a person than Maria José, the crown princess of Italy (born 1906), tried to arouse him sexually, only for him to fail at her bidding. The chauffeur, Boratto, mentioned a visit by an 'illustrious' female to the bathing hut at Castelporziano on the Roman Lido, grace-and-favour usage of which the royal family had given Mussolini in the 1920s. It had been an embarrassing moment, Boratto recalled, because the *Duce* was then entertaining Claretta, who had to be hidden away during a two-hour confabulation. Boratto maintained that thereafter 'successive meetings occurred ... of a more intimate character', when he would see princess and dictator go inside together wearing only their bathing costumes.[70]

Such allegation fitted the longstanding rumour that, although Maria José was regularly bearing children for the Savoy dynasty (Maria Pia in 1934; Vittorio Emanuele in 1937; Maria Gabriella in 1940; Maria Beatrice in 1943), she hated its austere and soulless lifestyle and found her husband, Umberto, cold or by preference a homosexual.[71] The idea that Maria José would seduce her country's dictator must nonetheless be severely doubted when there is more credible evidence that her circle, with aristocratic disdain, mocked Mussolini's dress sense, aggressive baldness and the premature white hair it disguised.[72] Maria José, who separated from her husband once the monarchy fell in 1946 and died in her nineties in January 2001, kept a lengthy diary but it is not to be made available to readers until 2071.[73]

What was Mussolini's version of the alleged affair, as disclosed (or fantasised) to Claretta? The date in her diary was 7 November 1937, a day suited to boasting since, that morning, Mussolini had signed the Anti-Comintern Pact with Nazi Germany and Imperial Japan, the countries set to be Italy's allies in World War II. Despite encroaching autumn, it must still have been warm since, in the afternoon, Mussolini and Petacci repaired to Castelporziano. At first they played ball but then she said she was tired and so they stripped off, lay down and sunbathed. And Mussolini began to talk about 'the princess'. She had shown up one time, he remembered, with only enough warning from an aide for him swiftly to pull on his towelling shorts. 'Am I disturbing you?' she had asked. 'But no, Your

Highness, of course not,' he replied deferentially. 'And then with a tug she let fall her dress and . . . she was almost naked, a pair of the briefest panties and two scraps of clothing on her breasts. I was quite at a loss,' he recalled dreamily.

Two courtiers had accompanied her. But she signalled them to leave, suggesting that she and the *Duce* should dive into the waves, since it was mid-August and boiling hot. She could swim well but, in the water, kept bumping suggestively into Mussolini's legs. Then they lay on the sand together and chatted about one thing or another. 'She isn't excessively clever,' the *Duce* pronounced, 'but she has a measured, not a flighty intelligence. Before understanding and replying, she likes to think it over.' So, Mussolini ran on, 'with any other woman who had come beside me in this condition of nudity, I would have seized my chance'. She may not have been totally beautiful but physically she was not bad. Anyway, in normal circumstance, he would not have refrained from acting. However, his penis gave no sign of interest. So, with evening darkening the sky, he told her that he had work to do. She commiserated about how boring it must be, but asked expectantly if she could come back the next day.

This time, Maria José 'was again here undressed, with still less on. She wore a green scarf on her head and sunglasses. Her breasts were all but jutting out.' She lay down and turned over and over; 'with her bum in the air, she wriggled and rubbed up against my legs and gazed at me'. But, again, according to Mussolini, he failed to rise to the occasion and was left to regret that she now believed either he 'was impotent or he was a complete idiot (*fesso*)'. On a third day she returned and quickly focused the conversation on 'sex and male virility'. But even that was a failure. 'Nothing. I was the head of government and she the princess'. And it was no different on a fourth and fifth occasion. Claretta by now was agog but Mussolini's chat drifted onto other issues, even if, perhaps aroused by the talk of his manhood, they did make love twice before leaving.[74]

On occasion thereafter the topic recurred, with Mussolini now deciding that Maria José actually was 'repellent', physically and intellectually.[75] More wistfully, he recalled, with his own coy euphemisms, that time when 'my little cock did not wake up, not at all, nothing. Rather, it went back into its cage. The more effort she made, the more he retreated.' His penis,

Claretta joked naughtily, must be a republican. Mussolini gave a laugh at that thought and went on to list his three failures to get an erection, the others being with Sarfatti (as already noted), and with a 'Russian' (perhaps Balabanoff?), when he was in Switzerland as a young man.[76]

It is hard to know what to make of the tale about Maria José, especially given that the lavish circumstantial detail of surroundings, dress and actions offers corroboration. Moreover, in 2011, it was revealed that, forty years earlier, Romano Mussolini had agreed, if a little vaguely, that the Mussolini family had always known of the 'intimate sentimental relationship' that, around 1937, had linked dictator and princess.[77] Yet, Claretta in her writings was recording her older lover's boasting, when he and she were preparing to have sex and arousing each other. Until the appearance of Maria José's diary, 'nonproven' may be the best verdict to give about the contention that the wife of the heir to the throne was ready and willing to be another of the dictator's partners.

* * *

Three further women in the Mussolini story need introduction, since he had children with each of them. His substantiated final tally of paternity was five legitimate children with Rachele, and illegitimate offspring with Fernanda Oss Facchinelli, Ida Dalser, Bianca Ceccato, Angela Cucciati, Ines De Spuches, Magda Brard (probably), Alice Pallottelli (probably two) and Romilda Ruspi: nine children from eight different mothers, while in 1940 Claretta Petacci did fall pregnant, but ectopically: no child resulted.[78] Here was a dictator who sought almost literally to be the *pater patriae*, a personal fount of national demographic growth. Somewhere in the background was his anxious desire, as expressed to his social superior Sarfatti, to be 'continued', almost as if he could not believe he had conquered without the proof of children. No doubt he insistently talked in a crudely patriarchal manner of 'taking' his women. Yet he tended to be solicitous of his lovers while they were pregnant and, in a majority of cases, kept some sense of paternal duty towards his illegitimate sons and daughters. He could be ruthless, especially with women whom he understood to be experienced and promiscuous and with whom he had not fathered offspring, although even then he scarcely made complete breaks with Brambilla and Tanzi and, in his way, with Sarfatti.

Of the mothers of his children, he imprisoned Dalser and sloughed off Oss Facchinelli. Yet, when the Second World War began to wreak havoc on his regime and nation and fret his personal sense of authority and purpose, Mussolini retained ties with Ceccato, Cucciati, Brard, Pallottelli and Ruspi, and conserved some knowledge of De Spuches. Even as the Petacci family added complications to his affair with Claretta, his other partners acted as though they belonged to Mussolini sub-families, and he did not disdain the thought. No wonder the most insistent theme in Petacci's diary is jealousy and Claretta's hope that she could drive her partner into simplifying his partnerships and their ramifications or, better, could absorb him into her own family.

Magda Brard may have been the most culturally talented of Mussolini's lovers, with the presumed exception of Sarfatti. She may also have led the most complex life, as revealed – somewhat obscurely – by the archives and in an interview that Roberto Festorazzi obtained from her in early 1998 when he admitted she was in mental decline (she died shortly afterwards, on 9 June).[79] Magdeleine Marie Anna ('Magda') Brard was born on 17 August 1903 (like Mussolini her star sign was Leo), in a town in Brittany. Her family was wealthy and established, with her father, Alfred, serving as a Radical senator in Paris, while enriching his family through a number of private and public business ventures. Probably a Freemason like most Frenchmen of his class, he was still in office in the 1930s. His two sons pursued successful military careers in the navy (Roger Brard rose to the rank of admiral) and air force.[80]

As a girl, Magda was a precociously talented pianist. She graduated from the Paris Conservatory at the age of twelve and began giving concert performances, touring the United States in 1919 and, in 1922, playing live at the Met in New York. Precocious in love as well as music, in March 1920 she was united in a high-society Paris wedding to Edmondo Michele Borgo, a rich motorcycle entrepreneur from Turin, where the couple soon based themselves. He was twenty years her senior.[81] They had a son, Reginaldo, in October 1926, and – more controversially – a daughter, Vanna, on 7 January 1932. From at least 1945 until her death, Brard would insist that Mussolini was a great lover and was the girl's father.[82] Whatever the case, by the time of this birth the Borgo marriage was collapsing, with a formal separation agreed in 1936. Six years later, doubtless as an indication of the social cachet of those involved, the Sacra Romana Rota approved dissolution on the grounds of *impotentia generale*, an unlikely determination given the two children. Magda was now pregnant with a second daughter (to be called Micaela), to Enrico Wild, a rich Swiss businessman and a believer in spiritualism. Transferring after the war to Nice, they married in 1947 (she was his fourth wife). Again the result was unhappy: Wild died suddenly in April 1955, amid rumours of mutual drug-taking and foolish investments by Magda; suicide has not been ruled out.[83]

Photos show Brard with somewhat untidy ringlets, although her elaborate hairstyles from girlhood suggest bourgeois expenditure on her appearance. She had dark eyes and, for her concert performances, favoured a silk gown and pearls. Another image exists of her playing ball in a modest period bathing costume, which displays a compact figure and shapely legs.

During the 1920s Brard had not accepted that marriage should signal her professional retirement. With the confidence of her class and rejecting Fascist blather about women preferring to be exemplary wives and mothers, Brard continued to give concerts, even when she was pregnant. So, during the summer of 1926 she was in Rome, and there had the self-confidence to write to the dictator suggesting a personal performance. Despite Ceccato's memory of him snoringly asleep at La Scala as *Aida* resounded, Mussolini liked to think of himself as a capable violinist – in 1927 regime propaganda published a tract entitled *Mussolini musicista* – and, throughout his life, he did play his instrument and grow emotional over it and other music. As his propagandist explained a little ambiguously: 'Mussolini is certainly not a musician in the strictly technical sense nor a virtuoso violinist. But he is something better and greater: an instinctual musician.'[84]

Whatever his skill, on the evening of 22 June Brard was invited to play at the Villa Torlonia. She did well. In a series of missives, Mussolini hailed her as 'a magician of the pianoforte' and, with more intimate slant, 'a woman who evokes perfect harmony'.[85] This being Fascist Italy, the police now began became interested in this French subject, with her high political contacts, noting happily at first that she was 'of fervent Fascist sentiments' and a great 'admirer of His Excellency Mussolini'. In February 1927 they added in stuffy bureaucratic phrasing that, evidently recovered from the birth of her son, she had spent an hour or so in 'the well-known apartment' in the Via Rasella, not leaving until after midnight. An anonymous spy now reported that she 'greatly feared the rivalry of another signora [Sarfatti]', who had begun to treat her with suspicion and jealousy.[86] There was also a further problem in Brard's career, since Mussolini took over the role of a patriarchal husband in discouraging her from performance and banning the Italian press from reviewing her concerts.

By December 1927 Brard was protesting vivaciously against such censorship, telling the *Duce* that, in his heart, he must comprehend that her 'art' was the 'fruit of years of hard work' and was what 'gave happiness to her family'.[87] Already, hostile informants had reported that Magda had disclosed at a reception in the French embassy that Mussolini 'ate like a pig' and 'other worse things'.[88] Rumours began to spread that Brard was a spy for her motherland, all the more after her concert career ended in 1931, just as she fell pregnant with Vanna. In March 1933 Umberto Ricci, the prefect of Turin, having earlier signalled the deplorable way she lived ostentatiously beyond her means, now accused her of being a 'con woman', 'who tried to exploit the friendship which she boasts of having here and in Rome for financial gain'.[89]

The police now threatened Brard with the loss of her PNF membership and the essential green light it gave to all profitable business dealings. She was only saved after she appealed – personally, vociferously, repeatedly and at length – to Mussolini. Invoking his 'sainted mother' as an initial rhetorical step, she talked of persecution and illness before growing ever more emphatic: '*I swear to you on my children's heads that I am completely innocent*' of any and every charge.[90] Her rhetoric worked. Her enemy, Ricci, was retired early and in November 1933 she regained her party card, with a positive judgement that she was 'a profoundly Italian woman', heavily and beneficially involved in business affairs.[91] She now successfully launched an Accademia della musica in Turin with state approval, and did not forget to send Mussolini personal thanks for his 'exquisite goodness' in her support.[92]

* * *

Brard remained the academy's director until 1943, with little sign of active involvement in politics or of new contact with Mussolini. In his bedtime musings with Claretta he only remembered her once, as a name in his list of multiple lovers at the Via Rasella.[93] Family gossip from the 1990s, taken seriously by Festorazzi, that, in 1940, she plotted to frame a deal whereby Italy and France could become allies in the Second World War, can be discounted.[94] Yet, in 1944–5, she did resurface in the archives of the RSI, to which she had adhered. At her Villa Roccabruna, above Como, she sponsored a salon of regime notables, including German generals and the minister of the interior, Guido Buffarini Guidi. There, in 1945, Gina Ruberti, the widow of Mussolini's son, Bruno, who had died as a test pilot during the war, and her parents found sanctuary.[95]

But Brard's new correspondence with the *Duce* (they had one face-to-face meeting at Gargnano in July 1944) revolved around her pleas to the dictator – whom she addressed in the proper Fascist manner as *Voi* (the second-person plural, rather than the more intimate *tu*, or the derided third-person singular *Lei*) – for special treatment. 'You have known me personally for twenty years,' she stressed, 'and you are aware of my sentiments about being Italian and my love for the *patria* of which you are the symbol.' However much approached with such grovelling phrasing, her sometime lover and possible father of her second child had now, in her mind, become the patron who owed his client something. So she wrote about her son, Reginaldo, who had been caught up in Germany and needed to come home. At the *Duce*'s obliging request, he did. After this little personal victory, as late as April 1945 Brard was still importuning Mussolini to bend the rules in accelerating state approval of her marriage to a foreign citizen whose third wife may have been Jewish.[96]

A few weeks later Brard herself was under arrest, held alongside Fascist chiefs who had survived the war in Como's San Donnino prison.[97] She was quickly released, however, following intervention by French diplomatic and military personnel. Was this a hint that she had after all been a spy? Or had she been the secret aide of anti-Fascists in difficulty during the war? Or, most likely, was it just that her French family were people who mattered in that country? In any case, Brard left quickly for Paris and then went on to Nice. She never returned to Italy. Ninety-five at her death, among Mussolini's lovers she had indeed been a woman of many parts.

* * *

In all the romantic literature about Mussolini's women, perhaps the silliest title, but one that well expresses the depth of nostalgia for the *Duce*'s body in Italy, has been given to a study of Alice Pallottelli, another woman, like Brard, with high cultural connections, if as an administrator not a performer. Whatever else Pallottelli may have been, she should not be hailed as 'Mussolini's Joan of Arc', as the subtitle of a 2010 biography had it.[98]

Alice de Fonseca was born in Florence on 6 October 1892. Her father Edoardo, known as 'Professor Fonseca', was the owner of a publishing house specialising in the figurative arts and music, that he would pass on to his daughter and her husband, Count Francesco Pallottelli Corinaldesi (born in March 1884, less than a year after Mussolini).[99] Alice Corinaldesi de Fonseca Pallottelli, as she was formally known after her marriage, was therefore much the same age as Rachele Mussolini, Giulia Alliata and Giulia Brambilla. Her first child, Virgilio, who was destined to accompany Mussolini and Claretta on their last journey along Lake Como, was born in Paris in 1917. According to Mimmo Franzinelli, Alice Pallottelli was 'tall, blonde, elegant, a fluent and correct speaker', who affected 'aristocratic style', whether in her successive 'luxurious residences' in Rome (most accessibly from 1927 to 1936 in the Villa Virgilio, Via Nomentana 377, just opposite the Villa Torlonia)[100] or in the family's Villa Gloria at Fabriano in the Marche, a town to which she and her husband long gave patronage.[101] A photo of her in the USA in 1923 shows her with bobbed hair, a stylish hat and well-cut floral gown and to have a pert nose, wide mouth and gleaming eyes; she plainly occupied a place many rungs up the class ladder from the determinedly rustic Rachele Mussolini.[102] Sexually she was no ingénue but rather, like the majority of the dictator's partners, experienced and worldly-wise. She was also a durable partner, fulfilling the role of what is best defined as a sub-wife.

Naturally, Mussolini got around to telling Claretta how their sexual contact had begun. It was spring 1938 and the *Duce* was feeling romantic.

'Look, the swallows are back. It is poetic to see them for the first time with you', he told his young lover in jovial affection, before ruminating on Pallottelli, with whom he was still having sex. 'As for Pallottelli, I never really loved her', he began. 'I knew her for the first time at Genoa shortly after I had taken office. She was in the hotel with her husband and sent me a posy of flowers with a card saying "From an Italian woman in gratitude". Then the next morning I met her in the lobby, we chatted, and little by little things started.' Following his move to the Via Rasella, he broke with her when she went off to stay for a week with D'Annunzio at his palace, the Vittoriale, on Lago di Garda (such a meeting could have had only one purpose). At first Pallottelli had not believed Mussolini's rejection but for five years they did not see each other. 'Then she turned up again saying she needed help for her son. So everything started again.'[103]

On Christmas Day 1932 Pallottelli was delivered of a son, Duilio, fifteen years the junior of Virgilio. A daughter, Adua (her name that of the Ethiopian town where Italian forces had suffered humiliating defeat in March 1896, later 'avenged' by Fascist arms in October 1935), followed in January 1936. Alice Pallottelli claimed each was sired by Mussolini and the *Duce* agreed, at least for most of the time, despite residual doubts about Duilio. He certainly could display paternal concern when he learned that one or other of the children were sick.[104] Duilio, he told Claretta, must be his given the way Pallottelli had grasped him at the moment of ejaculation, while Adua, he was sure, was 'the prettiest little girl in Rome. A real delight. Just like Anna [Maria],' his last legitimate child. Pallottelli, however, he assured Petacci dismissively, was now a 'stale crumb' (*vecchia ciabatta*), 'poor woman'.[105] Yet, despite her ageing, he did not cut off contact. In December 1940 Claretta was still chivvying Mussolini with the 'nausea' that she felt on realising that he had again slipped away to Pallottelli's flat (located conveniently near the Villa Torlonia).[106]

Of all Mussolini's partners apart from Claretta, Pallottelli has left the deepest archival trace. It provides evidence not so much about sex as business and, notably, the patronage that Mussolini's lingering lovers always expected that the *Duce* would provide for them and theirs. The story lasted through the Fascist *ventennio*. In 1923–4 Pallottelli was happy to act as the sophisticated woman with global cultural contacts, emphatic that she could benefit Fascism with her speeches on a tour of the USA. She duly earned thanks from Mussolini who told her that 'female propaganda always works the best'. The *Duce* also suggested beguilingly that she pass by his office before leaving so they could talk about 'final preparations'.[107]

Matters were not always so happy, however. In 1927 the file of scabrous gossip in Mussolini's desk drawer was expanded with anonymous denunciations of the Pallottellis, who were reported to be living off the elderly, eccentric and celebrated Russian pianist Vladimir de Pachmann (1848–1933). Pallottelli herself was reported to have established 'intimate relations' with such significant figures in the regime's cultural life as Giacomo Paulucci di Calboli and Senator Riccardo Bianchi. Both Pachmann and Count Francesco were said to be homosexual, a not uncommon claim in this literature, if one not necessarily to be believed.[108]

The business affairs of the Pallottellis deteriorated further following Pachmann's death, with the collapse of the family publishing company and the failure of other ventures in the concert world, despite many supplications for support from Mussolini. He was mostly accommodating. However, in 1932 he refused to back a scheme to have the Pallottellis' music review compulsorily sold to all visitors to the Mostra della Rivoluzione Fascista, as well he might have done if any credence should be given to the view in much current historiography that the exhibition was a pure expression of revolutionary culture. Mussolini's police chief, Arturo Bocchini, was independent enough in 1935 to rebuff a request from his *Duce* to get Count Francesco his driver's license back after a 'serious crash'.[109]

With the family fortunes plummeting, the solution for the Pallottellis became that which can be discerned in the imperial story of many European powers, that is, 'to go out and govern New South Wales'. With a recommendation from on high, by 1938 Count Francesco could rejoice in employment in the Fascist administration of Ethiopia, leaving Alice and her children in their flat in Rome. But dull governmental activity could not fill his days, so the count was soon trying to pressurise Rome into subsidising grand mining opportunities, which he claimed to have discerned in the new colony. In the interim he sought and won a pay rise. Alas for such entrepreneurship! The mining projects got nowhere and, in May 1940, the count chose a good moment to scuttle back to Italy. Thereafter he remembered to draw his pay but signally failed to resume labour in the colony[110] where, in any case, British imperial arms were quickly demonstrating that Ethiopia had been held by a Sawdust Caesar. Soon, rather than dealing with the grand world of empire, the Pallottelli files were focusing on the couple's dealings in Fabriano, with the perhaps happy news in December 1942 that Count Francesco had his driving license back since 'he was an agricultural producer of particular significance'.[111]

Alice Pallottelli was meanwhile deploying her historic connection with the dictator to urge that one citizen of Fabriano be let out of *confino*, a second off his taxes, a third allowed to transfer from the army to the air force, a fourth to move from the Greek front to home service near his family at Pesaro, and a fifth (a woman) to get a job as a school cleaner. Alice also asked that quite a large fund be found to assist in the restoration of a small local church, and urged that public telephones be installed in a number of *paesi* near Fabriano.[112] In May–June 1943 she confronted the graver problem of a report that her elder son, Virgilio, had been shot down on 23 May 1943 over Algeria and that it was not known whether he was alive or dead. Could government agents do everything possible to clarify the matter?[113] They did. Now happy reports arrived that Virgilio Pallottelli was alive. After the crisis of July–September resulted in the foundation of the RSI, he and his mother continued to have dealings with the *Duce* until April 1945.

* * *

Whereas useful detail survives on Pallottelli and a number of Mussolini's other lovers, Romilda Minardi Ruspi has left a meagre record,[114] except in Claretta's diary, given her recurrent jealousy over the sexual relationship between Ruspi and the *Duce* until the end of his life. Perhaps because of this durability, in 1945 Ruspi was well enough known to be included in a scandal sheet rushed out by anti-Fascists. She was there described as 'the daughter of a washerwoman . . . married to a printer from Frascati'. She had worked at the Villa Torlonia as a maid of some kind, attracting Mussolini with her 'bosomy figure'.[115] Claretta summed her up curtly as 'about forty, beautiful but mature-looking'.[116] No photograph of her seems to have survived. Ruspi was born around 1900 and her sister, Renata, worked on the staff of the Villa Torlonia and may have been the lover of Prince Giovanni Torlonia. Renata was confident enough in 1938 to make the recommendation that Mussolini intervene in favour of the Duchess Maria Torlonia in Sforza Cesarini in regard to a financial dispute that the duchess was having with a government agency.[117]

In the anti-Fascist account, Ruspi's husband, Giovanni Minardi, was annoyed at his wife's seduction but was mollified by being despatched to work in Paris on a party newspaper in a much better paid job than he had occupied in Rome. The family was also given a villa at Ostia Lido and other financial help, under the excuse of paying for the education of the three Minardi/Ruspi children.[118] Romilda Ruspi came from a lower class background than most of Mussolini's other lovers and, indeed, than Claretta. In attempted self-exculpation to Claretta, the *Duce* often made it sound as though Ruspi's presence on the staff of the Villa Torlonia had made sex with her inevitable. Once again, Mussolini continued to 1945 to feel some responsibility for her.

In 1939 the dictator dated the prime moments of his affair with Ruspi to 1927–9, claiming predictably that his only motive had been sexual, 'no love, no sentiment'.[119] Initially coitus seems to have occurred somewhere in the Villa Torlonia but later, in the 1930s, Ruspi was established in a flat in the Via Po, half a kilometre away.[120] A son, Massimo, had been born in 1929 and Mussolini sometimes, but not always, denied paternity.[121] However, he admitted to Claretta that the relationship with Ruspi by 1939 had existed for 'fourteen years' and it continued into the war, with Mussolini accepting that he must protect Ruspi and her children from untoward events.[122] Claretta's jealousy did not hamper the *Duce*'s sexual visitations to Ruspi's nearby flat, even if, on 11 July 1940, what the couple saw as a formally couched 'armistice' was signed between Mussolini (as 'Ben') and Petacci (post-dated a year). In this mock treaty the dictator swore not to allow Romilda Ruspi to 'enter . . . the Villa Torlonia for any motive at all', nor to 'see Signora Ruspi more than once per month without a single exception' and to ensure that any visits he made to her house were confined to 'twenty minutes'. The pact was a parody of that being arranged in the greater world with the surrender of France to the Axis powers, and was therefore viewed by the lovers as all the more amusing. A final clause noted that, if the terms were broken, 'hostilities will resume'.[123]

* * *

Given the number of women involved and Mussolini's readiness to treat them as though he were a ruling sultan, it is no surprise that a popular study of the subject is entitled *The Duce's harem*.[124] Yet there are some surprises in the story of Mussolini's sex life, where, at a moment of modesty, his tally to Claretta was a total of 'about thirty'.[125] Part of the current image of patriarchal sex is that the older man should seek young, slim, beautiful women as his partners. Whether true or not, such girls were certainly what Berlusconi liked to suggest were his bedfellows. Yet, with the exception of Bianca Ceccato and the office romance at *Il Popolo d'Italia*, Mussolini's other women were mature, experienced and married; divorce, unless managed through some special Vatican network, remained illegal within Italy. Most often the *Duce*'s partners sprang from a more elevated class background than his own (and certainly than Rachele's). A number were females of considerable culture, who evidently interested 'Professor Mussolini', the aspirant intellectual. A few were rapidly set aside by the *Duce* and all were the subjects of hasty denials to his new young lover that he had really cared for them at all; lust, he reiterated, was his sole motive. Yet quite a few retained contact, even sexually, with the dictator well into middle age. The majority could also rely on Mussolini's patronage if they fell into financial or other trouble and find a patron's protection for the children whom the *Duce* had conceived with them. So, perhaps, a harem is a fitting analogy since, while Mussolini remained married to Rachele, Pallottelli and Ruspi, Curti and Ceccato, in one way or another, continued to act as sub-wives, and neither they nor Mussolini saw much problem in so doing.

Another observation may be more important. Mussolini's sex life had curious parallels with his politics as dictator, given its combination of violence, unalloyed egoism and an acceptance of, or even a preference for, the established and traditional over the new and radical. Can the liaisons that the *Duce* undertook with a list of middle-aged, experienced and worldly-wise women have been the equivalent of his knowledge as dictator that, despite blarney about Fascist social and cultural revolution, he must get along with the monarchy, the Vatican, big business, large landowners and the pre-existing national establishment? For all his lustfulness, there was also something careful and predictable, even appeasing, about Mussolini's sexuality, and a curious unity between the unspoken assumptions of his public and private lives.

But what, it must now be asked, was a genteelly reared Catholic girl of the Roman bourgeoisie – presented with a sports car by her doting parents on her eighteenth birthday,[126] soon to be engaged to Riccardo Federici, a lieutenant in the national air force eight years her senior – to make of her induction into the dictator's life? Was she to be just another short-term sexual partner or another sub-wife? Or, as her ambitions expanded, could she oust Rachele as the wife of wives? What would her pious family, especially her ultra-Catholic mother, make of this relationship? Or was Claretta Petacci to be the female who would break the mould of Mussolini's lust, his modern, modernist or radical Fascist 'new woman'? What, in sum, would Benito Mussolini do to Claretta Petacci and what would she do to him, and how did that contact, which had begun with a passionate, girlish letter in 1926, expand into what, in 'wromantic' Italian representation, was the greatest, most tragic (and most Fascist) love affair of modern times? Indeed, was Claretta, as has been claimed, 'the most famous lover in the entire history of Italy'?[127]

3

AND SO . . . PAUSE . . . TO BED
Predatory Dictator meets Catholic Girl

In 1929 a new novel took the Italian literary scene by storm. Although initially published at the author's expense it rapidly sold out, demanding immediate reprintings. The book was entitled *Gli indifferenti* (eventually to be translated into English as *The time of indifference*).[1] Its author called himself Alberto Moravia, although his true surname was Pincherle. He had been born in Rome in November 1907, his rich and distinguished upper-bourgeois family residing in a comfortable flat outside the Borghese gardens, positioned less than a kilometre from the Villa Torlonia. An uncle, Augusto De Marsanich, was a Fascist dignitary who after 1945 became the second leader of the neofascist MSI. Moravia's cousins by contrast were the Rosselli brothers, Carlo and Nello, murdered in France in 1937 at the behest of Ciano in one of the regime's most public and brutal crimes. Moravia's mother came from Catholic nationalist stock in Dalmatia and his father from that world of assimilated Venetian Jews which incorporated the Sarfattis. Moravia was a sickly boy, diagnosed as suffering from a tubercular bone infection. He was often bedridden and so avoided public schooling at *liceo* or university. Still a teenager, he began writing *Gli indifferenti* while he was living for health reasons at Bressanone/Brixen in the Alto Adige/Süd Tirol, a town that Italy had annexed through its victory in the First World War.

After 1945 Moravia became a leading anti-Fascist, happy to be associated with that majority of intellectuals who fellow-travelled with the Partito

Comunista Italiano (PCI; Italian Communist Party). In 1947 he published *Il conformista* (filmed by Bernardo Bertolucci in 1969),[2] a novel expressing the ideas of psychologist, Erich Fromm, that Fascists were in their hearts people with a 'fear of freedom' (and, by implication, recalcitrant to fulfilled sex),[3] men (it was a male-driven ideology) afraid to understand or express themselves.[4] The Moravia of this era became an international celebrity. Under the regime, by contrast, Moravia did attract some controversy, increasing after the racial laws were implemented; nonetheless he generally fitted himself into Fascist cultural requirements, without ever launching into the more fervent or opaque efforts to talk up a political religion. His focus was instead on the barrenness of the bourgeoisie and their hypocrisy and vacuity. Members of the class who by the late 1930s the regime itself was abusing as 'slipper-wearing cowards' were exposed under Moravia's scalpel as bored and exploitative. Their sexual relations were loveless, fear-laden and patriarchal. Their jabber about family tenderness and commitment was false.

This visceral dishonesty was the theme of *Gli indifferenti*, amplified by the novel's setting in that soft and corrupt Rome that Italians mistrusted, with characters who were anything but bearers of heroic *romanità*. It was hard to detect in *Gli indifferenti* a whiff of stalwart Fascism. The plot revolved around a widowed mother, Mariagrazia Ardengo, mutinously entering middle age (like Pallottelli and Ruspi), her daughter Carla (not Clara), approaching her twentieth birthday, her son, Michele (not Marcello), attending university. Mariagrazia had for fifteen years been the lover of Leo Merumeci, a rich entrepreneur (Leo was Mussolini's star sign). As the book opened, Leo was tiring of Mariagrazia and aware (as she was, too) of her body's growing flabbiness. He therefore turned his lascivious attention to Carla and, by the novel's end, the young woman, under tormented pressure from her mother, agreed to bed him, all the more because Ardengo family finances were threadbare. Michele watched these bleak events with growing bitter realisation that lying and betrayal conquer all.

Here then may be evidence of a case where life imitated art. It might be suggested that the Petaccis in the 1930s played out in the real world what the 'realist' novelist, Moravia, had imagined a decade earlier as he surveyed from his sickbed, with youthful nervous insight, his bourgeois Roman world. Yet, as shall be seen over the next pages, 'real reality', what actually happened to the Petaccis, how they in fact comported themselves and how their lives fitted into Roman, bourgeois, Catholic and Fascist patterns of behaviour, offers a far richer canvas of human peccadilloes than Moravia's literary evocation of them. As in *Gli indifferenti*, the fate of the Petaccis is replete with hypocrisy, vacuity, exploitation, ennui, sex and death, but, at the same time, it is paradoxically warmed by family compact, belief, action, sacrifice and even love, somehow defined.

* * *

The story began on 24 April 1932, a sunny day in Rome. That afternoon, the Petaccis, by now residing even more centrally and respectably at flat 6, 326 Corso Vittorio Emanuele, decided they deserved an outing. Mother Giuseppina, little sister Myriam (not yet nine), Claretta (who had just celebrated her twentieth birthday) and her fiancé, Lieutenant Riccardo Federici (who may have boasted noble antecedents),[5] piled into their commodious, chauffeur-driven Lancia Astura limousine with its Vatican number plates.[6] For propriety's sake, Myriam was positioned as a sort of chaperone between Claretta and Riccardo;[7] among good Catholics, bodily contact must not become incontinent (and Myriam was destined often to repeat the protective role while her sister dallied with a different partner). What a good idea it was to go for a spin down the new Fascist motorway that led to Ostia, the beach and the Tyrrhenian Sea!

A similar pleasurable thought occurred to the *Duce*. After all, for some years, he had grown accustomed to utilising the bathing hut at Castelporziano, so graciously made available to him by the Savoys, with its direct telephone connection to his office, its shower and a bed. On 24 April, having given his chauffeur, Ercole Boratto, the afternoon off, he decided to drive himself in his red Alfa Romeo 8C, oblivious to the fact that Boratto judged his master a poor driver, too easily distracted at the wheel.[8]

After all, few clouds seemed to shroud the world that Mussolini bestrode. True, the fascistic Nazi party of the rather odd German *Führer*, Adolf Hitler, was gearing up for elections in July, where its vote was destined to expand exponentially, and the Depression was beating down on the German and most other European economies. But Italy seemed to have escaped the worst of the crisis through what was judged in many places its leader's genius. To reinforce his fame, over the last few weeks the *Duce* had granted a set of interviews to the Polish-born, Swiss-residing, German-Jewish journalist, Emil Ludwig. Their exchange went agreeably well, Ludwig being beguiled by what he described as Mussolini's good humour and mastery of detail when presented with more than four hundred questions. 'In conversation,' Ludwig reported, 'Mussolini is the most natural man in the world . . . I have no hesitation in describing him as a great statesman.'[9] Perhaps there was a hint of future concern when discussion had wandered onto some potentially treacherous issues, but the dictator, as yet no friend of Hitler, pronounced worthily that 'national pride has no need of the delirium of race'. The only worry came when, with the interview all but over, he philosophised in words, often to be repeated, that sounded almost wistful: 'fundamentally I have always been alone'.[10]

Only a few months before, on 21 December 1931, Mussolini had lost his brother Arnaldo, dead at the age of forty-six, the same as Mussolini's mother. Claretta would remember to send a comforting note on the first anniversary.[11] His father Alessandro had lasted until he was fifty-six. From now on, Mussolini's private meditations often turned to mortality. Perhaps the wistfulness was enhanced further by the fact that Edda, his elder daughter and favourite child, had been married to Galeazzo Ciano in a high society wedding at the church up the road from the Villa Torlonia on 24 April 1930, exactly two years before he met Claretta. Mussolini missed Edda, all the more when she swiftly departed to Shanghai, where Ciano had been appointed Italian consul. Distressing rumours soon suggested that the marriage had its tares, that Edda was indulging in the regrettable habits of gambling and drinking Coca-Cola, and that Galeazzo may have been bedding a sprC called Wallis Simpson,[12] while busying himself in promoting an arms trade between Italy and Chiang Kai-shek (Jiǎng Jièshí) and pro-Fascist elements in China.[13] Contact between father and daughter slackened. For a while Mussolini tried to correspond regularly by telegram[14] but intimacy had been lost; the two were drifting apart. Could Edda somehow be replaced by another?

Down the Via del Mare he drove; his masculine pride meant that Mussolini liked to go as fast as possible and his Alfa swept past the Petacci's Lancia with a derisory toot. But Claretta recognised the driver and, all a flutter, urged the chauffeur to pursue Mussolini into Ostia, where the two vehicles drew to a halt. Claretta leaped out and, at least according to her sister's much later memories, cried to her astonished fellow passengers: 'I'm going to pay homage to him. I've been waiting to do so for such a long time. There are no other people around. Riccardo, you come too, and speak with the *Duce*.'[15]

No police guards intervened. To Claretta's effusive greeting, Mussolini replied cautiously, enquiring about her family car's Vatican number plates. When Claretta told him who her father was, he, attuned to the nuances of status, politely claimed to have heard of Francesco Saverio Petacci as 'among the best-regarded doctors' in Rome. He added winningly that he knew Claretta, too, from her poetry and correspondence that his office had received. When addressing Federici, he more soberly elicited his rank and air base. Courteously, the *Duce* then said goodbye. More than satisfied, Claretta stumbled back to the family car in a state of high emotion, declaring that destiny had made the magical meeting possible.[16]

No doubt it might have been just an accidental rendezvous with no particular meaning or result. Mussolini was guiding his country through what his most comprehensive biographer, De Felice, called 'the years of [popular] consent' and expected his countrymen and countrywomen to love and adore him. Claretta, it is often contended, had been infatuated with the dictator from the time of Gibson's assassination attempt or earlier. Yet, there had been rumours that she had found a boyfriend, the son of a rich businessman, at Grottaferrata in the Alban hills in 1928,[17] and she was now engaged to Federici, whom she automatically hauled along with her in salutation. Even though Claretta's own obsessive version of her history would become that she had adored Mussolini from the very first, it was not yet wholly clear that her crush was anything more than that, nor that she had determined from her early teenage years to dedicate her sexuality, life and death to the *Duce*.

* * *

Three days later Mussolini, who was either predatory or missing Edda, was on the phone to the Petaccis. According to Myriam, who may well have added a sentimental gloss to the story, Mussolini asked to speak to Claretta, identifying himself theatrically as 'the man from Ostia'. Then the stunned family heard Claretta say: 'Yes, *Duce*. Yes, Your Excellency. Thank you, yes.'[18] When Claretta put down the receiver, she related that she had been summoned to Mussolini's office in the Palazzo Venezia. A pass was awaiting her. Mussolini wanted her personally to read her poetry to him.

Perhaps unsurprisingly, Giuseppina was perturbed at the call – as Myriam put it, 'Mussolini did not rejoice in a good name in regard to women' – but everyone in the family agreed that Claretta must accept the invitation. Mother, always the dominant personality in the Petacci household, took pains to decide what her daughter should wear: a brownish woollen dress, stylish shoes and matching bag, and a neat little hat. Soon mother and daughter were being driven by the family chauffeur the few hundred metres that separated their flat from the Palazzo Venezia. When Claretta went inside, Giuseppina sat in the car and prayed.[19]

Cliché would predict that, if Petacci were still a virgin, she must have emerged from her 'interview' one no longer, and Giuseppina's prayers must have been stimulated by that fear. But in fact, again according to Myriam, this first conversation stuck to banalities, with Mussolini remarking mildly that he had thought her much younger than twenty, perhaps still a schoolgirl of fourteen. Rather as if he were addressing a teenager, he turned the conversation to her interests, from culture to sport, and then sent her away with a suggestion to come back with the poems she had not had time to read on this occasion.

What is to be made of this meeting? An older man's preliminaries in seduction? Mussolini-style grooming? Very likely. Flattery was evidently involved, just as it had been in the encounter at Ostia. And, fifteen years earlier, Mussolini had seduced and abandoned the teenaged Bianca Ceccato, although since then his lust seemed to have been satisfied by older women. After all, there was another parallel, one with different implications in regard to Mussolini's motivation and behaviour. When, from Easter 1942, Mussolini revived his interest in Elena Curti, his illegitimate daughter, he similarly called her to his office or rang her late at night for regular chats, often about philosophy, partly hoping for congratulations about his own elevated intellectuality ('Professor' Mussolini again), partly with an apparent interest in a younger (female) mind and its preoccupations, and partly with an almost ingenuous pleasure in being able to be a young woman's patron.[20] He even asked that she address him as *tu*.[21] Elena Curti's Mussolini was more a sugar daddy than the violent Ejaculator of Gadda's imagining.

What, then, would be Claretta's fate? Meetings and telephone contact, once initiated, continued. A companion of his early days as a Fascist remembered Mussolini's calls graphically as 'febrile, wandering, nervous, calm, curious, pernickety, obsessive, acute, ingenuous, clever,' by no means narrowly focused in other words; the dictator certainly found time for very many conversations, every day.[22] As will be seen, Claretta was sometimes the recipient of a dozen or more during her waking hours. From November 1932 she began to record them in some detail, however banal their content. Quite often Mussolini's prime task was to explain to a precociously jealous Claretta why there were fallow periods in his attention to her. 'For two months,' she told him half accusingly, she had scarcely been away from the family phone in the hope that, at some precious moment, she would again hear his voice. If he did not ring, she wrote instead, obsequiously informing him that she was trembling with emotion as she put pen to paper. She, 'just a little thing', could not dare to approach him except for her 'immense desire, [her] joy to be able to see you again and because of [her] memory of your lovely goodness' (she habitually used the formal *Lei* to address him, a word choice about to be damned as effeminate and foreign by the new populist PNF secretary, Achille Starace).[23] Another phone call ended with Mussolini counting on his fingers the 'two months and two days' since they had last been in communication. 'How awful!' he said, perhaps lost for better words. 'Yes, it is really awful,' she replied and won from Mussolini a promise that he would call again the next day.[24]

Gradually, however, another theme began to enter their conversations, one that was familial in nature and where the initiative came from Claretta. When they were in direct contact, Signorina Petacci, rather than merely worshipping the great dictator, eagerly besought him for advantages to her father, her brother and her fiancé, for *raccomandazioni*, for special privileges, for financial gain, for promotion, for circumventing the bureaucratic system. (Party Secretary Starace had banned such behaviour on at least three occasions).[25] For the moment at least, Claretta did not mention the purist ideals of the Fascist revolution, with its strict hierarchical rules and pledged hatred of 'corruption'. Her family mattered more than her ideology (if she had one). As she petitioned her hero, Claretta began to seek reward for her devotion, rather as Italian Catholics have been found to view their ties with a local saint or with some emanation of the Madonna: godlike beings, yes, but ones that must forever prove themselves generous benefactors.

* * *

The new and momentous year of 1933 began. On 30 January President Paul von Hindenburg appointed Adolf Hitler chancellor of Germany, a rise to power destined to set Europe ablaze, and a change in government that, for the moment, Italian Fascists, including Mussolini, viewed equivocally.[26] At that time, the *Duce* still had every reason to think of himself as dictator major, even if, on 29 July 1933, he would pass the milestone of his fiftieth birthday. Photos from this period show a nuggety, fit-looking man, still possessed of a firm stomach – it was said that he weighed himself daily and hated the idea of running to fat.[27] Unlike most politicians of his era, he was ready to display his physique to his adoring public, for example when striding along the beach in his bathers at Riccione in the company of his client authoritarian leader in Vienna, Engelbert Dollfuss (1892–1934). The Austrian chancellor, a decade Mussolini's junior, was more fastidiously sporting a suit and tie, although the heat had forced him to remove his soft hat and carry his coat slung over an arm.[28] Even as Mussolini showed off his masculine athleticism, one small private sign of doubts about the future could be detected in the decision to shave his head. It was the sure way to hide the visible whitening of his hair. Mussolini was, however, still equipped with his famous jutting chin, fleshy mouth and burning eyes, these last automatically transfixing onlookers (a common talent of those said to bear charisma). A sometimes visibly happy dictator, he could still smile in public, not yet fully transmogrified into the stern, 'granitic' figure that he would become by the later 1930s.

For Claretta Petacci, 1933 was the year when her family celebrated her twenty-first birthday. She had a roundish face, quite a prominent nose and dark, on occasion heavily waved, hair. She was neither tall nor slender but her bust was well developed, and one – decidedly catty – upper-class critic conceded that she had 'beautiful legs'.[29] Her fiancé, Federici, was appreciably taller than she was and his hair was beginning to thin, although it remained youthfully black. Petacci was said to be a nervous eater but did love chocolates. Although possessed of a better swimming style than the *Duce*, she was not especially athletic, often happy to remain in bed, armed with a box of chocolates, well into the late morning. Jewels and furs could similarly improve her days. She liked Lanvin and Arpège perfumes,[30] Parisian products that broke the regime's rules on autarky and the compulsory use of 'made in Italy' products. Among high-society dames, Claretta was scarcely alone in such preference and behaviour. In most ways she was an unremarkable young bourgeois woman.

Yet she was also persistent. A record grew of her petitions to the *Duce* for special help to her father in a law case, and for early promotion for Federici. When Mussolini huffed and puffed in response, with sententious statements that 'in ten years I have never interfered with the course of justice, out of a deep sense of conscience', and that, even though he was the chief of all, he could not break the formal procedures of officer ranking, she did not back off. Rather she assured him that he did indeed have total power: could he not find some way to advantage her and hers? 'It's precisely because a law bans it,' she remarked blithely, 'that I have asked for your support. Otherwise it would just be stupid to disturb you.'[31]

On 15 December 1932 a lengthy phone conversation about such issues took a strange turn when Mussolini, perhaps trying to fob off Claretta and her importunities, asked her what she wanted to do with her life. 'Oh, I don't know,' she replied skittishly, 'to live, to do something, to achieve my possibilities, to do something, I repeat, that will fill my life.' Pressed further, Claretta retreated, saying 'I'm afraid of talking rubbish. You [she was still using the polite third-person form, whereas he used the 'intimate' *tu*, more as a reflection of their age difference than of genuine intimacy] are such a superlatively intelligent man . . . and I am just a child. You might just tease me.' Nonetheless she tentatively raised an idea that she must have read about somewhere of taking on a career as a secret agent. She could follow the path of people who had worked secretly for Napoleon (a personage destined to recur in their conversations). Mussolini – perhaps thinking of Brambilla or his desk drawer of secret denunciations or the Petacci family's Vatican connections – did not dismiss the idea. Rather, he warned her sapiently that becoming a spy must mean utterly changing her life. 'A dangerous activity and one of sacrifice'; once she entered the profession, she could not retreat, he added portentously.

When, perhaps struck by the absurdity of their theme, he began to hesitate and reiterate that she was just a child and he would have to wait until her understanding matured, she interrupted him with another strange query. 'And can these informers also have a husband? . . . Can they be faithful or must they by necessity . . .?' Here Mussolini, sounding sternly parental, cut her short. 'Ah no! Indeed no, Clara, if I'd thought you were going to propose such infamy, such a low and vulgar bargain, I would not have let you speak, I would not have let you continue. I respect you too much to make such a shameful proposal. Ah no! For you to sleep with men, no, never, Clara.' He then affirmed that, even in the greater world, with a few wartime exceptions, such things never happened. It was time to hang up. But Claretta managed to slip in a last request that he ring again soon, and to ask his judgement of her father, whom he had just met again. 'Excellent,' Mussolini replied automatically, 'he made a great impression on me.'[32]

At 7 p.m. on 30 January 1933, the very day that in Germany Hitler was sworn in as chancellor, Mussolini and Petacci had another of their increasingly cosy meetings at the Palazzo Venezia. As Claretta did not fail to record, Mussolini sat on the arm of his chair with his feet on its leather surface. In what was perhaps mock anger he raised with her a report that he had received, accusing Federici of flying too low over Rome, with an official request that he must therefore be rebuked, and then transferred after a week or two in military confinement. In response, however, Claretta switched the conversation to sex and corruption. The problem was, she reckoned, that a married captain had tried making 'shameful court' to her in the presence of her mother and father and although it was well known that she was engaged. She had rejected the propositioning of course. But from then on, a 'clique' had shamefully pursued a vendetta against her poor fiancé. It was a wicked world, it seemed, enough to make Mussolini stop teasing her about Federici.[33]

So their relationship continued as an odd couple. Most initiative came from Claretta. Only a few days after their talk about Federici, she scribbled down her thoughts on a train trip and sent them on to the dictator. Her spirit, she declared a little glumly, 'stays with you. My soul has been taken over. Only my body is here.'[34] On 18 April 1933 she wrote still more gushingly to say that she had just survived a dreadfully sad Easter but now the anniversary of the 24th was approaching. 'I know that you [*Ella*] have heaps to do but I don't know how to tell you that I'd love to come to Your [office] on the 24th, Monday. Do you not remember anything of this date? For me it was the happiest day of my life, the most precious moment when you spoke to me for the first time. I try to preserve for ever my gentle, sweet, shiver [of that day], that same violent emotion. How I trembled – do You remember? – but it wasn't the cold. Be nice, I beg You, and let me be near You on Monday.'[35]

Amid such effusions, she did not forget family duty. So she sent to the *Duce* copies of papers that her brother had written and pressed him for a positive reaction; before long, Mussolini rang to say that a good job was indeed coming Marcello's way.[36] Yet, mostly, her letters brimmed with her utter devotion, a sentiment harder and harder to separate from physical love, all the more so given that her conservative upbringing made it almost impossible for her openly to express sexual desire.[37] So she was left to beseech 'one little word from you' (now she switched to the party-approved *Voi* to address him, not the conventionally formal *Ella*). She could only compare him to the Sun God: 'I cannot live without your warmth,' she wrote. When she saw him at a parade, she explained that his presence aroused in her 'the ecstasy of my heart throbbing with affection. You who dominate the world gave me a smile. You were aware of me and so made me infinitely happy. Thanks.'[38]

In March 1934 another long conversation in the Palazzo Venezia potentially signalled a turning point in the contact between the two. Their conversation started predictably enough, with Claretta pushing the *Duce* for a change in Marcello's temporary and precarious academic status as a doctor and for an improvement in his pay. But a suddenly irritated

Mussolini broke in to ask her 'Why do you come? It is absurd, ridiculous, it does not make sense . . . I am old,' he added mournfully. 'You are a child.' But then Claretta had an idea. 'What if I were married?' she asked. Mussolini was struck by the suggestion: 'Well, then it would be different. You'd be a signora.' 'Well, then, let me get married,' Claretta suggested with surprising aplomb. 'Me?' Mussolini exclaimed. 'Yes, you.' 'But how?' the conversation ran on. There had been a development. 'He [Federici] has come back,' Claretta told the dictator.

No sooner was that information given, with its intimation that her fiancé had been flirting or worse with other women, than the conversation diverted into the fact that, as an officer, Riccardo Federici could not marry until he turned thirty, an event still more than a year off. Moreover, he did not really earn enough to provide for a wife of Claretta's social ambition and lifestyle. Could something be done? What about making him Mussolini's personal air adjutant, Claretta submitted, (in what sounded like a naive proposal for a *ménage à trois*)? 'No,' replied Mussolini, 'because they would say that he's been made adjutant because I am a friend of his wife.' 'But,' Claretta countered, 'Napoleon always looked after his girlfriends and gave them favours.' 'Yes,' was the pompous reply she drew, 'and that was one of his weaknesses.' Once launched, however, Claretta did not give up, not being sidetracked by a sententious Mussolini effort to underline how poor he had been as a young man. She could not cope with poverty. Rather she wanted decent pay, further promotion for her fiancé: 'Yes, captain, then major. It would be great and then?' she let the conversation meaningfully hang.

In response, she earned a grudging statement from Mussolini that he would see what could be done: she burst into tears of gratitude. Their conversation now became still more intimate. 'What do you see in me?' Mussolini asked. 'You're mad, you're stupid.' 'I love you and . . .' Claretta declared impetuously. 'You love me, me,' Mussolini responded incredulously. 'Oh, that's great. But I am old. You'd do better to love your fiancé Riccardo and live a quiet life.' Up and down they went, with Claretta again seeking advantage for Federici and Mussolini reiterating that his office made him a 'slave' of petitioners. 'But treat the matter as though I am your daughter,' Claretta urged. 'OK. But I can't. I always strike down my relatives when I can and never give them special help. That's just the way I am,' Mussolini retorted, propriety personified (while, in reality, lying shamelessly).[39] 'Help me,' Claretta again requested. Audibly tiring of the talk, Mussolini assured her one more time that he would do anything he could to assist her marriage to Lieutenant Federici, before suddenly asking whether she had eaten, intimating that it was time for her to depart.

Before she left, however, their conversation went down another track. 'Do you know what I shall do?' she asked. 'I'll be an artist.' 'Great,' the ageing dictator replied. 'What sort?' 'Cinema,' Claretta replied. 'I'll elevate the character of Italian cinema.' Mussolini reacted positively to this gambit. 'That's a good idea. You're by no means stupid and you have all that's needed to do it. You're beautiful. You've got a slim, elegant figure. You speak clearly and well. Yes, it's a great idea.' But Claretta had not finished with her love life and its complexities. If she worked in such a profession, with its disreputable image in the most orthodox circles, maybe Riccardo could not continue as an officer? And what about the other man who had talked to her of his passion? Mussolini, who may have been getting decidedly hungry, was left to protest that she was always raising issues that were 'tangled and difficult to resolve'. His real advice, repeated twice, was that she marry Federici and opt for a peaceful future; 'It is better,' he counselled sagely, 'not to leave the old road for the new . . . then you can see. *Addio,*' he finally managed to say.[40]

* * *

The marriage with Federici went ahead, being solemnised on 27 June 1934, a fortnight after the first confabulation between Benito Mussolini and Adolf Hitler at Venice, by no means yet a meeting of Fascist minds.[41] Within days, the Nazis, to Italian dismay, perpetrated the 'Night of the Long Knives' in Germany, murdering the most obvious of their opponents, whether in the Nazi party or not. On 25 July it was the turn of the Austrian chancellor Dollfuss to be killed; his wife and children were staying with the Mussolinis at the Riccione beach house.[42]

For upwardly mobile, snobbish Roman bourgeoisie like the Petacci family, however, such inauspicious horrors were merely noises off. Claretta and her Riccardo's wedding was held at San Marco, an elegant little church forming part of the Palazzo Venezia complex and said to date back to 336 CE (although it has been much restored since then). Claretta wore the ermine-fringed wedding gown that had once been her mother's. The officiating priest was the elderly Cardinal Pietro Gasparri (born 1852, he would die in November 1934); Francesco Saverio Petacci was his personal physician.[43] Gasparri had filled the high office of papal secretary of state, in charge of Vatican diplomatic dealing, from a wartime appointment under Benedict XV to 1930. He had thus performed a major role in the negotiation of the Lateran Pacts of 11 February 1929, the arrangement that formalised cohabitation between church and state in Fascist Italy. A more prestigious figure was hard to imagine, and the Petaccis were giving major public proof that Francesco Saverio was a person who counted within the Vatican. On 25 June, Pope Pius XI himself received the couple and gave them his blessing.[44]

Nor was the honeymoon a downmarket event. It began at the Hotel Danieli in Venice and proceeded into a fortnight's cruise around the eastern Mediterranean, with stops at Istanbul (where Francesco Saverio had been born), Jerusalem (where the couple's Christian devotion could prosper), Athens and Alexandria (where ancient civilisations could be admired).[45] By the second half of July the Federicis made landfall at Naples and, following a stop in Rome, moved to Orbetello and the air base where Riccardo was stationed. According to Myriam's memoirs, however, the marriage, despite its Catholic profile and socially ambitious trappings, had already slipped into crisis. The wedding night had gone badly. Federici had been bored to death on the cruise. And, no sooner were the couple back in Rome, than he was talking about a separation.[46] Can Riccardo Federici have immediately detected that a third person was involved in the couple's relationship?

It may be that hindsight made Myriam exaggerate the swiftness of the marital collapse. But, by spring 1935, Claretta's correspondence with Mussolini had revived, mixing an ever-heightening ecstatic worship and a practical devotion to family affairs. Now she philosophised about how, still a child at the time of the Gibson attack, she had dreamed of 'saving your life, with my only reward from you [*voi*] a kiss on my dying lips. To die for you and with you, a sublime concept of life, where light and dark merge, where one looks into the mystery with a smile of happiness achieved (and I accompany you on the sad journey with sweet caresses). You are like a powerful and beautiful god, whose light of love dazzles but does not burn, whose rays shine out over yourself but not just for yourself.'

Then came a sudden switch in her rhapsodic prose. She had a brother to defend. Marcello's boyhood heroism, she feared, had not been documented, yet was true, whether in Rome or Belgium, where by a miracle he had survived his savage anti-Fascist enemies. He had published and spoken publicly across a wide field, prepared his university thesis, and he and his father had just put together an important paper demonstrating that aluminium, so useful in the kitchen, did not cause cancer. Could the *Duce* see that he received proper and swift recognition?

But then another twist, and Claretta returning to her themes of infinite and undying love and her profound sadness at being locked far away in the Maremma – so boring compared with vivacious Rome – and there separated from Mussolini, and mostly frustrated when she did show up in Rome but failed for one reason or another to see him. Could he now organise the despatch of Federici to the Italian colonies in Africa Orientale Italiana (where the attack on Ethiopia that occurred on 3 October was being prepared)? That posting might allow him to rehabilitate himself, whether among his fellow officers or in the reputation for violence within his marriage, as yet hinted at rather than fully described by Claretta, and 'finally give me a bit of peace'. 'I feel so little, such a nullity compared with your grandeur, and it is only your patient goodness that gives me the courage to speak to you and to tell you that I love you,' she signed off beseechingly.[47]

The third anniversary of their first meeting, 24 April 1935, was a natural prompt to write again. But, on this occasion, family concern predominated. Her father's law case, being pursued against the Suore di Carità Figlie di Nostra Signora al Monte Calvario, was going badly. The nuns were the owners of the clinic, the Villa del Sole at Via Saffi 66, where F.S. Petacci was a consultant from 1914 to 1933.[48] They had parted in conflict and now it seemed that the case was to be hurried to a conclusion that would cost the Petaccis both financially and morally. Could Mussolini find a way to intervene? She sent him a folder with the details although, she concluded with studied innocence, 'I'm not really capable of talking to you about business matters.'[49]

In November came the good news that Federici had indeed been posted to the African war. But before he went – at least by Claretta's account, which also stressed that she was ill in bed with what she averred was 'meningitis' – he had slapped her, 'so violently . . . that I fell to the ground. I can't tell you my parents' reaction,' she ran on. 'This morning Papà wanted to go to the prosecutor's office, but I could not allow him to attract such humiliation and scandal. You [*Voi*] understand that a radical solution is needed. Tell me, I beg you, that you understand me. Make him leave within 24 hours for Africa and a destination where he will suffer,' she asked no longer such a demure innocent, 'where he will pay for the evil he has done me and the suffering inflicted on my parents. I beg you, if you care for me at all, don't abandon me. You are the only possible salvation.'[50] According to Myriam, Federici's savagery within his marriage had driven Claretta to stay in bed in convalescence for three months after initial treatment at Santo Spirito hospital in Rome.[51]

Claretta may have been unhappy in her marriage but the New Year brought unexampled triumph to the *Duce*, when, on 5 May 1936, Italian troops marched into Addis Ababa and proclaimed victory. From his balcony facing the Piazza Venezia, in successive speeches on 5 and 9 May, Mussolini exulted over 'our lightning victory', a triumph to be recorded as 'an uncancellable date for the revolution of the Blackshirts and for the Italian people who have resisted [their opponents] and not bowed to the League of Nations' and its attempted institution of punitive sanctions. Now and forever, Italy possessed an empire, the *Duce* boasted, 'a Fascist empire, an empire of peace, an empire of civilisation and humanity', an empire 'returned to the fateful [seven] hills of Rome'.[52] Now the diminutive Victor Emmanuel III could rejoice in the title of 'King and Emperor' and was also saluted by public demonstrations outside his Quirinal Palace. Now Mussolini had attained the apogee of his fame and power. Maybe he really was the modern equivalent of the Sun God, his propagandists urged.

Although the exact dating of the affair is uncertain, it was at this time of victory or its approach that Mussolini added another woman to his string of partners. In early April 1936, he granted an interview to a blonde French journalist who gave her name as Magda Fontanges and who had worked for *Liberté* in Paris and, during the Ethiopian war, been stationed in Rome by *Le Matin*. She appeared nattily dressed, wearing antelope-skin shoes and a silver fox fur, but her teeth were much discoloured by chain-smoking. She had pursued a career as an actor and would become a spy. Allegedly she had taken earlier lovers from the French and Italian elite; she certainly had been divorced some years earlier.[53] Her real name was Madeleine Coraboeuf (born 1905): she was destined to be promoted by Mussolini's memory to 'Countess De Fontanges'.[54]

He had other details to tell Claretta on a later occasion. 'She was one of those awful corrupt women who put an alternative before you,' he recalled on 13 March 1938, the day following the *Anschluss* in the wider world, the German annexation of Austria, which lost Italy all its strategic gains won in the First World War against Germandom. 'You could either take her or not take her,' he explained. If the latter, there was the danger that she would write you up as 'an invert or as impotent . . . So I took her twice.'[55] He continued:

> And the shameful woman went off to tell all to a paper. Exactly how it had all happened. She said that it had been so rapid that in my haste at pulling down her panties, they ripped with a strange sound. [Can Paris fashions not have been so sturdily sewn as their Italian equivalents?] And then it was so quick that she had not noticed when I had finished. She told everything, exactly everything. Not even a whore [Claretta still demurely wrote down 'p . . .' for *puttana*] would have had the courage and the lack of shame.

Mussolini only stopped his flow of details because Claretta went pale at his narration.[56] The by no means reliable Indro Montanelli claimed to have heard Fontanges's side of the story, where her main recollections were of the torn undies and the speed of delivery. Not a great lover, she reckoned: 'He is just like a Romagnol cock';[57] rapid and unfeeling.

Mussolini asserted ingenuously on another occasion that the whole business had put him off foreign women for ever.[58] For there was a sequel.

After the escapade, Fontanges was encouraged to leave Italy and not return. Her employers sacked her, perhaps troubled by her impropriety. She blamed the French ambassador, Charles de Chambrun, and on 17 March 1937 at the Gare du Nord in Paris shot him in the stomach, shouting a derisive *Merci*.[59] The bullet did not kill him, however, and at the subsequent trial her lawyer obtained for her a mere year in prison and a small fine. She emerged unrepentant and spent some years trying to get back to Italy while also proclaiming her faith in Fascism. Eventually she went over to the Germans, agreeing to spy for the Abwehr, activities which earned her a sentence of fifteen years' hard labour from the postwar French republic. She was released in 1952, again incarcerated in 1954–5, and, after further travails with drugs and mental instability, committed suicide in October 1960.[60]

* * *

The wild and embarrassing sexual bout with Fontanges over, might Mussolini now see Claretta as a woman and not a child? The *Duce*'s sister, Edvige, certainly remembered that she first heard of Signorina Petacci at much the same time as gossip was circulating about Fontanges.[61] During the months of colonial war, Claretta had continued her artless siege of her *Duce*. On 6 January 1936 she had sent him one of her pretty paintings, on the 28th she wrote about how she longed to leap into his arms like a happy child, on 16 February she hoped that nothing was troubling him. 'To you [*Voi*] perhaps it does not matter, but I suffer every little thing with you and I glory with you in every little greatness.'[62] To be sure there were still times when her adoration seemed unrequited. Mussolini might remember ancient empire and victory in Africa but he forgot her birthday on 28 February and Petacci did not fail to remind him of his failure. This time she sent a sketch of the seaside, 'your sea' as she defined it, and waxed lyrical about the recent Italian victory at Amba Alagi. How could she complain about the birthday, she wrote coyly? 'I am such a silly little girl. How can you remember such tiny insignificant things in your vast, marvellous work, where every precious instant is directed at creating power and glory'?[63]

Perhaps it was victory that made the change. Some time in the spring or early summer of 1936, Ben and Clara did finally become lovers in the physical sense. On 2 June (the anniversary of Garibaldi's death in 1882, also destined to be the date in 1946 that Italians voted out the monarchy, the foundation day of the republic), she used *tu* for the first time in their correspondence. In Claretta's mind, sex with a great man was indeed great. 'My great big love, how I adore you! You were so beautiful this evening. From your masculine face sparks of force seemed to light us up. You were as aggressive as a lion, violent and masterful ... I am overwhelmed with emotion. I see you as a giant of beauty and power. You are the man who triumphs over other men and over life. When I was thirteen, ignorant of everything, I had already offered you my whole life. Now I breathe your breath, I live sublime moments of dreaming near you and my whole life is yours. I love you,' she concluded in transport but then added in more homely sentiment, 'I hope that your little ones get better soon and you smile always.'[64] Five days later, she returned to her elation, reusing the intimate form *Tu* but giving it a capital letter to signify his dominance: 'I don't want to bore you, and you, every so often, like the sun shining between the leaves, can shine on me a ray of light and joy ... I'd like to kiss your strong hands, I want to be between your feet like a little unhappy cat and earn a caress now and again.'[65]

In June 1936 Mussolini might have been having sex with an adoring woman, much younger and prettier than his usual bed companions. But, in another sector of his private life, the euphoria of Addis Ababa had proved hubristic. Claretta's reference to his 'troubled little ones' had been vague. The actual problem was Mussolini's youngest child, Anna Maria, then aged six, who had been stricken with the incurable disease of poliomyelitis. By 10 June she was on the edge of death. Rachele looked unavailingly to quack medicines for solution. But Mussolini, in the crisis an anxious and paternal father, watched over Anna Maria through the nights and turned up at his office in the mornings, unshaven, red-eyed and exhausted. It was only in the next month that it became clear that Anna Maria would pull through. But she bore the burden of polio until her death.[66] Despite or because of this crisis within his legitimate family, on 11 June Mussolini found time to appoint his son-in-law Galeazzo Ciano, who was just thirty-three, as the youngest foreign minister in Europe: Edda's husband was soon fecklessly piloting Italy into what proved its costly and damaging intervention on Franco's insurgent side in the Spanish Civil War.

Claretta also had matters to confront, notably what was to happen to Federici now the third person in their marriage had become sexually active. In a letter of 31 May to the *Duce* she had bewailed her husband's reappearance from campaigning in Africa (where he had joined Mussolini's sons, Vittorio and Bruno, and son-in-law Ciano on care-free, murderous bombing raids against the all but defenceless Ethiopians). 'My God, what anguish,' she confessed. 'I am desperate. I feel a weight on my heart like an enormous stone. You [*Voi*] know the torture of my life with him and he hasn't changed. He's still got that terrible woman [there must have been a fourth in the marriage]. He's still the same.' Could he do something? she asked plaintively. Certainly, 'I shall do whatever you wish. Mamma is sick over the bad things he does to me.'[67] 'I don't know whether I detest or despise him the more,' she added a few days later, before insisting melodramatically again 'if they took me away from you, I'd have no reason to go on living'.[68]

A solution was arriving. On 28 July Claretta and Riccardo formally separated. To be sure, Federici did not altogether disappear from his wife's life, occasioning a long and hysterical letter on 16 October which either implied that he had returned to rape her in marriage (she wrote ambiguously that his 'beastly carnal instinct' had demanded 'his complete legal freedom') or was spreading tales of her promiscuity, charges that had annoyed the godlike *Duce* and upset her 'poor, dear mother'. 'Don't abandon me, don't let malice crush me again, don't refuse me a helping hand. I beg you on my knees for mercy from my love,' she adjured Mussolini.[69]

Mercifully, if quite a bit later, in autumn 1939 Federici was despatched to Tokyo as Italian air attaché. Since February 1938 Mussolini had promised Claretta that Japan was to be her husband's remote destination.[70] The mills of military and Fascist bureaucracy in this regard, however, ground slowly. Federici himself had in fact petitioned Mussolini for a transfer overseas in 1937, claiming that his wife's tie with the dictator interfered with his duty as an officer (and gentleman).[71] The solution of promotion, better pay and a distant appointment was one that Mussolini had already adopted for the husband of Romilda Ruspi. Myriam Petacci, not reckoning much with the

Tripartite Pact that by then bound Fascist Italy, Nazi Germany and Imperial Japan together, deemed the Tokyo posting the equivalent of relegation to 'the antipodes'.[72] Federici would stay in Japan until 8 September 1943, when he opted to support Badoglio and King Victor Emmanuel III rather than the RSI. He survived his subsequent harsh Japanese internment, returning to Italy only after 1945. Some years later, he married again and had a distinguished career as the commandant of Ciampino airport in Rome and eventually, having reached the rank of air general, worked as a representative of the national air force with NATO. He died in October 1972.[73]

* * *

With Federici fading into the background, Claretta thought that the magic of love had become real. But did Mussolini? Or did he view Petacci as just another female who had gone out of her way to be bedded? Did he even at a minimum share her artless effusions about their relationship? His record suggests that most likely he took the sex that was offered to him and scarcely shared his new partner's romantic outpourings. Yet, even at the beginning of their affair, oddities can be found. As a lover, Claretta came into the *Duce*'s life along with her mother and the rest of her family. On 29 October 1936, for example, a letter from Giuseppina Persichetti to the *Duce* survives in which Claretta's mother expressed her thanks to the dictator, 'with the devoted and grateful heart of a mother', for taking up her son Marcello's latest cause.[74] But this effusion was neither the sole nor the strangest connection existing between Mussolini and Signora Petacci.

Sources diverge whether the event took place at the Sala del Mappamondo of the Palazzo Venezia with the dictator erect in full dress uniform. But, according to Myriam's memoirs, it was on 16 October 1936 that the *Duce*, formally asked Claretta's mother: 'Signora, may I love your daughter?'[75] Giuseppina nodded her agreement, adding: 'The idea that she will be near a man like you [*voi*] is very comforting to me.'[76] Perhaps, long ago, Mussolini had made the same request to Bianca Ceccato's mother, who had also known of her daughter's affair. But Persichetti was an ostentatiously Catholic woman, a lay *terziaria* of the nuns of the Poor Clares.[77] While at home she was said to spend much of her time reciting the rosary or praying in her room to Santa Rita (the patroness of impossible causes)[78] or the Madonna of Pompeii (devotions which, as will be seen, she passed on to her elder daughter). Even if Claretta had separated from Federici (who, at his wedding ceremony, was claimed to have groaned that 'marrying her [Claretta], I'm really marrying her mother'),[79] Mussolini was still united in wedlock with Rachele, the mother of his five legitimate children. He and Claretta were doubly adulterers, damned by any reading of Catholic law.

And why too did Mussolini ask permission of Signora Petacci and not of Claretta's father? And why did Giuseppina take it as natural for that to happen? There can be little doubt that, for all the exclusion of women from the political life of Fascist Italy, this mother ruled the family hearth. Equally, Francesco Saverio may have been troubled by his daughter's affair with a man of his own age,[80] although he scarcely refused the advantages that he and his family would gain from it. Perhaps it is proof of the cheap corruption of the Petacci family,[81] a demonstration that they shared with Moravia's fictional characters in *Gli indifferenti*. Or maybe the story is evidence of the manner in which very many bourgeois Italians managed throughout the dictatorship to be Catholics, Fascists and familists. Certainly, through to 1945 and after the war, the other Petaccis, father, mother, brother and sister, would remain ever present in the relationship between Claretta and Mussolini.

Even as their sex life began, Claretta kept the dictator informed about family matters. 'Little Mammina' had been so ill that, for a while, she could not be moved, but now she was feeling better, she related cheerily.[82] 'Papà' was having trouble with the family landlord, who was driving them out of their flat in the Corso Vittorio Emanuele, causing trouble and expense and ensuring that his complaints got as far as 'Sua Eccellenza Pacelli' (later Pope Pius XII, 1939–1958), who had replaced Gasparri as papal secretary of state.[83] Could Mussolini intervene to do something? she was presumably again suggesting.

Sometimes their conversations took a homely turn. So, following a speech that had attracted the usual 'oceanic crowd' to Piazza Venezia, Mussolini wondered out loud about the need that mothers and children had for a comfort stop. 'One time there were hundreds of kids standing there for hour after hour and someone or other continued to talk, he never ended. Then I saw the kids shuffling from one foot to another and so I interrupted and said: "Tell me what you have to say, but now get them to break ranks and let the kids have a piss".' Next time he promised, too, with what a Prussian might read as unnecessary laxity, that he would make sure they were properly equipped, each with a bag containing a bread roll and prosciutto. Then they could eat and not get tired – words that gave Claretta the excuse to gush that, in his presence, no one ever tired.[84]

The New Year of 1937 solidified the relationship. By October Claretta moved on from what had been mainly succinct entries in her diary to record in rivers of prose every word that the two exchanged, whether by phone or when they were having sex in the beautifully frescoed and gilded Sala dello Zodiaco of the Palazzo Venezia. She gained access to the building from the Via degli Astalli, the service entrance. It stood around the back of the palace opposite the small balcony jutting out into the Piazza Venezia where Mussolini was accustomed to harangue applauding crowds. She was driven there by the family chauffeur, sometimes with her mother or father for company. Once inside, she would wait, often for some hours, for Mussolini to emerge from his office in the still more grandiose Sala del Mappamondo. The Sala dello Zodiaco was equipped with a divan bed and two armchairs, a gramophone on which (generally classical) music could be played, as well as a bar (although neither was a drinker). It possessed an annexe with a wobbly toilet, bidet and washbasin. There was no shower but Mussolini was old-fashioned enough to prefer to freshen up with eau de cologne[85] and did not always shave every day. While alone, Claretta would sometimes smoke, an activity that the older Mussolini disapproved of, although he had only given up cigarettes in the early 1920s (he similarly and fruitlessly had once tried to persuade Edda to avoid the noxious weed).[86] After sex, because of work demands or a speech needing to be delivered, Mussolini would sometimes depart abruptly, leaving Claretta in the darkened room.[87]

From February 1937 the Petacci car began its journey not from the nearby Corso Vittorio Emanuele but from the space outside the top-floor flat of Via Lazzaro Spallanzani 22. This street ran off the Via Nomentana; its haut bourgeois villas looked out directly onto the park of the Villa Torlonia. With the sort of historical resonance readily found in Rome,

AND SO... PAUSE... TO BED

Lazzaro Spallanzani (1729–99) had been a priest and pioneer in the medical study of reproduction.[88] With or without reflection on such history, Claretta joined Sarfatti, Ruspi and Pallottelli in living close to her lover; indeed she was the nearest of all. On 27 February, Claretta's diary recorded that they had made love, 'for the first time at my place. I shall never forget your emotion. You told me you were thrilled like a boy' (and it cannot have been difficult for Mussolini afterwards to stroll back across the road to his legitimate family's residence).[89]

Zita Ritossa, the partner, not the wife, of Marcello, wrote a bleak account in the 1950s of the Petacci family dwelling place. She and Marcello had met in Milan and, sometime in 1938, he had escorted her south to introduce her to his parents. 'My mother is the one who rules the family; she is our home *Duce*,' he informed her. My father is 'meek and mild and does not take any decision without first referring it to his wife'. When Ritossa entered the Via Spallanzani apartment, she met a woman whom she described as 'tall, large and dressed in black, with skin of an indefinable colour somewhere between grey and purple. She had a hooked nose and hooded eyes.'[90] This formidable de facto mother-in-law rigorously cross-examined Zita about her family background, politics and religion, with her responses being greeted for a time with evident disapproval. The flat, Ritossa recalled, had been full of heavy black furniture and seemed to her like 'a sumptuous family tomb, stuffed with enormous pots and vases and with gilded stucco everywhere'; in its taste, it clearly looked back to a Roman bourgeois past instead of expressing Fascist modernism. Eventually, however, Zita won Marcello's mother over to tolerance of some kind, although she continued to know that 'Mamma Giuseppina' was 'the great registrar of the life of her children' and would erupt like a volcano should there be any hint of trouble for them. Claretta by contrast, she remembered, 'practically lived in her bed' and often did not even come down for family meals.[91]

Maybe the elder Petacci daughter was tired out from her lovemaking, or by the other sporting activity that sometimes accompanied it. Mussolini, an executive with a generous measure of free time, spent quite a few of his winter days in 1936–7 at Terminillo, a ski resort a hundred kilometres east of Rome which, establishing itself as a major tourist venue, delighted in the *Duce*'s patronage. Claretta developed the habit of following him to the mountains, with thirteen-year-old Myriam in tow as a chaperone,[92] presumably on Giuseppina's command (Myriam was destined to grow up quickly). Although there could be problems – he might have his own youngest son, Romano, then nine, with him, or Claretta might prove an inept skier, fall and retire to bed, a place she always preferred to the ski slopes[93] – they did find a few hours together for sex in late afternoons in his hotel room. On other occasions they were restricted to exchanging glances, which she always nervously hoped were meaningful.[94]

Yet an idyll it was not to be. Claretta and her Ben made passionate love, but they also began to fight over Mussolini's other women and over nothing in particular. So, on 5 April, Claretta briefly recorded coitus but added that, afterwards: 'I cried so much. You wanted to leave. You were strange and nervous. You said awful things to me, then peace. But I was terrified. I thought . . . [here she could not continue] and I suffered so much'.[95] And Claretta was gradually realising that Romilda Ruspi retained her place in Mussolini's schedule, which was also frequently broken by his trips, whether official or familial. At the opera, he might still smile more upon his old lover than his new. Claretta tried an ultimatum: 'When you rang me, I told you to leave her. You [snapped back,] "No".'[96] Yet there were magic moments. On 8 July he took her to Castelporziano 'for the first time, after I had dreamed about it for so long. A magnificent day, unforgettable flashes of light.'[97]

But there was a problem of a different kind. On 13 July Claretta's diary read 'Terrible. The world is falling on me. I am dying.'[98] Mussolini, in a rage, had accused her of sexual disloyalty. He ignored her protestations of the next day that she had only sometimes met 'an old friend of Marcello's who, at my brother's bidding, saved me many times from my husband's violence' and who she had recently asked to act as a go-between with Federici with a view to having their marriage annulled. 'I really love you,' she ran on, 'I only live for you and from you. Since I was a child I have adored you and today and always you are my reason for living . . . I beg you on my knees with all the goodness that you have always lavished on me: don't abandon me, don't believe those who want to cut you off from me.' But on 15 July, Claretta received a curt message that she could pick up her paintings from the Palazzo Venezia; Mussolini was giving them back to her to signal the end of their relationship.[99]

The man involved was Luciano Antonetti, born at Alexandria in 1899. He possessed a minor curriculum vitae in Fascism (his father was *podestà* – Fascist mayor – of a *paese* in the province of L'Aquila). By the 1930s Antonetti was the owner of a failing small building company (one of Giuseppina's brothers, Guglielmo, was a more successful developer in Rome whose fortune grew after 1945).[100] Antonetti was also ill with TB and, in fact, died in June 1938. Already, the year before, the secret police were watching him and reporting to the *Duce* about his meetings with Claretta. On 15 July they advised that the Petacci family thought that Mussolini would get over his current determination to break with Claretta.[101] Eventually he did. But the resolution of the conflict saw a remarkably major role played by Claretta's mother, in this instance as indeed in many others *il madro*[102] (best, if inadequately, translated as 'The Boss' or 'She Who Must Be Obeyed'), the real head of the Petacci family.

In her own jottings, Claretta traced Mussolini's abrupt mood swings over the ten days between 15 July and his departure for a brief family holiday at Riccione. She did mention that, on the 17th and the 20th, her mother had gone with her to the Palazzo Venezia and, on the 18th, Mussolini had come to the Via Spallanzani.[103] But police reports offer more detail about a Catholic mother's supervision of a de facto sexual alliance. It was Mussolini who had taken the initiative to bring Giuseppina to his office on 16 July, where, insisting on speaking to her alone, he abruptly demanded: 'Is your daughter pure?' Mother assured him that she was. But Mussolini urged: 'Keep her under surveillance, monitor her constantly. I'm trusting you with her,'[104] almost as though he was translating to his private life a pattern of secret policing, which in the public world of Fascism was in the able hands of Arturo Bocchini, the head of the regime's secret police, whom the *Duce* saw most mornings.[105] One of the listed informants of the Fascist police state was none other than Edoardo Petacci, born in Constantinople in September 1895, the much younger brother of Francesco Saverio; it is not known, however, if his spying extended to his brother's family.[106]

However, when Giuseppina got back to the Via Spallanzani, where she summoned all the saints to the family's cause, Claretta was recalcitrant, bawling that she could not break with Antonetti when he was so ill. She also turned on her mother and blamed her for introducing her to Antonetti and encouraging her to see him alone and in public. Horrified, Giuseppina, perhaps seeing herself dragged off to prison, now demanded that the police put a tail on Mussolini's apparent rival. The next morning Giuseppina and Claretta were back at the Palazzo Venezia, for a confabulation with the *Duce* that lasted for two long hours from 11 a.m. In that time, Claretta did not speak. But her mother again emphasised the practical justifications that had inspired her daughter's meetings with this other man and insisted that their tie was no more than 'a simple friendship'. At that phrase, Mussolini burst out, in the Julius Caesar-style third person, very much on his high horse: 'Whoever has the privilege of being close to Mussolini cannot have either boy friends or girl friends' and shouted that he never wanted to see Claretta again.

That statement sent both Claretta and Giuseppina into floods of tears, with their violent passion persuading Mussolini to relent. But, when they got back to their flat, this time Francesco Saverio Petacci decided to get in on the action, entreating Claretta never to see Antonetti again and insisting that, if she did, they would have her put into a lunatic asylum. In his anger he threatened to slap her across the face or, as he phrased it, 'I shall slaughter you like an ox.' After such a pinnacle of hysteria, it was nonetheless agreed that Claretta could say goodbye to Antonetti at her dressmaker's. But that was to be it.[107] And it was, as perhaps Giuseppina told Mussolini in their next meeting on the 20th (for which no police report exists).

The crisis, then, had been surmounted. Soon Claretta was back to writing rhapsodic accounts of their sex life (and more jarring ones of their frequent squabbles). On 3 August, she noted they had had sex three times; what a man 'my great big love' is, she reflected contentedly. She was equally delighted to be taken to the seaside and sometimes they again made love back at her family house.[108] Although still very much an odd couple, they had confirmed their relationship. Somehow surviving Mussolini's deep egoism and his other sexual ties, the 'Ben and Clara' partnership would last till death.

4

SEX, LOVE AND JEALOUSY
Politics and the family

Petacci's first full diary entry featured her actions on 15 October 1937, an autumn day when it was still warm and sunny in Rome. The *Duce* was recently back from his trumpeted visit to Germany of 27–30 September, when, according to regime propaganda, the 'Axis' that tied the two countries in alliance had been mightily reinforced. To Claretta, Mussolini reflected, 'although the Germans are difficult to keep as friends, they are a fearful enemy' (there were in all 'one hundred million' of them) and so it was just as well that he had conquered them utterly, having stayed 'smiling and affable' throughout his trip.[1] True, Dino Grandi, the sometime Fascist *ras* (local boss in Bologna) and minister of foreign affairs who had been despatched in 1932 as ambassador in London, was sensing more negative ramifications, since British public opinion now viewed Italy as 'potential enemy number 1'.[2] But the new foreign minister, Ciano, was confident that he could win advantageous appeasement from Neville Chamberlain's government and steer his nation to increased international power.[3]

In Spain the civil war ground on, but the humiliating Italian defeat at Guadalajara in March had not led to further losses and, on 21 October, Francoist forces wiped out the last Republican resistance on the Asturias front, a region once a working-class redoubt. Within Italy, there were few hints of lingering anti-Fascist sentiment, with PNF secretary Achille

Starace assiduously driving newly totalitarian (or populist) policies along a line touted as 'going to the people'. In June, local fascists in France, sponsored by Rome, had murdered Carlo and Nello Rosselli, the most active leaders of émigré opposition to the Fascist regime. When a careful businessman warned the dictator against stretching national resources too far in his adventures at home and abroad, Mussolini grandly swept his doubts aside: 'You're wrong. Italy is rich and money there is. You just have to know from where to extract it. Anyway an economic issue has never arrested the march of history.'[4] In October 1937 there was every reason to believe that the Italian dictatorship, entrenched into the souls of the Italian people, was, as its propaganda stentoriously proclaimed, in irresistible rise.

That afternoon of Friday 15 October, a message reached Claretta to join her lover at the beach. Mussolini was the first to get to Castelporziano. 'Happy to see the sun', he entered the little room there and stripped off his working clothes (usually a battered blue suit rather than party uniform). 'Now,' he announced contentedly to his partner when she arrived, 'two or three hours of sunshine and freedom.'[5] She undressed too; a photographic record of her swimming costume survives, even if it now seems scarcely 'very brief', as contemporary critics judged it.[6] Two-piece costumes had been pioneered in Italy by the slimmer Edda Ciano.[7] Despite her three children, the *Duce*'s elder daughter, at the beach or in an evening gown at the gambling tables, scandalously resembled the image of the *donna crisi* ('neurotic woman') derided by Fascist propaganda. By contrast, Petacci's two-piece was a little bulky, and suggested that Claretta had a well-developed bosom and hips, with the rest of her body appearing sturdy as well. At a glance, she, unlike Edda, whom she growingly viewed as a rival,[8] looked like the natural *donna madre* (ideal mother), meant to be the norm for all Italians.[9]

Sunbathing stimulated meandering conversation between the two lovers, with the main initial topic being their family lives. Through his recent naval, academic and political activities, Marcello Petacci, Mussolini stated, would win applause, although he did warn Claretta that her brother should not be quite so outspoken in opinion and judgement. His private secretary Osvaldo Sebastiani, he confided, had told him that Marcello was 'a little exuberant but really very nice'. Sebastiani had therefore been, and by implication remained, happy to assist him in appointment and promotion as Claretta wanted.

Marcello's manifold dealings were destined regularly to preoccupy the couple (indeed, only ten days later, Claretta was earnestly defending her brother against a charge that he had flown illegally low in his plane and had to circumvent pious protestations from her lover that it would be improper for him to interfere in the case).[10] But, on this day, Mussolini wandered into a disquisition about Vittorio, his eldest son, who was currently touring the USA.[11] There, he was aiming to improve communication between the raffish world of Italian cinema – where Vittorio was, despite his youth, a leading figure – and Hollywood. As far as grand politics were concerned, Vittorio, his father observed complacently, had reported that Americans were afraid of the *Duce* but retained sympathy for his human character, whereas they simply detested Hitler. His clever son, he remarked, had not allowed himself to fall for the lures of the stars and starlets of US films. 'He says they are almost all ugly and any physical attraction that they have is due to the make-up artists ... They can completely re-fashion a face, add a bit to a nose, push out a cheek or a forehead. They create a face to fit the scene that the artist has to play,' the wide-eyed dictator continued, trying to seem knowing but actually displaying provincial innocence about the cunning skills of cinema and the rich wonders of American capitalism. Vittorio had also been to New York and slept on the 14th and the 17th floors of a skyscraper. But, his father insisted with family pride, he had not been over-impressed, since he was a tough, sensible, Italian boy, a Mussolini, 'not afraid of anything'. When he returned to Italy, his father published a piece of his in *Il Popolo d'Italia*. Entitled '*Cinema Americano-Cinema Ebreo*' (American cinema, Jewish cinema), the article gave Vittorio the chance to deride the communist penetration of Hollywood, denouncing the place for being 'as full of Jews as Tel Aviv'.[12]

Once launched into his family review, Mussolini was hard to stop. Anna Maria was still afflicted by polio, he mused. When she tried to walk by herself she often sagged to the ground. Then she would struggle up and say nothing but be visibly crestfallen, 'poor little thing'. As she recovered into a difficult life, Anna Maria mostly struck her father with her ruthless avoidance of sentimentality, unmoved by the sight of a lamb being butchered or a pet fish dying. It was the way of a modern child, he philosophised.[13] Anna Maria, he confided on a later occasion, reacted like a stone when, in March 1939, he took a tumble from his horse in front of her. 'She did not bat an eyelash, she showed no emotion.' 'Perhaps she has already suffered too much,' he added with paternal generosity and excuse.[14] In fact, there were few signs that his younger daughter had earned the place in his heart possessed by his eldest child, although Edda's wayward or independent behaviour also frequently made him grumble.

Most recently, Ciano's wife had been a worry, he told Claretta, since she had hired a German governess for her children who sought, 'in the Prussian manner', to discipline her elder son Fabrizio, ensuring that he ran wild whenever she was absent. In any case, Mussolini added, again sounding like the vehicle of popular prejudice, 'I disapprove completely since these foreigners brought into the home are all spies. My wife hates them,' he observed; Rachele may also be presumed to have damned Edda's bathing costume, in her view almost as deplorable as her son-in-law's effete fondness for golf. In her dress and in many other aspects of her high-society lifestyle, Edda was annoyingly intractable, which meant, her father lamented to his lover, that the regime could not give her worthy employment. Mussolini confessed that he sometimes wondered if Ciano doubted whether he should have married the *Duce*'s daughter. This comment elicited from the jealous Claretta a tart reply that Ciano owed everything to his father-in-law and, when Mussolini tried to point out that he was a bright boy, she told him ingratiatingly that 'he lives from your light, like all the rest'.

Then Mussolini, still a little ruffled, promised to calm such waves. 'I'll talk very clearly to my daughter. She's a really difficult woman, strange. But I dominate her.' Anyway there were other matters at hand, a late lunch and lovemaking, with a diversion into a discussion of the Petacci family plans to acquire land for what would become the Villa Camilluccia. The dictator was anxious that the building not be situated too far away from his office or the Villa Torlonia. 'I don't want to make love only once a week like a peasant, all the more since I am accustomed to you and to frequent sex and I hope you don't want to change the rhythm of things,' he retorted half jokingly. That thought stimulated them into intercourse instead of the kisses and caresses that they had been exchanging while they chatted. It proved to be, Claretta judged in what would become a habit of assessment, 'a mad embrace' and was followed by a walk before the dictator left at 4.20 p.m., after she had first helped him to dress. Once back in Rome, he rang her again at 6, 8, 9.30 and 10 p.m., on the last occasion to say that he was going to bed, signing off fondly 'Today has been delightful, divine. I love you.'[15]

When it came to sex, Petacci kept a record by writing the word *si* ('yes', thus underlined) into her diary, sometimes but not always followed by her assessment of the quality of their congress. Her *si* must have recorded orgasm on her lover's part, and presumably her own, although her Catholic education had left her ill equipped to provide much detail about the physical side of their lovemaking. Nonetheless, over the months, a history of their intercourse was registered. It mixed violence and satisfaction, gross patriarchy and stubborn love.

On 4 November, a national holiday celebrating Italian victory in the First World War, the partners, back at the beach (Mussolini sometimes got there to his boyish pleasure riding his own motorcycle),[16] squabbled over whether their intercourse was still 'up to standard' (*vibrante*). That debate was, however, enough for the *Duce* to curl up in her arms 'like a great big cat and shut his eyes'. Then he informed her that he really loved her and her flesh, initiating intercourse 'like a madman, like a wounded beast; it is divine'. Maybe the penile power that he had exerted prompted Mussolini, after they drew apart, to dream in Freudian manner of a 'colossal' monument to himself carrying a 2-metre-long drawn sword, of sufficient loftiness for children to gasp: 'This was Mussolini.'[17] On another occasion, the *Duce* persuaded her to sunbathe nude with him, presumably out of sight of police agents, in what he claimed was 'the Arab style',[18] and they also once made love, although not very rewardingly according to Claretta, in the sand dunes.[19]

Most of the time sex was energetic and pleasurable, even if, on one occasion, she recorded that her partner had left a deep wound in her ear by biting it hard during intercourse.[20] On another occasion, he scratched her nose painfully, with the explanation that, sometimes, 'I lose control. If it wasn't that way we'd be having sex like a married pair, tired out.'[21] During a third coupling he bellowed, 'I love you madly. I want to thrash you, harm you, be brutal with you. Why does my love express itself with such violence'? he asked. 'A need to crush and to break, it's a violent thrust. I am a wild animal. Every strong thing, every great sensation, gives me this sense of impetuous force,' he announced with brazen Fascist manliness.[22]

Whether such impulse to rape was his ordinary mode may be doubted but, when Claretta was less responsive than usual and he particularly savage, Mussolini chided her: 'you've been like a wife, paying your tax just as a wife does'. When eventually she helped him dress, his mood darkened and he murmured 'the Latin phrase: *post coitum*', an intimation of death that recurred on later occasions following their mating.[23] In April 1938 the *Duce* reacted violently to her comment that he was too tired and flaccid for intercourse, biting into her shoulder in a way that left his teeth marks on her skin.[24] On New Year's Day 1939 he verbalised his depression by upbraiding his young lover: 'You are inhuman. You really have let me down. It's true; I don't love you any more. It is all over and I have almost decided only to let you come [to the Sala dello Zodiaco] for important days, ceremonies and such things, like that for [Neville] Chamberlain [the British prime minister was due to visit during the following week in a last British attempt at appeasing the Italian dictator]. Afterwards, I'll just live alone. I like solitude. I'm getting old, really old,' he continued dismally. Why could he not find time to relax as Hitler did? he asked (with the sort of aggrieved sentiment that a neoliberal CEO feels when he finds he only earns 10 million per year while a colleague and rival nets 20 million). The Italian dictator was always working and far too hard, he muttered. But a siesta revived him and his spirits, and he and his biddable lover were soon having what Claretta deemed another 'loving' orgasm.[25]

Fiery sex, Mussolini philosophised in happier vein, was 'good for you, it refreshes ideas, expands the vision, helps the brain, makes a man perceptive, splendid'. 'I'd like to jump from here onto your bed like a big tomcat,' he added with his usual male bravado.[26] When he and his lover were apart, sex did not lose its charge. Rather Mussolini rang the Petacci household time and again, eleven times on 6 December 1937 alone, the last from the Palazzo Torlonia after midnight just to say that he could not forget her for an instant, bidding farewell with the thought that no one was more beautiful than she.[27] On 3 January 1938 his tally of telephone calls reached thirteen (at 8.45, 10.45 and 11.30 a.m., and at 2.30, 3, 3.15, 4, 6, 6.15, 7, 8, 8.15 and 9.45 p.m.).[28]

Here indeed was a national boss who did not always have government business at the top of his agenda. His sex talk could become crude. On Christmas Day 1937 he rang from his office where he was at work, perhaps grumpily so since he began by expatiating on a nameless earlier lover whom he had mistrusted and spied on to find she had betrayed him and so, he announced abruptly, 'I left her.' With that misanthropic warning off his chest, Mussolini continued in what may have been for him the Yuletide spirit: 'Darling, you are enough for me. Do you realise that I don't do anything except think of you? Morning, evening and night. For example, if at night I wake up and go down to piss [Mussolini was approaching his fifty-fifth birthday and such need may have been increasing], a lot of the time I am so drowsy that I do it on the floor. Then you come into my mind and I think: if only you were here and doing it [urinating] from the other place, wouldn't that be nice? I am really amazed that I think of you so much.'[29]

Yet, on occasion, their tie could become almost lyrical. On Sunday, 28 February 1938, after attending mass, Claretta reached the Sala dello Zodiaco at 3 p.m. to find the *Duce* reading the Romagnol poet Luigi Orsini, who intermingled localism and Fascism in his verses. Mussolini recited words about a dying boy asking his mother for his uniform until his own voice broke. With his eyes full of tears and unable to go on, he pushed the book over to Claretta: 'I bowed my head and placed my cheek on his and we read together in silence, united, filled with emotion. At the end we looked into each other's eyes and our souls came together in emotional understanding. We had tears on our eyelids just like kids. His soul is grand. He read a bit more from here and there to recover himself.'[30]

Often now, especially in the room that they utilised at the Palazzo Venezia, afternoon sex would be followed by a more practical snooze, with Claretta youthfully acknowledging that the *Duce* snored on such occasions.[31] On others he rehearsed in his sleep memories of his conquests of two decades ago,[32] in his devotion to history (of a kind) again characteristically mixing his private and public preoccupations.[33] Occasionally, when he woke, the couple had sex again. They did so for example on 13 March 1938, while Mussolini tried to digest the news from the outside world that the *Anschluss* was imminent and with it the ruin of Italy's strategic gains over Germanic Europe won in 1918. As Claretta recorded: 'we made love like mad, enough to make your heart sore, and then immediately afterwards we did it again. Then he slept, completely out of it and happy.'[34] On New Year's Day 1939, they also managed intercourse twice, once in the afternoon after he had taken a refreshing nap, and then again in the evening following a period when he had gone back into his office and reappeared, only at first to flip angrily through the French newspapers. That day had begun with five phone calls before Claretta reached the Palazzo Venezia at 2.45 p.m., but she was still inclined to grouse to her diary about his preoccupation with government business.[35] Trying to be generous, on 25 May 1938 the dictator assured his lover that, from now on, the Sala dello Zodiaco was hers to visit and use whenever she wanted,[36] although whether she might be bored and lonely while waiting for his attention was not a question that he asked.

Reading Boccaccio made him horny, as he confessed to Petacci with a degree of innocence on the phone: 'Yes, the pictures [in the book] are amazing. There's an image of a naked woman bringing plates to men sitting around a table. No, it doesn't interest me,' he added unconvincingly. 'But the style is pleasurable, interesting, always original.'[37] On another occasion, he divulged that, at the family farm at Villa Carpena, he had watched a bull mating with a cow, 'a grandiose spectacle'. 'In a few seconds' it was all over, he mused. 'It happens with bellowing, deep breathing, tremendous groans. Then the animal quickly gets down, melancholy, beaten as though he had been hit.' 'Isn't nature marvellous?' he concluded to his lover, whose genteel urban lifestyle did not normally take in such sights.[38] His personal sense of bullish power could even persuade him to reject artificial insemination of cattle as unfair to the animals involved.[39]

Sometimes, after intercourse, Mussolini simply went back to work in his office, on occasion after eating an orange or some other fruit, although there were also plenty of occasions when the couple listened to classical music together: their middlebrow bourgeois tastes took in *The Merry Widow*, Rossini, Puccini, Verdi, Vivaldi, Chopin, Wagner (*Tannhäuser* and

Lohengrin) and Beethoven.[40] On 26 December 1937 disconcerting static from the regime's growing anti-Semitism afflicted their pleasure when Mussolini muttered that Beethoven was great but it was 'a shame that he was a Jew. Great but still a Jew.' That 'knowledge' did not stop them from listening to the celebrated German romantic composer on other occasions, however.[41] Contemporary music, by contrast, they agreed was 'nauseating' (only a fool could prefer the celebrated contemporary, 'modernist' composer Alfredo Casella to Verdi, Mussolini advised his lover).[42] Indeed, the last act of *La Traviata* made the dictator sob out loud (although he tried to hide his tears and emotion from Claretta).[43] *La Bohème* similarly caused him to quiver with tearful sentiment.[44] For these lovers' emotional life, music was the natural partner of sex, and included occasions when Mussolini played his violin to her.

To be sure, sometimes Claretta jotted into her diary the news that the dictator was 'too nervous' at some political issue or other to attempt intercourse[45] or was 'slack' when they tried a second intimacy.[46] On other occasions, the pain from his ulcer made his performance of a kind that she reckoned was 'lacking in enthusiasm' and could be followed by his begging her for a bread roll to eat and so alleviate his stomach pains; in her memoirs Myriam recalled that the hampers that her mother packed for the lovers' picnics outside Rome were sometimes almost too heavy to carry.[47] Moreover, there were days when his passion was already spent, times when, as will be outlined below, Claretta was sure that he had already exhausted himself on another partner.[48] And, as he ruminated only too frequently, he was getting old. On 2 November 1939 he appeared before her unshaven and tired, to lament that his younger children were not starring at school. Bad-temperedly he pulled out of intercourse before attaining full satisfaction.[49] Then and earlier, enveloping European crises could demand Mussolini's presence elsewhere, but when, for example, he came back from the Munich conference, briefly convinced that it had been his personal triumph, the couple's passion in their renewed meeting on 1 October 1938 was great. 'It is 2 p.m. when I get there and he is waiting for me in an armchair in the dark. "Love, turn on the light. I'm here. You can't see me". He embraces me and kisses me like a madman. With our lips united we fall into the armchair. Never have we made love like this. Perhaps the first time. But now it is more perfect. With our clothes pulled down we make love twice. He says to me quietly: "I've suffered being so far from you."'[50]

Their conversation could take strange turns, as it did, for example, on Easter Day 1939, when Mussolini suddenly confided that in 1907 he had seen the Devil, 'a very tall black man dressed in evening clothes and notably elegant'. The spectre had offered the young Mussolini a choice, to be made within five minutes, of wealth, power or glory. Mussolini, with the Devil's approval, opted for glory and swore to his lover: 'I am in part a devilish creature and, for three quarters, a creature of God in whom I sincerely and profoundly believe.' Claretta did not register how her Catholic training judged such confession but soon they made love, 'with a tenderness and a passion equalled on few other occasions', only to quarrel afterwards about his infidelities, while he morosely let slip that he was ill with the flu.[51] Six months later, he repeated the story with some variations and a precise placing in a restaurant at Tolmezzo, where he had taught *scuola elementare* (early primary school) in 1906. The Devil was no longer black but was tall and dressed in evening clothes and had cloven feet. Again he gave Mussolini five minutes to decide but this time the *Duce* opted for power instead of glory, once more to the Devil's pleasure and approval but with a cry that 'your soul is mine'. Only the arrival of a friend, who recited the Lord's Prayer fervently to a stunned Mussolini, cut through the overwhelming tension that had filled the room and stopped the *Duce* himself from any appeal to God.[52]

With the outbreak of European war (they did manage 'savage' intercourse on the afternoon of 30 August, despite the dictator complaining that the Germans were out of hand in their warmongering and predicting that the Maginot Line would prove 'formidable and impossible to break'),[53] Mussolini grew sentimental, worrying that his and Claretta's love was not yet 'continued'. So, on 13 September, after what she described as 'a sweet and poetic' intercourse like few others, he told her that 'these are the embraces and divine moments' when a woman 'becomes a mother'.[54]

Six months earlier, Mussolini had warned his lover that war could severely dent their accustomed sex life.[55] Perhaps the *Duce*'s career as a sexual athlete was in any case in decline; Francesco Saverio Petacci sometime around now gave him a prescription for Hormovin, a German-made drug that was the Viagra of the time.[56] Certainly the diary now contained fewer descriptions of ecstatic sex, with Mussolini on 16 January 1940, for example, perturbed by the war, by Hitler's hopes to pull him into battle four years before he would be ready, and by his desire to help 'the brave Finns' in their winter conflict with the USSR (then the ally of Germany in the Ribbentrop–Molotov Pact). Popping in and out of the Sala dello Zodiaco the *Duce* saluted Claretta affectionately but somewhat distractedly: 'My love! What is my little one doing, waiting for her bridegroom? You are my darling little girl. We love each other with the tenderness of our first days, the poetry of our first days.' Though he was deeply moved by a rendition of '*Che gelida manina*' on the radio, Mussolini avoided sex. 'Now I really don't want it: I work and go to bed. Bye-bye, darling. This evening it will be Istituto Luce newsreels.' And so, at 8.30 p.m., he limped off to the Villa Torlonia.[57]

On 7 February 1940, after he was back in town from a trip to the Rocca delle Caminate, they did manage intercourse, but he slept deeply afterwards.[58] On 2 March they did it twice, but on the 3rd Claretta was left to scold her partner at their 'slack' congress that day; it was no better on the 4th.[59] In their bed-chat of the day before, Mussolini switched from a disquisition about the sexual habits of animals and birds – sparrows he admired as 'the most lustful of creatures' – to say: 'Oh my love, if you could succeed in having a child, you would be so happy.' He would be 'very sad', he disclosed, if she failed (keeping to his patriarchal insistence that reproduction was woman's business). The lovemaking that followed, according to Claretta, was 'of infinite sweetness'.[60]

Two months later, their lovemaking again failed to reach full conclusion on one occasion, and he refused sex on another, with further laments that managing military action would stop them seeing each other.[61] On 10 June 1940 Italy entered the Second World War on the German side, with Mussolini orating in (premature) triumph to a crowd that had been assembled by 5 p.m. below his balcony on the Palazzo Venezia. Ciano more dolefully scribbled into his diary: 'The adventure begins. May God help Italy.'[62] While such momentous events were occurring, Claretta was waiting in the Sala dello Zodiaco, where she had been summoned by three phone calls at 9.15 a.m., 9.50 a.m. and 12.15 p.m. She found the dictator 'twitching like a beast, shouting wildly, beside himself'. But she calmed him down and he was then so 'tender, loving and understanding' that she burst into tears. Mussolini gave assurance that he would still love her despite the war and left, without sex, at 9 p.m., only to ring her three more times once he was home.[63] In one of those conversations, the tap, kept by the secret police even on the dictator's phone, recorded a quarrel over whether current politics should outweigh 'love' in their relationship.[64]

With the great decision made, intercourse became more active, being 'violent' on 13 June and 'enthusiastic' on Sunday 16th, when Mussolini ejaculated twice (the two regularly had sex on the Sabbath, following Claretta's attendance at mass).[65] On the 21st they repeated their coitus, although Mussolini was troubled by sore eyes and overwork (he had long worn glasses in the office, if never when dolled up in uniform and in public). Buoyed by reports from France, on the 24th he predicted that the war would end in 'four days' time', preening himself with the news that Italian soldiers had fought well. Spurred by such happy auspices, they began sexual dalliance, but Claretta's record suggests that Mussolini then decided to pull out. She had been 'a precious little mascot', he told her patronisingly, but that evening he was 'tired', while he was again drooping and 'nervous' five days later.[66] Sex was better on 5 July but again 'slack' on the 6th, with Mussolini, despite picking up his violin to play to his partner, being 'depressed, worried and nervous'.[67] On 18 July they found time to go to the beach together and had sex twice, but Mussolini fretted about his absence from the office while Italian soldiers were dying.[68]

Battle was not after all over, the war had not ended, and Italy's pledge to run its own 'parallel campaign' was proving hollow. Meanwhile, before summer was out, a major crisis erupted in the lovers' lives; in his personal life, Mussolini's hope in 'continuation' with Claretta would be frustrated just as surely as the war was not bringing victory. Claretta was pregnant. But she was not destined to be another lover who would transmit Mussolini's blood to a new generation. Nor had she yet alerted the *Duce* to her condition. On 19 August he expected to see her, despite being crotchety after reviewing a parade of party sportspersons whose female members, he grumbled, had no experience of gymnastics and were hopelessly inadequate compared with the 'magnificent', 'tough' young men. After three phone calls she did arrive at the Palazzo Venezia, if more tardily than usual. She was feeling unwell and that made the egotistical *Duce* irritable and angry: he openly insulted her and said it was time to end their relationship. His crossness prompted her to burst into tears and she blubbered for half an hour without him offering comfort. Their tryst continued to go badly, with Mussolini distractedly mulling over accounts from the front in East Africa and eventually going home to watch a film.

Eventually realising that something must be wrong, he rang her flat at 10.50, 11, 11.30, 11.45 p.m. and midnight to find his lover in agony from what was quickly being diagnosed in her medical household as an extra-uterine pregnancy.[69] Over the next days, Claretta's condition worsened, while she was racked by 'atrocious stomach pains'. Mussolini, who knew something about physical discomfort in that part of his body, was aghast at his lover's fate, even if he could be distracted by fear that Rachele had overheard one of his phone calls. At 6 p.m. on 20 August he appeared at the Villa Camilluccia, where the Petaccis had moved the previous October amid congratulations from Mussolini to Claretta about her finding her 'nest',[70] to swear the depth of his love and to talk sentimentally about Edda and his grandchildren. On the 21st and 22nd he rang no fewer than twenty times each day. On the 21st he started at 6.15 a.m., excusing the dawn call with the information that he had been afflicted with insomnia, and offering Claretta the perhaps unhelpful counsel that she should try to sleep in till 9 a.m. Just after noon that day Giuseppina informed him that her daughter would have to have an operation, a recourse to imponderable medical experts for which he held a native fear. He dropped by the Villa Camilluccia again at 7 in the evening to swear: 'I have infinite anguish in thinking of your suffering. I'm suffering what you're suffering', failing as so often to move the conversation too far from himself.[71]

At 6.20 p.m. on the 22nd he was back again, 'smiling', announcing that she was looking better and declaring 'now I'll cuddle up close and that will cure you at once'. He then launched into a rambling conversation asking for the medical opinion of her father and describing the alleged failure of an air raid on the Caproni factory at his hometown of Predappio. 'I work like a black man, like a dog. I only have work and you: nothing and no one else,' he maintained. Despite the fact that he claimed to be worried about her moving in her bed of pain, Claretta performed some sort of sex act on him, whether masturbation or fellatio is unclear. He then went on to chat about his family and high politics, before further cross-examining Francesco Saverio about the coming operation. He left for the Villa Torlonia at 8.15 p.m., not forgetting to reward Claretta first with many kisses. He rang again at 8.45, 9.15, 9.45, 10.15 and 10.45 p.m., with a wish that she, and he, sleep well; he was off to 'beddy-byes', as he put it playfully before hanging up.[72]

* * *

Claretta's operation occurred on Tuesday, 27 August and her recovery from it was slow and probably debilitating; certainly she now stopped jotting her effusions into her diary until Christmas and beyond. It is probable that the surgeons' intervention (they were assisted by her father) meant that she could no longer have children, although, in December 1941, she was recorded by the secret police claiming again to be pregnant, a comment that led Mussolini to declare his pleasure and announce that he did not mind if the baby was male or female.[73] But it was soon clear that she was mistaken.

During her recuperation through autumn 1940, she and Mussolini exchanged letters and phone calls which allow their relationship to be charted, if without the detail of her diary. One day in October that he deemed full of 'the grave, gravest, great and important events' (Italy's humiliatingly unsuccessful invasion of Greece began on the 28th, without the Germans being forewarned), he rang her seven times in the afternoon, fitted in a game of tennis at the Villa Torlonia and reached the Villa Camilluccia just before 7 p.m. They engaged in sex of some kind (another *si* in her scribbles), before he talked over her condition with her father and then departed to ring again at 8.45, 9.15 and 10.25 p.m., promising to return the next day.[74]

By 11 December Mussolini's mood was blacker: the campaign in Greece and Albania lurched from one disaster to the next. Now he wrote to his lover beseechingly: 'Clara, listen. I love you as before and even more than before. But I beg you on my knees to leave me alone, alone with my struggle, alone with my thoughts, alone with the drama of my life . . . I must see, I must be at the helm and I cannot be disturbed . . . My nerves are aquiver: everything goes badly, everything is upside down. I'm on the phone from one minute to the next and God knows that I am at work trying to fix things up and get things done.'

Such rhetoric might craft an image of a stalwart dictator working away at his desk. But Mussolini's plea this day was at least partly inspired by the fact that on the 9th he had been forced to admit that he had spent half an hour with Alice Pallottelli. Love between Ben and Clara there might have been – and on 24 April 1941, the ninth anniversary of their meeting, he was to give her the gold locket and chain with the inscription: 'Clara, I am you and you are me. Ben.'[75] As noted above, she would carry it to her death. However, along with love, there was also jealousy, continued violent squabbling over Mussolini's failure to end his relationship either with Pallottelli or, more especially, with Romilda Ruspi. Then there was the fact that Mussolini was a married man, who, at the Villa Torlonia, lived for at least some of the year with his wife and (legitimate) children.

When it came to Rachele, the record in Claretta's diary is, for the most part, a highly predictable repetition of the vocabulary of adultery. In autumn 1937 Mussolini dilated on more than one occasion about his wife's limitations. She had 'never thought of me as a great man and never taken a part in my [real] life,' he growled egotistically. He was sure that, at the Villa Carpena, a local squadrist called Corrado Valori had been Rachele's lover for some years.[76] Sex acts between him and his wife, he reckoned, were down to 'seven or eight per year', with his sexual desire, but not perhaps hers, 'entirely spent'. Worse were her intellectual limits: she 'never reads anything; she doesn't know how to read'.[77] On 8 January 1938 he was still irritated by a furious fight that had broken out between them, lamenting that Rachele understood nothing about politics. He would not mind if she went out and enjoyed herself but instead, he groaned, she stayed at home and talked mutinously to the servants.[78] When he did pay his tax, as he put it, to his wife, he swore that, throughout the act, he thought only of his lover.[79] When he and Rachele sunbathed in spring sunshine in the park of the Villa Torlonia, all he noticed was how wrinkled she had become.[80] When he saw her in her bath, her nudity did not arouse him, he promised.[81] He had not slept in her bed since 1918 or thereabouts. Moreover, on the rare occasions when they made love, she never suggested that he stay for the night.[82] On 13 May 1940 he did report that he had been driven to have sex with Rachele for the first time for three months but, as for its quality, it was best to keep silent.[83] In any case, as he had explained cynically to Claretta three years earlier: 'Every man betrays his wife, even barber's boys do. All, without doubt, without justification. But I have justification,' he concluded self-righteously.[84]

As he assured his young lover in April 1939, he had only ever been attracted to Rachele physically; he had made the error more than once of mistaking lust for love, he added in typically careless betrayal of his wife. Now Claretta had taught him what love really was. 'I think of you, I suffer [over you], I desire you.' Their relationship was 'beautiful, different, sublime, great', in sum incomparable.[85] No doubt it was best if they hid their lovemaking from his wife – and Rachele would insist that she had no real understanding until July 1943 of the major role that Claretta had obtained in Mussolini's life.[86] With the predictable tactics of a half-guilty adulterer, he cut his young lover off when he feared Rachele was eavesdropping on a phone call,[87] and hastened to tell her to come when Rachele went away to the Villa Carpena or the Rocca delle Caminate. But, Mussolini insisted, Rachele was no competitor in his love for Claretta.

A melodramatic confrontation between wife and lover would eventually occur, but not till late in 1944. Rather than being preoccupied with the betrayed wife, Claretta's diary is replete with reference to her contest with Romilda Ruspi. It is a story full of weeping – even on a couple of occasions on Mussolini's part – and other high emotion, as well as of suspicion, surveillance and continuing disloyalty. The *Duce* found it impossible altogether to renounce his habit of sex twice a week with a woman who, in his mind at least, remained part of the fittings of the Villa Torlonia.[88] Meanwhile one hollow protestation that their affair was over succeeded another. Just before Christmas 1937, he notified Claretta that, after three recent encounters, he had broken permanently with Ruspi, who had burst into tears at the news, adding that she knew he loved Claretta as he never had her.[89] Two weeks later he repeated the pledge, urging that Ruspi was now as far off as 'Australia' from his life.[90]

Such promises were too good to be true, however. In any case, Alice Pallottelli still lived nearby. In April 1938 Claretta, who must have been watching from the Via Spallanzani, timed a Mussolini visit to her villa at twenty-four minutes, whereas he had clocked a rapid twelve and then tried to allay Claretta's jealousy with the comment 'All right, twenty-four minutes then. Listen, as a woman she's past it. After seventeen years, there's no enthusiasm. It's just like when I take my wife.'[91]

Nor had Ruspi disappeared, being duly exposed by Claretta's neurotic tracking of her presence at this parade or that ceremony or when she turned up at the Villa Torlonia to have lunch with her sister, who still worked there. A Mussolini boast that he had gone thirty days without having sex with Ruspi or anyone else failed to make Claretta feel secure. Another twenty-five minute visit to Pallottelli reduced her to insomnia and made her refuse to take her lover's apologetic phone calls.[92] But it was Ruspi who really alarmed and dismayed Claretta, it being clear that Mussolini had not in fact cut contact with her.[93] On 22 May 1938 he admitted two recent sexual encounters and told Claretta in what he must have deemed beguiling words: 'I'm a bad boy. Hit me, hurt me, punish me' but do not suffer yourself, 'since I love you'.[94] In November there was a fresh twist to the story, with Mussolini declaring that he had only gone off to Ruspi's flat after he rang Claretta and found her not at home. Once with Ruspi, he maintained, he had spent most of the time playing with her children and, with his common, rather innocent curiosity about the wider world, admiring their stamp collection and the geographical knowledge of Ruspi's daughter (not his) – 'Where is Uruguay? Where is Cuba?' he had asked.[95] When in more bitter mood, he bemoaned the fact that he had just handed over 60,000 lire to Ruspi and she was still sponging for more.[96]

In February 1939 Mussolini was himself 'peeved' to be briefed with the news that Claretta had been secretly tracking Ruspi to check where she went and whom she saw; the taxi Ruspi had hired was equipped with the number plate 223-33533, Claretta reported. Mussolini replied rudely that 'all women have a double or triple life'. Yet he rang Ruspi the next day to certify the detail, to be met with her denials, tears and protest that she had not seen him for three weeks and now her (that is, their) child was ill with a high fever.[97] On 2 July Mussolini did another of his tabulations of his virtue, assuring Claretta that he had been loyal to her for thirty-seven long days.[98]

The outbreak of the Second World War brought more urgent issues of his public life to the fore, but it was not long before the lovers were again bickering over the *Duce*'s inability to confine himself to Claretta, with Mussolini, on 14 September 1939, bursting out: 'God damn and curse her [Ruspi]', so drolly introducing the language of his public life into his private. His phrase was '*Dio la stramaledica!*'[99] Such usage had originated during sanctions in 1935–6, with the English then being the object of the curse, which would become a major part of wartime propaganda. On 12 October the *Duce*'s self-denial reached a new personal best of fifty-two days, even if he did explain to Claretta that his restraint had been caused by his preoccupation with Italian policy towards the European conflict.[100] But ten days later, he conceded he had bumped into Ruspi on her bicycle. In response Claretta wrote that her latest consent to intercourse was granted 'with the deepest disgust'.[101]

During the last weeks before Mussolini took Italy into the war, slanging matches recurred on more than one occasion, with Mussolini finding time to see both Pallottelli and Ruspi.[102] Claretta did not believe her lover's assurance that he was only visiting the latter to hand over more money to the mother of one of his children. On 24 May their spat was so serious that Claretta recorded herself refusing intercourse (*no* in her diary).[103] Faced with a sex strike, Mussolini took the time on 11 June – the morning after his declaration of war, when his desk must have overflown with political and military matters – to order Ruspi out of Rome.[104] She did not go however, and, four weeks later, Mussolini was still enduring attacks from Claretta about his surviving connection with her.[105] Matters only calmed a little with the remarkable seven-clause armistice treaty that the two lovers signed on 11 July (see chapter 2) and the turmoil of Claretta's extra-uterine pregnancy shortly thereafter. But, even then, Ruspi had not vanished from their lives. As will be seen below, to the very end in 1945 neither Ruspi nor Pallottelli had broken their bonds with the *Duce*.

If jealous outbursts about private dalliances filled the pages of Claretta's diary, she also gravely recorded her man's thoughts about the wider world and his public role as his nation's Fascist and totalitarian dictator, as well as his more covert desire to impress his young lover with his fame, brutality and foresight, offset, more occasionally, by his paradoxical queasiness at his destiny, emotions and self. After all, as the European powers moved to war and the Holocaust, Claretta was always there.

* * *

Scathing is the word that best defines Mussolini's estimation of his political opponents and, often enough, his partners. Here, indeed, was the dictator as misanthrope, vain, ill prepared, boastful, aggressive, angry, yet sometimes uneasy in his 'power'. The English, he advised, were 'a piggish and fallen people . . . a people who think with their backsides [Claretta wrote 'c . . .', not *culo*] and cannot admit anyone is better than them. They are egoistic, drunk, brainless; the most important part of their body is their bum.'[106] Their institutions, he informed her in December 1937, were riddled with Jews. Disraeli had been the great man of their empire; he was an Italian and 'the lover of Queen Victoria'; the rest were 'merely Jews and businessmen, tiny beings' and they hated Mussolini or anyone else risen from the ranks.[107] In fact they were all cretins, just like their French allies.[108] The British were murderous cynics, too. Once war began, they planned to starve the Germans with a naval blockade and would not mind if 'ten million' women and children died.[109]

The French, Mussolini was still hastier to damn. They had a Jewish prime minister (Léon Blum) and a 'black' president of the chamber of deputies (in fact this was the white Radical, Edouard Herriot, born in Troyes, and so Mussolini was again mistaken), while their women were all whores who only enjoyed sex with black men (how awful, Claretta recorded herself interjecting with unlikely sententiousness).[110] They were 'nauseous' as a people; wrecked by syphilis and absinthe (and their free press); 'thirty millions, brainless and cowardly'.[111] The only exception in his mind to French degeneracy had occurred more than a century before in the career of Napoleon Bonaparte, always his ideal historical figure, an admiration that reflected his early training in French language and culture, and his never wholly abandoned hope to be lionised in Paris. So, in March 1938, the dictator moaned that he was destined to die (relatively) young, as both

Napoleon and Caesar had done.[112] Nine months later he was more specific in his comparison and fantasies. Napoleon and he were the same, he affirmed, in eating vegetables and sleeping with the shutters firmly down, any chink of light banished.[113] The emperor only began to fail when his underlings fought among themselves.[114] That might also have unfortunate implications for the *Duce*. But, as Claretta always stressed to him when he was downhearted, he was the greatest of the great, incomparable in his dominance and grandeur.

From the mouth of such a titan she was not surprised to hear that little states like Czechoslovakia were hopeless, doomed to die.[115] Current-day Romanians, Mussolini explained to her nonchalantly, were the result of copulation between Roman legionaries and 'Slav whores' and so could never amount to much, while King Carol II made things worse by allowing his lover, Madame Lupescu, to dominate him.[116] The Poles as a people were beset by a 'suicidal mania'.[117] The king of Sweden was no more than a British 'slave'.[118]

The Germans, by contrast, were 'formidable, dangerous'. As he warned in February 1938: 'if that mass goes forward, it is terrible, compact, [fighting like] one man'.[119] When the Nazis imposed the *Anschluss* on Austria, Mussolini recalled the terrible death of Dollfuss in 1934 and wept with emotion when he and Claretta listened to *Lohengrin* together. But, in the *Duce*'s self-excusing opinion, the French and the Austrian chancellor, Kurt Schuschnigg, bore the blame for the destruction of Austria, despite the fact that Nazi 'fanaticism' during and after German occupation of the country was troubling.[120] One day there would be 800 million Germans, Mussolini predicted with his usual inaccurate 'mathematical certainty', and only the Italians could resist them.[121]

Some of Hitler's speeches Mussolini found disturbingly 'raucous'.[122] But, Mussolini maintained, the German *Führer* always deeply admired the *Duce*. 'Hitler's just a boy when he is with me', Mussolini related after the exchanges of May 1938. The German dictator had been tearful when he was parted from Rome and the Italian dictator. To Mussolini, Goebbels had an Italian soul, which he revealed when the two joked and laughed together.[123] At Munich, Hitler was similarly putty in Mussolini's hands, a 'teddy bear' (*sentimentalone*). The *Führer* had cried when he met the *Duce* there. During that negotiation, he – like the respectful and sympathetic Chamberlain and equally deferential Édouard Daladier, prime minister of France – simply followed where Mussolini led.[124]

By contrast the German seizure in March 1939 of the rump of the Czech state prompted Mussolini to philosophise about the impossibility of peace in Europe where there were 20 million too many Germans and where French and British women failed to keep up their nations' required birth rates. Already the Nazis had '30,000 chemists' at work on research. It was as well, he remarked, that, over the centuries, the Germans had so often been beaten by the Italians, which ensured that they would never attack them now. But 'it was necessary not to cling to illusions. It is very difficult to get the Germans to be viewed sympathetically by Italians. Indeed, for the most part, they detest them . . . I, myself', he explained with deep misanthropy, 'have no special sympathy for any people. Indeed, in the mass, I detest them all, none excluded'.[125]

European war did not stop Mussolini's vacillations towards his ally. Hitler, he lamented in October 1939, 'suffers from hallucinations, is hotheaded, a visionary'. All would be much better if only he had followed Mussolini's counsel. The German people were turning against their chief, the *Duce* predicted with his usual inaccuracy.[126] Two months later, he inveighed against the atrocity of German occupation policies whether in Austria, Czechoslovakia or Poland; they were of 'unparalleled cruelty, I am nauseated'. The SS were to blame; they are 'beasts, beasts', he expostulated to Claretta who, in her political ignorance, was unable to recognise the name of their chief, Heinrich Himmler.[127] The Ribbentrop–Molotov Pact could lead to no good and must only advantage the Russians; Italians would love a war against the latter.[128] Only in May 1940 did Mussolini fully swing round to express support for the German cause. Even if he was a little disturbed by the thought that Hitler had 'won the war by himself', the Nazis, he now decreed, had a right to defend themselves 'with all necessary violence'.[129]

If the Germans were a quandary, his Japanese partners in the Tripartite Pact could scarcely be loved or admired. Their population grew by a million a year and their economy expanded at a rapid rate, but only because they were 'like monkeys, they imitate everything'.[130] Moreover, their decision-making process was sluggish, their emperor weighed down by tradition and, although they were good soldiers, 'we do not need them in order to march'. After all, they were 'a different type, they live within a different mentality'; they sprang from 'other races'. Of course they loved Mussolini but that did not mean they were loyal. 'They pursue their interest as every people does,' he summed up for Claretta with his usual fondness for Machiavelli and *Realpolitik*.[131]

The Spanish, by contrast, even those with whom he was allied in their civil war, were 'like Arabs' (racist phrasing that belied his waving of the 'Sword of Islam' on a visit to Libya in March 1937); their armies could never match Italian élan.[132] Their *Caudillo* Franco was 'an idiot'. The rival sides in Spain during the civil war shot their enemies out of hand, he declared in some amazement, and Dolores Ibárruri, the communist who proclaimed that the Francoists would not pass, had bitten a man to death and sucked his blood. Her behaviour was, to the *Duce*'s mind, 'typically Spanish'.[133]

In most circumstances, despite the Fascist fanfare about empire, Mussolini's map of Africa lay, like Bismarck's, in Europe, while Claretta showed no interest in Libya or *Africa Orientale Italiana*. The *Duce* was never actually to visit Ethiopia and, in his bed-chat, was left merely to congratulate himself that the Italian empire had been won at a trifling loss of 1,200 lives and, on occasion, to show his lover pictures of Italian road construction or to applaud other colonial building work there.[134]

The act of fighting, he, the old soldier from the First World War, remembered – by no means in heroic mode – as a time 'when a man really becomes a savage, enjoys killing and ignores that another life is involved'.[135] The (Fascist) bombing of Barcelona in Spain was 'terrible' and killed women and children without mercy or halt. War was never fought for ideals (or ideology). 'No people,' Mussolini pronounced, 'makes war to please another, but only for its own interests, because it is thinking of the booty available.' He himself would always endeavour to be the last to enter battle, unless he was somehow 'forced to act'.[136] Yet men were born to destroy. It was a shame. But such desire to kill was a fundamental truth. War was as natural to men as motherhood was to women, he stated in echo of a regime slogan.[137]

SEX, LOVE AND JEALOUSY

In regard to Fascist propriety, he did ask when Francesco Saverio Petacci had taken out his party card: 'certain formalities are necessary'.[138] But his comrades among the PNF bosses were scarcely men to admire. Rather, he imparted cynically to Claretta in March 1939, they were courtiers like any others, people who gave 'a friendly smile' all the better 'to stab a colleague in the back'. He might be an untrustworthy lover, he conceded, but as a man he was 'straight as a die' and so completely unlike his underlings and the rest of humankind.[139] At least in the Petacci diary record, this dictator was scarcely the vehicle of totalitarian ideology. He was instead a bleak Machiavellian. As he had reported to Claretta back in December 1937 with classic misanthropy: 'All the world is against me and I am against all the world.'[140]

*   *   *

Cynicism apart, the ideas which surfaced most regularly in his conversations with Claretta between 1937 and 1938, if seldom thereafter, were anti-Semitic in nature, along with the linked conviction that he must preside over a racial revolution and allow ideology to drive him. His diatribes about Sarfatti have already been noted. The Jews, he bellowed at his lover in April 1938 while reading a 'Jewish review', were 'pigs, a people destined to be wiped out completely'. They deliberately refused to have a country of their own and instead were always traitors within the gates of those places where they lived. 'I detest them.'[141] He himself, he assured Claretta six months later, had been a convinced anti-Semite since 1923. His aim now was 'to purify the race and get Aryans into all the posts that have been exploited [by Jews]'.[142] 'I shall massacre them like the Turks did,' he promised Claretta in between caresses at the beach on 11 October. 'I have imprisoned 70,000 Arabs in concentration camps. I can do the same with 50,000 Jews. I'll put them on a small island and shut them all up there . . . I shall kill them, every one,' he swore.[143]

On occasion he remarked on the conflict that smouldered between Nazism and the Vatican, in December 1937, for example, favouring the Germans while he explained that he himself was 'an apostolic Roman Catholic but not a Christian', although he did add that he always tried to

133

attenuate his German partner's racial fanaticism.[144] German hostility to attendance at Mass was, he pronounced in different tone in July 1938, 'antipathetic, highly antipathetic'.[145] Yet, three months later, it was Pope Pius XI whom he deemed 'a calamity' for trying to defend Jews and blacks. He had 'lost Germany completely' and 'had mistaken utterly the spirit of the times'. 'As a Catholic,' he told Claretta, whose father still acted as a papal doctor, 'worse than this pope' he could not imagine.[146] Yet a few months later when Pius died, a phone tap recorded the *Duce* mentioning to Claretta blithely that he had been the 'pope of the concordat'. His death was to be regretted. With Pius XI, Mussolini now declared, he had almost always felt secure, although he also admired his 'highly cultivated and diplomatic' successor, Pius XII.[147] Similarly when the dictator was in expansive mood, King Victor Emmanuel III he judged a monarch whom he appreciated, even if he hated the formality, falsity (and softness) of the court.[148]

Yet, for all such seeming moderation, Mussolini was ever ready angrily to lament the failings in his eyes of the Italian people. That same day that he let Claretta know his intention to round up the nation's Jews, he launched into a bitter attack on 'merciful and cowardly Italians', whom he claimed to have been studying for 'thirty years', a period that was even longer than his vaunted anti-Semitism. There were at least 'four million' such fellow citizens, he reckoned. Every one was a descendant of slaves from classical times. Their blood had stayed vile for 'fifty generations'. Already a few months earlier he had ascribed cohabitation between Italians and Ethiopians as caused by the 'heirs of Roman freedmen', who had 'no racial consciousness, no dignity'.[149] Now, if they showed any sign of rising, he shouted, 'I shall destroy them all, I shall exterminate them'. They were the Jew-lovers. 'Everyone has his or her own Jew to defend', not excluding Cornelia Tanzi, poet and his sometime lover, he observed. Such racially degenerate Italians talked feebly about being afraid of Franklin D. Roosevelt. In regard to race, he now declared, it was Hitler who had the right ideas. When it came to implementing tough policies, he bragged, 'I am like a train, once I am started, I cannot be stopped.' An alliance of 120 million Germans and Italians would quickly destroy all their enemies. They would not be blocked by a Jew like Anthony Eden (again Mussolini was mistaken in this racial attribution). Throughout the next war, every Italian man, he proclaimed, would have to fight, and women too would work. He had already primed Bocchini, the head of the secret police, to compile a list of any who might refuse, and he would 'shoot them one by one'.[150]

Such ferocity may well have lain engrained in the *Duce*'s soul. But, even if legal restrictions on the nation's Jews continued to be toughened, and, after 1943, the Germans did use the details that had been recorded by the Fascist bureaucracy to implement the Final Solution in Italy,[151] Mussolini did not continue to fill his lover's pages with his passion against the Jews or, indeed, against the church and the nation's bourgeoisie, among whom the Petacci family and Edda and Galeazzo Ciano might naturally be numbered. Rather than preparing his own final solutions, the dictator could still on one occasion sound almost soft when, in October 1939, he read out to Claretta petitions from Jews against rulings of the now established Racial Tribunal, stating a little sadly that 'it is a tragedy for some'.[152] With different emphasis, earlier he had bewailed the actual limitations of his power. 'I am not a dictator, but a slave,' he groaned, one who was unable even to command within his own family; there appeasement was his common line.[153]

* * *

If the *Duce*'s stance on the international and national issues and ideologies of the day had its vagaries and his children remained ready to speak up for 'their Jews', Claretta never forgot that she belonged to the Petacci family. Nor did they forget her. The other Petaccis cast a constant shadow over the relationship between the dictator and his lover. One of the more obvious quiddities of the sex acts that Claretta so fulsomely wrote into history is that, quite frequently, her young sister, Myriam (always then called 'Mimi' by her elders), who turned fifteen in May 1938, accompanied the lovers on their trysts, at least to the beach or the mountains. Frequently, while standing somewhere not too far away from the lovers and their sexual encounters, she would be carrying in homely fashion a toothsome snack that her mother had prepared at home. Through to 1945 she would wryly call herself the *paciera-vivandiera* ('peacemaker and butler') or, with rougher humour, the *piccola idiota* ('little idiot'), from those times.[154] In her mother's imagining, Myriam may have been performing the role of chaperone and so sustaining Claretta's honour, despite the immorality of her affair with the *Duce*.

In turn, Myriam's presence provoked rumours that Mussolini enjoyed her favours as well as those of her sister (indeed, along with her sister), a scandalous charge made immediately after the collapse of the regime in July 1943[155] and reiterated first by Margherita Sarfatti and again by some recent popular historians.[156] But, even though in May 1938 Claretta recorded Mussolini looking at Mimi with a frighteningly 'male eye' for the first time,[157] there is no direct proof that the younger sister ever had intercourse with her sister's lover, and circumstantial evidence is strongly hostile to such suggestion. Myriam herself certainly took pains to pass on to her sister pledges by the dictator about the depth of his love for Claretta, while mostly confining her conversation in their presence to a deferential 'yes' and 'no'.[158] When still only fourteen, she was asked by the *Duce* to articulate his assurances to her sister that he did not really love Ruspi.[159] Whatever Myriam's self-interestedness and cynicism in personal relations (and, as will be seen below, they were considerable), it is all but impossible to believe that the jealous Claretta would have tolerated a sister in her bed and, as has been noted, Mussolini was not a man much given to collecting teenage lovers.

As the 1930s drew to their close, the member of the family more likely to preoccupy the lovers was Claretta's father, Dr Francesco Saverio Petacci, with the dictator generously ready to give counsel about his fortune and career. On 31 October 1937, for example, Mussolini offered Claretta priggish advice to give her father: Dr Petacci needed to 'make more of a splash and creep out of the shadows', Mussolini suggested, especially since the *Duce* wanted to elevate him to the Senate (a promotion destined never to happen). Everyone pushed themselves forward, Mussolini remarked, and Dr Petacci should hold more public conferences, thereby getting himself better known. To quite a degree, he could fix matters, Mussolini added encouragingly.[160] Meanwhile, the *Duce* did quickly exploit the advantages of having a doctor in house, explaining late in November to Claretta, who was feeling ill, that her father knew that his ulcer had been caused by the 'psychic damage' of the Matteotti affair: she must not allow herself to be swayed by her own phobia about disease.[161]

Soon the topic of favours for her father recurred in the lovers' bed-chat, with Mussolini promising that a senatorial toga would arrive in '1939'. But, in the interim, the dictator had arranged for Dr Petacci to be hired by the Rome daily paper, *Il Messaggero*,[162] as a regular expert medical commentator, with a healthy remuneration of between 2,000 and 2,500 lire per month. He would also get Claretta's brother, Marcello, promoted, he pledged in giving mode, and bring him to Rome along with his patron in Milan, Professor Mario Donati. It might be a disadvantage that Donati was Jewish but he had a Christian wife and children, Mussolini had noted, and so the dictator, setting aside his anti-Semitism where the family opposed it, could back him with money and influence. 'I shall always do what I can,' he assured Claretta in disarmingly loving (and less than racist) mode.[163]

As for the contract with *Il Messaggero*, that was a simple matter of a nod and a wink from the *Duce*. On 9 January 1938 the Sunday edition of the paper duly carried a less than punchy piece by '*Dott.* Francesco S. Petacci' on 'Somatic disharmony' and the functioning of the heart, with lessons on how a balanced lifestyle could keep it in prime condition.[164] The story goes that Mario Missiroli, one of Italy's most celebrated journalists and a regular but generally unacknowledged author of the paper's editorials, rang the owners, Mario and Pio Perrone, to protest against the 'incomprehensible medical articles' which were now being published. When he was told that the author was 'Claretta's father', he turned so green that Dr Petacci had to be urgently summoned to his aid.[165] Mussolini, by contrast, assured Claretta warmly that her father's piece was 'really excellent, bursting with sentiment and science'.[166]

In March Dr Petacci moved on to 'the use and abuse of wine' in an article headed 'Defence of the race'. The regime, he was glad to say, closely monitored the health of the nation and was especially aware that the young were vulnerable to excess. Yet, he enthused, 'the Italian of today has a firm pulse and a will of iron and has largely surpassed other races in his chastity and sobriety'. Such progress was displayed in the fighting spirit of Italian soldiers, the devotion to labour of Italian workers, in women's fidelity to maternity and all Italians' 'deep and united devotion to the family'.[167]

A number of commentators have remarked that Francesco Saverio was nonplussed by what was happening and would continue to happen within his own family.[168] Certainly the worthy sentiments that he expressed in his writings, with their laboured mixture of Catholicism, Fascism and science, made few concessions to his elder daughter's life choices (nor to those that Myriam would soon make). In the spirit of the times, Dr Petacci was painfully ready to salute his country's dictator, writing in the aftermath of the Munich conference, for example, that 'no one more than a doctor can appreciate the extension and grandeur of this victory of civilisation [under the regime's governance] through the Italic genius made flesh in the *Duce*'.[169] As in this case, most of his moralising was decidedly unoriginal; without knowing about the crisis that would afflict his daughter in August 1940 (or evincing any sense of the continuing poverty of many Italians), he advised sapiently in April 1939 about taking convalescence from an operation seriously and being sure in those times to keep clean, eat well and avoid high emotion.[170]

Dr Petacci was deeply impressed by new research on vitamins, declaring that a balance in their intake was crucial for bodily health (and, as will be seen, he was ever ready to inject the *Duce* or members of his family with what he deemed appropriate supplements to their diet in that regard).[171] In May 1939 he was sufficiently self-aware as a citizen of the new Roman Empire as to find time to reflect on 'colonial health consciousness', arguing in phrases that few European imperialists would have eschewed that doctors must pursue a mission to the Ethiopians. 'To educate and cure the indigenous means to protect the European [settler], too; human reclamation [*bonifica*] and the reclamation of the soil can transform vast regions into the Promised Land,' he wrote with hackneyed metaphor. 'After freeing the natives from slavery,' he added, 'it is necessary to raise their spirit and consciousness from centuries of brutalisation.' There were plenty of other health dangers in the tropics, he admitted, but the Italian, with his 'natural frugality' and preference for vegetables over meat, was better equipped than the British to rule such places.[172]

Dr Petacci was a Fascist, at least in the sense that, in October 1940, he wrote personally to the *Duce* to cheer on the attack against Greece and urge revenge of the early losses.[173] However, his articles in *Il Messaggero* did not overtly mention the Jewish question despite being composed at the height of the anti-Semitic campaign. Nor did the outbreak of war do anything to arrest Petacci's earnest scientific expositions to what may be assumed were his less than numerous readers. It was typical that his first article after Italian entry focused on an accurate definition of the various blood types; his next piece reviewed issues raised in the diagnosis and treatment of high blood pressure.[174] Apart from his colonialist thoughts, the nearest he went to overt racism was an article in January 1941, where he explored what he viewed as the British mistrust (and exploitation) of Australian soldiers, with their convict blood and fiercer fighting qualities.[175] He was still writing naively in March 1943 to praise the way that war promoted science, while urging that, in 'this world pervaded by destructive madness, civilised man' drew his fighting spirit from a union of love of the *patria* and faith in God, best illuminated by 'one light only, that of Rome'.[176]

In 1940 Dr Petacci was encouraged further to raise his professional profile through a book entitled *Life and its enemies*.[177] Sales were helpfully guaranteed by a government order to purchase by all hospitals, public libraries, school libraries and *dopolavoro* (Fascist after-work) clubs. Similarly, the director of the Banca Nazionale del Lavoro was persuaded to distribute the work as part of his institution's advertising campaigns.[178] The book's content must have surprised few who had absorbed the articles in *Il Messaggero*. Mussolini was inevitably hailed, in particular because of his achievement of the draining of the Pontine Marshes outside Rome: 'in only fifteen years of the Regime, the formidable will, the profound sense of humanity, the understanding of one Man, has brought to fruition what was long the platonic aspiration of doctors and health-workers' (plainly, in Dr Petacci's mind, the best of prophets). The achievement in the Rome hinterland amounted to a marriage of the spirit of St Peter and that of Mussolini, Petacci concluded in not altogether obvious concatenation.[179]

When it came to the detail of his text, Dr Petacci's sentiments were still more detached from the reality of his own family's behaviour than were his press articles. Some present-day women, he wrote, deplorably deviated from their 'holy mission' of maternity, surrendering to a 'neurotic instinct for pleasure and an anxiety to live'. Such indulgence was dreadfully bad for 'the moral, political and social power of the nation'. Church and state must combine to prevent it and to educate young women better. Cities, he ran on with less blatant hypocrisy, except that related to his lifetime in an expanding Rome, could grow too big and thereby prevent citizens from seeing the sun and bathing in the sea in what was the naturally healthy fashion. Lazzaro Spallanzani had already preached about the way the sun killed bacteria in 1769, he added in what reads as a yearning for his flat in the street named after that medical pioneer, instead of the grandiose new family dwelling on Monte Mario.[180]

After some sardonic comments on the male tendency to a Faustian search for perpetual youth (but with no reference to prescriptions of Hormovin), Dr Petacci did include a chapter on race, with warnings against the degeneracy to be found in every 'coupling between a white man and a Negro'. Similarly, he added briefly, 'if a marriage occurs between a Jew and an Aryan, it will not be fecund'; the 'Jewish race', he assured his readers, had been enfeebled by over-frequent intermarriage. Yet Dr Petacci drew the line at Nazi ideas (though he did not specify them as such). He was emphatic that 'state-fostered breeding' was abhorrent and unnecessary. Given the natural purity of Italian women, the natural virility of Italian men and the general national commitment to the family, he was sure that 'the Italian *patria* will continue to multiply its hearths'.[181]

Not through his own daughters, hindsight might remark. Already by the end of 1940 Marcello and Myriam were behaving in a way that brought them negative attention in the highest circles of the regime, however much they were favoured and protected by the dictator. As 'Ben and Clara' continued to negotiate their relationship in wartime (Mussolini also had Alice Pallottelli and Romilda Ruspi to consider, and would soon expand his multiple family 'duties' via renewed contact with Angela Cucciati and Elena Curti), the Petacci family were tracing their own way through a complex world where a devotion to Fascist ideology did not fill all of their lives; a world where, for the moment, their social rise proceeded as planned and where more than one tragedy was in the making.

5

WARRING IN PUBLIC AND PRIVATE LIFE

Sadly for Mussolini's treasured hopes to be greater than Napoleon – and his confident predictions to Claretta in June 1940 that the war would be over in 'four days'! – by 1941, despite the waves of regime propaganda, it was clear for all to see that Fascist Italy was incapable of waging a 'parallel war' as an equal partner with Nazi Germany. Defeats were occurring on every front. The new empire in *Africa Orientale Italiana* had quickly proved a mirage, despite the dictatorship's killing fields there. On 18 May the viceroy, Amedeo, duke of Aosta,[1] who had initially commanded more than 370,000 men, surrendered the main Italian force to what was little more than a rag-tag British imperial army, aided by Ethiopian irregulars; an Italian residue fought on until defeated at Gondar in November. In Libya, British troops swept the Italian enemy out of Cyrenaica by the end of January 1941, leaving Fascist power to be resuscitated by Erwin Rommel and the Afrika Korps, who reached Tripoli in the following month. In Greece, the Italian attack had quickly been blunted, with Chief of Staff Pietro Badoglio sacked in retribution by the *Duce* in November 1940. Only when the Germans moved into the Balkans in March 1941, taking Athens on 27 April, could Fascist forces, the 'ignoble second' of the Axis,[2] claim the most hollow of victories.

With every month the war was becoming more deeply ideological and global and therefore less adjusted to the compromises, ambiguities, parochialism and falsity of Fascism. The Germans attacked the USSR in Operation Barbarossa on 21 June and the Japanese bombed Pearl Harbor on 7 December, Italy in each case following obediently where its greater partners led, with Fascist troops brutally doing the Nazis' work for them in the Russias.[3] For a time, in 1941–2, victory seemed possible, while the Germans swept ever further east and the Japanese advanced across the Pacific. However, the vicious battle for Stalingrad, which raged from August 1942 to January 1943, led to Nazi defeat and the falling back of Axis forces towards the west. Similarly, the Japanese thrust began to be repelled after the US success at Midway Island in June 1942 and, although continuing to fight with bitter determination, Imperial Japan thereafter went into retreat. By the beginning of 1943 it was very likely that, unless the liberal–communist alliance broke, the USA and the USSR, and such lesser allies as Britain, were going to win the war.

Well before then, perceiving no way to stop Anglo-American armies advancing across Libya until, finally, on 9–10 July 1943, they landed their forces in Sicily to paltry Italian resistance, Mussolini sought to persuade Hitler to arrange some sort of compromise peace with Stalin. The grim news entering many Italian households from their emigrant relatives in the USA – that, after Pearl Harbor, Italy had gone to war with 'paradise' and forced Italo-Americans to abandon their past enthusiasm for Mussolini – made the situation worse. Italian soldiers, often enough peasants more committed to their families than to the nation or the dictatorship and its ideology, longed to go home.[4] By 1943 Italy's claims to be the least of the Great Powers were plainly feebler than they had been during the First World War, with Fascism less able than liberalism had been to steel a national fighting spirit, marshal a modern war economy and identify war aims. Militarily speaking, Mussolini had indeed proven a Sawdust Caesar and had enough self-knowledge, somewhere beneath his denials and ascription of Fascism's failures to anyone but himself, to realise the fact. To July 1943 Italian casualties amounted to a little over 200,000, high enough for family mourning but scarcely on the scale of the horrendous tolls that were afflicting, and would continue to afflict, other combatants in the Second World War.[5]

If the Italian military were less than brilliant abroad, Fascism similarly staggered on the domestic front. One secretary of the Fascist Party succeeded another: Ettore Muti, who had ousted Starace in October 1939, was a year later replaced by Adelchi Serena. Despite Serena's reputation for administrative efficiency, he was dismissed after a short fourteen months, replaced by Aldo Vidussoni, a twenty-seven-year-old of slight experience and worldly knowledge but with a fondness for boxing. Vidussoni lasted until April 1943, when Carlo Scorza, a Tuscan 'Fascist of the first hour', took over, soon to report that the party was in a state of dissolution. 'Laxity and confusion', Scorza advised, were the disastrous actual watchwords of the national war effort.[6]

Typical was the fact that the regime had proved unable or unwilling to impose a fair system of rationing on its people – bitter proof of which was given when, at the time of Scorza's appointment, the prefect of Turin, the nation's most industrialised city, banned the killing of cats for food since they were needed to keep the rat population under control.[7] As the leading British economic historian of the war summed up, 'Stagnating production and raging inflation soon made Italy's situation hopeless'; its production of the crucial weapon of the war – aircraft – was, he underlined, 'risible'.[8] No wonder Walther Funk, the Nazi economic chief, told Goebbels just as the titanic battle in the east was launched: 'The Italians are a thorn in [my] flesh. Always demanding more than they are entitled to, and indulging in state-sponsored black market currency dealings. What a nation!'[9] By the time the Fascist Grand Council turned against their *Duce* on the night of 24 July 1943, Mussolini was a dictator who had lost his regime's and his nation's plot.

* * *

As will be seen further below, among those accused of business misdemeanours was Marcello Petacci. Meanwhile it was not the Petaccis but the Mussolinis who endured a death in their ranks. On 7 August 1941 the *Duce*'s second son, Bruno, was killed as a bomber test pilot in the skies above Pisa.[10] Mussolini had only infrequently shown much personal interest in his two elder sons, although the files of his secretariat did preserve secret police reports on them.[11] On the rainy day that Bruno married Gina Ruberti on 29 October 1938,[12] the dictator had slipped away from the ceremony to his office, to find Claretta ready for him by 7 p.m. in the Sala dello Zodiaco. Earlier, she had been in the crowds who cheered the celebrities as they processed into the church of San Giuseppe on the Via Nomentana and had nervously registered that Mussolini had smiled at the comely wife of Colonel Pessutti, who was also there.

But that wedding evening, her main rebuke fixed itself on Pallottelli and Ruspi, with an irritable *Duce* stating coarsely that he would have sex with the latter whenever the spirit moved him and do so in the same spirit that drove him when he went to the toilet. Eventually, however, the dictator grew maudlin about the events earlier in the day, vowing that he felt greater tenderness for Bruno than Vittorio. 'He's still a child,' Mussolini fretted:

> He's married too early, he could have waited . . . But now there is no more Bruno. From the head of the table I shall look at his usual place and it will be empty. A great melancholy. Yes, it is true. He'll be back. But it's not the same thing. The family is breaking up. Soon we [he and Rachele!] will be left alone.

As the evening passed the *Duce* did not manage to shrug off his gloom at the decay of his career as paterfamilias. There was no comforting *si* for Claretta to register. Instead, at 9 p.m., her lover slipped away to watch *Snow White and the Seven Dwarfs* at a city cinema, a bruised and melancholic patriarch in need of light entertainment.[13]

Bruno was enough of a dictator's son to enjoy driving fast cars and motorcycles, and had been involved in a fatal accident in April 1938 when he ran over a poor, elderly woman. Police investigation (Bruno was another whose phone was tapped) concluded, however, that the accident had been the victim's fault. At much the same time, Bruno escaped a charge from a serving maid that he had made her pregnant, allegedly excusing himself with the remark that his father had often behaved similarly; nothing should therefore be made of it and he did not intend to help the woman involved. In January 1940, despite what a romantic biographer has called his 'timidity', Bruno did accept the office of president of the National Fascist Boxing Federation, and earlier had given every sign of enjoying his bombing raids over Ethiopia and Spain. He was also alert to the possibility of making money from his flying skills. However, in February 1941, in something of a dampener, his father sent Bruno a lengthy file of commentary from the English press on his 'stupidity'.[14]

Whatever the distance between father and son in actual life, Bruno's death struck the *Duce* hard. According to Roberto Festorazzi, the *Duce* 'was never the same man again'.[15] Certainly, in the aftermath of his son's demise, Mussolini swiftly produced a seventy-page statement of grieving entitled *Parlo con Bruno* ('I talk with Bruno'). Sales were pressed on the public (the secret police detected at least one Italian complaining resentfully how the papers carried on and on about Bruno, but 'when one of us dies, they don't even bother to publish the name'),[16] and translations into a number of foreign languages were urgently arranged.[17] Other family pieties manifested themselves. The secret police reported that Bruno's widow had collected the sheets and pillows on which he had slept during a last night at the Albergo Nettuno in Pisa and presented them as a holy relic to his sorrowing mother.[18] *Parlo con Bruno* was an odd mixture of personal eulogy and Fascism, couched in a rhetoric that owed much to Catholic versions of sainthood. Bruno, readers were told by their *Duce*, was 'a Fascist born and bred . . . intransigent in his faith', he had lived a perfect life cycle from one war to another. The sacrifice of his blood was immense, 'worth more than all my own, present, past and future'. 'Only blood raises a man to the purple of glory,' the dictator insisted.[19]

But Mussolini's lamentation over his dead son was not confined to his legitimate family circle. News of the air crash arrived just as the *Duce* was readying himself for another of his seaside trysts with Claretta. Deserted for the moment, she prayed that 'God help my love in such torment. God give him the strength to endure.' Over the following weeks, she continued to offer herself as a support, in reward being employed as subeditor, examining the text of *Parlo con Bruno* before publication.[20] It was not a task that anyone thought of asking Rachele, or indeed Ruspi, to do.

Claretta did her best to combine respectful sorrow and sexual solace. On Christmas Eve 1941 she gave her partner a miniature of his son in a silver frame, a present that moved him deeply and elicited a promise that it would stand on his desk in perpetual memory.[21] The next day, however, Mussolini was growling churlishly that he hoped by Christmas 1942 to be 'dead and buried' and thus 'no more filled with disgust at this contemptible humankind'.[22] On 28 December it was Bruno's loss that depressed him most, with him telling Claretta that, at home, he could not shrug off his dismay at his son's absence; evidently he was a Fascist dictator worse afflicted by family loss than by the death toll being endured by his people.[23] The Germans, he predicted, making a characteristically misanthropic link between private and public disaster, would deservedly lose the war in the USSR, where many of their soldiers were being frozen alive.[24]

Throughout 1941 and 1942 Petacci's diary entries were mostly short and as fixated as ever over Mussolini's 'betrayals' of her with Ruspi (his dalliances with this partner Claretta usually reckoned to be confined to fifteen minutes), Pallottelli and other women. Claretta was never assuaged by the *Duce* agreeing, for example, that Alice Pallottelli was a 'viper' and swearing that he would have long ago given her up but for the fact that he had fathered her daughter and youngest child.[25] For all Claretta's editorial work on *Parlo con Bruno*, and for all the information that she received about the regime's military losses, the private not the public dominated her world. When, in early March 1941, Mussolini toured the Albanian front and phoned her regularly with excitedly positive detail of the fighting qualities that he found in the soldiery there and affirmation that direct experience of battle was making him a boy again, most important for her was his pledge that, for almost a week, he remained 'chaste, totally chaste'. Naturally, such virtue did not last, with him confessing, 'after five days I could not resist any more . . . and the first woman to offer herself I took'.[26]

Claretta was anguished as usual at the news. After she put the phone down she wrote that 'her heart had swelled with bitterness and pain'. Sometimes she now spelled out her own feelings in the diary with greater detail than in the past, reflecting, for example, a few days before Mussolini's escapade in Albania, that she needed a longer convalescence from her operation: 'So many things have wrecked my illusions and peace of mind and I am tired: tired, tired of thinking, seeing, feeling, suffering, in short, [tired] of everything.'[27] Yet, despite the depression seeping into each of their minds, the couple did not break their relationship. Rather there were a few signs that the dictator was beginning to rely on his partner for something more than sex (where, in any case, her *si* had become relatively infrequent). To be sure, on 12 June 1941 they enjoyed sex twice, 'in the afternoon, a full one'. On 6 August they managed to get away to the seaside and had coitus there, but Claretta diagnosed in his distracted technique a recent new betrayal.[28] On 26 October he kept her waiting for hours at the Sala dello Zodiaco and, when he appeared, he was tired and cranky over a quarrel with Rachele. They did have sex, but, Claretta noted, 'without any desire on my part; I didn't have the courage to refuse him'. Then he settled down to sign photos of himself (sent out in their hundreds every day during his regime). 'You can be my secretary,' he remarked with what may have been a patronising acknowledgement of her skills as a scribe.[29]

Even Petacci's Catholicism might be useful. Albania may have been bracing but the Italian march to Athens did not go as Mussolini had hoped and, when he returned from the front, he asked Claretta, almost plaintively, to 'go to church and pray. All the auspices [at the front] are good and everything promises well, but it is good to pray. Will you do it? Great.' In reward he added that he had returned from his military mission 'purified'. He could therefore swear (as he had so often done before): 'I shall love you as you want, with tenderness, absolute dedication and a great purity, a new love, a boy's love. I shall love you in a way that you cannot imagine.'[30] Three weeks later, however, Claretta was bitterly registering the meetings that he had with Ruspi, Pallottelli and Elena and Angela Curti (whom he rudely called 'the cow from Milan'). The couple's wrangling resumed.[31]

Nonetheless, on 22 January 1942, the *Duce* grew mournful at the Villa Camilluccia while he and Claretta listened again to Beethoven's 7th Symphony together. Added to a recurrent depression were frequent wartime bouts of flu and other minor illnesses, for which Dr Petacci was ever ready with useful diagnoses. Music could soothe Mussolini's troubled mind and Bruno, his father was sentimentally sure, would have been equally moved by the Beethoven.[32] But Claretta was a substitute. His relationship with her could allow some private sweetness to offset the bitterness of what he had half admitted was his failure as a Fascist dictator: 'You are a comfort to me. I've always been a loner, I don't have friends, I don't have brothers . . . I did have one, my friend [Arnaldo] and I lost him and my son [Bruno]; he, too, left me. I am always alone, really alone. I only have you,' he repeated obsessively. He then took up his own violin to play a little of the Beethoven, hymning Claretta sentimentally: 'My darling, my little darling, who shares my tormented life with me.'[33]

* * *

The multiple disasters of the Fascist war effort were now drawing critical public attention to Mussolini's affair with Claretta, blatantly a liaison more serious that his earlier sexual adventures. Late in May 1941 Ciano and Bottai – two sleek, bourgeois Fascists of the new generation who frequently met in the comfortable clubhouse of Rome's Acquasanta golf course – spoke on the subject. The former made a record of the conversation. Bottai, Ciano wrote, 'is pessimistic about our internal situation which, in his opinion, is characterized by the formation of two groups that . . . are extra-legal with a strong and dangerous influence on the *Duce*'. Donna Rachele and her friends constituted one such faction, he underlined, and 'the Petaccis and their satellites' the other. 'Like all *outsiders* [Ciano wrote the word in English], these people intrigue against those who hold legal and constitutional power.'[34] Six months later, Ciano was more specific, documenting the charge by Guido Leto, the head of OVRA (the secret political police), that Marcello Petacci's schemes and escapades were 'doing the *Duce* more harm than fifteen [lost] battles'.[35]

The Petaccis were not the only people who sought advantage from sexual bonds with the *Duce*. Claretta's diary regularly recorded monies that Mussolini was arranging to pass, with no observable dent in the national budget, to Ruspi and Pallottelli, no doubt to assist his illegitimate children but not merely for that. As already noted, the business deals of the Pallottellis have left a substantial archival record in the variegated worlds of musical performance, mining in Ethiopia, clientelism at Fabriano and the recovery of a driving licence after a fatal accident. From 1938 Edda Ciano was also receiving 3,000 lire per month to spend charitably and without budgetary review.[36] But the Petaccis were a greater object of gossip, one reason being their transfer to the Villa Camilluccia, which stood out in its grandiosity and social ambition, and through the fact that, whenever Mussolini wanted to visit his lover there, he had to drive across the city as he had not had to do when Ruspi, Pallottelli, Claretta and, before her,

Sarfatti, resided in the immediate environs of the Villa Torlonia. Mussolini may have been trying to adjust Claretta's role in his mixture of public and private life in a positive sense. But regime opinion increasingly read rumours of the affair as a sign of their ruler's physical and mental decay.

As the young architects had promised, the Petacci property was built in a way that 'was decisively non-traditional' for a 'genteel' dwelling place.[37] A historian has estimated that the villa cost 1.73 million lire, 'a robust tally' and proof that the Petaccis had joined the high-society whirl.[38] Contemporary rumour contended that a Bechstein piano was added to the place's furnishings during the war at a cost of 130,000 lire.[39] Claretta's papers do contain a copy of a thirty-year loan that her mother took out with the Banca Nazionale del Lavoro for 226,838.27 lire in regard to the purchase of the villa.[40] Giuseppina Persichetti, with her family background in real estate, was pleased by the transfer from rented accommodation, with Claretta noting wryly that her mother thereby 'had won the thirty years' war'.[41] She was thought to be especially delighted by the vast *salone*, although the modernist effect was contradicted by its twenty armchairs and the placement of large nineteenth-century furniture there and elsewhere in the house, as well as such family treasures as small tables made in the Republic of Venice.[42] There were accompanying rumours that Dr Petacci had been left deeply in debt.[43] A more common assumption, however, was that the dictator (that is, the nation) and not the Petaccis had paid for it.[44]

The architects did give their services for free,[45] presumably hoping that, in their profession's world of patrons and clients, one good turn at the social heights of the regime would deserve another. They were certainly destined for success after 1945, with their best-known work being at the Italian capital's Leonardo Da Vinci airport and the Olympic village that housed athletes during the Rome Games of 1960. Back in the war years, perhaps the provision of an underground level – technically an ample servants' quarters but also equipped as an air-raid shelter in a city notoriously lacking in them – enhanced the notoriety of the Villa Camilluccia and the Petaccis. The place was an obvious target for resentful sack after 25 July 1943 and, even before that, one courageous and sarcastic graffitist scrawled on its walls *Scuola di Mistica Fascista* ('School of Fascist Mysticism': a genuine regime organisation with that pompous title had been launched in Milan in 1930).[46]

Mussolini himself, predictably under-impressed by 'Fascist modernism' up-close and a natural heretic towards the regime's architectural ideology, muttered that the building looked 'a little Bolshevik', and he probably did not use the grand mosaicked bath, standing isolated on the floor of the bathroom. Presumably he relaxed better in Claretta's bedroom, with its pink furniture, baby-pink telephone and king- (or *Duce*-)sized bed, although the mirrors on every wall may have been off-putting.[47] His own visits were confined to afternoons and evenings. He and Claretta did not spend a night together there, although when the villa was occupied by the Carabinieri in July 1943 it was reported that they found an extensive supply of Hormovin in the medicine cabinet.[48]

* * *

By 1942 another member of the family was gaining notoriety in the news and gossip of the regime: Claretta's sister Myriam, the sometime *piccola idiota* and chaperone. She had turned eighteen in May 1941, being thereafter launched into Roman high society and the louche world of cinema, with its trumpeted Fascist centre at Cinecittà out along the Via Tuscolana. According to one star, Doris Duranti, who by this time was the very public lover of Alessandro Pavolini, promoted to become the radical Fascist secretary of the party under the Salò Republic, cinema was a world of champagne, sex and cocaine. No hint of rationing restrained such 'joys' in wartime, she contended, while in 1942 she boasted that she was the first Italian woman to show (some of) her breasts on screen.[49]

Film, then, might not seem the ideal career path for a gently reared Catholic girl or a sternly Fascist one. But it was for Myriam. Always 'Mimi' within the family, she adopted a number of different professional names, from the humble Maria to the aristocratic Miria di San Servolo, eventually becoming in her Spanish exile Miria Day. Some say that it was Mussolini who suggested the aristocratic-sounding Miria di San Servolo,[50] with its hint of a Freudian reference to the lunatic asylum on the island of San Servolo in the Venetian lagoon, a place where, by the 1930s, only males were confined; women like Ida Dalser suffered their cruel fate at the nearby island of San Clemente. More starchily the Petaccis maintained that San Servolo referred to a castle near Trieste, which family legend stated had once belonged to their ancestors, the Petazzis, nobles under the Holy Roman Empire.[51] A little naively, Marcello liked to maintain that the family's escutcheon was composed of twelve gold coins set on a red background.[52]

Myriam's Catholic mother allegedly nourished the ambition that her younger daughter could prove the Eleonora Duse of the regime;[53] Duse had been an internationally celebrated actor in Liberal Italy and a durable and generous lover of Gabriele D'Annunzio. Giuseppina's phrasing was unfortunate, however, since Roman wits mocked Myriam as a potential Eleonora *Duce*.[54] After all, before she turned to cinema, Myriam, despite a lack of training in formal singing, had made an appearance as the maid in Cherubini's one-act comic opera *La locanda portoghese*, with the performance twice broadcast on Fascist radio at dictatorial command.[55]

But cinema offered more prestige and better financial return than comic opera. Adapting an established pattern to new circumstance, Giuseppina Persichetti chaperoned Myriam's visits to Cinecittà, sitting herself in a corner and reciting her rosary throughout filming. Piety was her constant comfort although, when bombing threatened and she descended to an air raid shelter, she kept up her confidence both by telling her beads and by sipping from the flask of brandy she always carried with her.[56] Film boss Luigi Freddi, writing after his own career as a Fascist had been superseded by anti-Fascism, remarked cattily that, at Cinecittà, Giuseppina looked like a 'mixture of a boxer and a caryatid', embodying the 'resolute and interfering matriarchy' of the provinces.[57] Freddi was equally dismissive of Myriam's acting skills and physical attractions, stating that she was a child of the 'petite bourgeoisie, full of its incorrigible habits, with an artificial vivaciousness and an insipid gaiety', incapable of taking on the style and character of anyone but herself. She was, he thought, the sort of girl who popped up in 'second-class hotels' at 'Cortina, San Remo, Stresa, Rapallo, Capri and Rimini', and that her only appeal lay in her ample breasts and seductively swinging hips.[58]

Myriam's first film role was in *Le vie del cuore* ('Paths to the heart'), directed by Camillo Mastrocinque (born 1901), a distinguished director who earned greater fame after 1945 with an eclectic mix of horror and comedy; the great Totò became one of his stars. *Le vie del cuore* was a historical romance, set in the 1870s. Myriam played Duchess Anna, a wronged noblewoman, who lost her own child in melodramatic circumstances and was rendered barren. By the film's end, however, she had reconciled with her (elderly) husband, agreeing selflessly to mother the son of another woman. Reviews varied, growing much more hostile after 1945 than they had been before. The comments of two sometime-Fascist journalists, one positive under the regime, the other afterwards not, were typical. From his viewing in 1942, Guido Piovene prophesied fawningly that Myriam would take 'an elevated part in the coming growth of our cinema'.[59] Aldo Palazzeschi, in 1948, noted instead her 'tubby figure' and 'stubby neck', dismissing any future for her as a star.[60]

Le vie del cuore was one of the films chosen for official screening at the 1942 Venice Biennale, an event rendered less lavish than in the past by the war but still boasting the presence of Alessandro Pavolini (at that time minister of popular culture) and Joseph Goebbels.[61] Scuttlebutt suggested that the applauding audience at the premiere of Myriam's film was composed largely of secret police and sailors stationed at the port; the latter were dragooned into attending by Marcello Petacci, who held a position as a naval surgeon there.[62] However, the local paper, *Il Gazzettino*, gave its readers mixed messages about the film. A first review on 4 September hailed Myriam as gifted with 'a singularly artistic temperament and refined sensibility'; she took her place among recent 'precious acquisitions' of the nation's cinema. A more extensive account nine days later, by contrast, found the plot unconvincing and the screen work inadequate, politely hoping that Myriam could find a better role next time. Viewers of *Le vie del cuore* soon fell away in numbers, and no Venice prize was won.[63]

But Myriam's career continued to blossom; she appeared in three more roles over the next twelve months. Again she was cast as a young noblewoman unhappily married to an older man – this time instructed in the ways of the world by 'an expert in women's psychology' – in the 1942 *L'amico delle donne* ('Women's friend'), directed by Ferdinando Maria Poggioli. This comedy, loosely based on a story by Alexandre Dumas, *fils*, elicited some ironical gossip about its title given the Petacci family

1. Claretta enjoys the seaside.

2. Leda Rafanelli as new woman.

3. Margherita Sarfatti, confident bourgeois.

4. Ida Dalser, bringing Paris fashion to Milan.

5. Benittino, son of Ida Dalser and Mussolini's unluckiest child.

6. The Mussolinis as they settled in the Villa Torlonia.

7. Edda marries Galeazzo and the social pages are delighted.

8. Ingénue in the office? Bianca Ceccato.

9. Mother with staying power: Angela Cucciati.

10. Elena Curti, philosophy student, loyal to the end.

11. Alice Pallottelli as a young woman.

12. Magda Brard, the *Duce*'s pianist.

13. Cornelia Tanzi rebutting postwar allegations of horizontal collaboration.

14. Giulia Carminati as stern Fascist.

15. Magda Fontanges with the snap in her prose.

16. Every inch a princess: Maria José.

17. Mussolini and female admirer (the image was suppressed under the dictatorship).

18. Rachele making a rare public appearance with the *Duce*.

19. Nonno *Duce* (another officially suppressed image).

20. Claretta around 1940, putting on weight and respectability.

21. Claretta the cartoonist, with herself as doggie listening to her master's voice.

22. Marcello Petacci and car.

23. Zita, Benghi and Ciccio.

24. Villa Schildhof, Naifweg, Obermais.

25. Francesco Saverio and Myriam on her wedding day.

26. Myriam and Armando marry in Santa Maria degli Angeli.

27. The mature Claretta, with the heavy and non-modernist furniture of the Villa Camilluccia.

28. Myriam and Armando with fags (in the Camilluccia grounds).

29. Claretta soulfully reading a Mussolini autobiographical piece that ignored her and her family.

30. Villa Fiordaliso and Claretta's bed ready for the next guest.

31. Claretta facing exposure, 1945.

32. Ben and Clara hung.

33. Francesco Saverio, Giuseppina and Myriam at Claretta's reburial in Rome, March 1956.

34. Claretta and the now mouldering Petacci tomb, Campo Verano.

35. Rachele Mussolini contemplates the past.

connection, and this reached the ears of Giuseppe Bottai.[64] An anonymous reviewer in Vittorio Mussolini's magazine, *Cinema*, observed ironically that Miria di San Servolo was most occupied during the film in changing outfits.[65] According to Luigi Freddi, screenings in Rome cinemas were interrupted by the throwing of stink bombs and the shouting of imprecations linking *peto* ('fart') and Petacci; the film closed within a fortnight.[66]

Poggioli re-employed Myriam in his next film, *Sogno d'amore* ('The dream of love)', but work on it at Cinecittà was unfinished in July 1943, when Mussolini was sacked by King Victor Emmanuel III. On this occasion, tittle-tattle alleged that completion had been slowed by Miria di San Servolo's flightiness. Poggioli committed suicide by gassing himself in Rome in 1945.[67] Myriam's final role was in *L'invasore* ('The invader'), directed by Nino Giannini with assistance from Roberto Rossellini. The film, another historical romance where aristocratic husband and wife (Myriam) were reconciled after much derring-do, was ready for screening in 1943,[68] but not actually shown until 1950. By then Rossellini, who had become a leading anti-Fascist through such celebrated works as *Rome: open city* (1945), adapted it for new times. Giannini, by contrast, openly backed the Repubblica Sociale and did not resume a directorial career after 1945, although he lived until 1978.

* * *

Myriam's stardom under the regime was therefore confined to historical romances in the *Telefoni Bianchi* ('White Telephone') vein that much Fascist cinema preferred. The majority of the regime's films aimed at schmaltzy entertainment: at forgetting present troubles as much as remembering the Fascist revolution. Certainly Myriam's roles were scarcely vehicles of overtly totalitarian propaganda.[69] Historical research has nonetheless shown how Cinecittà pullulated with secret police, evidence that someone in the regime feared that film could express seditious unspoken assumptions,[70] even if raffish actors were not always punished for their vagaries.[71]

Myriam's cinematic career was one source of public gossip. At least as great a source of scandal was her early marriage, her first husband being the 'Marchese' Armando Boggiano. They met at the elegant ski resort of

Cortina when Myriam was still only eighteen; two months later they were engaged. Boggiano was more than ten years her senior and had already gone almost completely bald. He must have been smitten, however, and was soon writing her a thirty-two-page love letter.[72] Oddly the Boggiano family is not listed by the main Italian repository of noble descent, the *Libro d'oro della nobiltà italiana*.[73] But, as Doris Duranti snobbishly recorded, the cinema world was beset by a circle of counts and marquesses whose titles were sometimes more assumed than real.[74] Maybe Boggiano was one of them. For Claretta, ever more obsessively imagining the Petacci family supplanting the Mussolinis (except for one), there may have been pleasure in this demonstration that Galeazzo Ciano, from his father's death in 1939 2nd count of Cortelazzo and Buccari, was matched in title by Myriam's partner.

Whatever the authenticity of his noble status, Boggiano was the son of a rich textile magnate in Liguria, with an associated import–export cotton business, trading with the east.[75] Money was not his problem; according to Myriam, in 1942 he readily lent her brother 1.5 million lire so that, in April 1943, Marcello could purchase the Villa Schildhof at Obermais – looking out over the town of Merano and the surrounding Alps – from Francesco Paolo Conte Pálffy and Rodolfo Conte Erdödy, men belonging to the top echelon of Hungarian aristocracy. Popular memory is today sure that Mussolini frequently visited Claretta there, despite little actual evidence of such meeting.[76] (Recollection of sexual athleticism is not confined to 'Ben and Clara', with contemporaries also claiming that Count Pálffy retained five local women friends, each being granted a separate garden space in the villa's extensive grounds to work on during his long absences.[77])

Boggiano was even more generous to his wife than he was to her brother, buying her more than one fur coat, including the leopard-skin she wore at the wedding reception.[78] As an elegant young man about town, the marchese did not bother to join the Fascist Party until around the time of his marriage and, malicious observers maintained, was most renowned for what he regarded as his especially clever cat (a preference for felines over canines being something he shared with Mussolini). The cat's name was Nerone-Caligola ('Nero-Caligula'), with his owner suggesting he carried imperial blood. As a matter of respect to this noble creature, Boggiano insisted that his friends and lovers write regular letters to it. Nerone-Caligola, he maintained, was cheered by personal mail.[79]

Despite wartime rationing, Myriam's and Armando's wedding was celebrated in style on 22 June 1942, with a religious ceremony at Santa Maria degli Angeli (still today a nationalist church, proud of Italian imperialism), up the Via Nazionale from Dr Petacci's medical practice. Giuseppina and Claretta took pains to don rich furs for the occasion, despite the summer heat, while Francesco Saverio – whose hair had by then gone white (perhaps a reflection of his stressful family life) – wore a cutaway morning coat. Wedding photos show Myriam luxuriously attired in lace (Marcello Petacci's partner stressed that it was 'ancient and Venetian' in origin and had belonged to the Boggiano family); her dress was said to be her mother's and it was equipped with a very long train.[80] However, although possessed of blue eyes and golden-brown hair and capable of looking beautiful in her publicity photos, Myriam had the disadvantage of a rather plump figure.[81] Both she and Armando smoked.

On 22 June the vast interior of Santa Maria degli Angeli (once the Baths of Diocletian) was covered with sweet-smelling flowers.[82] Afterwards guests stepped around the corner to the nearby Grand Hotel, where, it was later recalled, mountains of ham and caviar, cakes and chocolate, were washed down by the choicest wines and the best champagne. Official rationing rules were ostentatiously ignored. Made hungry, at least in their fears, by wartime austerity, high-society guests consumed the offered comestibles like locusts but had remembered to provide rich gifts to the new couple, Mussolini sending an elegant set of twelve silver plates. Rumour said that the dictator phoned *Il Messaggero* at midnight after the wedding to be informed just how the paper's social pages intended to describe the event; as a prominent Fascist remarked morosely: 'Mussolini took more interest in the marriage of the Petacci woman's sister than in the marriages of his own children.'[83] A honeymoon at Budapest followed. Myriam claimed in her memoirs to have become pregnant within a year, only to lose the child after a 'banal accident' in April 1943,[84] but rumour whispered that sexual relations had not long prospered.

The marriage was riven with greater problems. Myriam upbraided Boggiano for being drunk on their wedding night and maintained that the two were living largely apart by the end of 1942, although were partially reconciled by a ritzy skiing holiday at St Moritz (by no means prevented by the war).[85] Despite such marital contentment, Myriam had not given up living in the Villa Camilluccia,[86] and was equally determined to proceed with her career as a film star. Moreover, Giuseppina Persichetti was soon lamenting that she, to her disgust, was expected to become a loyal correspondent of Nerone-Caligola.[87] By July 1943 relations between Myriam and Armando were precarious and were not to be assisted by the Badoglio regime's rapid sequestration of the Boggiano family's landed property.

Gossip published in the Italy that had been liberated by the Allies contended that Boggiano was 'a pure-blooded nobleman, good at sport, vain, and an idiot', while hinting that his chief erotic predilection was not heterosexual.[88] Under the RSI the couple formally separated in April 1944 (and eventually had a Swiss divorce in 1951) but, according to Myriam, remained good friends, an attachment that lasted until Boggiano's death in September 1985. Certainly the terms of his settlement with her look generous, with rich Boggiano family jewels to a composite value of 1.4 million lire passing into her hands and Armando agreeing to pay 10,000 lire per month as an allowance. The legal agreement in this regard was signed on 25 June by both Myriam and, typically, Giuseppina Persichetti.[89]

* * *

In her memoirs, Myriam remarked that her family always believed in the slogan of the Dumas *père* character d'Artagnan: 'One for all, and all for one.'[90] They did indeed frequently hunt as a pack, familism outweighing Fascism in their lives. But the Petacci making the greatest public splash before and during the war until July 1943 was neither Claretta nor Myriam, but Marcello. Over the years he has had a bad press. The chief witness in his defence has been his father, who, in 1961, edited a collection of Marcello's scientific papers as a doctor; they covered such topics as the social origins of TB, prostate cancer, the cardio-renal effects of syphilis, heart attacks and ulceration brought on by twisted veins, and in other matters where his expertise as a naval surgeon had provided insight (and there is a half-hint of relevance to the *Duce*'s medical problems).[91] Francesco Saverio provided these studies with a glowing biographical preface, which included positive references from such distinguished doctors as Mario Donati, Giuseppe Galli and Antonio Ciminata, and a list of hundreds of successful operations that Marcello had performed on patients who ranged in age from two to seventy-six.[92]

According to his father, Marcello graduated young from Rome University in 1932 (he must have transferred from Pisa) and thereafter concentrated on clinical work in the Italian capital. The younger Dr Petacci was equally devoted to the regime's institutions, worthily instructing about 150 members of the Balilla (the Fascist male scouting organisation) in 'anatomy and first aid'. His trinity, his father swore, was composed of 'science, *patria* and family'. In March 1935 Marcello joined the navy and was called up for the Ethiopian war. He did not serve there, however, rather remaining in Italy on a lecture circuit. Thereafter he passed a series of exams promoting him up the officer ranks of its medical service. In 1937–8 he was based in Milan, working under Professor Mario Donati and acquiring further expertise at the Umberto I hospital at Monza, even when that post entailed operating late at night. Donati was a distinguished figure of international reputation, a converted Jew, expelled from his university position in 1938 because of the racial laws, but able to survive in wartime Milan running a private clinic, his persecution regretted by Francesco Saverio in his eulogy for his son.[93] Mario Donati's brother Pio had been a socialist member of the Chamber of Deputies between 1919 and 1923 and was an avowed anti-Fascist, perishing in exile in Brussels in 1927. Under Nazi racial threat after September 1943, Mario Donati found sanctuary in Switzerland, returning to Italy following the war. He then regained his university and hospital posts, only to die in 1946.[94]

It was while Marcello was working in Milan that he began his relationship with Zita Ritossa, a woman who did not belong to the highest social classes of that city. She had been born to the Ritosch family at Parenzo in Istria on 23 September 1914 (now Poreč, Croatia) and her father was said to have remained even in the late 1930s uncertain how to express himself in formal written Italian. He was, however, reasonably well off and had an international profile in the wine trade.[95] His daughter shared her first name with Zita of Bourbon-Parma, married in 1911 to the Habsburg Archduke Charles of Austria-Este, who, in 1916, was crowned as the (last) Habsburg emperor. The name suggests that the Ritosch family, at the time of her birth, were not yet Italian nationalists. Parenzo and Istria were annexed by Italy through the Paris peace settlement (to be lost again after 1945). However, by the 1930s, Zita, who had been educated by the Ursuline nuns at Gorizia, had Italianised her surname and worked for her living as a seamstress at the Sartoria Ventura, which is still open for business in Milan.

In her postwar memoirs, Ritossa disclosed that she met Marcello by accident in 1937 when she was suffering from tonsillitis. At first she found him annoyingly fond of boasting of his success with women, and immediately jealous of her. However, they quickly decided to live together and, in 1938, he took her to Rome to meet his family, meticulously planning the event, she observed, like a 'pilgrimage'. There she received the grudging approval of Giuseppina Persichetti, who told Zita sternly, in her 'hoarse voice', that Marcello needed 'guidance', his mother being always the best person to supply it.[96]

Zita, who was proud of her own independence, retreated to Milan – perhaps to avoid such maternal instruction – where she and Marcello started a family: their son Benvenuto Edgardo was born on 5 December 1939. This name allegedly tied the Petacci heir to his aristocratic Petazzi ancestors in Trieste,[97] but the child was always known in the family as 'Benghi'. The delivery occurred at the couple's Milan flat in the presence of both Dr Petacci senior and his wife, with the latter supervising her grandson's premature arrival, Zita remembered, while fervently fingering her rosary beads. Marcello's father, by contrast, was usually 'meek' and mild, although he did once pursue Zita around the family home toting a large syringe, determined to inject her with some health-giving liquid.[98]

Shortly after the birth Benghi suffered a cerebral haemorrhage, which left him with learning disabilities: he would remain under his mother's care until his death in 1977.[99] His condition may have been worsened by his alleged observation of his father's execution at Dongo in April 1945. His younger brother Ferdinando – 'Ciccio' to the family – grew more sturdily and is still alive in 2016.

* * *

By the outbreak of the war Marcello had acquired joint qualifications to serve in the navy and in Italian universities. In August 1941 he was promoted to the rank of major and stationed thereafter at Venice where, his father proudly reported, his skills as a surgeon saved many lives.[100] Back in January that year, on a day when Mussolini was absent, admiration for her brother set Claretta off on what she must have thought was deep reflection in diary commentary that characteristically mixed family, Fascism and her obsessive love for the *Duce*: 'The sky is grey like my heart and soul', she wrote:

> Only Benghi can make me laugh. [But so can] Marcello, that big boy, full of enthusiasm, with lots of projects always off and away, bold and energetic. I start thinking, thinking of how he dreams of working for Italy and has done seven hundred operations for you [Mussolini] without a single death. I understand that it is possible to be a doctor and an Italian at the same time, just like the heroes of the Risorgimento and the young devotees of your revolution. When the *patria* is in need, there is just this one powerful mother who as never before sets moving the living, breathing blood, who drives [us] forward and makes demands [on us]. I think with infinite sadness of the evil done by the cowards who surround you and of how many young lives have thus been swept away, and my throat constricts with pain.[101]

It has already been noted that, even before she had sex with Mussolini, Claretta zealously advanced her brother's career with the dictator and thereafter regularly kept the *Duce* abreast of Marcello's multiple schemes. In March 1938 Mussolini told her hearteningly that her brother's writings beautifully demonstrated 'the Fascist sentiment' of the Petacci family. 'Very good. You must keep these carefully. They're very important,' he advised.[102] Similarly, the *Duce* took pains to congratulate Claretta on the promotions that Marcello won in the navy, predicting that one day he would reach the elevated rank of medical general; 'you see, I do everything you want,' he added as a generous patron might.[103]

In January 1939 the Petaccis contrived to have Myriam and Marcello accompany their sister on an assignation with Mussolini to the ski slopes of Terminillo, with some preoccupation from Claretta that the *Duce* might display too much interest in Myriam. Marcello proved an incompetent skier, but he was offered avuncular dietary advice by Mussolini, who pronounced, from his own medical knowledge bank, that 'nutrition must vary with age'. The ideal, according to the *Duce*, was 'to eat a lot of spaghetti at twenty, less at thirty, to move towards vegetarianism at forty and to give up meat almost entirely at fifty'.[104] Mussolini was not always so genial. In September 1939 he passed to Claretta a police report on scandals where Marcello was allegedly involved. Whether true or not, the dictator said, he must not in future allow himself to be accused of 'nepotism', a charge fostering gossip that he was declining into a 'second childhood'.[105]

Records do exist intimating that Marcello was not a wholly austere practitioner of medicine. Nino D'Aroma, a journalist responsible for many of the regime's newsreels, stated after the war that the younger Dr Petacci was 'a kind of eternal burbler, full of a hundred thousand deals', a man 'lacking any brake and hence insufferable, ready to spice his conversations with the grossest lies'.[106] One fantastic scheme that he favoured was a 'scientific' process that would automatically regenerate the oil used in automobile engines.[107]

Another contemporary, less friendly to the regime, castigated 'the "Petacci group" of racketeers', who, in exploiting the dictator's senile passion for Claretta, had organised in Italy and in the Iberian peninsula 'a network of dubious but highly profitable commercial enterprises. He [Marcello] was despised yet feared even in the most Fascist circles'.[108] A third remembered how irascible Marcello was in his dealings with officialdom, always ready to decry their failure to applaud his brilliant understanding of politics and opportunity.[109] According to Zita Ritossa, Marcello publicly claimed that, 'with a bit of money, I can do everything', and she added that, before July 1943, he had compiled for Mussolini a detailed list of the 'traitors' who were undermining the regime. To derail their sinister plots, he proclaimed, a band of young men, including himself, stood alert and ready to fight for Fascism.[110]

Given Marcello's lack of diplomacy in his dealings with the established elite, it is no surprise to find Mussolini's secretariat collecting negative stories about Marcello well before the outbreak of war. In May 1938, for example, to the scandal of sticklers for bureaucratic propriety, he had written a letter suggesting names for the committee established to judge his application for a university post. In doing so, he was, he explained in another letter, 'following the Chief's wishes'. Lest any mistakes be made in that regard, appointment to his selection committee some months later came with evidently ironical bureaucratic advice of the *Duce*'s 'benevolence' towards him and hope in his success.[111] His promotion to captain in the navy was similarly assisted by recommendations from on high.[112]

Files also grew on Marcello's tendency to absent himself from naval duty and involve himself in such escapades as an incident on the Via delle Terme di Diocleziano in central Rome, where, during a public stoush, his dog bit a journalist. The fracas was reported in *Il Messaggero* but without naming names.[113] Only ten days after this case, Marcello weighed into a brawl with five locals in the centre of the tourist resort of Abbazia (Opatija) in Istria. When the police intervened, they alleged Petacci was drunk, although Zita Ritossa, who was with him and had courageously come to his physical assistance, denied this. A fortnight later another rumpus broke out. On this occasion, Admiral Ildebrando Goiran, in charge of the base at La Spezia where Marcello was meant to be serving, judged him blameless, but added that he could not ignore earlier advice that Marcello's actions at Abbazia demanded 'the severest reproof' and a review of his officer status.[114]

Following Petacci's transfer to Venice, his lifestyle did not become any calmer. Soon he was involved in a loud public quarrel with Countess Donatella Parisi, from whom he had rented a house, a dispute which saw the duke of Genoa, long the most prominent royal in Venice, intervening against Petacci.[115] The purchase of the expensive Villa Schildhof, with its ample grounds, added to Marcello's notoriety, supplying further evidence of the Petacci family's desire to insert themselves into the highest circles of society, whether Italian or wider European. Its actual purchase price, which included the villa's furnishings, was 1.625 million lire. Scandal shortly after the war suggested that the deal with the Hungarian owners had lacked transparency and, as early as 9 May 1945, Counts Pálffy and Erdödy managed to have the sale declared null and void, with no indemnity being conceded to the surviving Petaccis.[116] An appeal from Myriam and her parents, which reached the supreme court, the Cassazione, in October 1949, failed, as did a further legal recourse by Zita Ritossa in 1953–4. At the end of the decade the place was sold to a German family.[117] Readers will have to decide for themselves whether the (modernised) villa's current address, Naifweg 3, Obermais, is appropriate.[118]

* * *

Despite the official austerity of wartime, Marcello's effrontery in 1942–3 had known few bounds. In February 1943 he felt able to send the *Duce* a memorandum impetuously sketching a full scale reworking of national war aims and military strategy. Anglo-American forces, Marcello began by stating, outweighed Italy in North Africa by ten to one. Something had to be done. Spain could be the first target. A secret embassy should proceed there to ensure the Franco regime launched an attack from its sector of Morocco. The best delegates would be people who had good contacts in the Spanish army and clergy, as well as with the papal nuncio and in the Vatican. A careful reader might have been able to come up with a worthy candidate.

But that was not the end of Petacci's imaginings, fantastical in their span but also traditional in their Machiavellian basis in *Realpolitik* (rather than in any Nazi-fascist race theory). Marcello was nothing if not global in his scheming. The South American states could be brought into the present conflict. Turkey could be persuaded to invade the USSR and China could do the same. Chiang Kai-shek, Marcello wrote, was a convinced admirer of Mussolini and Japan could divert its warring from China to the rich oil fields of the Dutch East Indies (Indonesia) and the vast empty lands of Australia. It could be possible to win Stalin to Italy's side, for example by offering him India to rule. Marcello had a good friend who could be the special agent in that regard. Britain, too, might be converted to an agreement reviving its rule over Canada and the USA. Samuel Hoare, the British ambassador in Madrid (and an ex-British agent in First World War Italy and financier of *Il Popolo d'Italia*),[119] was a prospective friend of such amendment. Only the USA was likely to be really tough over any division of the world under Italian guidance, since the Americans had everything to gain and nothing to lose in the present war. Germany and Italy, Petacci suggested without going into too many details, could split Africa and the Middle East. If some of these contrivances failed, it was always possible to raise the Arabs against the Jews, arm the Indians against the British and persuade the Berbers to massacre their colonial masters in French North Africa.[120] No evidence of a dictatorial response to such a memorandum has survived.

A matter causing wider immediate scandal was Marcello Petacci's social, political and financial visibility, and especially his dabbling in the gold trade. Among Marcello's contacts was Santorre Vezzari, a long-serving secret agent of OVRA. Having been first employed in Switzerland in 1924, Vezzari worked as a spy in Madrid from 1931 under the newly installed Spanish Republic, where he devoted himself to developing a network of friends. He also displayed skills in covert currency-dealing across the border with France. His career did take a dip in early 1941 when he was arrested but, by November of that year, he was installed back in Franco's Madrid as the attaché dealing with trade and exchange. Marcello, meanwhile, pressed him forward as the next Italian ambassador there.[121]

The Petaccis also developed excellent relations with Admiral Arturo Riccardi, the elderly under-secretary for the navy 1941–3 (he had been born 1878), having assisted the admiral's son, Roberto, gain entry to a diplomatic career in 1939, after a two-year campaign featuring, his father wrote, 'some disillusion and anxiety'. Roberto Riccardi remained in service after 1945, becoming an ambassador (to Luxembourg) in 1971. Admiral Riccardi was in compensation a useful support to Marcello's officer status in the navy, and the Petaccis asked for his intervention in their favour when Marcello's affairs became complicated.[122]

By contrast, the minister for trade and exchange, Raffaello Riccardi, an old squadrist who does not seem to have been related to the admiral, led the attack, complaining in November 1941 to Ciano that Marcello was a 'crooked speculator' and, the next year, expressing his disgust at Vezzari's appointment to Spain.[123] A few months later the minister blamed Marcello and his clique for the sudden sacking of the director of the Banca Nazionale del Lavoro, Arturo Osio, after the banker had been rude enough publicly to label Marcello *Lorenzino dei medici* ('the doctors' little Lorenzo').[124] By May 1942 Riccardi had compiled a ten-page document setting out

Marcello's dubious financial ventures through a company he had established called the Compagnia italiana scambi estero ed Europa (the 'Italian exchange company with Europe and abroad'). Myriam in her memoirs damned this Riccardi for behaving like a 'rabid dog' over the matter.[125]

Marcello Petacci's business gaze extended almost as widely as it would do in his strategic 'plan' of 1943. Profit for the company and advantage to the nation, he urged, could be won with a takeover of phosphate reserves in Algeria, fresh and salted fish purchase in Spain, the sale of old and disarmed Italian ships lying immobile in neutral ports and the acquisition of rubber held in Portugal. Such business was to be done through back alleys and via personal deals. Finally there was the despatch by Vezzari through the diplomatic bag of 100-million-lire-worth of gold, weighing 16 kilos.[126]

In June 1942 Riccardi took the story to Mussolini who, Riccardi told Ciano, was indignant at Marcello's behaviour. The dictator promised to warn Claretta's brother off such schemes in future and, indeed, from 'trafficking' of any kind.[127] The gold meanwhile, on Ciano's initiative,[128] was taken into the custody of Carmine Senise, the chief of police, where it remained, still the object of rumour and scandal, in July 1943. In his postwar memoirs, Senise provides a sardonic account of having to deal with the speculations of 'the brother of that sister, do you get me?' (as he phrased it to an underling).[129] Ciano led the anti-Marcello faction, proof that the dictator's relationship with Claretta was causing increased worry to his legitimate family, among whom, for example, his capable sister, Edvige, gossiped to Ciano about 'the shady business dealings of the Petacci clan', which, she said, had become a 'national problem'.[130] Edda Ciano bearded her father over the matter, only to receive characteristic intimation that Marcello's real fault was his foolish openness in his business dealings.[131]

Marcello's extravagances prompted growing dismay well beyond the Mussolini family. Among the regime elite, Giuseppe Bottai, who had so long tended his own crush on Mussolini, bewailed the fact that Claretta was an inferior imitation of Madame de Pompadour. Nor was it only leading Fascists who viewed the Petaccis as demeaning the *Duce*. In March 1943 Bottai was irritated enough to record a joke circulating in aristocratic circles which had Claretta finding Mussolini in his bath examining his genitals. 'Why are you doing that?' she asked. Her lover's reply: 'Because it is the only prick still attached to me.'[132] Among people in the know, especially in Rome, Mussolini's sexual obsession with Claretta (rebuked by Ciano already in July 1940)[133] was an ever-greater factor in the decay of the dictator's image and in public rejection of the notion that Fascism should any longer frame their identities.

Amid the undergrowth of party rivalry and plotting, Marcello and his sister had relied (and would soon rely again) on the support of Guido Buffarini Guidi, since 1933 the under-secretary for the interior and a rising figure in the regime's hierarchy, once a client of Ciano but now scenting a higher position.[134] Perhaps Mussolini was seeking an escape from such dirty warring when, in February, his ministerial reshuffle dismissed Ciano, Raffaello Riccardi and Buffarini Guidi, the last not even saved when Claretta publicly burst into tears at the news.[135]

* * *

Between 1941 and 1943 these eddies of Petacci family life and ambition complicated Claretta's relationship with Mussolini at least as much as had the *Duce*'s manly refusal or emotional inability to cast off Ruspi and Pallottelli. The first year had contained one major step, when, in March 1941, 'Clara Persichetti' as she called herself tellingly, travelled to Budapest in the company of the family lawyer, Gino Sotis, to petition for divorce. Perhaps assisted by the fact that Marcello's business arrangements embraced Hungary (he was seeking involvement in oil production in Transylvania),[136] the decree was granted on 29 December 1941, having also been approved by Riccardo Federici from Tokyo.[137] From then on, somewhere in Claretta's dreams (and very likely those of her mother) lay the hope of a second marriage for both her and the *Duce* and thereby a victory of the Petacci family in the war that they now openly contested with all the Mussolinis. In February 1942 Claretta turned thirty; the photographic record shows her to have developed a mature figure, often partly hidden beneath flowing ankle-length gowns. In quite a few ways she may have remained infatuated with the *Duce,* but Claretta Petacci was no longer an ingenuous teenager.

In her diary she had begun the year by wishing sentimentally that the sun would rise again on her lover's fortunes, so that 'a smile can return to [his] handsome face today veiled in shadow'.[138] Such happy expectations proved barren, however. In their first meeting of the year, Mussolini – who, Claretta did not fail to record, had already seen Ruspi from 8.30 to 9 a.m. that morning – rambled on about the Four-Power Pact that had earned some diplomatic praise back in 1933, and which in regime propaganda was dubbed the *Patto Mussolini* ('Mussolini Pact'). Its provisions, the *Duce* pronounced with his usual cynicism towards an ideologically driven Axis, had arrayed Britain, France, Italy and the United States (his memory was deficient in this last regard) in a system that could have kept German dynamism under control.[139] Five days later, by contrast, he swung around to deem the current conflict a 'war of religion' and ideology, while whingeing about a flu that was afflicting him and, during a visit to the Villa Camilluccia, seeking a proper prescription from Francesco Saverio. Mussolini was also disgusted by what he heard of weak-kneed Italian military performance in Dalmatia and by the inability of the regime's authorities to repress the black market at home.[140]

It is almost a surprise to find Mussolini dropping in on the Petacci family on Sunday, 10 May, before he was due to leave for a tour of inspection in Sardinia, in order to have sex twice, on the second occasion, in Claretta's judgement, in a pleasingly 'frenzied fashion'. Her own sensual joy did not last, however, and she was soon in tears from nameless fears about what might happen to him on his journey (he did return, but with another bad cold).[141] By the end of the month she was telling him dolefully that she was just another of his concubines and whores, while urging him desperately to buck up and 'rediscover his [real] self'.[142]

During these months Claretta did occasionally venture away from Rome, for example spending time in September 1942 with Myriam in Venice and Arenzano (where Boggiano met them), to the *Duce's* jealous irritation. When she travelled by train to Milan, he almost sounded like Giuseppina in his spartan view of family life, as he pressed Marcello into joining the trip as a chaperone.[143] As far as the wider world was concerned, the *Duce's* mood darkened further. On 30 November he told Claretta in lachrymose phrasing: 'Nothing matters to me anymore; I am deluded and tired. Everything is the reverse of what I awaited and hoped for . . . Nothing and nobody interests me; not even you.' How much better it would have been, he concluded, if he, and not Bruno, had died in 1941![144] To be sure, two days later, after he spoke to applause in the Fascist parliamentary chamber – his tone, he congratulated himself, had been 'symphonic, Beethovian' – there were moments of optimism (and swift intercourse).[145] But on 4 December he revived familiar complaints about how young Claretta was compared with him, how certain she was to betray him, and how dissatisfied he was with Edda's conduct and attitude. They did manage sex but not until he had taken some 'heart pills' (perhaps Hormovin).[146] By now Dr F.S. Petacci was required to appear at Palazzo Venezia in order to inject him every second day with what were probably vitamin supplements.[147]

Just before Christmas 1942 Claretta took a new line in a long conversation that she recorded, expressing sentiments destined to become more prominent in her mind over the last two and a half years of their relationship. Here was a Claretta who was getting on top, a woman whom some would eventually call *La Ducessa* ('the female *Duce*'). Mussolini awoke on Saturday, 20 December, in terrible pain and, after injecting himself with sodium bromide, he took another, stronger, anti-spasm pill and almost became unconscious until Claretta, who had arrived, calmed him with a massage. He told her, however, that he was finished and it was time to leave office. Claretta refused to accept such logic and demanded he must not 'yield to the English and the priests'. They then put on a recording of their favourite, Beethoven's 7th Symphony. When it reached its second movement, Mussolini was deeply moved and cried 'for the first time since the death of Bruno, crying in great gulps, lying stretched out on the ground, with his eyes covered in the dark'. That burst of emotion made Claretta sob as well and set off a further long excursion into the failure of his life and works that not even the playing of Vivaldi's 'Spring' from *The Four Seasons* could arrest.

When he resumed his theme – the need in sackcloth and ashes to approach the pope and the English in order to have Rome declared an 'open city' and so be saved from bombing – Claretta grew almost stern with him, transmuted into a mother unable to tolerate weakness or backsliding.

He must not accept a 'spiritual suicide', she declared. He must not bow to 'subtle manoeuvres by "Anglo-priestly" forces'. He must not allow the nation's capital to lose its 'Roman and Fascist' imprint and limply consign it to the Vatican and 'priestly power'. He was 'the chief' and could not 'yield his command' nor 'go into exile'. He must stand up against the 'sheep and canaille', the pathetic beings who were betraying him. Rather than obeying corrupt generals and a cowardly monarch, he should summon to his cause 'the authentic Italian people'.[148]

If ideology mattered, Claretta's outburst made her sound like the most fanatical Fascist 'new woman', a fervent adept of a new political religion. It was quite a change. Until then her politics had been little more than a reflection of her love of, or obsession with, Mussolini's person. Her family had similarly been more engaged in their own social advancement that in devoting themselves to the belief system of Fascism. Giuseppina had clung to her rosary beads, Francesco Saverio to his papal contacts, Myriam to her career and noble connection, while always protected by her sister's readiness to announce that 'any friend of Mimi is a friend of mine'.[149] Marcello, who had been pleased by the patronage of Mario Donati, was doubtless polishing his contacts with Franco's Spain or Admiral Horthy's Hungary, but had seemed more interested in profit than ideological purity. However, from 1942, the private hopes of the Petacci family were to become ever more enmeshed with Fascism, its factions and fate. Private and public life were destined to become ever-more entangled.

* * *

For the moment, however, Claretta's radical sentiments, whatever her Fascist zest, did not revive her *Duce*. His railing against his lot and the inadequacy of the Fascist armed forces only intensified. Officers, he charged, surrendered in droves without fighting, disgracefully happy at their 'complete lack of racial decorum and national dignity'. Throughout history, Italians could not and would not fight, as Napoleon had rightly understood. 'The empire' was 'entirely undefended'. Such forlorn sentiment was enough to earn another rebuke from Claretta. Baffled by the depth of her lover's pessimism and misanthropy, she swung all but automatically into her never-ending remonstrance against his promiscuity and failure to give her the love that she deserved and needed.[150] He was, it was hard to deny, a public and a private failure. The year of 1942 was not ending well.

The New Year proved worse. Not far beneath the surface of the regime a battle was raging over how to get Italy out of the catastrophic war with the least damage. Among those who had long opposed the German alliance was Ciano, who, in the reshuffle of February, lost the Ministry of Foreign Affairs but was sent instead to be ambassador to the Vatican, with a prospect there, never fully developed, to manage an Italian exit from the war. In so doing he might turn from what Claretta sarcastically defined as 'The Dauphin' into Mussolini's successor.[151] In practice, however, Ciano failed to take his chance and the major plotters to remove the *Duce* were Grandi, Bottai, the former chief of staff, Badoglio, and the aristocratic advisers of King Victor Emmanuel III.

Failing to find an escape from Fascism's glaring public failings, Galeazzo and Edda Ciano and other members of Mussolini's family circle instead augmented their campaign against Claretta, helped by the scandals that eddied around her brother. The public, it was rumoured, were joking about a *Santa Chiara, protettrice degli affari poco chiari* ('Saint Clara, protector of dubious business affairs'), while, disgracefully, Marcello was thought to have free entry to every place of power and financial advantage in the country.[152] It was time therefore, the Cianos insisted, for the relationship to end, with Edda, according to her memoirs, extracting from her father a lunchtime promise in November 1942 to break with all the Petaccis, and a dubiously pious pledge that 'no woman' other than Rachele had 'ever meant anything to him'.[153] In response, Claretta stoutly fought her corner in this family war, hardening her overt posture as a convinced Fascist. She warned of the threat from Badoglio and other generals, pleading with her lover to accept that 'your general staff is a nest of filthy snakes'. They and their traitorous friends, she maintained, had won over the dwarf king. Galeazzo and Edda worked for them. Scorza was a sad joke; what a shame it was to have dropped Buffarini Giudi in the February changes. To stop the conspiracy, Mussolini, she implored her lover, must remember the revolution and arm the Fascist militia.[154]

But Mussolini by now lacked the fortitude to accept either her advice or the not dissimilar – if cruder – counsel of his wife Rachele, who was demanding that 'we must make some heads roll'.[155] Instead there came the sudden news in May that, in future, Claretta was to be banned from entry to the Palazzo Venezia. In the unpublished biography that the journalist Paolo Monelli prepared in the 1950s (but refrained from publishing after he lost a law case to the surviving Petaccis over a taster he had sent to *France Soir*), it was maintained that the Ben–Clara relationship was then at breaking point. Had Mussolini's sacking been a little delayed, Monelli speculated, the Petaccis would have lost their place in history.[156] Certainly, Claretta's emotions knew no bounds as her private life again overwhelmed her Fascism. 'You have tried to free yourself from me in the most brutal and definitive manner, creating a scandal,' she cried in admonishment. She had suffered the humiliation of being turned back by the police. 'You have treated me like a thief and a prostitute.' She would die, 'crushed by the pain for ever'.[157]

Yet she had not forgotten her other campaign. The nefarious plotters, and especially Ciano, she asserted, lay behind her expulsion. They had taken advantage of Mussolini's present weakness and depression to tell the people that he was 'useless, past it, defeated'. He must react. He must resume his natural role as 'the titan, the giant, the world dominator'.[158] He must reclaim himself (and Claretta). In her campaign, she had her mother by her side. Giuseppina wrote to Mussolini that he must not for a moment believe the calumnies of Ciano, his wife and their associated 'canaille'. 'Claretta's life,' she stated, 'lies in your hands'; her love for him had no limit.[159]

In his diary, Bottai, perhaps with the male jealousy of one who, for so long, had been transfixed by Mussolini's charisma, was pleased to hear of the ban, hoping that this time Claretta's departure was 'definitive'. An attempt to expel her earlier in May had soon collapsed.[160] Nor, this time, did the relationship cease, even when, on 14 July, for the third time, Claretta was officially stripped of automatic entry to the Palazzo Venezia.[161] In reality the 'Ben and Clara' affair drifted on, despite ever more open discontent among the Italian elite with Mussolini's leadership and everlouder mutterings about the whole Petacci family. On 21 June a rumour had swept the sets of Cinecittà that the grocery supplier of the Petacci family was to be arrested for ration-breaking, but that Myriam had intervened to save him.[162] From among the plotters, General Quirino Armellini recalled in his memoirs his disgust that the Villa Camilluccia promiscuously housed Francesco Saverio, Giuseppina, Myriam and Boggiano and Mussolini's lover, 'a family of whores'.[163] On 16 July the *Duce* ignored advice from Scorza's radical chef de cabinet to shoot Ciano, Badoglio and Marcello Petacci out of hand or risk losing all popular support.[164]

Skirting the latest ruling against her occupying the Sala dello Zodiaco, Claretta characteristically translated the troubles of the nation and the regime into her private world, on 18 July informing her lover melodramatically that, 'if you fall like a Myth, like God, the only thing left for me to do will be to kill myself'. The issue was not just political. Mussolini had rung Ruspi from the Villa Camilluccia and had not ended his contact with Pallottelli. 'I tell you that today all that exists is my tragedy, my pain, my delusion. You have the right of life or death over me; the sentence must be worthy of our love.'[165]

But politics kept surfacing, too. On 20 July Claretta warned her Ben against attending the meeting of the Grand Council scheduled for the evening of the 24th. The army, Freemasonry, the royal house, Badoglio, 'Grandi the Englishman', all were preparing the 'major coup', she prophesied, all would pull him down. They duly did, with Mussolini going like a sleepwalker to dismissal by the king on the late afternoon of the 25th, after the Grand Council, meeting late into the previous night, had terminated his rule – almost as though he were not a dictator but just another parliamentary politician beset by a cabinet crisis. Before Mussolini drove to the palace, both Rachele and Claretta (whom a telephone tap recorded being rung at 3.45 am)[166] gave the same advice, despite their different peasant and Catholic bourgeois cultures and despite their womanhood: 'Arrest them! Kill them all!' 'You alone are the judge,' Claretta added emotionally. 'No one has the right to give you counsel or suggestion. Don't destroy yourself to satisfy those who do not understand you and wish you evil. Remember who loves you and who never tires of giving herself to you.'[167] But, on 25 July 1943, Mussolini did not listen. The Fascist regime, mark I, had collapsed. Could Claretta and the rest of her family find a path to a Fascist regime mark II? And what would Mussolini and his legitimate wife and children make of such a prospect?

6

THE WINTER OF A PATRIARCH AND HIS *DUCESSA*

On 29 August 1943 *Il Messaggero* carried a banner headline: 'Filmed: a life as it was lived.' A subheading added 'The Petacci family in Novara prison – How the fortune of Claretta Petacci and Miria di San Servolo was made and passed on.' In the small print of wartime, the front-page story was lavish in details. It began with the looting on the morning of 26 July of the medical practice of Francesco Saverio Petacci on the Via Nazionale. Furniture, books, white medical gowns, microscopes and stethoscopes had all rained down onto the street below. The crowd, it was reported, had joined the assault with 'knowing laughter and graphic commentary'. How, the paper asked artlessly, could someone who had written in its pages attract such hostility? Such a short time before, Dr Petacci's contributions had 'aroused scant or no interest', the account continued in more sardonic vein, even when, for example, they had respectfully attributed the following remarkable skills to his 'benefactor' (in the coy phrasing of the time):

> intuitive power (that is, the ability to foresee events), concentration, analysis, calculation, judgement, readiness in planning and decision-making, wide perspective, solid memory, iron will, self-control, energy, tenacity, firmness, resolution, imperturbability, a proper approach to all great issues, administrative skill, loyalty, eloquence, staunch psychic resistance and an excellent arterial system for nerves, lungs and brain.[1]

As a result of such ample 'knowledge', *Il Messaggero* observed, *Dottor F.S.P.* had been 'well looked after and protected' before July 1943 by 'a personage of the highest status'. Yet that *altissimo personaggio* had not cared so much about the doctor's medical science as about his 'cute daughter, Claretta by name'. She had presented herself one day to this 'most elevated personage' [still unnamed in the article] on the Roman Lido in a 'teeny bathing costume that allowed view of her by no means displeasing figure' and 'bronzed bosom'. Once introduced, this young woman had gushed about the poetry she had been accustomed to send him, while adding guilelessly that she loved flowers. In all honesty the man had struggled to remember her verses. But the next day they were back in contact and soon 'the personage' was inviting Claretta to 'visit his garden' at the Villa Torlonia, not a tiring trip since her house lay on the Via Spallanzani. In gratitude the man in question organised an exhibition of Claretta's paintings at the Collegio Romano in the Campus Martius, although, since Claretta had talked of art but not actually painted, the family had to rush around to hire someone else to daub some artwork that could be shown. The hired hand did so at a rate of four paintings per day.

Thereafter their mutual infatuation 'spread with the fury of a fire'. The protector, despite being of a certain age, was 'completely smitten'. Claretta, as a 'worthy daughter' of her family, did not want to keep the *altissimo personaggio* for herself alone but happily shared him with her sister, the *bel canto* singer and film star 'Miria di San Servolo'. While such generous apportioning prospered, the Petaccis moved into a 'delightful villa on Rome's periphery'. There, or on trips to the Adriatic, Giuseppina Persichetti, 'the mother', 'followed the twists and turns of the happy idyll' with approval and support, even if the unnamed personage's jealousy now 'locked Claretta away [in the Villa Camilluccia] for weeks on end'.[2] On 25 July the Petaccis speedily left Rome for Milan, whence they soon fled to Boggiano's family castle at Meina on the Piedmont–Lombardy border.

According to the additions in Paolo Monelli's unpublished biography, news of Mussolini's fall had sent Giuseppina into a rage against the King and Badoglio, while Myriam wandered around the Villa Camilluccia crying (in a curious ordering of her thoughts) that the mob would kill everyone and rob them of all that they had accumulated.[3] At Meina, on

12 August, Claretta, her mother, father and sister were arrested. They were then escorted to the Castello Visconteo-Sforzesco gaol in Novara, to much gossip and censure in the town, focusing on their 'corrupt' dallying with the *altissimo personaggio*.[4] (Boggiano had earlier been confined at the Regina Coeli prison in Rome.)

Thus was the scandal salaciously narrated, with journalists ignoring Marcello, who, from 20 August, had also been imprisoned at Forte Boccea in the capital after initial confinement by the naval authorities at Taranto. He was threatened with immediate trial and, at least in his frightened imagination, execution under charges of corruption and unacceptable association with the *Duce*.[5] However, he was released by the Germans on 12 September and escorted to a meeting at their embassy with such regime notables as Raffaello Riccardi, Attilio Teruzzi (minister of colonies 1939–43), Guido Buffarini Guidi's brother and General Renzo Montagna of the Fascist militia (to become police chief under the new regime). According to Montagna, he and the other Fascist bosses were appalled at having their lives linked to Marcello's; they loudly demanded that he be treated as a separate case and expelled from their presence.[6] Marcello was able quickly to get out of Rome, find Zita and his sons in a safe haven on Lago di Garda, transport them to Meina and then go down to Novara to discover what had happened to his parents and sisters.

* * *

In their denunciation of the Petaccis' sins and their glorying in their retribution in Rome, the newspapers failed to report the fate of the Villa Camilluccia, which was ransacked more thoroughly than the clinic in the Via Nazionale. By August Ursuline nuns of the Most Holy Crucifix had taken it over as an orphanage, despite what they described as its battered state. They found room for fifty children in its generous interior.[7] For the time being, the Petaccis accepted this situation, although they compiled a long inventory of stolen property. It included fourteen pairs of shoes (they were recovered), a beaver-fur jacket worth 60,000 lire, belonging to Claretta, and three other furs, Myriam's property, the richest of which – of white ermine – was claimed as costing 150,000 lire; they were lost for ever.

So, too, were many silk negligees and quite a bit of beachwear. Numerous plush items of furniture also vanished.[8]

In regard to assaults on their persons and property, the Petaccis were treated worse than the Mussolini family, most of whom left for Germany on 27 and 28 July.[9] The Cianos, after a month of house arrest and in the face of rising public opprobrium over their wealth and its allegedly corrupt sources, were ill advised enough to follow them on 27 August, a fatal choice for Galeazzo.[10] Mussolini himself, after being bundled away from the royal palace, was confined first on the island of Ponza, taking over quarters that once housed an Ethiopian prince, and then at the naval base of Maddalena in Sardinia, across the water from Caprera, Garibaldi's island of retreat. There the fallen dictator received a belated sixtieth birthday present from Hitler of a complete twenty-four-volume German edition of Nietzsche's works, enough to keep him going for some time, it might be thought. Finally, from 28 August, Mussolini was escorted to Campo Imperatore, high in the Apennines east of Rome and south of the Terminillo resort, where, in their salad days, he and Claretta had disported themselves, sometimes with Myriam and Marcello in tow. It was from Campo Imperatore that, on 12 September, the *Duce* was rescued by an SS glider team, and delivered to a reunion with his legitimate family near Munich.[11]

* * *

The post-Mussolini regime, headed by Pietro Badoglio and lasting forty-five days, gave few indications of stirring a revolutionary tide among the Italian people, who wearily looked to the king and officer corps to chart a way out of a hopeless war. No one much protested when the new chiefs kept the word 'totalitarian' as a positive in their political vocabulary, went on executing peasant soldiers for 'desertion'[12] and did not immediately cancel anti-Semitic legislation. Revenge killing or other onslaughts against Fascist bosses were few, the shooting in mysterious circumstance of ex-PNF secretary Ettore Muti near the Roman Lido on 24 August being the exception.[13] Terms of surrender to the Allies were agreed on 3 September, but Badoglio and King Victor Emmanuel bungled the revelation of this deed and management of its military consequences.

On 8 September the two men skedaddled from Rome to Brindisi, while the vengeful Germans seized control of the country down to Naples and beyond. Thereafter Italy descended into civil war, fought between those willing still to call themselves Fascists and anti-Fascists from a wide political spectrum; one early victim was Claretta's cousin, Raffaele Persichetti,[14] who died near the Ostiense station in Rome on 10 September. There a road is now named after him, skirting a number of Fascist buildings and running alongside what from 1938 to 1944 was the Viale Adolf Hitler. The bitter conflict, often as in this case splitting families and friends, continued for twenty long months while Anglo-American forces slowly pushed north. During that time, a resuscitated Fascist Republic – with Mussolini as puppet dictator and equipped with a constitution after a meeting at Verona in November 1943 – shared governance in the north with the ever-more ruthless Germans. Killings of soldiers and civilians multiplied on the ground, while a regular toll of victims was exacted through what our neoliberal leaders now euphemistically call 'aerial strikes'; by 1945 more Italians had died from wartime bombing than Britons, despite the entrenched memory in that country of the Blitz. Some 200,000 Italians had perished in the conflict until July 1943; more than 250,000 fell between then and the advent of peace in May 1945.

The hostility aroused by the Petaccis during the forty-five days of the new regime deserves notice, indicating deep popular resentment at their social climbing and rumoured corruption, as well as a dislike and perhaps envy of the dictator's unrestrained and flaunted sexuality (one popular curse against the *Duce* during the war had been that he be punished by someone cutting off his balls).[15] Nonetheless, the Petaccis' experience at this time turned out to be an ill wind that blew some good, at least until April 1945, all the more so since Romilda Ruspi and the Pallottellis may have had a few unpleasant weeks but they escaped the punishment inflicted on the Petaccis. In the Novara gaol, the irrepressible Claretta was scribbling away at a prison diary; it would become a useful document after the Petaccis' eventual release and, during the Repubblica Sociale, the regular emphasis on family distress and sacrifice that she depicted shored up her connection with the dictator. Mussolini's sister remembered her brother saying after the Petaccis' release that he could not break with Claretta after she had suffered so much for him.[16]

As the anonymous editor of a 1946 edition put it, Claretta's prison diary constituted 'a document of exaltation and morbid passion which history, more than the news, should not ignore'.[17] It combined in characteristic fashion Catholicism, the family, Claretta's infatuated love for Mussolini and a politics, half fanatically Fascist and half self-interested, that trickled down into and from it.

The first entry was on 12 August, with Claretta imagining herself narrating to 'Ben' her and her family's sad fate as they were dragged into Novara, an arrival that coincided with a violent air raid. Their property was seized, they were strip-searched, the three women locked in a small, dirty, dingy cell and Francesco Saverio separated from them. 'I've always been terrified of prison,' Claretta confided to her pages, 'my mental state wavers; may the great and good God help and save us, we can do no more'.[18]

The second day brought further deterioration. Giuseppina was collapsing under the conditions; the mottled skin, which Zita had once noted, may have been a sign of high blood pressure, and she had been treated for heart trouble since 1940. An undated appeal by her to the Novara police chief during her imprisonment, requesting the return of her fur coat to keep her warm (despite it being August), contains an impressive list of other illnesses including lingering pleurisy, throat blockage, ear pain provoked by a radical mastoid surgery with frequent re-intensification, chronic inflammation of the colon (a legacy of another botched operation) and appendicitis. 'I cannot put up with the cold and the humidity,' she wrote, 'and have an absolute need for covering at night.'[19] She equally found time to list the 'family jewels' taken from her; they had belonged to her father, she stressed with studied ingenuousness.

While awaiting charity, the Petacci women summoned Francesco Saverio to their aid. He must have been allowed to keep his black bag on his admission to prison and arrived to give his wife an injection.[20] He was then escorted back to his cell but that night the family came together in the prison air raid shelter. 'I've never seen Papà cry,' Claretta observed first sadly and then vengefully. 'May this unmerited evil fall on the head of whoever has struck us down.'[21]

On Sunday, 15 August, Myriam fainted at the pain and disgrace of her treatment, while Claretta meditated wrathfully on the 'injustice' that had 'thrown into prison people who have never done anything wrong to a living soul . . . What will happen to us? What has happened to Armando [whom she knew was in gaol in Rome] and Marcello?' 'Why, Ben, why?' she asked her imagined interlocutor emotionally. 'Is it perhaps a crime for us to have loved as I did you in purity? Where are you? What are you doing? At least if you think of me, I shall be less alone,' she reasoned hopefully.[22]

The Petaccis' prison days continued. On 16 August Giuseppina endured a worse cardiac attack, a crisis due to which, according to Claretta, even the nuns and other detainees wept over her sad condition. Claretta feared her mother was dying: 'Mamma was leaving us, everything was collapsing all about us, everything to do with us was finished if she died.' 'It's atrocious what is happening, Ben,' she expostulated, still writing as though he were in the next room. 'You loved your Mamma and can understand me, can grasp the atrocity of these moments of supreme anguish.' Such thought reminded Claretta of her own medical crisis in 1940 and of Mussolini's solicitude for her during that time. 'Your caress, your love, your voice were my medicaments,' she scrawled again a few days later, seeking self-consolation in her prose.

Only Dr Petacci's injections seemed minimally to steady Giuseppina's health, and her husband was allowed to stay the night perhaps because, as Claretta stated, the head of the prison was both moved and alarmed by the Petaccis' evident tribulation.[23] The fleas and cockroaches, the 'fat, black scorpions' in the cell, reminded Claretta of the plight of Silvio Pellico, whose memories of Austrian imprisonment constituted one of the school textbooks of Risorgimento history.[24] She herself was ill with fever, she groused. Myriam had spent a whole day in tears. The other female common prisoners were noisy, ugly and horrible. As she remarked, they sang constantly, either 'of the most obscene matters' (unsuitable to a genteel Catholic ear) or 'a sad, lugubrious dirge' (which demonstrated how far their class culture was from hers). Only the nuns were good: 'little, delicate, thoughtful: a breath of human sweetness amid so much bitterness'.[25] When on the 22nd Claretta knelt in piety in the prison church, however, it was for Mussolini and not for her mother whom she prayed. He also dominated her dreams on the two following nights.

Yet her family did not lose its prominence in Claretta's life. So, she registered fearfully on 25 August, there was a threat to send her to another prison, perhaps back in Rome, and 'to divide us one from another'. 'To leave Mamma without Papà would kill her, do you understand Ben?' she wrote. 'Kill her. She needs continuous injections, she weeps, she is mistreated and overcome. Oh! My Ben. What have you done and what have we done to be shut in like this?' That evening, however, she and Myriam were feeling more sparky when they took their daily walk in the prison courtyard. 'Mimi and I did the goose step [*passo romano*] up and down and sang Fascist songs, especially the one about *Battaglione M*, and *Giovinezza*, and that which finishes "*Duce, Duce, Duce!*"' she recorded just a little vaguely.[26] Such behaviour 'really irritated the sentinels and the guards but we did not give a stuff at all about that and kept going as long as we could, thereby comforting ourselves'. They even did some gymnastics, reminding Claretta romantically of her sportive days with 'Ben' by the seaside at Castelporziano.[27]

On 29 August there was a new, deeper, 'great pain' to be endured. A copy of *La Gazzetta dello Sport* had come into their hands and it repeated the scandalous account of the Petaccis in *Il Messaggero* and other mainstream papers. How disgusting it was to read of Myriam being dragged into the affair, Claretta whined. 'It really went beyond the bounds of decency' thus to be exposed to 'popular derision'. 'Can you imagine, Ben,' she asked her missing partner, 'the effect on Mamma and Papà, from whom we failed to hide the paper? They wept all day. I swallowed my tears as usual and so did Mimi. Then, that night, Mimi was struck by a terrible attack of stomach pain . . . We were in despair. I cried for Armando about whom we know nothing. Can you believe it, Ben, I seem to live a life beyond reality, in a tough arena where neither logic nor intelligence reign?' All Italians had gained so much from two decades of Fascism, Claretta maintained defiantly. But now its credo was deemed 'utterly horrendous'. Only the lost war had provoked such a reversal in attitudes. As usual, however, it did not take her long to switch from public to private thoughts. 'The suffering has cut years from my life – my hair is going white,' she protested. Once 'Ben' had hoped to see 'snow in her curls'. But where was he now, as she sought him 'in every light and shadow and every dream'?[28]

The days limped by and her invocations of 'Ben' and her love for him grew still more intense. 'Our heart,' she wrote with an unspoken opposition to the science of her medical family, 'commands our nervous system, our very fibre, our will, our desire, anxiety, memory, sense of pain.' Such emotions, with 'the ability to wait and hope, live, breathe, tremble', lay beyond any 'power, effort or brake'.[29] She was a total prey to them; they commanded her being. Nor was her jealousy quite overcome. On 4 September she wondered at the current fate of Ruspi, Pallottelli, their children, Rachele and even Cesira Carocci, Mussolini's housekeeper at the Via Rasella during the 1920s. Was she the only woman in his life to be wracked by such torment, Claretta asked pathetically, again unable to stem her tears? If only he were keeping to that slogan of once upon a time: *Nec tecum nec sine te vivere possum* ('I can neither live with you nor without you').[30]

* * *

By 7 September Claretta calculated that she had endured 'twenty-seven sleepless nights', perhaps hyperbole given the regularity with which she welcomed Mussolini's appearance in her dreams. Giuseppina was ill again on the 8th and Francesco Saverio was only permitted briefly to bring comfort, leaving Claretta to make the camphor injections that her mother needed: 'I trembled at the thought of messing them up,' she confessed anxiously. Her nerves were a wreck until she slept. But she woke more happily to think herself back in the Sala dello Zodiaco, with the taste of her lover on her lips.[31]

Two days later, the news of the armistice with the Allies belatedly arrived at the prison, with Claretta bewailing the fact that 'it is the end, it is the end. The end of our Italy, of our grandeur, the end of empire, of everything'. Communism, she prophesied fearfully, would take over, unless the Germans advanced in time to seize the whole country. And where was Mussolini? What had the 'traitors' done to him? While she waited for answers, her family, she lamented, were not being fed anymore; the authorities were behaving towards them 'with a Russian-style cruelty'.[32]

Still no information percolated into the gaol from outside. One torrid day and night succeeded another. Now Claretta told 'Ben' that, for twenty-seven days, the Petacci women had been praying, morning and evening, to the Madonna of Pompeii (*la Beata Vergine del Santo Rosario di Pompei*; her religious site had been founded in the late nineteenth century and expanded notably under the regime) 'for your safety, for your liberation'. 'I have faith, I have faith,' she swore emotionally, readily fusing her Catholicism and her Fascism as her comforters.[33]

By Monday, 13 September, the Germans had reached Novara, the imprisoned Fascists had been released, with some immediately taking over guard duty at the Visconteo-Sforzesco prison. But no succour arrived for the Petacci family. Perhaps it was Freudian of Claretta to record her dream that night that Mussolini was betraying her with a 'foreign woman', with people depressing her with stories that he did so every day. Setting aside heretical thoughts about her lover, now she transmogrified her Christian God into a human God; she prayed to 'my Ben: free me. Today,' she added, 'I learned by chance that Hitler called you "his most faithful friend", and I wept with joy and emotion.'[34] Two days later, still lost and abandoned, she was flustered lest Mussolini was angrily staying away in dread that she had become a '*Presidentessa* like Sarfatti'. 'But do you not realise the gulf between that woman and me?' Claretta remarked with radical Fascist propriety. 'Race, only race. Race which dominates all the rest!' When, in May and June, she had warned him against the traitors enveloping his life and regime, it had only been for his good. He must not count her foresight against her. Feeling cosier with that thought and ideologically armed for a Nazi-fascist republic, she cried herself to sleep.[35]

Finally, on 16 September, came the promise of release, but not – as in Claretta's dreams – following her lover's miraculous arrival. First to reach the prison was instead Armando Boggiano, Myriam's husband. 'I cannot describe to you,' she explained as if Mussolini were near, 'how their reunion went. They fell on each other. They held each other in their arms, crying. Pallid, emaciated, destroyed. Fifty days of prison [for Armando], with no food, [except for] bread and water and soup, a quarter of a hour's walk, a small hole in the ceiling to let in air, and all alone, alone, like a beast raddled by fleas and other such things.' Then Marcello, who had actually been the one to contact the Germans and arrange the family's exit from gaol, turned up. How well the Petacci family had resisted their cruel fate,

Claretta crowed, however fretfully, even as they waited until the next morning actually to walk free.

'And you, my Ben, you naturally have forgotten me completely. Not a word for me,' she groaned. Nor had there been any kindly message for the Petaccis, whose family life had been 'destroyed' for him. 'What will happen to us?' she asked plaintively. 'I put up with everything, I suffered everything, I struggled not to die and now, now, the end awaits me. Without your love, it is the end.'[36] When they finally made ready on 17 September to go to Marcello's Villa Schildhof, she again mentioned to her lover how she kissed first the images of Santa Rita the Madonna of Pompeii, and then his photo. Maybe, she hoped, again prostrating herself to his grandeur, 'you will understand me'.[37]

Travelling northeast the next day proved a troubling wartime journey, with three tyres blown out before they got to Bergamo. They had stopped to find a replacement Fiat Balilla at a Nazi-controlled air base when the news came that Mussolini was to hold forth on the radio at 9.30 p.m. from Germany. They stayed to listen[38] and Claretta's emotional effusions (and sensuality) boiled over. 'You speak, you speak to the people still . . . but to me it seems you speak also to me. Your soul passes into mine in drops and I feel you within me as before. I am transfused as always! Your unique words, your touching phrases, your way of speech, so human, simple, precise, poetic.' When he finished, she fainted to the consternation of the rest of his audience, and had to be revived with cognac.

They went back to their car and, with a military escort, drove into the night: 'I was in ecstasy, shuddering with love and poetry, transfixed by melancholy and adoration, with fat, slow, hot tears pouring down my face while I begged Santa Rita desperately to let me see you again.' In Claretta's sensibility, the very stars glittered as they had never done before. They reached Marcello's villa only to find he had forgotten the keys. But they knocked up the German garrison and were told to move instead to the Albergo Parco in Merano, which they reached, exhausted, at 6 a.m.

The Petaccis were safe; even Zita Ritossa now joined them, narrating how she had had to flee from one sanctuary to another during 'fifty' days, avoiding arrest at Trieste by a lucky ten minutes. Boggiano, who had not taken well to imprisonment and the concurrent sequestration of his property, and had had enough of his wife's family, went off by himself.[39] Soon it was clear that, despite the poignant embraces in the prison of a few days before, his marriage to Myriam was disintegrating. But the more important questions, certainly for Claretta, were whether her relationship with Mussolini survived, and how it could be fitted into the new politics of what was becoming the Social Republic.

* * *

In his oration, said by some to have been delivered in tired and depressed tone, Mussolini spoke in terms that his Nazi rescuers applauded. He had been betrayed, he maintained, by those same forces that had always held back his regime. Now 'the state that we want to institute will be national and social in the highest sense of these words; that is, it will go back to the origins of Fascism,' he proclaimed. It would also be bloody; its prime task was to 'annihilate the parasitic plutocracy'.[40]

Naturally enough there was no room for talk of love on such occasion. Nor did Mussolini admit any influence from his relationship with Claretta in a short memoir that he, ever the able journalist, rushed out to portray his imprisonment. Indeed, in his *Pensieri pontini e sardi* ('Thoughts on Ponza and in Sardinia'), he was categorical in rejecting demeaning suggestions that he had been prey to women. Females, he repeated, 'have never had even a minimum effect on my politics'. He was not finished with the subject, however, adding somewhat perplexingly: 'Perhaps that was an advantage. Yet, thanks to their delicate sensibility, women are more far-sighted than men.'[41] Thoughts of both Rachele and Claretta warning him in July 1943 to 'kill them all' may have been lurking beneath the patriarchal phrases, while he hurried on to another cliché about himself. He was a 'loner', he bragged; in his whole life he had never had a friend and been all the better for that lack.[42]

In the weeks following his release, Mussolini had much to decide. Rapidly he was detached from Rachele and the children, travelling to see Hitler at Rastenburg near the Eastern Front. The *Führer* made it known that, should the *Duce* prove unwilling to return to command, German vengeance on the Italian people would be drastic.[43] In any case, like many a politician, Mussolini, for all his depression and pessimism about the war, had not lost a sense of his own indispensability. The Nazis were telling him what he wanted to hear when they continued to applaud him as the only possible *Duce*. Meanwhile, German doctors fussed about, seeking a remedy for Mussolini's ulcer; eventually Georg Zachariae was appointed as a court medical expert who stayed with the *Duce* almost to the end, and later published an apologetic memoir about his experience, full of admiration for Mussolini's intellect and human generosity.[44]

On 27 September Mussolini re-entered Italy, initially staying at the Rocca delle Caminate, with plans already drafted to create what, in November, was formalised as the Repubblica Sociale Italiana.[45] It became known as the Salò Republic, after the small town on Lago di Garda that housed some of its reconstituted ministries, although others were scattered across Venetia, with the Ministry of Foreign Affairs, for example, based in Venice itself. By 11 October Mussolini had taken residence in the Villa Feltrinelli at Gargnano, halfway up the lake's western shore. The large and elegant structure stood in an estate of 8 acres owned by the publishing family, with space for an orchard, a tennis court and a guardroom to house the thirty members of the SS who defended and monitored the restored *Duce*. The villa became a combined office for a puppet dictator and residence for his extended (legitimate) family, with Gina Ruberti and her little daughter Marina, Vittorio Mussolini, his wife and children, Arnaldo's son Vito, and various other relatives finding continuous or sporadic shelter there. By one estimate, after October 1943, more than two hundred people related to Mussolini had taken sanctuary at the villa or in other quarters near Lago di Garda.[46] In one of his letters to Claretta in January 1945, Mussolini noted that family food supplies were bolstered by the presence of a cow, a newborn calf, two pigs – one live, one recently slaughtered – a few dozen egg-laying hens, some rabbits, three dogs and two cats. Despite such rural joys, Mussolini almost always ate alone, he told her, ostentatiously solitary even at his table.[47]

On 8 November Rachele returned from Germany with the two teenage children, Romano and Anna Maria, to be greeted by Mussolini with what his new secretary, Giovanni Dolfin, judged to be 'deep affection'. Rachele charitably enquired about her husband's health and then moved more aggressively to curse those who had betrayed him, notably their son-in-law, Ciano.[48] Here, then, was the major issue of the moment, another matter where private and public life intermingled. A fortnight earlier, Mussolini had conceded to Dolfin that universal hatred was being directed at Ciano 'in order to strike me'. Ciano, he affirmed, was no worse than many another, a conclusion that he was inclined to voice with the appearance on 20 October of Edda, her unauthorised arrival prompting quibbles from the SS to what they obviously viewed as their Italian underlings.[49] Despite her 'open marriage', Edda was another woman fixated on saving her husband, rather as both Rachele and Claretta had been in regard to Mussolini on 25 July.[50]

But Mussolini, for all his overriding egoism, knew two things. Ciano's fate was sealed. Both the Germans and the radical Fascists were determined that his son-in-law must die. His death was a punishment for the 'treachery' of 25 July, as well as for Ciano's deep doubts since 1939 about the Axis alliance. Yet, at the same time, Ciano had to face the executioners because of the inadequacy of the dictatorship; because, for all its propaganda boasts, it had proved neither totalitarian nor revolutionary. Ciano may have been at heart a young conservative who donned a black shirt in deference to the fashion of the times. But the real failure, the person who in fact had allowed the 'Italian dictatorship' to remain 'Italian' – coursed by many historical currents and not only those of a total modern ideology and political religion – was Mussolini. He lived on. Ciano was shot at Verona on 11 January 1944. During the three months preceding that event, Mussolini feebly accepted that he could do nothing to stop it, a failure that came at the cost of severing his ties with his favourite child and with a bright young man who had so often been his sounding-board in matters of war and peace.

* * *

By January 1944 then, Arnaldo, Bruno and Galeazzo were dead, while Edda brooded in self-imposed exile in Switzerland. As has been repeatedly remarked, Mussolini was given to congratulating himself for being a loner. Yet, throughout his life, he gave plenty of indication of needing human company of some definition. Once Galeazzo and Edda were gone, Claretta Petacci filled an evident vacuum. Mussolini may have treated the Petaccis during their imprisonment as though they had never been. But, under the Salò Republic, despite the objections of Rachele and a faction of radical Fascists, who, in April 1944 and again at the year's end, plotted to murder Claretta and end her dalliance with the *Duce*,[51] Claretta and the rest of her family were reinforced as mainstays of the dictator's life, and Claretta transmuted from being mainly a sex object into a cherished counsellor.

Contact between the lovers had resumed on 4 October with a phone call from the Rocca delle Caminate to Merano. In Claretta's diary version, it mainly consisted in a long whinge from Mussolini about the treachery that he had suffered, his bad health, disgusting diet and depression, before moving on to arrangements to secure further contact, either by phone or letter. The *Duce* did not forget to salute 'Mimi' and the rest of the Petacci family and to regret the devastation of the Villa Camilluccia, while slipping in a jealous enquiry whether Claretta had anywhere been 'molested'. He and she, he declared, must accept that most people hated them. Finding a refuge for her would be vexing. But he would write soon in full detail about what might be done for her and her loved ones.[52] Given the malfunctioning of the phone system at Salò, the fact that it was no secret that the Germans tapped all calls to and from the *Duce*, and the difficulty that the lovers had in seeing each other physically, from now on letters became their chief vehicle of contact and expression. Between October 1943 and April 1945, Mussolini communicated with his young partner about twice every three days, often at considerable length.[53] She responded even more copiously (often, it was said, with her mother automatically reviewing her prose).[54] Giuseppina and Myriam conducted their own correspondence with Mussolini. By the time they were established in their own accommodation on the lake, their typist was Zita Ritossa's eighteen-year-old brother Giuseppe, who must have been protected from military call-up for this important war work; according to his sister, he often acted as a secretary for his de facto brother-in-law, Marcello.[55] It was another case of matters being kept in the family.

The first actual meeting of the lovers occurred on 28 October under close German surveillance and with Claretta, when she travelled towards her partner, praying to 'God and my Santa Rita to help me and look after me as they always have done', while through other spare moments she recited the rosary, as she now claimed to do every evening. Once they were in each other's company, the lovers talked for an hour and more about the double theme – public and private – of the 'martyrdom' that each had endured and the tragedy inflicted on the 'crucified' nation. Eventually they went to bed presumably for sex (but Claretta recorded the orgasmic *sì* no more) and chatted 'through the night without a single interruption'. Inevitably Mussolini's thoughts turned to Ciano and his likely sad fate, even if their conversation found no cure for his concern. The *Duce* lamented that it was sadistic of people to 'see if you are brave enough to eliminate your son-in-law' (and dishonour his own grandchildren). 'He will do what he must. I feel that he is profoundly upset and sad, and I understand him,' Claretta wrote trying to be helpful, or to seem such.[56]

This night of love was very much the exception in their lives. By 15 November Claretta was being instructed by post that she and her family must accept housing at the Villa Fiordaliso at Gardone Riviera, some 20 kilometres south of the Villa Feltrinelli. At least it was better there than to be rusticated to Malcesine far off on the other side of the lake, as the Germans had initially planned.[57] The quickest method of communication was by a fast motorboat but it is unclear how many times Mussolini was able to use such a method to join his lover. The Renaissance Torre San Marco on the shoreline, reachable across the lake from the Villa Feltrinelli, was an occasional venue for sex;[58] Claretta's double bed in the villa seldom.

Claretta's diary now omitted her sexual encounters with the Duce almost entirely, except for the occasional lament that a meeting had been hurried and unsatisfactory: 'the joy and intensity of an instant' was 'succeeded by the desolate sadness of a brevity' which prevented any 'interesting talk'.[59] Such emphasis on a now more mature and political relationship is, however, contradicted by immediate postwar claims that the two still had trysts 'two or three times per week'.[60]

The Villa Fiordaliso was not large. Space in it had to be found for Claretta and her parents, her youthful, perhaps worryingly manly, SS guard, Franz Spögler (who had been born in the Alto Adige), and Ono

Shichiro – correspondent of the *Mainichi Shimbun* from Tokyo and son-in-law of the Fascist propagandist Shimoi Harukichi – and his family.[61] Ono and Claretta became friends, according to his postwar account, with him remembering that she often ate a solid breakfast on the terrace while reading the papers of the day, thereafter lying in the sun to improve her tan. He also recalled that she had regretted not being Japanese since, in his country, 'belief and trust' still 'meant something'.[62] The Petacci papers show Ono acting as a delivery boy for messages from Claretta to the *Duce*, thereby avoiding the ban, which Vittorio Mussolini, endeavouring unsuccessfully to cement a major role in his father's political life, tried to impose on Claretta and her family[63]

Mussolini's further advice to Claretta (whom he now always addressed as 'Clara') as she settled into the Villa Fiordaliso was guarded: 'I beg you to lead a completely reserved and absolutely quiet life. Don't let anyone see you. Don't seek out anyone. Have yourself forgotten.' But he did end romantically: 'There is, however, one whom you should not forget and will never forget because he remains always the same. Your Ben.'[64] In other letters around this time Mussolini counselled Claretta and her family to flee while it was still possible to do so, not to Switzerland, where there were too many 'renegades', but best to Hungary, although she must be aware that the roads were 'infested with partisans' and insecure, while the widely bruited scandal of the Villa Camilluccia continued to heap up popular hatred against the Petacci family. She must always destroy his every letter, he insisted (ineffectually).[65]

By 19 December the two were discussing an elaborate project, which sounded as though Marcello may have been its progenitor. Could Marcello be made the RSI's commercial attaché in Budapest, given that Hungary was a country with which diplomatic relations survived, Claretta had suggested, perhaps under the name Signor Colfosco-Schwagenek? It was all a little intricate, Mussolini replied gently. It would be better for Marcello just to go to Budapest on a 'service passport' and establish a 'centre for economic and political information' for which, the *Duce* noted drily, 'he had a disposition'. Could he not choose a more Italian name than Schwagenek, since it would only arouse queries? Yet he did insist that the Petacci name possessed the same notoriety as his own, warning Claretta that it was 'of the highest danger that you are such a short distance away'. In a postscript he added wearily that it was quite absurd for her to start worrying again about other women. 'You must not complicate my life,' he admonished her, 'if you want to save your own.'[66]

Mussolini however was not being entirely frank with his lover over his contacts with his sometime partners. In October Alice Pallottelli had written a letter addressed to 'my dear Prime Minister', rejoicing in his liberation and expressing anguish at his affliction, while declaring 'the flame of hope' still burned in her heart and predicting 'further miracles'. Through Dolfin, Mussolini offered advice to her to leave Rome for the north where she and her children would be safer.[67] Virgilio Pallottelli had returned from his time as a POW and, during 1944–5, won a prominent place in Mussolini's personal entourage, with his mother sounding maternal as she asked Dolfin to remember that Virgilio was 'an exuberant young man who sometimes needs a brake and protection'.[68] In May 1944 Virgilio sent the dictator a copy of a memoir that he had prepared of his air crash and imprisonment, underlining the hatred of the enemy for 'our race now that it is finally tired of being enslaved'.[69] He was destined to be a member of the final convoy that took Mussolini and Claretta to their deaths in April 1945, when he was known to be a friend of Elena Curti, Mussolini's illegitimate daughter, who, it has been noted, had engaged in regular contact with her father since 1942, ties that were not broken under the RSI. She, too, would be there in April 1945.

Romilda Ruspi had similarly not lost her connection with her long-time lover, even if the archives do not allow exact tracking of her life after July 1943. In April 1945 she was at Monza, near Milan, but she was one of Mussolini's harem who herself did not go – nor have a family representative present – on the last convoy. Throughout the RSI, however, Claretta certainly could not, and did not, forget her, as shall be seen below.

* * *

When the New Year of 1944 dawned, for Mussolini the great issue was the fate of his son-in-law and elder daughter, a tragedy which, he wrote, was 'shaking him profoundly'. After 1945 surviving members of the Petacci family would portray a magnanimous Claretta who had tried to persuade Mussolini not to accept Ciano's execution, the most romantic story being told by Zita Ritossa, which sounded as though it might have been influenced by an opera plot. In this version, Claretta wanted Ciano to be substituted by another man justly condemned to death and hidden away until he could be led out to execution. But the plan was frustrated by alert German security.[70] In reality, however, Claretta had tried malevolently to stiffen Mussolini against his 'traitor' son-in-law, guilty, as she wrote, of having been 'systematically devoted to the [Fascist] system's disintegration'. For Claretta, Ciano deserved no mercy. Edda, in her judgement, was no better and her lover must not let himself feel sorry for his wayward daughter.[71]

In a cascade of letters following Ciano's execution, Claretta tried to ginger her lover into being a 'real dictator' again, while not forgetting to urge him to accept her protector, Guido Buffarini Guidi, as his leading counsellor. Equally the *Duce* should not forget that Hitler loved him. He must arrange soon to meet the *Führer* and obtain from him the 'understanding and help' that he and the RSI needed and deserved.[72] In such advice, Claretta envisaged a quadripartite alliance of herself (and, presumably, Marcello),[73] Buffarini Guidi, Mussolini and Hitler to dominate the new order. Despite her many retreats and her flaunted humility, Claretta had become a woman willing and anxious to assume a political role.

The other Petaccis had not disappeared, with Giuseppina writing early to Mussolini emphasising the 'holocaust' [*sic*] that her family had undergone for him at Novara, and urging him to make use of their 'pure and intelligent youth'.[74] In January 1944 she demanded more specifically that a position be found for Marcello, by implication a rewarding one that would safeguard 'him and his little angels [her grandsons]'.[75] She did not say so, but Boggiano had been paying the family bills at Merano, and the Petacci lifestyle, even at this stage of the war, needed replenishment.[76] Francesco Saverio kept in character, too, when he opened correspondence with the *Duce* from the Villa Fiordaliso, but merely enclosing a detailed weekly diet. It entailed an intake of from four to seven pills per day and a nightly injection.[77] Dr Petacci himself did not carp about the curtailment of his medical career but, on 21 February, Claretta chided her lover for ignoring her father's 'moral misery into which he has fallen because of us'.[78]

Myriam, although only just approaching her twenty-first birthday, was as practical as her mother and more forthright in rebuking the *Duce* for not paying enough attention to her sister, thus allowing her to sag, to become 'tired, deluded, prostrate, absent, in sum incoherent and exasperated'.[79] But Myriam also had Armando to consider and her rocky marriage. 'In spite of every effort,' she informed Mussolini, 'Armando has not been able to revive his textile factory and believes that he will never succeed in doing so.' No doubt, Mussolini's benevolent help had allowed him to restore his *palazzo* in Milan and systematise some of his other holdings. Yet more could be done for him. 'Now listen to what I am asking you,' Myriam charged. 'As you know there are official places available to control the sequestration of Jewish textile concerns.' Could not Armando become a '*commissario* or some such' in that activity and take over a large business with lots of workers? Such a post would allow him to 'rediscover his equilibrium after many painful events have struck at him so badly and then he could in a happy tomorrow return to being my husband in the real and noble fashion in which I had believed and dreamed'. Buffarini Guidi, she was sure, could deal with the details and thereby achieve 'the definitive systematisation of Armando'.[80]

Myriam's casual anti-Semitism, harnessed more to family advantage than ideological purity, is notable. However, the archives do not provide information whether this request to seize Jewish business was successful and, by spring 1944, Myriam and Armando had separated for ever, with Claretta's sister finding a new partner in the lawyer Enrico Mancini, apparently a close friend of her husband. By then Myriam's letters to the *Duce*, when they were not berating him for mistreating Claretta, sought with more direct self-interest his urgent intervention with Goebbels or others so that she could resume her film career. Fernando Mezzasoma, the RSI's Venice-based minister for popular culture, she dismissed rudely as 'a priest who says Mass at any altar going'.[81]

Marcello joined in the correspondence as well, notably in a long letter sent to Mussolini at the end of May 1944; he presumably did not know that, a month earlier, Mussolini had protested to Claretta over an 'unpleasant visit' from him, when Marcello (whom the dictator sardonically called 'Colfosco') had expatiated on a set of 'absurd and impossible proposals'.[82] Claretta's brother began his letter with yet another rebuttal of libels about his family reaching the *Duce* from their many enemies in what he plainly understood as a Darwinian world. 'The Petaccis have remained like few others with you and are capable of dying with you and for you in spite of the flames, the wreckage, the guns put to necks, the advance of the Anglo-Saxons and Bolshevism.' 'For millennia,' he ran on with bold assertion of historical significance, 'the Petaccis have taken their modest place solely as the fruit of their work and thought, and so today have a prime right to breathe freely notwithstanding the Badoglio people, the Fascists in bad faith and the imbeciles of every race.' Mussolini was the most powerful genius of the times and Claretta the greatest saint, racially sprung from the Santa Chiara of 1200, Marcello urged expansively. There must be no conflict between them and he was there to ensure it.[83] Mussolini simply must 'above all defend the woman who alone has followed you in pain and fortune and will follow you tomorrow whether to the calvary of defeat or the bright light of victory'.[84]

Late in January 1944 Claretta fell ill, receiving solicitude from a distance in Mussolini's regular letters.[85] But in early February she was strong enough to communicate at length, again summoning Mussolini to radical action. 'Today is the time for the revolution in the revolution. You are reborn.' The *Duce* must understand that 'you cannot live without me and I cannot live without you'. Nothing must be permitted to stand in their way. It was excellent that he was soon to meet Hitler and he must not in any way feel himself an inferior of the *Führer*. 'You are always Mussolini and he is Hitler. Nothing has changed ... He is your dearest friend.' They must stand together. 'You are two dictators struggling with the world. You must follow the same idea and pursue it to the end,' Claretta argued firmly.[86]

Occasionally she remembered sex. On 14 February Claretta wondered whether her Ben was yet asleep: 'I cannot as yet,' she mused. 'I want to sleep with you in the big bed as on 28 [October]. I desire to pass a whole night with you and I believe this will happen. Our love is stronger than everything and everybody.'[87] Less than a week before she had been imagining a solution to their sexual drought whereby Rachele ('your wife') would move out of the Villa Feltrinelli, either back to the Rocca delle Caminate or onto an island in the lake.[88] But the events of the war could always enhance her new political extremism. When Montecassino suffered a massive Allied aerial strike on 15 February, Claretta excoriated Pope Pius XII for his acceptance of such barbarism. The pope was vilely genuflecting to 'dollars and gold'. 'Ah our wretched Lord, our wretched religion. Today this pope is absolutely a figure without honour or dignity . . . Is it perhaps the end of the Christian religion? . . . I don't understand anything anymore,' she cried.[89]

But the epistolary exchanges with Mussolini brought little satisfaction, full as they were of the *Duce*'s deep depression, physical debility and psychological certainty that he now counted for nothing. On 23 March Claretta found the depression contagious as she complained: 'I cannot be and do not want to be in your cabinet.' She might express political views but they did not lie at the heart of her relationship with Mussolini, she contended. Or maybe jealousy of his other family was the real issue: 'I want to leave. I'm tired. I don't want to live like a prisoner, like a slave, like a beast in a cage', especially when those dwelling at Villa Feltrinelli – full, as she sarcastically put it, of 'Olas, Vitos, Idas and Ginas' – were in practice lording it over her.[90] When another of Marcello's schemes broke down, Claretta grumbled that she and her family were victims not merely of Badoglio but of 'you and yours'. He would react to her scolding merely with fudges as he always did, she predicted. 'Nothing remains for me but to abandon the field, in a totally just reaction to so much infamous wickedness, incomprehension, injustice, lack of courage in response to our courage. My love is being transformed into hatred and vendetta.' '*Addio*, Ben', her letter finished melodramatically.[91]

Mussolini hastened to calm her, although his prose soon wandered into his own depression, and he fixed a tryst with her for the following Sunday. But that proved impossible, all the more so because he had to get Party Secretary Pavolini to deal with a plan to kidnap or murder Claretta that had been brewing among radical Fascists, with the support of some of the *Duce*'s own family.[92] When Ben and Clara could arrange an assignation, their contact was always short and likely, as Mussolini observed, to be shredded by 'bitter' news from the war.[93] Claretta herself described how, 'to the joy and intensity of the moment, is added the desolating sadness of a brevity that prevents any interesting talk', although that did not stop her from writing to counsel the *Duce* to get closer to the Japanese through Ono Shichiro and Japanese ambassador Shinrokuro Hidaka. 'Listen to my advice,' she insisted yet again. 'Avoid the error of overvaluing the merits and capacity of your family circle,' especially Vittorio. He and his louche friends had cost his father 'the sympathy of all the Germans who love us'. The family circle was equally responsible for Mussolini's weak refusal to impose capital punishment on his opponents. All was not yet lost. He should work with Buffarini Guidi, who knew Himmler well, while Marcello was always worth a discussion, Claretta advised.[94]

Despite her rarely leaving the Villa Fiordaliso, it was now common for Claretta to endeavour to galvanise her partner into ever more brutal policies. It would be good to imagine another 25 July, she wrote, when, this time, Mussolini killed his enemies himself, as the German dictator had once done.[95] As he prepared for a meeting on 22 April with Hitler at Klessheim, the first since the foundation of the RSI, Claretta sent him composite preparatory material: detailed political notes, a photo and a holy image of Santa Rita. He must not bow to the *Führer* but instead simply assume 'absolute parity' with the Nazis and display 'a sharply defined and developed programme from which you must not even minimally diverge'. No German interference into Italian politics could be tolerated.[96] When he returned with paltry achievement and ruin grew closer, Claretta conjured up Fascist phantasmagoria as she imagined their death, 'buried under the wreckage caused by drunken negroes, Jews, plutocrats, and those sold for pleasure to these priests without a *patria* or religion, only because their chests are filling with dollars and pounds sterling'.[97]

* * *

For all the violence of Claretta's opinions, the relationship remained boxed in between the rival villas on the lake, with Mussolini supplicating his lover after his return from Germany: 'I beg you to have complete faith in me and in what I do and shall do. You must stay where you are, whatever happens.' There could be no ban on their love as had been attempted in May–June

1943.[98] Yet their meetings remained rare. Even when they happened, squabbling was likely to result, as for example after Mussolini on going home failed to phone Claretta with a love message. At the Villa Feltrinelli, Rachele still campaigned unrelentingly against her husband's lover, while among the Petacci family Myriam did not refrain from rushing off a letter to the *Duce*, again inveighing against his mistreatment of her sister. Giuseppina wrote attacking Rachele more directly, whom she accused of 'having entered *a state of insanity with murderous ideas based on a senile post-menstrual phobia*', entertaining 'mediocre, uncultivated and unscrupulous men', who defamed Claretta and planned worse actions.[99] As his women warred rowdily around him, Mussolini accepted the persona of puppet dictator, endeavouring without hope or strategy to appease each side.

In May 1944 Myriam despatched another broadside, maintaining that Claretta had decided to take Mussolini at his word when, in his weakness, he had asked to be left in peace and quiet; now she intended to separate herself from him. 'Love for you has reduced a woman to a state deprived of will and dignity. [Claretta] has been allowed to reach the pit of humiliation when she should possess the right to have near her the person who understands and comforts her and gives her a sense of life and a constant and devoted tenderness. She has not had one decent hour; nothing more than anxiety, punishment, vexation, calumny, gossip, betrayals.' It was intolerable, now that his wife was back from a trip to the Rocca delle Caminate, for there to be no communication with Claretta for a fortnight. 'I, *Duce*, just do not understand you anymore,' the twenty-one-year-old declared in an intrepid manner (not designed to appeal to all dictators), 'unless it is simply true, as Claretta keeps repeating, that now you have lost any love and any desire'. Could he at least ring her sister, she asked?[100] Further letters of this tone and sentiment followed, sometimes with an added request that more be done for Marcello,[101] who continued, generally to Mussolini's annoyance, to demand interviews with the *Duce* and to pursue his complex business affairs as though he had support from on high.[102]

For Mussolini, who was watching the Allied armies approach Rome, the onslaught from Myriam and the accusations from Claretta provoked minor rebellion when, on 22 May, he charged his lover over her single-mindedness and blindness to his multiple woes. 'The dominant note and in normal times the beauty of your love had been your egocentricity, your egoism driven to insurmountable limits. Nothing exists except it,' he protested. 'That the English are at Formia, Gaeta, Terracina and threaten Rome; that Italy is in flames and ashes; that I am trying to work amid a thousand difficulties, and with a thousand idiots and bastards, none of that has anything to do with you. You don't give a toss. You want what you want even if it means your and your family's ruin.'[103] Such retort did little to divert Claretta from her now accustomed rhetorical course, however. In regard to Rome, Claretta urged simplistically, he must rouse Hitler in the Eternal City's defence: 'Two Chiefs, two men, two friends, *alone* [sic].' It would not matter if, in grandiose battle, Rome was razed to the ground, she pronounced imperiously. What was important was that the two geniuses unite to defend it to the last.[104] Claretta's virulence about the fate of her own birthplace may have been exacerbated by the news that Mussolini had seen Ruspi again (only because – he claimed – her eldest son had died as an airman above Florence, after heroically refusing to dodge the draft).[105]

Over the summer the content of exchanges between the two did not vary much, although Claretta did sketch a series of charming cartoons of herself as Mussolini's 'little puppy dog' (sometimes being booted out of the august presence),[106] perhaps as much to while away her empty hours as to win her lover's applause for her artistic skill. In more solemn vein, she continued to push the crumpling *Duce* forward, somewhere and somehow, in order to defeat the 'war criminals', Roosevelt and Churchill: 'You are a Man of world stature. If today the Great God could allow you to sit at a table negotiating a just peace . . . You and you alone could give us and the world light and truth . . . Speak to Hitler, telegraph, write, communicate in some way . . . But courage, Ben,' she ended before a typical personal twist and the recommendation that above all 'you love me while there is still time'.[107]

* * *

On 15 July Mussolini set out by train on another visit to Germany, destined to coincide with the attempt five days later by Claus von Stauffenberg to blow the *Führer* to smithereens at his Wolf's Lair headquarters on the

Eastern Front. Mussolini should have been there too, but his train was late, delayed in Munich by Allied bombing. There could have been another reason for Mussolini's good fortune, since the anxious Claretta had again insisted that 'you do not forget the wallet with Santa Rita' in it, before hastening on with her familiar message to 'remember that you are alone, the only person who can save the world situation'. Despite such hopes she was terrified, she conceded, that he would not come back. She would 'kill herself' rather than falling into the hands of 'the English or the rebel Italians', she promised.[108]

When he did return, a little chuffed to find that Hitler had experienced his own '25 July', she declared: 'I prayed a lot. Santa Rita has again saved you for the good of this poor humankind.' He was happy enough to agree that the saint must have been useful, sentimentally assuring her he had been cocooned by her love and by her ability to act as a lightning rod for what was occurring both near and far off.[109] Claretta, more vengefully, tried to use the fact that Hitler, as well as Mussolini, was now one of 'two Great Men, betrayed in their certainties, work, and immense struggle', to demand that the *Duce* strike down his enemies inexorably, whether dissidents like Roberto Farinacci or – she did not say aloud – Rachele and the Mussolini family circle.[110]

* * *

For some months, the two lovers had been discussing where a refuge might be found for the Petacci parents with, as yet, no concrete result. But Myriam and her new partner had transferred to Spain in June, having first tried to organise the *Duce* into finding some well-rewarded job, for example as cinema or commercial attaché, for Enrico Mancini. 'The air [on Lago di Garda]', Myriam wrote in her usual blunt manner, has become 'impossible to breathe and, if I do not leave this madhouse as soon as possible, everyone will go mad'. That confession off her chest, she did not hold back from lambasting Mussolini's 'cruel indifference' towards her sister. He should come clean about his new lover (here perhaps were renewed suspicions about Elena Curti). He should ask why he permitted Rachele to drive him mad and so render everyone else insane. 'Examine your own conscience,' she urged, 'and do so serenely without false pride and egoism. Then you will find grave, the gravest wrongs and you will accept that I am right.' He had only himself to blame if Claretta made the sensible choice finally to leave him.[111] When Mussolini objected to such scathing words, Myriam gave no ground, instead further chastising him over her sister's 'prostration', before peremptorily adding that 'you must organise [matters in Spain] with the maximum seriousness, everything'.[112] Moreover, she was leaving in his charge her parents, Marcello and his children, and he simply must do more to free her brother to utilise his 'intelligence and devotion' in one or other of his excellent schemes.[113]

Once in Barcelona, Myriam wrote to Claretta to persuade her to join her and Mancini (Jesus would assist her to get there, she suggested), with Mancini adding a note that, deprived of her sister, Myriam spent every day weeping.[114] Petacci emotions, it seemed, swelled ever more abundantly. Myriam had taken with her some film rushes, hoping to transfer her cinema career to Franco's Spain, while Mancini pursued business interests, armed with a personal recommendation from Mussolini and the title of Italy's 'film commissar' to Spain.[115] Perhaps the *Duce's* visible backing helped pay the bill at the Hotel Ritz in Barcelona where the couple, as *Avv. Mancini and signora* ('Lawyer Mancini and wife'), first took residence.

Matters were complicated, however, by the Spanish regime's cautious failure to recognise the RSI and by the fact that the new Italian ambassador from the pro-Allied 'Kingdom of the South', Tommaso Gallarati Scotti, did not actually reach Madrid until February 1945.[116] Myriam and Mancini cast around but openings for them were few and Italians on the ground reported the fact that the two had brought no capital with them and found none in Spain.[117] In regard to Claretta's sister's career and well-being, Mussolini preferred to lie low but, in September, he did agree to write to Ramón Serrano Suñer, the retired minister of foreign affairs and Franco's brother-in-law, on her behalf. Serrano replied politely, but no financial advantage followed and, by Christmas, Myriam – who claimed to be suffering from appendicitis – returned to Italy with her partner.[118]

Her mother missed Myriam badly while she was away, as Claretta pointed out to Mussolini when there was further talk of some eventual sanctuary for the family.[119] One suggestion in July was that Claretta should follow her ex-husband, Federici, to Japan.[120] If her parents were to join Myriam in Spain, as was also projected, Claretta requested a hefty subsidy of 20,000 Swiss francs ('they only accept Swiss francs, dollars or sterling', she explained); that sum would allow them to live well enough for six months.[121] What, too, she did not fail to ask, should be done for Marcello's 'kiddies', for whom he was seeking some refuge?

But even as she fought for her family's good, Claretta was opening a familiar old front, that where Mussolini engaged with Ruspi. To Claretta's disgust, on 22 July 1944, the two had met again. He must see what a contrast, Claretta wrote in anger, Ruspi was, compared with herself, a woman 'dedicated to him as far as the holocaust'. Ruspi had set up at Varese, was living cosily with another man, and happily cashed the money that Mussolini over-generously passed to her. 'I tell you, with extreme frankness, Ruspi must be liquidated from your life,' Claretta exclaimed. 'If she has any need of financial help (in spite of the industrialist [her new partner]), she can go via your personal secretary. There must be no taxes [that is, coitus] of any kind paid and no excuses of any colour.' She was watching, she promised menacingly[122] (and, later that month and again in September, Mussolini had to fob off an ever-alert Claretta's irritable charges that he had seen his ex-lover, who herself had launched at least one tirade against Marcello and Petacci family 'corruption'). But, the *Duce* retorted listlessly, 'there is no new woman in my life' adding that, to his mortification, Claretta was wasting her time and money spying on Ruspi.[123]

In September the Petacci parents did transfer to Marcello's Villa Schildhof in the Tyrol, where, as Mussolini told Claretta, not altogether comfortably, the zone was 'for the moment, quieter' than Lago di Garda. In reality, he added gloomily, 'the internal situation worsens from one day to the next. The audacity of the partisans grows with every further demonstration of our *impotence* [sic].' As he had explained bleakly the day before: 'my nights are very long . . . I don't care if I die. I am an utterly ridiculous person.'[124] Not long after, his mood grew Stygian: 'Goodbye darling. If I could blow up the world with a load of dynamite I would do it and [take] *us* with it.'[125]

By late in the month Allied troops were marching across those regions where he had been born: 'Goodbye Rocca delle Caminate! Goodbye

Romagna! And, in not too long, goodbye Italy!' Soon, he thought, orders would come to flee to Germany. '*You must go and join your family* in Merano, from where you can come afterwards to where I go,' he counselled. 'I embrace you and am always Ben.'[126] Spain remained another possibility and Mussolini assumed the role of an elderly teacher when he tried to persuade Claretta that learning a new language would be easy, that he had already mastered it and that there was a great overlap in vocabulary with Italian. To speed her progress, he sent her a Spanish magazine to read.[127]

As one disaster followed another at the front, private and public still intermingled. On 10 October Mussolini wrote Claretta a review of his love life. 'Many women have fallen out of my life. I scarcely remember them,' he assured her. Although it turned out that he had seen Ruspi again a few days before, he pledged that she was only of interest because her children thought of him as a father; indeed, 'with my help, as was their due, they are now grown up and established. They have followed their destiny.' Pallottelli was living on Lake Como in straitened circumstances. Giulia Gangi was 'interned I know not where'. Giulia Brambilla had finally disappeared. Even Elena Curti had moved to Milan. Whatever had happened in the past, Claretta was his only love, Mussolini maintained: '*You are you and you are not comparable to any other being in the whole world. You are in my heart. You alone.*'[128]

* * *

Mussolini's harem may have threatened dissolution under the impact of war. But Rachele had by no means surrendered her man to his lover. Like Claretta, she had a team of spies at work and, on 28 September, upbraided her husband for seeing 'the pimp' Marcello, who, she griped, always worked on his sister's part. Four weeks later, the cold war that had rumbled on between the Villa Feltrinelli and the Villa Fiordaliso burst into flames. The first salvo was fired on Sunday, 22 October when local police chief Emilio Bigazzi Capanni burst into the Villa Fiordaliso, with personal orders from Mussolini to check if Claretta had been copying his letters to her. The dictator had repeatedly demanded that she tear them up, but she had disobeyed him and indeed copied some, although seemingly with Mussolini knowing that fact. When the police knocked at her door, Claretta, according to one romantic account, rushed to her bedroom, emerging to threaten the intruders with her revolver but fainting rather than firing a shot. She was revived with brandy and some heart medication. Incriminating evidence not being hard to find in the confined space of the Villa, Bigazzi Capanni left carrying Mussolini correspondence, but without arresting Claretta, despite what may have been instructions to do so.[129]

Back at the Villa Feltrinelli, Rachele was enraged at the evidence that yet another of her husband's compromises was in progress. So, according to a memoir account, on the morning of 24 October she marched into the office of the portly Guido Buffarini Guidi, until that moment a man who had tactfully persuaded both Rachele and Claretta that he was the privileged agent of each to the power elite of the RSI, equipped with the guile of 'not saying things out loud but letting them be understood'.[130] Now, however, Rachele commanded that he find a car and military support, and take her to her rival's villa. Nervously Buffarini Guidi agreed. Since Rachele was also by now a little stout, the two crammed into the back seat of a Fiat Topolino with an armed driver and headed south along the lake at 'a mad pace'. Once they arrived at the Villa Fiordaliso, Rachele pulled out her own revolver and, since the gates were locked, forced Buffarini Guidi to crawl through the fence, tearing his trousers in the process.[131]

Claretta came to the door, dressed as usual in a negligee (she was said generally to get up at 10 a.m. and then spend two hours grooming),[132] to be greeted by Rachele with a volley of insults, vociferated in 'the most expressive' Romagnol dialect; the word 'whore' was used more than once. Rachele pushed her way into the villa, shouting 'Signora, I am no longer young and I know it. But, believe me, if the *Duce* saw you at the moment, without all the make-up', he would 'not consider you any more as his idol'. Under such physical and verbal assault, Claretta burst into tears and fainted more than once, readily revived by a sip of the brandy that Buffarini Guidi had been quick to locate in the house. She doubtless thereby confirmed Rachele, who was proud never to have shed tears,[133] in her contempt. To exacerbate the pandemonium, Mussolini was contacted by phone, with accounts disagreeing whether he was rung by Claretta or Rachele or whether he himself, apprised of the confrontation, had used the line to try to calm the conflict between his wife and lover. Finally Rachele, after a couple of hours of abuse, yelled a lame if prescient imprecation: 'You will come to a bad end' and stalked out, pulling Buffarini Guidi with her.[134]

They then drove back to the Villa Feltrinelli where – in the account of German interpreter, Eugen Dollmann – Buffarini Guidi, 'breathless, dishevelled and bathed in perspiration . . . tottered in and flung himself down on the sofa with a groan, having first . . . tossed aside something which looked suspiciously like a revolver. Then he moaned: "*Queste donne, ah, queste donne*" ['These women, ah, these women'].'[135] Mopping his brow, he proceeded to relate to Dollmann all that had transpired.

From his own office Mussolini rushed off a letter, ingratiatingly telling Claretta how happy he was to hear from a third party that she had agreed to move further away. 'In your new "place of retirement" you will settle back down. I shall find a way to communicate with you, by phone and letter, and to see you. We must change [the] system,' he emphasised, 'since everything is now known and put under surveillance. I give you infinite thanks for allowing things to go ahead and I send you every tenderness,' he concluded, with what he hoped were winning emotions, and there was space for the last advice: 'Destroy this,' and then again on the back of the page 'Tear it up! Tear it up! Tear it up as soon as you have read it.'[136]

Alas, these hopes of a more peaceful private life were short-lived! On the morning of 25 October Mussolini scribbled another note to Claretta: 'This morning there has been an attempt at suicide. Immediate intervention. Nothing alarming but a serious [medical] crisis . . . I have the impression that the only intended aim was not to break me from you which is impossible but to put a greater space – territorially speaking – between you and me.' While he was in the act of writing, Gina Ruberti burst in to inform him that 'the poisoning is grave and there are moments of delirium'. Even if, in another display of his personal cowardice, Mussolini did not mention Rachele by name in his letter, he ended with a crabwise request to his lover for appeasement. 'I, too, am very disturbed [by the act] and hope that it does not have a dramatic epilogue. If your momentary move away somewhere is necessary, you will do it, I think, as you already have done in the name and sign of our love.'[137] After this open skirmish, would it prove impossible in future to sustain the uneasy historic compromise between Mussolini's legitimate family and his lover and her kin? Claretta, for the moment, feared so. She wrote back accusingly: 'your wife and your family have won again as they always do'.[138] Yet, in fact, battle immediately resumed. The melodrama of the Petacci and Mussolini families could not be calmed by an armistice, an unsurprising situation since, over recent months, Claretta (and her family) often seemed made of sterner stuff than was the fading dictator. A *Ducessa* (of some definition) bid fair to outlast the *Duce*.

7

DEATH IN THE AFTERNOON

On 25 October 1944 it may have appeared that Mussolini's life had reached a personal turning-point. Appearances, however, were misleading. Rachele survived her attempted suicide. At the Villa Feltrinelli life returned to its customary edginess, and the long war between the Mussolini and Petacci families, in a curious parody of the world conflict, smouldered on. All that really happened was that Claretta moved out of the Villa Fiordaliso, thereafter being housed across the road and up the hill at the Villa Mirabella, part of the estate of Gabriele D'Annunzio's pompously named Il Vittoriale degli Italiani. D'Annunzio, dead now for six years, had left behind a widow, Maria Hardouin di Gallese, principessa di Montenevoso, a title in which she continued to rejoice, despite many years of separation from the sexually athletic poet.[1]

The princess was willing to welcome Claretta (and her SS guard) as tenants. Claretta shared the new quarters with Count and Countess Cervis, the couple with whom, in April 1945, she left her diary and other family papers.[2] Through the depressing months ahead, Claretta may have been troubled by the view from the windows of the villa of the prow of the torpedo boat *Puglia*, cemented into the hillside above at D'Annunzio's command in 1923, with the Germanophobe message that Italians would never again allow the lake waters below to be called *Gardasee*.[3] The Petacci parents had removed themselves from Claretta's presence some months earlier, thereafter residing mainly with Zita and Marcello's children in their more modest but still commodious villa at Merano; from the viewpoint of Giuseppina Persichetti, its great advantage may have been its attractive chapel where she could continue her regular Catholic worship.

While these minor changes in location were occurring, Mussolini composed reams of words to Claretta aimed at ensuring peace in his time between wife and lover, or at least a lasting armistice. Perhaps, he did not dare to hope openly, a solution to these private battles could be somehow replicated in the world war? As usual, when he put thoughts down on paper at Gardone, Mussolini found it hard not to be sorry for himself. He had, he admitted, been swept away by jealousy when told both about Claretta copying his letters and about 'an [alleged] Italian lover', and so had ordered the police requisition of the Villa Fiordaliso. But that was only the beginning of his woeful list. 'Then came the scene on Tuesday [with Rachele], another horror.' Then Wednesday morning and the suicide attempt from which his wife would need a long convalescence. 'In the midst of the greatest dangers,' he drifted on, 'I have never lost my head, but now I [have] lost it. I confess and ask your forgiveness. Hence the proposal to have you hidden away for a while.'

But any scheme that he and Claretta should for a time part had not advanced far, he interjected hastily. His own life had been foul, the family disputes having filled the Villa Feltrinelli with rage and imprecation. It was awful to have to live 'in this wretched little village, full of gossip and spies'. Yet, switching to a more sentimental key that he must have hoped would charm Claretta, he declared, 'I thank fate that has allowed us to live near to each other. *I love you*. No doubt troubles wear love down. But love will find a way ... We have overcome other obstacles ... I embrace you tenderly and I beg you to *tear up* every piece of paper,' he concluded, combining (tepid) warmth and (feeble) command.[4]

A second letter that day contained a similar mixture of emotion, self-interest and persuasion. Claretta should not put herself in the wrong by objecting to his latest plan. 'You must understand my situation. My soul is rocked by a tempest. I send you my every thought,' he pledged unconvincingly, with reiterated instruction to destroy that letter, too.[5] On the next day he composed a longer appeasing epistle, which started with good news before venturing into bad. 'You have given your youth to me and it is fair that I give you the rest of my life . . . I shall not permit anyone, and I mean anyone, to raise a scintilla of doubt about your crystalline faith as a Fascist and Italian woman – as a courageous Fascist – from your adolescence on,' he vowed. Yet, he revealed, he (not she) might have to move away – his polio-stricken younger daughter, Anna Maria, was, he claimed with what sounded a palpably cheap excuse, in declining health. And, he acknowledged, he could not overcome his suspicion of Claretta's relationship with the young SS guard, Franz Spögler. What did the German's habit of using the phone in her bedroom entail? A man and a woman, he knew in his soul, could only come together in private for one purpose. Yet his peroration attempted upbeat as he concluded virtuously, 'I have practised passive resistance [to his suspicions and those of others] and I am sure that I shall save our love.'[6]

Hardly had this note reached Claretta than she composed a bitter reply, accusing Mussolini of being swayed by the 'unworthy and cowardly campaign' against her in her new quarters at the Villa Mirabella. 'You have not defended me,' she charged, 'nor do you ever defend me. I must look after myself . . . I do not believe in you anymore . . . They have won but you have lost and you will understand the matter when it is too late.' By now, she was, she confessed, 'in a complete state of collapse . . . Reflect before you do something. Think before you act,' she ordered with more telling command than his.[7] A Mussolini–Petacci family armistice still lay – at least in her mind, it seemed – some way off,.

Faced with Claretta's stubborn opposition, Mussolini began to retreat, even if there was further discussion of transferring her to a villa near Vittorio Veneto. While the debate swung to and fro, the poor *Duce* had caught what might reasonably be diagnosed as 'man flu'. Despite being ill, he wailed, he was having to work very hard – twenty interviews on just one afternoon, thirty on another. But, he added with attempted brightness, he had not forgotten his responsibilities towards Myriam in Spain (a return flight from Madrid, even under German protection, might prove difficult and dangerous, while the Germans did not accept that Myriam and Mancini deserved priority in their air travel schedules). Meanwhile his cold ground him down further. He feared that his health had been utterly broken by his approval of the house invasion of 22 October; he could not believe he had been silly enough to think his Claretta had been behaving badly. When he looked in the mirror he was sure he could see new wrinkles on his face that had not been there before. Mournful thoughts about his public and his private life tangled depressingly in his mind.

After a fresh salvo from the Villa Mirabella, he now had to promise that he had not been seeing other women and that he had had nothing whatever to do with Ruspi, while at the end of the month he had to rebut furious objection from Claretta about Elena Curti, whom she was sure had arrived from Milan for sex. He was sorry to learn that Claretta, at least by her own account, had now also fallen ill. But soon Rachele, who must have been recovering more speedily than was initially predicted, was back on the attack, and likewise Vittorio Mussolini. Did it really make sense for Claretta still to live nearby, the dictator asked plaintively? Over and over again he hinted at her departure, but Claretta showed no sign of moving. Rather her relationship with the puppet dictator meandered on in its accustomed fraught way, even as Scottish soldiers marched in mid-November 1944 into Forlì, capital of *la provincia del Duce*, and the town where Mussolini had once been an eager socialist journalist and the lusty abductor of young Rachele from his father's and her mother's tavern.[8]

Although a couple of assignations were now successfully arranged between the two at their lakeside tower, with some presumed sexual satisfaction, perhaps more to the relief of a bored Claretta than to Mussolini, contact mostly remained indirect and, on 7 December, news of the death of the Futurist chief, Marinetti, deepened the *Duce*'s gloom. 'I love the telephone when there is not a storm between us,' he confided, 'and I detest it when we fight because I am convinced that there is someone listening and noting it down. Today I am empty in body and soul. Today – *really* – I would like to be dead. As will soon happen,' he whined with yet further urgent instructions to tear up his letter.[9]

* * *

With the rival residences on Lago di Garda continuing in their tussle, Claretta tried to divert her lover into choosing a centre of last resistance, which, at the time, she thought should be the Alto Adige. She still hoped in a 'miraculous intervention' that could somehow save Italy's cause in the war. But the real problem, she insisted, was that Mussolini was again being weak and failing to listen to her, a repetition of his error on 25 July. He was too uncertain in his decision-making, too optimistic about his Italian comrades, too fearful of being as violent as he should be, and too humble in dealing with Hitler. In that last regard, the public and the private again mixed in her counsel as she urged that he must make it crystal clear to the German authorities in Italy how much she mattered to him and how, if he must be shifted somewhere, so must she.[10]

In a succession of letters through December, Claretta pressed on with her psychological siege. His sexual performance was, she chivvied him, so 'tired' that she knew that, when he did come to her bed, he had just left another woman's side. Such limpness was clear proof that he had abandoned her. If amatory thrust was not the issue, then it was the constant 'malignant campaign by your wife and friends'. 'I experience your decay, your tiredness,' she wrote in attempted, if self-obsessed, understanding. 'I feel they have exhausted you.' But he must be strong. He must not let Gina Ruberti, his daughter-in-law, seduce him with her beguiling glamour and fondness for dubious business dealings, Claretta now warned (in curious reversal of the rumours circulating about the Petaccis and still at that time doing the rounds among radical Fascists).[11] He was not eating enough and what he ate was not good for him, she counselled maternally. 'For all of us you still represent everything, the banner, the Idea, the Credo,' she pronounced in more political terms. 'Either you are with us, for us, and the man whom we believe in and love, or we – and I, too – will head for the hills and rebel.' There could be only one 25 July. He must prevent another. He must persevere in backing Buffarini Guidi (Claretta had not detected any double play from that party boss on 24 October). He should also at once organise a workers' pay rise of '25 lire per day, otherwise you will find yourself in serious trouble,' she suggested with surprisingly precise detail.[12]

Amid the encircling gloom one chink of light glimmered when Mussolini returned to Milan and, on 16 December, broadcast a public speech from the Teatro Lirico. It combined a history of the 'betrayals' of 25 July and 8 September, a propaganda blitz about a Fascism which had returned to its origins in the RSI and was committed to the 'socialisation' of profit and land, and predictions that the war could still be won via a breakup of the 'unnatural' liberal–Bolshevik alliance or the sudden impact of some new weapon. With its 'third way', Mussolini bellowed, almost as if he were back on the balcony of the Palazzo Venezia, the Social Republic could yet strangle communist internationalism and Judeo-Masonic cosmopolitanism in the interests of the Italian people.[13]

Claretta may have griped before her lover left for Milan that he should have consulted her about the speech's wording,[14] but no one was more impressed and enthused than she when she heard the speech. Her language became almost girlish again: 'Ben, for the first time after 14 months I am not sure that I am finding the best words for you,' she gushed. 'I feel as though I am starting again and I am suddenly a part of a shining life that has already done much but now seems new, more beautiful, more grand, more ours.' 'I am stunned, astonished, happy and unhappy,' she continued. His speech had meant a 'physical return to *your people, always yours*', who knew they were being offered his 'unchanged and completely pure soul'. For so long his depression had made plain to everyone that he did not believe in himself. But now 'you have found yourself in yourself and in your people'. 'On my knees before your voice,' she avowed, 'I sustained you with my soul, with the violent beating of my heart as I listened, enraptured . . . At every pause, a shudder froze me, and I cried, throbbed, spoke with you, word for word, phrase by phrase, breath by breath.' When he left the stage in Milan, back at Gardone, 'I collapsed into unconsciousness'.

She hoped a phone call might confirm such mystic identification with her lover and his politics. Alas for Claretta, nothing. Yet, she wrote with personal infatuation (and wilfulness) fusing with ideology:

> this is my day, these hours belong to me, they are mine, mine, from my love, my desperate faith, my certainty, my constancy. They are mine, from my sacrifice, my torment, my humiliation. They are mine from my devotion, my oblation, my renunciation, my suffering.

But her moment of hysterical celebration soon switched to besotted self-abnegation. He mattered; she did not. Now that with her help he had rediscovered his true path, off he must go. 'You could make a gesture to me and my love; it could re-inspire me with hope and put the lie to evil. But you do not know it and will not do it. Goodbye, my great Ben, my credo, my faith, my useless but huge love. Clara', she signed off disconsolately.[15]

But in the 'Ben and Clara' relationship, times of transport, however sublime, could only be fleeting. Within days, Claretta had detected another, less empyrean, feature of the Milan trip; while there, Mussolini had managed to meet Pallottelli, Ruspi and Elena Curti. Soon he and Claretta were quarrelling in familiar manner over the phone about the implications. As Mussolini tried to explain with jaded self-justification, he had seen Pallottelli and Ruspi very briefly, for old time's sake, to hear of their current troubles and anyway they were now too old for sex. He had told Curti to go away (the fact that Elena Curti was actually his daughter was not accepted by Claretta until the last journey in April 1945). But how could Claretta spy on him, he expostulated, and how could one of his entourage act as her spy! 'It is really humiliating and I beg you not to do it,' he adjured her with his usual hollow force, before moving back to vainglorious boasts about his courage in touring around Milan in an open car where, finally, he trusted, 'a little sunshine has reappeared on the horizon'.[16]

Back at Gargnano, the momentary optimism of Milan vanished and he soon slipped back into depression, not helped by his decision on Christmas Day to read over the proceedings of the Verona trial that had cost Ciano his life (on 10 January, the anniversary of the execution, in his egoism Mussolini recalled downheartedly what a 'dramatic day' it had been for him).[17] Again, he announced glumly, 'I am tired, totally stuffed with too many skirts. But not of course yours since I love you,' he remembered to add.[18] By 27 December his letter virtuously revealed that he had refused to see Ines De Spuches, mother of his other dead son, who had come looking for him; naturally, mention of someone she labelled the 'dirty woman' reignited Claretta's jealousy, with her extracting from her partner another denial that De Spuches possessed any significance for him a few weeks later.[19] Trying to absolve himself from blame and return the focus of their exchanges to politics and war, Mussolini lamented that 'the magnificent flame of Milan is turning into a pile of words reduced to ashes', before promising that he could fit in a meeting with Claretta on New Year's Eve. And, he added trying yet again to find a positive, at least Myriam was back from what had not been a very successful venture to Spain.[20]

Claretta did not take a step back as she drafted a seven-page charge sheet against his current self-absorption, reiterating her disgust about Ruspi and her lover's many failings, while again reprimanding the *Duce* for not taking sufficient advantage of the alliance with the Nazis. Now only the Germans could 'defend our land', she told him peremptorily. She had changed her mind about the place to resist. A retreat to the Alto Adige would be useless. Milan was the city where he should make a last stand.[21]

In his response, written after the New Year dawned, Mussolini endeavoured to be blunt in emphasising that he did not welcome such advice from his lover. Their last meeting had gone badly. She had lain on the ground shouting imprecations at him, humiliating him. 'You think too much. You're too cerebral,' he charged. She should ask herself how best to receive him when he saw her, he suggested 'With some enthusiasm?' 'I embrace you, in spite of all, your Ben,' he concluded in some lightening of tone, followed by another order to destroy the letter.[22]

But Claretta was not going to let him get away with such rebuke. 'There is no danger in getting bored at your place,' she wrote sarcastically, 'especially given your marvellous and unique ability to adapt.' His charge that she was 'cerebral' ignored her love, sacrifice, devotion and acceptance of his betrayals. It was no way to enter what should be the happiness of the *Befana fascista* ('Fascist Epiphany', a regime festival of gift-exchange in better days), and, with her own feminine gesture of appeasement, she did remember to send his granddaughter Marina a doll.[23] She had also not forgotten her dedication to Santa Rita (indeed, while Myriam was in Spain, she had adopted the pseudonym 'Rita Colfosco' for their correspondence), and she continued to hope for divine help for Italy and the Repubblica Sociale.[24] But Mussolini's mood did not lift. 'I am fed up with being a fool,' he grouched on 7 January, 'I am just a ridiculous person. I am a grotesque puppet.' Only death could bring release and he desired it 'ardently'.[25]

* * *

As winter drifted into spring – with what seemed to the pair, who for so long had lived in Rome, culpable tardiness – the tone and topic of exchanges between the two lovers, each now often claiming to be ill, altered little in its fusing of private and public catastrophe. Mussolini noted wryly that he had taken so many pills that he felt as though his bones were dissolving, but then he always did exactly what doctors told him to do;[26] can he have been subtly contemplating whether he was prey to the medical expertise and obduracy of the Petacci family? For her part, Claretta alternated between the role of counsellor, trying to stiffen her *Duce* for one last effort at bloody resistance, and an hysterically jealous lover convinced, as for example in early February, that 'you have betrayed me, you are betraying me, you will betray me' with Ruspi. 'I believe,' Claretta predicted with what proved foresight, that, 'in dramatic circumstances, you will go away with your people, including the intruder [Curti], without caring a jot for me and without making a minimal attempt to find a place in the world where we can still see each other.'[27]

Every now and again, Mussolini tried to obtain the upper hand, telling Claretta on 31 January for example that he was in a complete fury towards all the women around him and that he would add her to his list if she continued to chide him so unmercifully.[28] Only a few days before, his wife had grabbed him as he emerged from the air raid shelter to castigate him for an hour about Claretta. Gina Ruberti then disclosed to him that a rumour (which Mussolini was sure must be false) had reached the Villa Feltrinelli that Claretta had petitioned the German ambassador to confine Rachele to a home. Being shouted at was one problem. Just as bad was the fact that the Mussolini women had taken to table-turning to discern the future; with his own misreading of history, the *Duce* wondered whether life would not be better as a prisoner in the Tower of London.[29]

An ever-more pathetic old man, in mid-February Mussolini fussed that his weak eyesight meant that he was having trouble with Claretta's handwriting even when using his glasses: could she make sure her future correspondence with him was typed?[30] That wish prompted an unsympathetic response from Claretta, who told him firmly that her writing was only bad when he had made her 'nervous', 'apathetic, irritable, tired and bored, bored with everything'. Once launched, she did not stop: 'Everything is useless. With you, for you, for me, for everyone. I can read your heart and know that you will only do for me what does not disturb your so-called family quiet and your marvellous and ineffable egoism', before she moved back to sentimental memories of their early days together in the sunshine, and signed off excusing herself and requesting his 'comprehension'.[31] His sacking of Buffarini Guidi from the Ministry of the Interior on 21 February similarly earned him flinty rebuke from Claretta; she wrote three letters in a single day to try to save Buffarini Guidi or to have him placed in charge of RSI foreign policy: he was the only person tough enough to stand up to the Germans and their growingly evident desire to remove themselves from Italy.[32]

The loss of Buffarini Guidi, a man whom she regarded as her political patron, stimulated Claretta to a ferocious statement of her own radicalism and *romanità* (however tinctured, somewhere beneath the words, by her willingness to sacrifice anything for love). 'I declare that I am an anti-Semite by racial instinct,' she told Mussolini on 25 February. 'Really I am a patrician – in my blood there is not a single drop of impurity – and I feel a profound pride that springs from my utterly pure stock. I do so, not so much from aristocratic sensibility but in [my natural] rectitude in behaviour, in honesty, [in devotion] to the safety of and love for the *patria*, understood in the widest terms.' She then went on in more Machiavellian mode to explain away the charge that the RSI's deputy police chief, Eugenio Apollonio, who had fallen with Buffarini Guidi and been arrested by the Germans, was stained by Jewish blood (his enemies were charging that he was racially contaminated by a Jewish great-grandparent).[33]

* * *

Claretta was still seeking the best words to craft a path through the murky high politics of the RSI as her own domestic affairs remained in turmoil. Myriam's return from her unsuccessful venture to Spain had renewed Petacci family solidarity, with Myriam recommencing her lengthy and critical letters to the *Duce*. In February 1945 Claretta's young sister, still short of her twenty-second birthday, detailed a familiar register of error and blame. Once she had been the sweet child waiter and food provider, she began. She had not changed and neither had her sister. He, however, had bowed to 'the obnoxious connections that surround you'. He was failing to recognise Claretta's love and sacrifice. He simply must get rid of 'those reptiles who . . . fill you with poison', notably 'your wife who uses any dire means to strike at Claretta', Myriam demanded, not mincing her words. Only yesterday, Rachele had spent two hours filling Paolo Zerbino, the new minister of the interior (he had replaced Buffarini Guidi), with lies about Claretta and her family. Mussolini must understand, as Myriam and all the Petaccis understood, that 'Claretta has always been right' (*Claretta ha avuto sempre ragione*; Myriam was, consciously or unconsciously, parodying the regime slogan: *Mussolini ha sempre ragione*). The *Duce* must listen to his *piccola idiota*, now reduced to being an 'unhappy little person beset by destiny'. He must make sure to see Claretta on her birthday and then concentrate on a proper reconciliation with her.[34]

Amid her fervent pleas for her sister, Myriam did not forget her own concerns and pressed Mussolini to ready passports and letters of recommendation to Franco and others, should she and Mancini return to Spain, this time in the company of her parents. It also might be sensible for them to have a contact with the Japanese ambassador in case of need; with what sounds like superb geographical ignorance, Vittorio Mussolini and his friends were allegedly around this time thinking of transferring Mussolini by submarine to the 'security' of the East.[35] Myriam had no knowledge of such fantastical schemes and urged with more humdrum purpose that Mussolini must write 'a clarifying letter to Claretta about the intention that you presently have for the morrow since, to me, it looks very dark for Claretta without the understanding, tenderness and gratitude that Claretta merits'.[36]

From late February 1945 much of Mussolini's correspondence to Claretta was duly devoted to plans to get the Petaccis away safely to Spain, with helpfully false names on their passports and with German backing, however grudging.[37] But for the moment no action followed and instead Mussolini again intimated that he should move back to Milan for some sort of final resistance, perhaps in the city, perhaps in the Valtellina on the border of Switzerland. For Claretta, all such sketches meant was that he was doing what his wife and Ruspi wanted: he was paying no attention to her. In Milan he could be killed by any stray bomb, while chat about the city as a final bulwark was an absurdity. On 18 March she wrote at length to say that intimation of his imminent departure meant that she had come 'to a final decision to leave you cost what it may'. She had stayed with him without 'fear', 'mental reserves', 'false shame' and despite his own odious 'cowardice'. She had fully merged her 'faith' and her love, her politics and her life, her public and private self. But he did nothing for her and was not even brave enough to break with Rachele, who had done nothing worthwhile for him for thirty-five years. He was not big enough for her 'love and offering', she had decided. Yet perhaps he still carried potential power as the *Duce*, she concluded in final sentimentality.[38]

Predictably, Claretta had not really shaken herself free from her lover, nor had Mussolini accepted that she had sundered their ties, sending a reply insisting that they both should move in short order to Milan, while complaining again about his time being wasted listening to Marcello's wild schemes and tolerating the 'canaille' who were his friends (Marcello had taken on occasion to elevating himself to the nobility as conte di Colfosco). The dictator had, however, readied matters for the departure of Myriam and Mancini,[39] although, with her family loyalty ever at the ready, Claretta accused him a few days later of failing to appoint Mancini Italian commercial attaché in Madrid and assured him that he was completely wrong to doubt the political commitment to Fascism of Myriam's new partner.[40]

As wintry weather lingered and Mussolini caught another cold (it hampered fidgety plans for a sexual encounter),[41] the two lovers continued their epistolary wrangling, for example over who was spying on whom.[42] On 29 March Mussolini expostulated how 'grotesque, sublime and humiliating' it was, 'at a moment when the old and new world are burning', that 'I must talk to you about Elena Curti'.[43] By early April he disclosed that he was working on the assumption that, although Franco's Spain was becoming steadily less welcoming to its old Fascist friends, he could still get the Petaccis, including Claretta, away there.[44] Maybe, he wrote with what might have been a flicker of lust, there was in fact a last sexual opportunity somewhere near the lake, even if the bed would not be supplied with sheets; better at his place than hers and their tryst could last a whole night, he claimed.[45] In the meantime, it went without saying, he maintained, that he was '*chaste* in the most strictly literal meaning of the term'.[46] As far as the wider world was concerned, the news of the death of Roosevelt, 'the greatest criminal', might yet be a good omen.[47]

At around that time, Claretta compiled another of her lengthy despatches, ranging freely over her dissatisfaction with Mussolini and tabulating his inadequacy in public and private life. He must read the letter twice, she urged. She devoted a whole page to his failure to treasure Marcello Petacci, a man who had sacrificed his professional life and his naval career, in which all his promotions had been won strictly on merit, to the *Duce*. Mussolini had not noticed how Marcello had kept 'his faith intact and totally pure since adolescence', as was appropriate for the 'first-born' and heir of a family name that was '*flawless, honourable, innate*'. As she painted her lyrical portrayal of her brother, Claretta was working herself up to a conclusion that was an even more definite declaration of family loyalty than the pronouncement of her racism a few days before. 'Now, I tell you. One day it will finally be the time of reckoning. I do not believe that I shall expire beneath a bomb or be riddled by a machine gun or anything else. The day will come when you won't recognise me anymore. Then you will see how I know how to defend the honour of my father, my mother, Marcello, Mimi and all my family.' Such a final reckoning could only be avoided if he at last perceived how much gratitude and justice he should grant 'to a whole family condemned to death by Badoglio for your sake and by you and today condemned to civil death by you'.[48]

* * *

On 18 April Mussolini penned his last letter to 'Clara'. It contained mixed news. Entering Spain was more and more problematic. Those who arrived on a clandestine flight would be interned and have their plane seized. He was off to Milan, where he would have no time for thoughts about women. He hoped eventually to get back to Lago di Garda. If she herself somehow reached Milan, he would hope to see her there. With a hug and a final message to tear up the letter, that was all.[49]

Claretta replied twice at greater length and with heavy emphasis on her accustomed themes. She began with sarcasm: 'to help me you have decided to *leave, not to see me, not to speak to me, to leave me alone to consume myself*'. Despite his trying for the hundredth time to escape the issue of her role in his life, she would follow him to Milan: one last kiss might be enough, she wrote romantically before again charging him with wanting to fix some arrangement there with Ruspi. 'I now consider my life over, my cycle closed . . . Everything is finished for me as for all those who give everything with no reward,' she announced bleakly before wishing him 'Goodbye'.[50]

In her second letter she concentrated more on trying yet again to ginger the dictator into drastic action against all those whom she believed were plotting against him. As for herself, 'never as now have I known that I am definitively *alone*, alone in my faith and my pain *that I alone know* . . . Today in my desperation, *I can do everything. I have overcome everything. I am beyond good and evil*,' she scrawled with what may have been suicidal intent. '*If you do not seek me, I shan't seek you*,' she repeated before a final digression into patriotic politics and the reminder that Trieste was another place that had to be defended to the last since, from the First World War, it throbbed with Italian 'blood' and Italian 'heroism'.[51]

At its end, therefore, Claretta, in her correspondence, managed to fuse fervent Fascism, familism, infatuation, devotion and 'love'; as so often, the public and the private. She avoided any analysis of what might now seem the contradictions of such ideas, even while she so often excoriated Mussolini for his own weak failure to choose between her and his legitimate family, his ideal public policy and the bad part of his private life. Now, inevitably alone and with Mussolini giving few thoughts to her, she hastened on the evening of 18 April to organise her own departure from the Villa Mirabella. Contrary to romantic accounts of their love story, it was still by no means certain that 'Ben and Clara' would die together. But they had fewer than ten days left to live.

***

At dawn the next morning, Claretta left for Milan, taking pains over what she had described to her man as 'little feminine things'. So she asked that her bag be packed with 'her cardigans with pink buttons, eight of her best blouses, two negligees, one black, the other velvet with fur trimming, plus an orange one to wear on getting up from bed in the morning, and some summer ones' (which could be found in a separate suitcase). She also wanted to be equipped with stockings, shoes, toiletry and sanitary absorbents. Her father's chestnut-leather bag must similarly not be forgotten. As two contemporary historians have noted: 'it was not a list for a woman expecting to die at any minute'.[52] She had, however, left her diaries and other papers behind, perhaps indeed with a sense of consigning a legacy to history. She arrived safely later that day at her sister's flat in Milan, still, according to Myriam's memoirs, accompanied by her SS guard, Spögler.[53]

Over the previous fortnight, Myriam had kept up her barrage of letters to Mussolini, especially when it became clear that she, Mancini and her parents were finally going to flee the 'inferno' that lay all around in 'martyred Italy' and abandon the equally 'martyred' Claretta to her lover's by no means trustworthy hands. Marcello and his children also required succour, Myriam did not forget to remind the *Duce*. They belonged to a family of virtue. By contrast, Rachele, a woman of 'criminal insanity', and the rest of his legitimate kin deserved to be cursed and cursed again. They never ceased their plotting to get rid of Claretta and even to murder her 'in the medieval manner'. They were literally driving him 'mad'. But Mussolini had utterly lacked courage in dealing with his wife, Myriam lamented in sentiments that her correspondent had so often heard from Claretta, and so treated her sister 'like a dog or a donkey'. How could a man of his 'intelligence and good sense', Myriam protested, leave her to get herself alone to Milan in the current dangerous world? No wonder her poor sister now had the beginnings of an ulcer to add to her other woes, an illness she could share with him.

Just as was true of Claretta's correspondence, in Myriam's prose there was space for aggression and space for peace. So, Myriam requested beseechingly, could she take with her a recent photograph of the *Duce* for remembrance's sake, and would he make sure to write at once to Serrano Suñer, so she and her parents could 'avoid the bureaucratic path and arrive straight to Franco without need to call on people whom we don't know and may be full of gossip'? Or maybe Portugal was a better venue. In whichever sanctuary, it would not be good if the Petaccis were subject on arrival to police or customs inspection.[54] 'You know how to write without me telling you', the *piccola idiota* (as she again winningly called herself) wrote with some temerity. It was not good enough for him to be rude to Mancini, when the lawyer arrived to fix final passport (and presumably financial) arrangements. 'Today I think of Claretta as a Saint [*sic*] and a heroine, if still, in spite of everything, she has decided to follow your destiny, which she rightly considers her destiny,' Myriam pronounced, once more slipping into accusatory mode. 'She is split in two, in three. You and the *patria*, Mamma and Papà, me, Marc[ello] and Benghi. Too many, too much for just one little heart.' Sadly, time and again, Claretta had won no real understanding or comfort from Mussolini, her sister wailed. But, perhaps at the last, he would comprehend how 'Great [*sic*], absolute and sublime' was the love that Claretta had given and would always give him.[55]

Myriam was not the only scribe among the Petaccis. On 10 April Giuseppina Persichetti typed her last farewell to the *Duce*. It was unfortunate, she conceded a little smugly, that, since the events of 25 July 'bound together our tragedy and your tragedy', the Petaccis had been forced to live from 'your oxygen', 'contrary to our principles of fairness and dignity'. Now she was trusting in God's help to get them 'safe and sound to their destination'. But she was leaving behind Claretta and Marcello, 'with their rooted faith, their generous acceptance of holocaust, their ardent love for poor Italy and you'. As a mother who had given her own child to him, she nourished one last wish: 'Take care of her as the most sacred thing that you possess. Protect her, defend her with the sense of responsibility that her sacrifice of Love demands. Do not ignore how delicate, sensitive and fragile she is and how she needs understanding, loyalty and tenderness.' He simply must recognise that Claretta was the most beautiful and worthy aspect of his life, her mother demanded in vow and prayer.

The Petaccis had gone to prison and sacrificed their civic life to him, Giuseppina reiterated. So she was certain that he would ensure that Marcello did not suffer any more 'humiliations' and be ashamed of his name. Mussolini must recognise that her son was 'one of the few faithful left to you'. Marcello's 'intelligence, energy and versatility' made him an ideal potential minister at the highest level, his mother remarked on the evident principle that she should never give up. Departing to Spain, she was not sure whether her son had succeeded in 'making his little angels safe and secure', she added with a frisson of fear. But she knew Mussolini would offer every assistance to them. So she signed off, 'with tears in my eyes, as that most tragic being, a mother and an exile, I kiss your hands and thank you'. With her whole heart, she hoped they would meet again and God would help and bless him. Then, in unfeigned invocation, she recommended Claretta to his love and devotion one last time.[56]

The only Petacci to stay silent through these weeks was Francesco Saverio, perhaps demonstrating how justified was the conclusion of one contemporary that Claretta's father had remained 'bemused' by the whole affair.[57] Another sympathetic account states that, even before 1943, the doctor had lost patients through his daughter's notorious behaviour and his wife's snobbery. He had been left silently to hope for a fate for him and his family that was not too horrid. In his world, away from the official Fascist gender order, the women led and he followed, less the appeaser and more the servant.[58]

* * *

The Petaccis' flight from Malpensa airport outside Milan was finally organised for Saturday, 21 April. But the times were difficult to say the least; delays blocked departure, and the family finally reached Barcelona in the early evening on the 23rd – whereupon they went straight to the Ritz Hotel – after a bumpy four-hour trip in a plane with false Croatian markings. If Myriam's romantic recollection can be trusted, they were furnished with only 8,000 lire, £10,000 and a few 'jewels'. They did carry with them, however, 'some letters of recommendation'. As Mussolini had predicted, the Francoist police seized the plane and interned the crew.[59] According to Myriam, Claretta had written her a lengthy farewell letter. It combined marital advice – she should view Mancini as her 'father, brother and friend' – final good wishes for her parents, and the announcement of her firm determination to 'follow my destiny which is also his [Mussolini's]'. 'I shall not destroy with a cowardly gesture,' she swore, 'the supreme beauty of my offering' of love and devotion.[60]

Marcello's actions during the concluding weeks of the Fascist regime cannot be fully charted. Their detail is confused by the numerous conspiracy theories since constructed about what he may have been doing, with the leading one marshalled by his surviving son, Ferdinando. It claims that, by 1945, and in all likelihood well before that, Marcello had been working for Winston Churchill and the British secret service as an agent under the code-name 'Fosco'.[61] No sources in the United Kingdom have ever been found to justify this claim. Marcello's partner, Zita Ritossa, did say in her memoirs that she, their children and Marcello successfully crossed into Switzerland on 18 April (conspiracy theorists allege some last-minute compromise with the British minister there, Clifford Norton).[62] But, perturbed by the thought that the Swiss would hand him over to the Allies as a 'war criminal', Marcello soon decided to return to Milan where he and his family were together on 23 April.[63] His choice to punt on Italy, Mussolini and his sister was a fatal one.

* * *

Mussolini had left Lago di Garda for Milan without briefing the German authorities in Italy, who were, in any case, seeking their own independent peace with the triumphant Allied armies. By 24 April, however belatedly, he took care to send Rachele, Romano and Anna Maria to sanctuary at a villa on Lake Como owned by the wealthy silk industrialist Mantero family. In the very early morning of 26 April Rachele tried to cross the Swiss border with her two youngest children at Ponte Chiasso, but was refused entry by the border guards and returned to her refuge at Como. Over the previous days in Milan, the *Duce* had begun a scattergun series of negotiations with Cardinal Schuster, the archbishop of Milan, with the partisan leadership, with men who might or might not fondly remember Mussolini's socialist origins, with his own surviving *repubblichini* (devotees of the RSI) and with his regime's military commander, Rodolfo Graziani. There was still talk of a last redoubt and a final heroic fight but, whenever an attempt was made to count arms and men, it became quickly clear that such talk was in vain.[64]

With the evident failure of his efforts to find a compromise, on the evening of 25 April Mussolini left Milan, which was promptly liberated by armed partisans. He reached Como some hours later. With Graziani now taking his own path, in the wee hours of the next day Mussolini's convoy moved on to Menaggio, where there was a crossroad to Lake Lugano and the Swiss border. There the dictator again dithered, going part of the way west and then turning back. Claretta, Marcello, Zita and the two boys now caught up with the *Duce* in their yellow Alfa Romeo 6C 1500 (from which fluttered the Spanish flag, with its claim of diplomatic immunity). Marcello had extracted from the friendly Spanish vice-consul in Milan a passport stating that he was Don Juan Muñoz y Castillo, a businessman. There were other children in the convoy but most had been left behind at Como; Marcello's motivations remain imponderable. He may have been trying to protect his sister and to act as head of the Petacci family. He may have been engaged in one last adventure. He may have been unable to perceive an alternative to uniting his destiny and that of his partner and sons with Mussolini's.

Whether he wanted to be or not (and perhaps to his mute surprise), Mussolini was now reunited with Claretta. The couple had time for one final noisy quarrel over Elena Curti, who had also joined those remaining with Mussolini to the last, as had Virgilio Pallottelli.[65] Romilda Ruspi, however, had remained at Monza. At dawn on 27 April, now assisted by a retreating German anti-aircraft unit commanded by Lieutenant Hans Fallmayer, the convoy reformed and headed further north along the lake. Claretta, wearing a rich mink coat and a neat and stylish turban-style hat, again travelled with Marcello and not with Mussolini. One partisan later reckoned that she was carrying with her 150,000 lire, 30,000 Swiss francs, some gold coins and:

> a quantity of foreign paper valuables, two gold watches studded with diamonds and rubies, 16- and 9-carat-diamond gold rings, two white gold and silver earrings with drop pearls, a necklace of cultivated pearls, a 2-carat solitaire diamond, two flower-shaped clips and two heart-shaped ones with diamonds and opals, and a little gold bracelet set with rubies.

Such treasure again did not suggest craven surrender to imminent death. It was later found that she also was concealing another ancient family ring, a gold locket with a rosary crown from the shrine of Santa Rita, and another with diamonds forming the intertwined letters C and B, plus a miniature of Mussolini inscribed with the motto: 'Clara, I am you and you are me. Ben 24 April 1932–24 April 1941.'[66] Zita Ritossa and Marcello Petacci had similarly brought much cash and jewellery with them.[67] Little of this impressive collection was ever returned to the surviving members of the Petacci family.

* * *

The convoy's passage – whether towards Switzerland, the Valtellina or Germany – was interrupted at 7 a.m. on the morning of the 27th. Just north of a village called, as it happened, Musso, and just short of the town of Dongo, the well-armed Nazi–Fascist vehicles were halted by what was only a small force of partisans. Negotiations began.

While talks proceeded, some of the Fascist chiefs in the group began to identify themselves, one being Ruggero Romano, the minister of public works, who may have been trying to save his wife and adolescent son (he was successful). By the afternoon it was agreed that the German troops could proceed but the Italians must stay behind and accept their fate. Now, in the confusion, with Claretta's desperate shouted blessing, Mussolini agreed to don a German greatcoat and conceal himself with Nazi soldiers in the back of a truck that moved off with the other German vehicles. At Dongo, however, when there was a further inspection, Mussolini's identity was revealed. He was arrested and dragged into the small local town hall. The Germans then finally moved away to the north.

Marcello and his family had also been allowed to travel on from Musso: the flag of neutral Spain had done its job. However, at the village of Germasino, their journey ended, with some dispute remaining over the cause. According to Walter Audisio, a communist who had fought alongside anti-Franco forces in Spain, 'When I addressed him [Marcello] in Spanish, I might as well have been speaking Ostrogothic. Not only could he not understand but he did not know a single phrase in Spanish.'[68] A rival partisan account suggests that Marcello's passport bore in different sections two different birthdates – 1912 and 1914 – and was palpably false.[69] A third claim is that partisan suspicions were raised by the children chattering in Italian to each other about how 'stupid and bad' those who resisted Mussolini were.[70] The partisans decided that 'the fair-haired, well-built man with a small birthmark on his fat chin'[71] must be Vittorio Mussolini, an ironical fate given the enmity between Marcello and the real Vittorio.

Audisio allegedly slapped the face of the man whom he identified as Vittorio Mussolini, with a threat to shoot him there and then 'like a dog'; in the interim he seized from his jacket a gold cigarette case, a gold fountain pen and an ordinary propelling pencil. Such violence rapidly elicited from Marcello outraged yelps that he was not Mussolini's eldest son. Rather, he maintained, without yet providing a name, that he had always been an anti-Fascist at heart and was, in fact, 'the head of the intelligence service in Italy'. When that grand contention was greeted with incredulity and he was dragged off to see a priest for final absolution, Marcello tried yet another of his fantastical stories. 'It is because of me,' he averred, 'that the Germans never succeeded in using secret weapons.' He asserted, with some echo of an earlier scheme, that with an engineer friend he had discovered a way to have water replace petrol in combustion engines, an invention which, had it been deployed by the Axis, could have changed the course of the war.[72] His story won over the Capuchin to whom he had been brought, either out a priestly ignorance of science or priestly hope in finding grounds for mercy. But Marcello's lofty pretensions to be an inventor – the last throw of a fantasist – cut little ice with the partisans.

While Claretta's brother struggled to avoid execution, that destiny was what awaited fifteen Fascist bosses who had been identified in the convoy. They included Party Secretary Alessandro Pavolini, who had attempted an armed escape and been wounded in the resultant fire, Ruggero Romano, Paolo Zerbino and Nicola Bombacci, never a Fascist minister but an old friend of Mussolini from his socialist days, whose personal contact with the *Duce* had been restored during the Repubblica Sociale in an effort to counter Mussolini's loneliness and isolation.[73] They, Marcello, Zita and the children were now driven back to Dongo by their partisan guards, with death creeping ever nearer.

* * *

The radical Fascists were, in fact, briefly to outlive Mussolini and Claretta. After his identification, arrest and interrogation at Dongo, Mussolini was imprisoned for the night of 27 April in a decaying barracks at Germasino; it belonged to the Guardia di Finanza, a specialised police force targeting smuggling to and from Switzerland. The defeated dictator now asked that his best wishes be sent to a female friend, whom he admitted to be 'Signora Petacci', travelling with 'that Spanish gentleman', as Mussolini cautiously phrased it.[74] Once he had returned to Dongo, the liberal partisan chief, Pier Luigi Bellini delle Stelle, separated Claretta from her brother – she had been fussing about a broken nail and had asked for cognac (to be given only a sip of more humble brandy)[75] – and conducted what he recorded as an hour-long interview with her.

Bellini acknowledged that, he had, until then, thought of her as 'an adventuress who had attached herself to a man of power out of pure self-interest'. But, in the course of the conversation, she earned his commiseration through her emphasis on how Mussolini had been surrounded by 'wretches', whose only thought had been 'saving their own miserable skins'.[76] After she had made plain her dislike of the Fascist diehards, Claretta tried to suggest that the best course of action for the partisans would be to hand Mussolini over to the Allies. This idea remains the source of massive and continuing conspiracy theorising, often connected with the alleged 'Churchill letters' noted in the introduction of this book; that controversy will be avoided here.

When Bellini replied that he was too patriotic an Italian to allow national responsibility for the Fascist regime to be subordinated to the Allies, Claretta rejected the idea of a trial as a humiliating 'torture'. 'It would be better for him to die at once,' she wailed. Under further questioning, Claretta denied that she had been a key 'adviser' to the *Duce* and began to sob, arousing a combination of sympathy and suspicion from her captor. As she dried her tears, she related to Bellini just how deeply she had loved Mussolini and how different she therefore was to his other women. She had offered, she pledged, 'true love, absolute devotion, complete dedication, love such as would have soothed him in moments of rest and loneliness and relieved his mind in moments of stress and worry'.

Obscuring her family's past and continuing squabbles and the longstanding struggle between them and the Mussolinis, switching to her private and renouncing her public persona, and perhaps convincing herself in the process, Claretta affirmed that recently she had won her lover over and brought him to her side. 'I never entertained the idea of entering into politics or government affairs, let alone advising him,' she ran on with a virtue that seemed as much directed at her absent partner as her partisan interlocutor. 'If I have ever used my influence over him it has been to recommend to his notice someone who had asked me to plead his cause, officers, party leaders and other important persons who had fallen into disgrace, people who wanted recommendations for a job or what have you. I simply tried to help them all because I always tried to do good to everyone,' she remarked disarmingly, before moving on to the claim that she had never been especially 'jealous' but had rather always forgiven his foolish women and tried to do her best for them, too.

Having preached her case with ability and care, Claretta 'suddenly leaning forwards slightly . . . grasped my hand and said imploringly, in a voice choking with emotion: "Put me with him!"' Bellini was not sure how to reply to this tearful appeal and, before he did, Claretta interrupted to cry that what the partisans intended was to shoot Mussolini, meeting protestations from Bellini that the matter was not yet decided. Claretta was not naive enough to believe his attempt at neutrality, and pressed on to her final point and a demand that he make her one last promise: 'I want to die with him. My life will mean nothing once he is dead. I would die anyway, but more slowly and with greater suffering. That is all I am asking: to die with him. You can't deny me that.'[77] With that request, the interview was over.

After midnight and in pouring rain, the partisans decided to permit Claretta to be reunited with her lover and, at the same time, to transfer him from what they feared were the insecure barracks at Germasino to an isolated peasant house owned by the De Maria family at the settlement of Bonzanigo, back southwards down the lake, on the hill above a village called Giulino di Mezzegra. It was after 3 a.m. when they arrived. Ben and Clara were found accommodation in a peasant-style, iron double bed, the first they had shared since 28 October 1943. According to her popular biography, however, Claretta was menstruating and no final sex act was possible.[78]

DEATH IN THE AFTERNOON

* * *

It is from now that the story flows into many rival streams, flooded with (dubious) detail, with one commentator who remained nostalgic of Fascism publishing a two-hundred-page study of 'Mussolini's last five seconds'.[79] The books, articles, interviews, films and TV documentaries on the *Duce*'s death are mostly blatant in their contemporary political colour, usually anti-communist and sympathetic to a degree with Fascism. They are probably more useful as primary sources in the analysis of conspiracy theory, especially as it attaches to Mussolini, than as secondary sources on the history of 1945. They will not preoccupy this book.

Still the simplest and most credible account is that provided by the communist partisans who, however much prompted by Partito Comunista Italiano chiefs, were the first to tell the tale. Here the chief figure is the man who then called himself 'Colonel Valerio' but was actually Walter Audisio (although a vast conspiracy literature denies such identification), a middle-ranking communist official and Resistance fighter. He had been chosen by the CLNAI (Comitato di Liberazione Nazionale Alta Italia) – the de facto liberation government in Milan – on the evening of 27 April, to go as quickly as possible to Dongo and there execute Mussolini, in advance of what may have been (rival American and British) Allied secret service plans to capture the dictator and send him to trial.[80]

* * *

According to Audisio's memoirs, when summoned on the afternoon of 28 April by her executioners from the bed on which she lay already dressed, Claretta had trouble tottering to the partisans' Fiat 1100 in her black chamois-leather high heels.[81] Another account claims that, when roused, she could not find her knickers, only to be roughly told by her lover: 'it doesn't matter. Come as you are. You shouldn't worry so much about whether you are properly dressed.'[82] When, not long after at around 4.15 p.m., she and Mussolini awaited the final shots at the gates of the Villa Belmonte, Audisio's version maintained, Claretta was 'out of it, completely stunned, moving erratically'.[83] Others of greater piety or sentimentality say that, at the last, she had time to kiss a cross and admit that she had sinned against 'Heaven and Earth'.[84] Still more romantic versions depict her throwing her body in front of the *Duce* when the fatal shots rang out, attempting to grab one of the executioner's guns in a loving attempt to save him, or the two collapsing together in a final embrace.[85]

There is a considerable and growing literature emphasising the injustice and illegality of the killing of Claretta along with her lover. No doubt, strictly speaking, this claim is correct. Yet late April 1945 was not a time of much legal nicety, whether in Italy or other parts of Europe. Nor was Claretta the only Fascist woman then to die; the Marchese Carla Medici del Vascello, the aristocratic last lover of the ex-party secretary Roberto Farinacci, for example, was also shot along with her partner 'while trying to escape' in these days.[86] And, given her iron determination – reiterated on so many occasions – to stay loyal at any cost to her version of her relationship with Mussolini, however far from reality it was, perhaps death at Giulino di Mezzegra was indeed the kindest fate for Claretta Petacci and her obsession.

At Dongo, when the news came of the shooting of Mussolini and Claretta, the time of execution for the fifteen Fascist bosses and Marcello had arrived; Virgilio Pallottelli and Elena Curti, although arrested, were not deemed significant enough for the death penalty. Claretta's brother had been allowed to say farewell to Zita, who, along with their sons, had been put in a room in the small Hotel Dongo. When Marcello emerged from there and was led towards the shoreline and the place of execution, the Fascists greeted him with hostile screams that he was a 'spy' and a 'traitor';[87] they must not have their ideological purity impugned by dying in his company, they shrieked. There was a moment of hesitation among the partisans, with the communists favouring immediate death for all, and the liberals suggesting Marcello should be killed alone, with eventual agreement that the firing squad should direct its bullets against the fifteen first. Twelve of them made the sign of the cross before they died; three – including Bombacci – did not.[88]

A few moments later, as he was pushed, terrified, towards the row of corpses, Marcello, detecting in his captors a moment of distraction, took his chance to struggle free. He ran first towards the hotel and his family, was grabbed there by four partisans, but again broke their hold on him. 'Still yelling he ran to the water [of the lake], threw himself in and swam out with powerful strokes,' Bellini recalled. 'He did not get far', however, but was mown down by a hail of bullets from 'submachine guns, rifles and revolvers'.[89] According to more melodramatic accounts, his family watched his last dive into the lake from their hotel window, with allegedly devastating permanent effect on the mental health of Benvenuto. In her memoirs, however, Zita remembered rather that, late on a busy afternoon, her two children were taking a siesta, while she watched the horror alone.[90] A recent 'anti-anti-Fascist' history claims that, after her husband's death, Zita was raped by the partisans, who imprisoned her for a couple of days, but there is no contemporary evidence of such assault.[91]

While blood spread on the surface of the lake in a large red stain, the local priest proffered last rites of a kind by directing the prayer of absolution towards it.[92] After floating back to the surface, Marcello's corpse was pulled to the shore and dumped on top of the dead Fascist bosses in the back of a truck that already contained the remains of Mussolini and Claretta. Its engine spluttered into life and at around 8.20 p.m. it and its macabre cargo headed for Milan. All that was left at Dongo, Bellini recalled, was a pool of coagulating blood and a smell of powder.[93] Myriam later clung to a theory that the body extracted from the lake was not actually Marcello's. He had preserved himself somehow under water, reached a friendly shore undetected and some day would, like a sleeping Barbarossa, reveal himself to his sorrowing family; his coffin at the family tomb in Campo Verano, she contended in her memoirs, stood in fact still 'empty'.[94]

* * *

The truck reached Milan after 3 a.m. and was directed to the Piazzale Loreto, one square down from the railway station. The stopping place had been chosen because, at 6.30 a.m. on 10 August 1944, fifteen anti-Fascists had been taken out of the San Vittore prison to be publicly executed at the Piazzale by a Fascist firing squad composed from a paramilitary force calling itself the Legione Autonoma Ettore Muti, after the party secretary killed in Rome in August 1943. The corpses were then left to rot in the sun for the rest of the hot summer day and only handed to their sorrowing families that night after a merciful intervention from Cardinal Schuster. Now, eight months later, was the time for vengeance.

The evident popular thirst for retribution has stimulated quite a lot of unhistorical moralising about the crowd's behaviour. Sandro Pertini, for one, remembered being shocked by the 'rancour' on display and set a track that others would follow by distinguishing between Mussolini, 'a war criminal' who had received his just desserts, and Claretta, 'a courageous and loyal woman' who had won his 'respect'.[95] Again, however, judgement needs to be put in the context of a war that had killed at least 50 million Europeans, a tyranny, however erratic its practice, which was responsible for a million premature deaths at home and abroad, and a still unfinished civil war, which had provoked more death and destruction than the rest of the Italian war effort.

The photographic record shows the nineteen corpses laid out on the square (added to those brought from Dongo was Achille Starace, who was executed after being found jogging in a state of mental confusion around the city) before a jostling crowd. Mussolini's body was the object of special abuse. He had part of his head kicked in so viciously that brain matter began to seep out of it and his left eye was dislodged from its socket. At some stage his head was laid on Claretta's breast, bloodied by the shots that had killed her. The dead dictator was given a phallic Fascist *gagliardetto* or sceptre to clutch as symbol of what has been called 'the most derisive [last] orgasm'.[96] As a more sensitive onlooker recalled of this rough humiliation of the lovers: 'They looked flabby . . . Their faces were bloated and anonymous, as if they had never lived, cadavers that had not been cleaned up by undertakers.'[97]

Eventually, at around 11 a.m., seven of the bodies were strung up from their heels on a steel stanchion 4 metres above some Esso petrol pumps at the side of the square. Claretta was set next to her lover. Since she had no underwear, her skirts were first pinned up by a charitable priest, who had found someone among the crowd with a safety pin, before being secured with rope.[98] At 2 p.m., following intervention by the US military authorities, the bodies were taken down and all nineteen corpses were taken away. Mussolini's body went first, to suffer the last abuse of an autopsy ordered by the Americans, certain that their science could help them understand a dictator's errant psychology. Claretta and Marcello, soon to be joined by Benito, were taken to the central Musocco cemetery in Milan[99] and interred in anonymous graves. The troubled 'Ben and Clara' relationship had ended, perhaps in tragedy, perhaps in bathos, although, as was reported in the introduction to this book, its ghost continues to walk abroad.

* * *

In her last hours at Dongo, Bonzanigo and Mezzegra, Claretta had at last seemingly shaken off her family, in the past so insistent a cushion to, or distraction from, her 'love' for the *Duce*. Certainly she made no last-minute attempt to save Marcello from his brutal destiny, another whose execution was scarcely 'legal' in the narrow meaning of the word. With the deaths of Claretta and Marcello, Myriam and her parents were left to work out their own futures; they would, however, never want, nor be able, to renounce their connection with Mussolini's lover.

After they moved from the Ritz Hotel at Barcelona to Madrid, the Petaccis took up residence in the Calle de Lagasca 122, in a bourgeois zone of a city still not fully recovered from the vicious fighting (and Fascist bombing) during the Spanish civil war. As the family's main money-earner (although Giuseppina was soon ready to publish in Spanish a memoir of Claretta),[100] Myriam resumed her cinema career, starring in nine romances between 1946 and 1950, one of which, *Cita con mi viejo corazón* (1949), was directed by Ferruccio Cerio, a Fascist director who had supported the RSI and also sought sanctuary with Franco, before returning to Italy and soon dropping out of the film business.[101] For these Spanish films, Myriam took the pseudonym 'Miriam Day' in place of Miria di San Servolo. If her career in Spain eventually came to a dead end, Myriam declared virtuously that, after the Second World War ended, she had rejected 'fabulous sums' offered by Hollywood, one of which was to star as Claretta in a film of the Mussolini love story.[102]

Beset by much confusion, Myriam divulged in her memoirs that she did not hear about Marcello's death until July 1945 and, fearful of her mother's weak heart, kept the unhappy news from her parents for some months after that. In June 1948 they were joined in the Spanish capital by Zita Ritossa. But a permanent stay there proved impossible for Zita when she could not find a decent school for the psychologically damaged Benvenuto. Nonetheless, the two boys did take their first Communion in Madrid in 1949, with family influence presumably helpful in obtaining the presence at the service of the papal nuncio to Spain.[103]

Myriam returned to Italy to live in 1951, quickly taking a leading part in a succession of legal proceedings, as well as in a controversy that had begun earlier over whether the body buried under Marcello's name at Musocco was really his.[104] She resumed residence in Spain from 1956 to 1959. After this third retreat, she joined her parents in a rented flat in Rome.[105] More lawsuits followed, including one against her de facto sister-in-law, Zita Ritossa.[106] Francesco Saverio, although never able to regain his position at the Vatican, survived well into his eighties, outliving his wife by almost a decade. Myriam, in declining financial circumstances, lasted until 1991, leaving Ferdinando, an emigrant to the USA, as the only survivor from her immediate family

For the rival Mussolini household, 'alike in dignity' to the Petaccis in our story, the deaths at Mezzegra, the abuse in Milan and the history of the Italian dictatorship left a legacy from which it was difficult to shake free but which offered richer rewards than were allowed to the Petaccis. On 29 April 1945 Rachele had been arrested and spent some days in the San Donnino prison, where other prisoners included the widow of Roberto Farinacci and their children. Mussolini's legal wife may have been disgusted to find that one repeated topic of conversation among party loyalists was whether the *Duce* had demeaned himself, his ideology and regime by dying in Claretta's company.[107] Yet, the greatest contempt at the way Mussolini had perished was scribbled by his sometime deep admirer, Giuseppe Bottai, by then disguised as an anonymous soldier in the French Foreign Legion in Algeria: 'That detail of Petacci "facing justice" at the side of Mussolini struck me very hard. It had been easier to pardon him as a man than to forgive him for his brothel-style condemnation that he had brought upon himself.'[108]

One Fascist confined at San Donnino was Buffarini Guidi; he was soon released, then arrested again and, in July, executed for his political crimes.

For Rachele, however, there was a transfer on 2 May under Allied auspices to a military camp at Terni, northeast of Rome, followed from 25 July by a comfortable enough period of *confino* on Ischia, where – according to one sentimental journalist – she took pleasure cooking bean soup for her children.[109] Eventually she returned to the family estates in the province of Forlì, welcoming the final interment of Mussolini's corpse in the family tomb at San Cassiano outside Predappio on 1 September 1957. Rachele died at the Villa Carpena on 30 October 1979.

Among those who dwelled at the Villa Feltrinelli not long to survive the war was Bruno's widow, Gina Ruberti. In April 1945 she found refuge with friends at a lakeside villa near Como where she sought to live a quiet life with her small daughter. However, on 3 May 1946 she died late at night when the speedboat that she was sharing with two British officers sank, sparking predictable gossip about what she had been getting up to with her foreign friends or, indeed, whether the British secret service had murdered her. In death she was thus fitted into the huge tangle of conspiracy theories that continue to be woven about anything, however tangential, that might be imagined to bear connection with Mussolini's last days.[110]

In 1944–5 Edda Ciano spent months in a Swiss clinic, revealing, according to her Swiss psychiatrist, 'a profound disgust for all sexual matters'.[111] She was returned to Italy at the end of August 1945 and was sentenced to two years *confino* on Lipari, the largest of the Aeolian Islands, where, by one questionable account in denial of the Swiss analysis, she enjoyed a passionate affair with a local communist.[112] Soon amnestied, she spent the rest of her life in houses at Capri and Rome, dying on 8 April 1995. She remained an advocate of dictatorship[113] but was never fully re-integrated into her surviving family.[114]

After 27 April Vittorio Mussolini, his wife, children and cousins were hidden for a while by sympathetic priests near Como. Over the next months Vittorio was piloted along Catholic networks to Spain, back to Genoa and then on to Argentina, under its friendly dictator, Juan Perón. The *Duce*'s eldest son reached Buenos Aires shortly before Christmas 1946. Twenty-one years later, he moved his life to Italy again, married a second time and died on 12 June 1997. The two youngest Mussolini children, Romano (born 1927) and Anna Maria (born 1929), had different fates.

Romano became an internationally acclaimed jazz musician, and did not die until February 2006. As was noted in the introduction, Romano, perhaps encouraged by his politician daughter, Alessandra, during his last years favoured the development of a pious memorial site to his father linked to the family estate at the Villa Carpena. His polio-stricken sister, Anna Maria, had a much shorter life, dying on 25 April 1968, but did leave behind two young daughters.[115]

* * *

In quite a few ways, then, the more prolific Mussolinis retain a presence in contemporary Italy that the Petaccis do not. Had they thereby won the family war? Yet, when it comes to ghosts, image and 'mythistory', Claretta's impassioned and doughty 'love' may have found a deeper place in Italian souls than anything that genuinely survives of Fascist ideology and practice, ensuring that, in our own times, Mussolini's body matters more than his mind. It is a result that could already have been predicted during the events near Lake Como. On 28 April 1945 the partisans killed a bewildered and defeated old puppet dictator who had long outlived his aspirations and whose public ridiculousness had been clear for a time; alongside him they killed a youngish woman utterly determined upon a private sacrifice that would never die.

CONCLUSION
A diarist's tale

I have told my tale. Or should I say Claretta has told hers? She is the real narrator of my book: so many of the words that I have inscribed are her own. I have translated them from the diary and the letters that she so persistently, stubbornly, self-righteously, obsessively and even hysterically wrote. I have added where necessary material from the numerous messages that Mussolini sent her, especially in 1943–5, and the correspondence that members of her family, led by her thrusting little sister, Myriam, were always ready to dash off to the *Duce*. With the assistance of such rich sources I have portrayed a love story of a kind. It has been replete with emotion: lust and sensuality, jealousy and passion, infatuation and manipulation, devotion and sacrifice, fear and hatred, kisses, love bites and orgasm, snoring and insomnia, cowardice and commitment, betrayal and forgiveness. In the 'Ben and Clara' relationship high sentiment mixed with grosser bodily functions, the extrusion of semen and vaginal fluid, tears and sweat, piss and spit, blood menstrual and vital. This romance led not to true happiness but rather death, if not a death exactly planned and arranged. My book might be best read with the *Sturm und Drang* of Clara and Ben's favourite music, Beethoven's 7th Symphony, playing loudly in the background (the couple did not seem to care that the composer, once a fan of Napoleon Bonaparte, Mussolini's hero and historical competitor, was by his 7th Symphony composing for the emperor's counter-revolutionary enemies, the Habsburgs).

Armed with a vast verbal record, I have been able to depict a dictator and his lover, and their surrounding family members, who, as they piloted themselves through the first totalitarian state, were driven by Fascist zealotry. At least at first sight, Mussolini's sexual record – five legitimate children and at least nine illegitimate (from eight different partners) – and his hasty and brutal sexual habits might seem proof that he was, as Gadda derisively called him, the 'Great Ejaculator', the supreme embodiment of Fascist disdain for, and exploitation of, women. Yet more nuanced conclusion is possible.

Certainly their attachment to the intrusive modern ideology of Fascism did not exclude Claretta and her family from being moved by Catholic piety and ingenuous religiosity, medical science and academic pretension, class arrogance and ambition, social climbing, *romanità*, whether in its regime or its older, more manipulative and venal, versions, timid fatherhood and unyielding matriarchy, rampant egoism and blind oblation. Above political commitment and even sometimes, it seemed, beyond her adoration, Claretta remained tied to her family, whose members were doughtily linked to her. Following their favoured (if clichéd) slogan 'One for all, and all for one', the Petacci family unrelentingly pursued their advantage and profit. Over time, such pursuit was shadowed by Claretta's increasing determination one day to overthrow and replace Rachele, the *Duce*'s legitimate wife. Although the evidence is slighter on their side, the Mussolini family were equally staunch in resisting Claretta and the other Petaccis' attacks, similarly convinced that they constituted a fortress in an imponderable and dangerous world. By 1943–5 the romance had become one of 'two households' warring to the death, almost as though they were a microcosmic parody of the bitter international conflict which saw the Italian dictatorship bring nation and regime to destruction. In such circumstances, the likelihood became steadily greater that this 'pair of star-crossed lovers' must also face their doom.

Not that Claretta for a moment accepted that the Petaccis and the Mussolinis were 'alike in dignity' or sincerity of devotion to the *Duce*. She knew that her family were good, her rivals bad. In her simplistic Darwinian reading of the world, there was a further complication since Mussolini had possessed so many women, comprising what has been well called his

CONCLUSION

'harem'.[1] To Claretta's constant disgust and dismay, he treated two of its members, Romilda Ruspi and Alice Pallottelli, as though they were sub-wives, from whom he was no more capable of his own free will fully to break than from Rachele. Mussolini continued to have sex with them, describing it to Claretta using the same deprecatory term that he used for coitus with his wife: from time to time, he stated, he must pay his taxes.

Both Ruspi and Pallottelli had borne illegitimate children to the dictator. Such paternity meant in his mind that they were part of his 'continuation', again to use his own terminology, one rooted not so much in contemporary Nazi-fascist racism as in traditional familism. Mussolini's comprehension of fatherly duty and obligation extended into the harem, if rather more in his later than his earlier days. While he was still a journalist and not a political chief, his cruel persecution of Ida Dalser and their son, Benito Albino, is notorious, while his seduction and abandonment of Bianca Ceccato reads mainly as a banally patriarchal case of office exploitation. By contrast, from 1942, pushed by her mother, Angela Cucciati, who had never renounced contact with the *Duce,* Mussolini welcomed his illegitimate daughter Elena Curti into his personal circle, perversely without fully explaining to the jealous Claretta who Elena was. He had similarly not forgotten Ines De Spuches, mother of a son of his killed in the war. With Curti, as with the children of Ruspi and Pallottelli, including ones who were not his, Mussolini did not gainsay responsibility for their financial wellbeing, or, when they were old enough, employment. Fitting this familial pattern, when his sometime partners, even Bianca Ceccato, were in childbirth, he was likely to be less harshly dismissive of them than at other times. Anthropologists used to talk about the deep significance within the Italian family of *sistemazione* (finding a place in life); Mussolini, with an extended family of greater breadth than the orthodox version, is a case study in that regard, a pattern not unknown among aristocrats of an earlier generation and Mafia bosses, then and later. The *Duce* was both more and less than a Fascist patriarch.

When it came to producing children, Claretta, after her extra-uterine pregnancy in August 1940, was a failure. Their hopes for what Mussolini told her in July 1940 was the 'infinite joy' of fatherhood proved barren.[2] Her illness and Mussolini's solicitude during her suffering, if a little wavering, became engraved into her history of their relationship as a moment of pure love. Mussolini, too, looked back on her travail and his reaction to it with nostalgia. In their relationship, there may have been no blood 'continuation', but perhaps there was a presence of the 'child that never was', ensuring that they could not part.

* * *

In recent years, emotions have become a modish topic of historical research. Jan Plamper, a leading theoretician of the subject, has dated interest in them to the French *Annales* school of the 1930s, underlining that Lucien Febvre was alerted to the subject by the emotionality of the crowds who applauded Mussolini and Hitler.[3] Plamper's predictable assumption is that dictators whip up those dark passions left inert in better societies. Yet it is worth noting that Mussolini, too, and not just his fans, was prey to a visible array of emotions. Lust may often have been the strongest but Mussolini could also sob while listening to *La traviata* or *La bohème*, be translated in mood when playing his violin or, as his circumstances declined during the Second World War or he reflected on a dead (legitimate) son, howl in desperation and frustration and bewail the crumbling of family life.

Most literature on dictatorship concentrates on high politics, assuming that the public thought and action of tyrants are what matters and that the private is of secondary significance, scarcely worth review or merely the natural and inevitable result of a perverse childhood.[4] Such attitudes are reinforced by the fact that Hitler, the supremely wicked artificer of the Holocaust, stands unchallenged as the prime model of a modern dictator. This all but automatic assumption detracts from our understanding of the type, among whom Mussolini was the twentieth-century and European pioneer. Yet, in most literature, the *Duce* is reduced to being a rather laughable clone of the *Führer*. When, in 2016, some Americans sought to ridicule Donald Trump, they readily highlighted an alleged parallel with Mussolini (prompted by the Republican candidate's ingenuous citation of a Fascist propaganda slogan: 'It is better to live one day as a lion than a hundred years as a sheep') and labelled him 'Il Douche'.[5]

CONCLUSION

As a man, Hitler combined a profound fanaticism, determined utterly to liquidate 'Judeo-Bolshevism', with a limply petit-bourgeois, *Biedermeier*-style sociability. Or perhaps, as a recent culturalist study has argued, it was merely his propaganda machine that constructed this banal persona.[6] Maybe the public prim formality hid what were deeper currents. Yet Hitler's arid dealings with Eva Braun bear little comparison with Mussolini's tumultuous relationship with Claretta. Certainly, the *Führer* gave no sign of caring about his physical 'continuation'. According to his latest biographer, Volker Ullrich, Hitler was certainly still a virgin at the end of the First World War and by 1924 had decided never to marry. He did like to be admired by much younger females, including Eva Braun, born, like Claretta, in February 1912 and therefore twenty-three years younger than the *Führer*. Ullrich explains in some detail the impossibility of knowing whether the two had sex.[7] But what is patent is Hitler's patriarchal certainty that women were too irrational to be taken seriously, a cliché of masculinity that Mussolini too expressed and yet, as has been shown, in practice gave his private life nuance and variety beyond the German dictator's ken.

Hitler's tedious personality is well expressed in his collected 'table talk'[8] and could run to his 'knowledge' that Italian women owed their beauty to their regularly carrying their property on their heads.[9] On any given night, Hitler chattered away into the wee hours with his entourage, who were forced to listen to his disquisitions on such matters, unable to admit the truth that he was a boring little man (in his frequent meetings with the *Führer*, Mussolini typically swung between being cowed by Hitler's power and fanaticism and being derisive of the German dictator's strangeness and loquacity).

Joseph Stalin, the second great tyrant of interwar Europe, was a different personality, mixing the cruel ideas and practices of a bandit with an entrenched belief in Marxist ideology, coloured by the literalism of the swiftly or partially educated. Because Stalin – unlike Mussolini and Hitler (with the exception of the murders within the Nazi party on the 'Night of the Long Knives' in June 1934) – directly eliminated many of his immediate political circle, his behaviour with his entourage was never free of menace. Nonetheless, as historian Sheila Fitzpatrick has recently illustrated, there was a 'Stalin team' and it did involve sociability of various kinds from family exchanges to deep, most often all-male, drinking. At their happiest before the purges, she has noted, 'the Stalins and their guests [at their dachas] played tennis, billiards, bowls, and chess; skied; went horse-riding; danced to the gramophone; sang; drank Georgian wine; and played with their own and other people's children'.[10] They nourished a profound attachment most of the time to others in the team, while possessed by a greater loyalty and an unmeasured respect for Stalin.

By contrast with the other two dictators, Mussolini was a man of some human span, curiosity and intellect, if doubtless better at tactics than strategy, time and again making the wrong overall choices in his life, and, in very many senses, a failure (perhaps more interesting because of that; most dictators 'fail'). In regard to personal emotions, Mussolini commonly bragged that he was a 'loner', being much given to misanthropic gibes at his closest Fascist colleagues, the Italian people and humankind. He did all that he could to avoid socialising with such comrades as Roberto Farinacci, Giuseppe Bottai, Italo Balbo and Dino Grandi, although they served his regime in many different posts throughout the *ventennio*. There was no intimate Mussolini 'team'. The *Duce* was the reverse of the Italian who likes to stroll arm in arm with his friends in a daily *passeggiata*. He was never a touchy-feely person and neither took tea nor drank wine with his 'friends', a word he did use but always in terms of such people's immediate utility to him.

Mussolini's standard position therefore was to be proud to be alone in a wicked and treacherous world; his arrogance always suggested that no party colleague could come close to matching his authority, drive and intuition. Yet, especially as he grew older and as the war enhanced his depression, particularly once he had to endure being a puppet dictator at Salò, Mussolini did on occasion grumble about his solitary fate. Such melancholy could lead him to remind Claretta wistfully of people with whom he had once had human contact. They were not party colleagues but instead family members: Arnaldo, his brother, with whom every evening he had talked on the phone until Arnaldo's early death in December 1931, Bruno, his dead son (here often embroidering the truth of their actual distant relationship), Edda, his eldest and favourite child, Galeazzo Ciano, her husband, admiring interlocutor, and, by the mid-1930s, implicit dauphin, despite the fact that the son-in-law was a soft gilded youth and no rough and tough Fascist boss.

There were also his bed partners. Again the *Duce*'s reiterated line was that women were constitutionally inferior to men and that no one could ever take their views seriously. When it came to bodily matters, Mussolini sounded like a patriarch of the old school, a man for whom sex could only be nasty, brutish and short. Yet, as Christopher Duggan archly noted, 'Though Mussolini endeavoured to keep his lovemaking as perfunctory as possible, there is little doubt that his relations with women consumed a huge amount of his time.'[11]

The Petacci diaries and other papers, the stream of phone calls and letters, certainly confirm that they did, whether in her direct regard or in his regular reflection to her on his other love affairs (by preference in historical recounting), even if, typically, his memories were overwhelmingly misogynist. Despite such lordly maleness, Mussolini more and more mixed his public and private activities, allowing Claretta space under the RSI to become a *Ducessa* of a kind, just as once he had engaged in massive correspondence with, and accepted counsel from, Margherita Sarfatti (while later so volubly despising both her and his weakness in listening to her), Leda Rafanelli and Angelica Balabanoff. Contrary to his loud pronouncements about female inferiority, Mussolini often mingled his decision-making in high politics with his emotions.

In that regard, as Italo-British historian Giuseppe Finaldi has acutely suggested, the *Duce*'s life and attitudes as expressed in his speeches bear less comparison with Hitler or Stalin and more with Winston Churchill, that other overflowingly emotional journalist-politician of the interwar.[12] Finaldi does not endorse the fantastic theories about a lost Mussolini–Churchill correspondence. But he does draw attention to the parallels that exist between the voice of an Italian, risen to power from 'below' at thirty-nine, and an impecunious and imperialist English aristocrat, held from the most glittering of prizes until he was sixty-five. Through the interwar and indeed his life, much of Churchill's emotion was directed at his gambling with financial fortune (and in minimising tax on it),[13] rather than on the lust for sex that occupied so many of Mussolini's hours. But each politician is difficult to understand without a constant reckoning with his emotions.

CLARETTA

* * *

If rage, passion and disquietude were a common part of Mussolini's mind and a regular trigger of his actions, hardly an hour seemed to pass without Claretta giving play to her emotions. Hysteria was a daily matter. Claretta regularly relied on stereotypically female floods of tears, a ready swoon in times of crisis, a devoted religiosity to Santa Rita and emanations of the Virgin, a huge repertoire of the melodrama of love and infatuation and a reviving sip of cognac. At the same time, she retained the primness of her class training, which stopped her from writing out such horrid words as 'bum' and 'whore'. No doubt she did list her sexual acts and, over time, frequently added an assessment of Mussolini's performance during them. Yet her *si* was not enlarged into more detailed description of how she and the *Duce* intermingled during their sexual congress. Claretta Petacci was no Henry Miller; at least in her descriptions of sex, she followed the missionary method.

As has been noted, except during her last hours, Claretta's emotional life was never fully detached from that of her family and, in turn, her father, mother, brother and sister reacted emotionally to her life choices. Francesco Saverio anxiously clung to his medical profession. Giuseppina Persichetti told her rosary beads and implored the Virgin for support, even while she approved or fostered the irregular lifestyle of each of her daughters. Marcello gave rein to his vivid ambition as doctor, thinker and moneymaker. Myriam belied her years in her importunity. Only Zita Ritossa, with available evidence the most shadowy member of the family, behaved like an 'exemplary wife and mother', devotedly cossetting her damaged son, Benghi, until his death in his thirties; she herself lived ten further years before succumbing to a heart attack in 1987. She had also been a good daughter in finding a residence for her parents – refugees from Istria in what was now Yugoslavia – in Merano, where, despite the postwar loss of the Villa Schildhof, they stayed until their deaths.[14] Yet, despite such conventional female attention to duty, even Zita was 'modern' or independent enough never to complete a church or state marriage with her partner.

Among the Petaccis, Myriam is of special interest, growing from an early teenage chaperone, *piccola idiota* (and object of lascivious side glances) to an ambitious film star, fleeting wife, and cocksure client determined to make the most of her opportunities in dealing with the grand patron Mussolini, not minding being, on at least one occasion, anti-Semitic in the process. It is Myriam who found the words that best expressed the potency of the Petacci family unit when she told the *Duce* that he must accept that Claretta *ha avuto sempre ragione* ('has always been right').

The ubiquitous slogan of the Fascist regime was, by contrast, *Mussolini ha sempre ragione* ('Mussolini is always right') and it hangs over the historiography of the Italian dictatorship as summation of a system where the *Duce* ruled alone and untrammelled. The corollaries typically are that Mussolini was hell-bent on empire and war. As a fascist must be (the small 'f' removing any idea that his ideology and practice were merely Italian), he preached and practised violence and murder. Seeking total power, he was a damnable enemy of human freedom, a purpose summed up in the regime's totalitarian determination on a system where all 'was for the state, nothing was against the state, no one was outside the state'. At the same time he was an adamant enemy of female liberation. Under the theory of Fascism, women were returned to the bedroom where their only serious role was to make children for the *patria*. Neither politics nor thought was for them.

There is much that is justified in such interpretation. Certainly in the long run, the dictatorship did not improve the wellbeing of its subjects, male or female. Its wars in Africa and Europe brought a million victims prematurely to their graves (almost half of them the peoples of Libya and Ethiopia). Fascist Italy was also an active participant in the Holocaust, that nadir of human civilisation. The image of a bloody, 'modern', patriarchal Fascism, killing freedom with totalitarian determination, is deeply inscribed in current historiography. It was well expressed in the American historian Michael Ebner's important recent study of the sanctions imposed against anti-Fascists under the dictatorship, published as *Ordinary violence in Mussolini's Italy*. Ebner entitles his introduction 'the Fascist Archipelago', thereby apparently establishing a connection between the Italian regime ruled by Mussolini and Stalinism.[15] It may be that the Rome-based historian Emilio Gentile was the intellectual pioneer of the reassertion of a genuine totalitarianism in interwar Italy.[16] But he has had a legion of disciples, especially in the United States and especially now when, in the practice of history, a culturalist methodology has triumphed over what, during the 1970s, was still the leadership of social history.

There is something intriguing about the chronology of such argument since, as Francis Fukuyama first perceived in however stuttering prose,[17] with the fall of communism and the certainty that its economic and political models were both bad and incompetent, we live under a hegemony of neoliberalism. We therefore subsist with what might almost seem a totalitarianism in reverse, wherein 'all is for the market, nothing is outside the market, no one is against the market' (at least in regard to government policy). Such a terrible simplification of budget-making is conditioned by identity politics and its ideal of a thousand flowers blooming (as distinct from the rigidity and narrowness of class). Since fascists are practitioners of a state religion, it is usually maintained, they must be bad guys; was it not the residue of French fascism that trickled into the (rival) Baathist regimes of Saddam in Iraq and the Assads in Syria that made them so much 'worse' than the Kingdom of Saudi Arabia, for example?

Since, the argument continues, Mussolini instituted a regime of untrammelled state power, there can be no reason to limit its present condemnation. Even if, in reality, Fascism rose to destroy Italian socialism, especially as implemented by the unionised poor peasantry of the Po valley (admittedly with an addition of hyper-nationalism aroused on the nation's expanded borders through victory in the First World War), it must have fundamentally been a dictatorship viciously opposed to freedom. Liberalism, not Marxism, must have been its real enemy; indeed, as totalitarianist theory in the liberal USA of the 1950s urged, communism and fascism were in fact opposite sides of the same evil modern coin.

Again I am willing to accept quite a bit of such analysis, despite wanting to note wryly that any governor of Texas executes more of his citizens in a single term of office than Mussolini did throughout his rule in Italy in peacetime, and that the victims and 'collateral damage' of neoliberal imperialism must by now be threatening the tally of those killed in its fragile empire by Italian Fascism. I might also wonder at the claim to unsullied virtue of our neoliberal present, as expressed, for example, in its euphemism of 'taking out' (that is, murdering with no hint of legal process) 'bad guys' and any unlucky enough to find themselves near the 'strikes' inflicted on them by anonymous drones or distant pilots. Should we really assume that our times and our side are virtuous and, thus armed and equipped, move on to liquidate fascism historically?

Setting such moralising aside, in the narrower arena of history writing, the point needs underlining that, in offering an understanding of life under the Italian dictatorship, the totalitarianist version offers sight of half the glass but not its entirety. As the senior Italian historian Roberto Vivarelli, himself once a young and fanatical Fascist and later a liberal patriot, Italian-style, has noted in some puzzlement, Mussolini should not be assumed to have been just another Hitler or Stalin. The Fascist chief was, Vivarelli contended, 'rather more moderate, more malleable, alien to fanaticism, deprived of all the most repugnant traits of those bloody tyrants'. Crude, vain and cynical Mussolini no doubt was; yet he was also a recognisable Italian man, Vivarelli urged. This dictator required less fanatically religious belief from those he ruled and more 'obedience and conformism, an individual's renunciation of his own dignity and character'. The main practical ideology of the regime therefore was not so much deep theory as 'vulgar Machiavellianism'. Given such reality, Vivarelli has asserted, perhaps remembering his own liberalism, 'Fascists and fascism were not the same thing . . . a negative judgement on the phenomenon, a historical judgement, does not necessarily extend . . . to all those who were, in various but active ways, then actors of the phenomenon.'[18]

If a close reading of Mussolini's character elicits mixed messages, study of Claretta Petacci is little different. Her writings show her to be an unrepentantly Fascist racist (whether in her drastic assertion of her timeless and 'noble' purity of blood or her anti-Semitism). Equally she frequently urged her lover into greater violence, while advocating the closest ties with Hitler and Nazi Germany. Read literally, her words suggest that she was the model of a 'new Fascist woman', a true believer in the radical fascism that was enunciated as the purpose of the Repubblica Sociale or, if her subordination is read as involving the confinement of her mind, no more than her master's voice.

Yet the most fanatical political chiefs of the revived revolutionary promise of the RSI regime despised and hated Claretta and her family, as was made crystal clear when Marcello awaited execution with fifteen of them beside Lake Como. They were right after all to be suspicious since, as has been noticed, even in its most passionate expression, the Petacci version of Fascist revolution was conditioned by family loyalty, Catholicism, class, a Roman setting and a number of other factors. At the same time, it may be suspected, when the deep beliefs of Pavolini, Starace, Bombacci or any of those whose bodies were destined to be exposed in Piazzale Loreto are reviewed, there, too, currents of Fascist ideology were mixed with other ideas and actions.

Much social history of the Italian experience of the regime remains to be written. It will need carefully to distinguish deeds from words, the practical from the ideological. It will perforce examine the functioning of family life, not merely that of people of the Petaccis' class and urban background but of many different sorts of Italians.

Yet bringing Claretta's family story into focus is a start. Taking them at their own word, the Petaccis were Fascists, racists, anti-Semites, fans of Hitler and Franco, nationalists, Catholics, clients and patrons, capitalists and Roman bourgeois, possessed of a snobbish ambition to rise into the nobility and a staunch class identity. In their firm family solidarity, the Petaccis, old and young, saw no contradiction in such amalgam. They were not atomised individuals who had surrendered their agency to an all-powerful state, despite the fact that, in April 1945, their family crumbled away as a result of Claretta's connection with Mussolini in a love story that was less tragic than it was pathetic. In their multifarious, complex and ambiguous thought and action, Claretta and the rest of her family hold a telling place in contemporary history. Their story illuminates much about what life was like in the first avowedly 'totalitarian', yet decidedly Italian, dictatorship.

ACKNOWLEDGEMENTS

This book owes its conception to Christopher Wheeler who, almost two decades ago now, won me over to the idea that I should venture to write a biography of Benito Mussolini. In the new millennium, I gradually became aware of the existence and eventually the public availability of a massive new source on the regime and its dictator, stimulated first by contact with Mauro Suttora, the editor of the initial collection from the Petacci diary. It was published in Italian in 2009 and, to our frustration, has not been translated into English. I was further encouraged by my long friendship with Mimmo Franzinelli, the most productive Italian historian of his generation, and an extraordinarily honest one. Franzinelli edited a second collection from the diary and prepared still unpublished extracts for a third. He generously gave me access to these. My book, supplemented by further material from the Petacci family papers, is dedicated to him.

Helped by Mariapina Di Simone and her expert staff, I read further in the family papers at the Archivio Centrale dello Stato, that emblematically Fascist building in the Fascist model suburb of EUR. I had already spent quite a bit of my research life there and had collected material on other characters in the story to be related in this book. The ACS, as every historian of contemporary Italy knows, is a delightful place to work; expert archivists, ample and well-lit research space, cheap coffee and two excellent

ACKNOWLEDGEMENTS

'fasts' to choose from for lunch. In Rome, my investigations were reinforced by the helpful and efficient staff of other libraries, notably the Biblioteca Nazionale, Biblioteca di Storia Moderna e Contemporanea, Biblioteca Baldini (where Silvia Concina was especially helpful) and Istituto Gramsci. When visiting the Eternal City, I have grown used to staying at the British School at Rome, where there is another excellent collection of books and journals as well as an array of scholars of wondrous variety in interest and place of origin, where sociability and intellectuality are deftly sustained by the director, Christopher Smith (no narrow classicist he).

I may be a stubborn Roma-phile. But I have on occasion strayed to other places in Italy and must especially acknowledge the help over the years of the staff at the Biblioteca Nazionale Marciana and Biblioteca Querini Stampalia at Venice and the Biblioteca Classense and Biblioteca Oriani at Ravenna. In my search for a place in the world, I have found the most delightful of sanctuaries in Oxford for five years now: imagine living in a house fifteen minutes' walk from the Bodleian (with lunch to be had at a college two minutes away). An old man in paradise! Every now and again I have searched out books elsewhere, and so should add my thanks to the Taylorian Institution Library, the Vere Harmsworth Library, Worcester College Library, the British Library and Reading University Library.

I have had other generous assistance in tracking down places in Italy where the Petaccis resided or had connection. I owe particular thanks to Giovanni Minelli for continuing legal advice and Susanna and Patty for meals and joys at Venice, to Max Tosetti and the staff of Villa Fiordaliso at Gardone for my tour of the villa there and a fabulous lunch, to Camilla Bettoni for twice escorting me to the Vittoriale degli Italiani and its environs, to Alessia Micheletti for showing me around the Villa Feltrinelli at Gargnano, to Verena Vok for allowing me to inspect her Villa Schildhof, to Georg Schedereit for smoothing that visit (and more generally for acting as a sensitive and generous host when I visited Merano/Meran), and to Fabio Malusà for assisting my locating of the Petazzi chapel at Trieste. I am also in debt to Simon Levis Sullam at Venice, Gustavo Corni at Trento and Dante Bolognesi at Ravenna for assisting my researches there, as well as to Patrizia Dogliani for a reminder visit to Predappio, now quite a few years ago.

ACKNOWLEDGEMENTS

My brilliant and hard-working colleagues at Jesus College have been wholly welcoming to an elderly historian of Australian birth, incapable of long resisting the chance to chatter about Claretta. John Krebs, the college principal until 2015, could not have been more helpful to someone with claims to act as the oldest 'nut boy' in Jesus history. The college's 'real' historians, Patricia Clavin, Alex Gajda and Sue Doran – women who, unlike me, still fill their hours with teaching and yet find time to research and write – are splendid colleagues (even if I sometimes feel guilty at my inactivity compared with theirs).

Daniele Baratieri, Gianfranco Cresciani, Christopher Duggan (so sadly lost to us in November 2015), Mark Edele, Giuseppe Finaldi, David Laven, David Lowenthal, Joe Maiolo, Ross McKibbin, John Pollard, Mark Thompson, fine historians every one, have corrected at least some of my errors and infelicities and helped me remain active as a writer and researcher. Gerald Steinacher confirmed a footnote; Reto Hofmann deserves thanks for two.

As ever I owe a massive debt to Michal. Our fiftieth anniversary fell just as I was about to start writing this book, but that did not stop her being, as ever, my first critical reader. I am similarly happy with and proud of our children, Mary, learned and active Oxford professor of criminology, and Edmund, now an Irish banker. My agent, Clare Alexander, pushes me effectively into readable topics and Heather McCallum, Rachael Lonsdale, Samantha Cross, Lauren Atherton, Heather Nathan, Maha Moushabeck, my copy-editor Jacob Blandy and the rest of the fine staff in the London office of Yale University Press put up with my vagaries as a historian and produce books of high quality that do not look as though their only purpose is rapid sale.

In every way, my life devotion to modern Italian history has been a fortunate one, and I like to think that, even when portraying such flawed human beings as Benito Mussolini and Claretta Petacci, my exploration of humankind leaves me, now as ever, more an optimist of the will than a pessimist of the intellect.

ENDNOTES

Introduction

1. Emblematically a recent popular evocation of the last days of the war in Europe starts with the deaths of Mussolini and his lover, and dwells upon the 'anarchy' of Piazzale Loreto. See Nicholas Best, *Five days that shook the world: eyewitness accounts from Europe at the end of World War II* (Oxford: Osprey Publishing, 2012).
2. Anon, *L'ultima favorita: Clara Petacci* (Rome: Editore Francesco Mondini, 1945), p. 14. In fact, exhumation would show she had a broken tooth, a damaged jaw and other bruising, most likely received on the ground at Piazzale Loreto, although other, conspiratorial, explanations exist.
3. Mirella Serri, *Un amore partigiano: storia di Gianni e Neri, eroi scomodi della Resistenza* (Milan: Longanesi, 2014), p. 125.
4. Anon (ed.), *Mussolini giudicato dal mondo* (Milan: Universus, 1946), pp. 250–2.
5. Ezra Pound, *The Pisan cantos* (London: Faber and Faber, 1949), p. 7.
6. Wladislaw Potocki, 'Clara Petacci: "io sono la Petacci, voglio morire col Duce"', *Plush*, 1964.
7. *The Times*, 10 May 1975.
8. Throughout my text, I shall call Petacci 'Claretta' in order to distinguish her from the other members of her family. Over their last years together, Mussolini did generally call her Clara but she was almost always Claretta within her family. She called her lover 'Ben', after initially using *Gattone* ('Big Pussy Cat') as her term of endearment.
9. Robert D. MacDonald, *Summit Conference* (London: Amber Lane Press, 1982), pp. 8, 24. For a review of its first staging at the Glasgow Citizens Theatre in 1978, see *The Times*, 21 January 1978. Recently, the popular historian Arrigo Petacco has written a less-than-compelling joint biography of the two. Analysis goes little further than his introductory note that each was an Acquarian, each died aged thirty-three and the two never actually met. See Arrigo Petacco, *Eva e Claretta: le amanti del diavolo* (Milan: Mondadori, 2012).
10. *The Times*, 19 March, 29 April 1982.
11. *The Times*, 13 August 1977, 16 May 1978, 30 May 1984. An offspring then finished second in its maiden contest behind a colt called Falstaff.
12. Steiger reprised the role in *Lion of the Desert*, directed by Moustafa Akkad (1981). The film's exploration of Italian colonial genocide meant that it was long banned in Italy.

13. *The Times*, 15 February 1972.
14. For an apolitical account of Cardinale's career as a 'dark, shapely and sensual' star, see Réka Buckley, 'The emergence of film fandom in postwar Italy: reading Claudia Cardinale's fan mail', *Historical Journal of Film, Radio and Television*, 29, 2009, pp. 523–59.
15. Again the name of this Petacci, as will be noted further below, came with variations of name and its spelling. I shall use Myriam throughout since that was what she chose to call herself in her memoirs. In the family she was generally known as 'Mimi' or 'Mimmy'.
16. Roberto Olla, *Il Duce and his women* (Richmond: Aline Books, 2011).
17. Nicholas Farrell, *Mussolini: a new life* (London: Weidenfeld & Nicolson, 2003), pp. 20; 227.
18. *Guardian*, 5 December 2014.
19. FO 371/23825/R1805, Foreign Office to Lindsay (Washington), 17 March 1939.
20. *Daily Mail*, 5 February 2015.
21. *Il Corriere dell'Umbria*, 4 July 2015. There, it was emphasised that Claretta on more than one occasion had visited the tourist town of Spello.
22. *Il Corriere di Brescia*, 18 October 2012.
23. See http://www.museodisalo.it/it/repubblica-sociale-italiana (accessed 9 October 2015). For my more general assessment of Italian memory and its gaping lacunae, see R.J.B. Bosworth, 'Victimhood asserted: Italian memories of the Second World War' in Manuel Bragança and Peter Tame (eds), *The long aftermath: cultural legacies of Europe at war, 1936–2016* (New York: Berghahn, 2016).
24. The 'B' and 'P' that appear on the Petacci bed thus have nothing to do with Ben and Petacci. For D'Annunzio, see the English biography, Lucy Hughes-Hallett, *The pike: Gabriele D'Annunzio, poet, seducer and preacher of war* (London: Fourth Estate, 2013).
25. For a visual version, see https://www.youtube.com/watch?v=9sGaIytJ-WI (accessed 3 February 2016).
26. Roberto Festorazzi, *Claretta Petacci: la donna che morì per amore di Mussolini* (Bologna: Minerva Edizioni, 2012), pp. 285–6.
27. Roberto Gervaso, *Claretta, la donna che morì per Mussolini* (Milan: Rizzoli, 1982).
28. See reports in *Alto Adige*, 1 November 1949; 26 April 1950. I owe this reference to Professor Gerald Steinacher of the University of Nebraska–Lincoln.
29. Fondo Monelli, b. 139. According to Monelli, Francesco Saverio would have preferred a villa on the more decorous Aventine Hill but the family could not afford it.
30. For a newsreel image from 1947, see http://www.britishpathe.com/video/clara-petaccis-villa (accessed 11 October 2015).
31. *The Times*, 7 March 1960.
32. Francesca Romana Castelli and Piero Ostilio Rossi, 'Una villa per la "banda Petacci"', *Capitolium*, III, 1999, p. 89. Cf. the photographic representation in *Casabella*, October 2011, with much praise for the young architects Amedeo Lucchienti and Vincenzo Monaco.
33. For the story, see R.J.B. Bosworth, *Mussolini* (rev. edn; London: Bloomsbury, 2010), pp. 335–6; for an autobiographical account by the body-snatcher, cf. Domenico Leccisi, *Con Mussolini prima e dopo Piazzale Loreto* (Rome: Edizioni Settimo Sigillo, 1991).
34. Ministero dell'Interno Gabinetto 1957–1960 [hereafter MIG], b. 43, Ministero dell'Interno to Direzione Generale di Pubblica Sicurezza, 8 January 1954. *The Times*, 17 March 1956, did report the presence of the Francoist Spanish press attaché at the interment, while 'Prince Farouk', perhaps the exiled Egyptian king, sent a wreath.
35. See http://www.ilmessaggero.it/roma/storie/il_verano_tra_museo_e_palco_pellegrinaggio_dai_grandi_artisti/notizie/217502.shtml (accessed 12 July 2014).
36. See http://www.vivisanlorenzo.it/News/News_gennaio_2004/visite_verano_san_lorenzo.htm (accessed 12 July 2014).
37. For this subject, see my analysis in R.J.B. Bosworth, *Whispering city: Rome and its histories* (London: Yale University Press, 2011).

38. For Rachele's complaint about the matter, see Bruno D'Agostini, *Colloqui con Rachele Mussolini* (Rome: OET, 1946), p. 86.
39. The tomb thereby seems to affirm the view of historian of emotions, William Reddy, that modern 'Western romantic love is particularly unusual insofar as love continues to stand in contrast to lust' and is typically armed with 'spiritual expectations'. See W.M. Reddy, 'The rule of love: the history of Western romantic love in comparative perspective', in Luisa Passerini, Liliana Ellena, and Alexander C.T. Geppert (eds), *New dangerous liaisons: discourses on Europe and love in the twentieth century* (New York: Berghahn Books, 2010), p. 51.
40. *Il Tempo*, 28 October 2015.
41. *Il Giornale*, 22 August 2016; *Il Tempo*, 8 September 2016.
42. See http://www.ok.com/permalink.php?story_fbid=301569753224072&id=1081804125 63008&stream_ref=5 (accessed 14 July 2014).
43. See http://www.storiainrete.com/7237/rassegna-stampa-italiana/morte-mussolini-lanpi-modifica-la-targa-a-giulino-a-modo-suo/ (accessed 11 October 2015).
44. MIG, b. 43, 23 February, 5 April, 5 September, 1 October 1959, 18, 27 February 1961.
45. MIG, b. 43, 19, 20 September, 22 November 1962.
46. For a curious example, see Paul Ginsborg, *Silvio Berlusconi: television, power and patrimony* (London: Verso, 2004) and his warning that Berlusconi was creating a Fascistoid following and state.
47. For its standard history, see Piero Ignazi, *Il polo escluso: profilo del Movimento Sociale Italiano* (Bologna: il Mulino, 1989); cf. also his *Postfascisti? Dal Movimento Sociale Italiano ad Alleanza Nazionale* (Bologna: Il Mulino, 1994).
48. For their website, see http://www.casapounditalia.org/ (accessed 3 February 2016).
49. For a recent typical example, see the six-month diary *Benito Mussolini: lo stato sociale nel Ventennio: pagine di storia dimenticata* (Rome: I Libri del Borghese, 2016). It includes only one image of the familial *Duce*, with wife and five children. There is no sign of Claretta.
50. Vittorio Mussolini, *Vita con il mio padre* (Milan: Mondadori, 1957); *Mussolini: the tragic women in his life* (London: NEL, 1973). The first account ignored Claretta. By the second she had risen to share billing in 'tragedy' with his sister and mother.
51. Edvige Mussolini, *Mio fratello Benito: memorie raccolte e trascritte da Rosetta Ricci Crisolini* (Florence: La Fenice, 1957); and cf. Benito Mussolini, *Opera omnia* (ed. E. and D. Susmel) (36 vols) (Florence: La Fenice, 1951–62), vol. 36, pp. 479–80, which does list Claretta in a chronology of Mussolini's death. An additional eight volumes, still without Claretta, were added in Benito Mussolini, *Opera omnia* (ed. Edoardo and Duilio Susmel) *Appendici I–VIII* (vols 37–44) (Florence: Giovanni Volpe Editore, 1978–80).
52. Emilio Settimelli, *Edda contro Benito: indagine sulla personalità del Duce attraverso un memoriale autografo di Edda Ciano Mussolini, qui riprodotto* (Rome: Casa Editrice Libraria Corso, 1952).
53. Edda Mussolini Ciano, *My truth (as told to Albert Zarca)* (London: Weidenfeld & Nicolson, 1977); *La mia vita: intervista di Domenico Olivieri* (ed. Nicola Caracciolo) (Milan: Mondadori, 2001).
54. Fabrizio Ciano, *Quando il nonno fece fucilare papà* (ed. Dino Cimagalli) (Milan: Mondadori, 1991). This Ciano died in 2008.
55. Romano Mussolini, *Benito Mussolini: apologia di mio padre* (Bologna: Rivista Romana, 1969); *My father Il Duce: a memoir by Mussolini's son* (New York: Kales Press, 2006).
56. For background on the highly fissiparous neo-fascist zone in Italy, see Andrea Mammone, *Transnational neofascism in France and Italy* (Cambridge University Press, 2015).
57. Scandal never ended. In 2015, for example, it was reported internationally that her husband, Mauro Floriani, an officer in the Guardia di Finanza, allegedly known to his friends as 'Captain Mussolini', was to be prosecuted for 'paying for sex with teenage prostitutes'. See *Daily Telegraph*, 26 June 2015.

58. See www.casadeiricordi.it (accessed 3 February 2016).
59. Maurizio Ridolfi and Franco Moschi (eds), *Il Giovane Mussolini 1883–1914: la Romagna, la formazione, l'ascesa politica* (Forlì: Neri Wolff, 2013).
60. See, for example, Claudio Mussolini, *La parentesi: 1914–1924 dall'entrata in guerra alla presa del potere: le vie del fascismo: un esame di bibliografia comparata* (Milan: Baldini e Castoldi, 2002).
61. See *La Repubblica*, 5 September 2006; and a campaign, launched by Guido, eldest son of Vittorio (died 2012), to exhume Mussolini again and restart a trial of the details of his death.
62. Davide Fabbri has some local celebrity as *Davide il Vichingo*, a rightist satirist, and has at times talked of somehow replicating his antecedent's March on Rome or, perhaps, Perugia. See *Il Tempo*, 23 February 2011 and http://www.ilfattoquotidiano.it/2014/04/29/forconi-a-bologna-ce-il-pronipote-del-duce-tiro-le-banane-al-ministro-kyenge/968156/ (accessed 15 October 2015). In the initial lessons, Fabbri was reported to be supported by another relative, Benito Moschi. See *Libero*, 25 June 2006.
63. Rachele Mussolini, *La mia vita con Benito* (Milan: Mondadori, 1948). Cf. *The real Mussolini (as told to A. Zarca)* (Farnborough: Saxon House, 1973). The latter book contained a photo of Claretta's lavishly furnished bed at the Villa Camilluccia. The earlier Italian account did not.
64. Anita Pensotti, *Rachele e Benito: biografia di Rachele Mussolini* (Milan: Mondadori, 1993), p. 9.
65. Rachele Mussolini, *La mia vita con Benito*, p. 273 and cf. pp. 250–3.
66. Francobaldo Chiocci, *Donna Rachele* (Rome: Ciarrapico Editore, 1983), p. 12.
67. See, for example, Bruno D'Agostini, *Colloqui con Rachele Mussolini*; Anita Pensotti, *La restituzione dei resti di Mussolini nel drammatico racconto della vedova* (Rome: Dino Editore, 1972).
68. Posthumous journalistic biographies have not demurred. See Francobaldo Chiocci, *Donna Rachele*; Anita Pensotti, *Rachele: sessant'anni con Mussolini nel bene e nel male* (Milan: Bompiani, 1983); *Rachele e Benito* (1993); *Le italiane* (Milan: Simonelli Editore, 1999); Elena Bianchini Braglia, *Donna Rachele: con il Duce, oltre il Duce* (Milan: Mursia, 2007).
69. In regard to reality, see Ruggero Zangrandi's celebrated account of his own passage to the Resistance after a gilded teenage life in Rome and a friendship with Vittorio Mussolini. Ruggero Zangrandi, *Il lungo viaggio attraverso il fascismo: contributo alla storia di una generazione* (Milan: Feltrinelli, 1964), p. 20, where he remembered Rachele, almost always in her apron, feeding the two bread and butter, just as his own mother did.
70. Cristina Baldassini, *L'ombra di Mussolini: l'Italia moderata e la memoria del fascismo (1945–1960)* (Soveria Mannelli: Rubbettino, 2008), p. 5.
71. *Ibid.*, p. 14.
72. Silvia Pizzetti, *I rotocalchi e la storia: la divulgazione storica nei periodici illustrati (1950–1975)* (Rome: Bulzoni Editore, 1982), p. 80.
73. Cristina Baldassini, *L'ombra di Mussolini*, pp. 2–6.
74. Silvia Pizzetti, *I rotocalchi e la storia*, p. 70.
75. Luigi Cavicchioli, 'Il testamento di Claretta ha commosso il pubblico: Al processo di Brescia Clara Petacci è risultata una donna fedele e coraggiosa', *Oggi*, 10 July 1952.
76. Myriam Petacci, 'Questa è la mia storia', *Oggi*, 14, 21, 28 April, 5 May 1955.
77. Myriam Petacci, *Chi ama è perduto: mia sorella Claretta* (ed. Santi Corvaja) (Gardolo di Trento: Luigi Reverdito Editore, 1988).
78. See *Cronache*, 20 October 1945, as preserved in Fondo Monelli, b. 139.
79. Zita Ritossa, 'Mia "cognata" Claretta Petacci', *Tempo*, 7, 14, 21, 28 February, 7, 14, 21, 28 March, 4, 11, 18, 24 April, 2, 9 May 1957; 'La mia vita con Claretta Petacci', *Oggi*, 9 April 1975.
80. See http://www.jus.unitn.it/users/pascuzzi/privcomp00-01/topics/3/Cass_1963.htm (accessed 18 October 2015).

81. Cristina Baldassini, *L'ombra di Mussolini*, p. 278.
82. Anita Pensotti, *Le italiane* (Milan: Simonelli Editore, 1999), p. 8.
83. Rachele Mussolini, *La mia vita con Benito*, pp. 267–8; Benito Mussolini, *Opera omnia*, vol. XXXII, pp. 267–8.
84. See, notably, Sergio Luzzatto, *Il corpo del duce: un cadavere tra immaginazione, storia e memoria* (Turin: Einaudi, 1998), pp. 197–8, based on a reading of Anita Pensotti, *Rachele e Benito*, pp. 126–7. The account, itself decidedly vague, is repeated from Anita Pensotti, *Rachele*, pp. 118–19.
85. Anita Pensotti, *Le italiane*, pp. 12–14.
86. Elena Bianchini Braglia, *Donna Rachele*, pp. 22–5.
87. Renzo De Felice, *Mussolini l'alleato 1940–1945*, vol. I, *L'Italia in guerra 1940–1943*, part 2, *Crisi e agonia del regime* (Turin: Einaudi, 1990), pp. 1069–78.
88. *Ibid.*, pp. 1536–40. There is a slightly different version in Fondo Monelli, b. 139.
89. For my own account at the end of the 1990s, see R.J.B. Bosworth, *The Italian dictatorship: problems and perspectives in the interpretation of Mussolini and Fascism* (London: Arnold, 1998). For more up-to-date commentary on Italian views, see *Studi Storici*, 55, i, 2014.
90. Here see the massive and important comparative work, Paul Ginsborg, *Family politics: domestic life, devastation and survival 1900–1950* (New Haven: Yale University Press, 2014).
91. See, for example, *Guardian*, 12 September 2003. Cf. *La Repubblica*, 27 January 2013 after Berlusconi chose Holocaust Memorial Day to downplay Fascist anti-Semitism.
92. See *Daily Telegraph*, 9 November 2011.
93. Roberto Festorazzi, *Claretta Petacci*. The book sought to replace the earlier accounts of Roberto Gervaso (see n. 27 above) and Franco Bandini, *Claretta: profilo di Clara Petacci e dei suoi tempi* (Milan: Sugar Editore, 1960). Festorazzi doubled the dose with a book about Mussolini's women in general but gave quite a bit of space to Claretta. See Roberto Festorazzi, *Mussolini e le sue donne* (Varese: Pietro Macchione Editore, 2013).
94. Roberto Festorazzi, *Il nonno in camicia nera* (Como: Il Silicio, 2004).
95. Roberto Festorazzi, *Claretta Petacci*, pp. v–vi; 111; 129–30.
96. *Ibid.*, p. 283.
97. *Ibid.*, p. 286.
98. Benito Mussolini, *A Clara: tutte le lettere a Clara Petacci 1943–1945* (ed. Luisa Montevecchi) (Milan: Mondadori, 2011). Apart from the editor, Elena Aga-Rossi and Giuseppe Parlato provided polite commentary following a preface by Agostino Attanasio.
99. Ermanno Amicucci, *I 600 giorni di Mussolini (dal Gran Sasso a Dongo)* (Rome: Editrice 'Faro', 1948), p. 18.
100. Roberto Festorazzi, *Claretta Petacci*, p. 129.
101. Anita Pensotti, *Le italiane*, pp. 37; 60–1. By the time she found refuge on Lipari in 1945, Edda herself only weighed 42 kilograms. Marcello Sorgi, *Edda Ciano e il comunista: l'inconfessabile passione della figlia del Duce* (Milan: Rizzoli, 2009), p. 35.
102. For the most authoritative version, see Galeazzo Ciano, *Diario 1937–1943* (ed. Renzo De Felice) (Milan: Rizzoli, 1980). The English version is *Ciano's Diary 1937–1943* (ed. Renzo De Felice) (London: Phoenix Press, 2002). For the latest English-language biography of Ciano, see Ray Moseley, *Mussolini's shadow: the double life of Count Galeazzo Ciano* (New Haven: Yale University Press, 1999).
103. See Giuseppe Bottai, *Diario 1935–1944* (ed. Giordano Bruno Guerri) (Milan: Rizzoli, 1982); Bruno Bottai, *Fascismo famigliare* (Casale Monferrato: Edizioni Piemme, 1997). For a forgiving biography of Bottai, see Giordano Bruno Guerri, *Giuseppe Bottai: un fascista critica: ideologia e azione del gerarca che avrebbe voluto portare l'intelligenza nel fascismo e il fascismo alla liberalizzazione* (Milan: Feltrinelli, 1976).
104. Edvige Mussolini, *Mio fratello Benito*, p. 163.

105. Mimmo Franzinelli, *Autopsia di un falso*: *i Diari di Mussolini e la manipolazione della storia* (Turin: Bollati Boringhieri, 2011).
106. *Ibid.*, pp. 11–41.
107. *Ibid.*, pp. 41–53.
108. *Ibid.*, pp. 56–7.
109. *Ibid.*, pp. 60–6.
110. *Ibid.*, pp. 68–73.
111. *Ibid.*, pp. 74–6.
112. *Ibid.*, pp. 82–3.
113. *Ibid.*, pp. 196–8.
114. Anon, 'Introduzione', *I diari di Mussolini [veri e presunti] 1939* (Milan: Bompiani, 2010), pp. 12; 29–30; 42.
115. But cf. a deeply negative analysis, approved by Franzinelli in a foreword, Nicola Ciccolo and Elena Manetti, *Mussolini e il suo doppio: i diari svelati* (Rome: Pioda Editore, 2012).
116. Mimmo Franzinelli, *Autopsia di un falso*, p. 180.
117. *I diari di Mussolini [veri e presunti] 1939*, pp. 68–70.
118. *I diari di Mussolini [veri e presunti] 1937* (Milan: Bompiani, 2012), pp. 73–4.
119. For a lively popular account, see Robert Harris, *Selling Hitler* (London: Faber and Faber, 1986).
120. See Arrigo Petacco, *La storia ci ha mentito: dai misteri della borsa scomparsa di Mussolini alle 'armi segrete' di Hitler: le grandi menzogne del Novecento* (Milan: Mondadori, 2014).
121. Inevitably they do feed conspiracies nurtured around Churchill, with regular 'proof' of how close he and Mussolini were. See, for example, *I diari di Mussolini [veri e presunti] 1937*, p. 368; *I diari di Mussolini [veri e presunti] 1939*, pp. 344; 484.
122. See, for example, *I diari di Mussolini [veri e presunti] 1939*, p. 531 (cited by Mimmo Franzinelli, *Autopsia di un falso*, p. 139). The diaries also contain no reference to Margherita Sarfatti or to those other women (see following chapters) who were, during these years, his sexual partners.
123. Claretta Petacci, *Mussolini segreto: diari 1932–1938* (ed. Mauro Suttora) (Milan: Rizzoli, 2009).
124. Mauro Suttora, 'Questo diario', in Claretta Petacci, *Mussolini segreto*, p. 8. For Re, cf. Emilio Re, *Storia di un archivio: le carte di Mussolini* (Milan: Edizioni del Milione, 1946), where, p. 32, he did agree that Mussolini may have kept a diary.
125. It is published in Roberto Festorazzi, *Claretta Petacci*, pp. 308–24.
126. Avvocatura Generale dello Stato, *Ecc.ma Corte di Appello di Roma per il Ministero dell'Interno patrocinato dall'Avvocatura Generale dello Stato (avv. Salorni) contro gli Eredi di Clara Petacci, patrocinati dagli avvocati De Pilato, d'Amico e Luciani* (Rome: Tipografia Consorzio Nazionale, 1953), pp. 9; 16; 32–3; 37.
127. For background, see R.J.B. Bosworth, *Whispering city*, pp. 197–9; 252–4.
128. *La Repubblica*, 20 August 1991.
129. *Ibid.*, 22 August 1991.
130. Rizzoli are again meant to be the publishers.
131. Federico Robbe, 'Il neofascismo delle origini e l'ossessione antibritannica', *Nuova Storia Contemporanea*, 19, 2015, p. 99.
132. Mimmo Franzinelli *L'arma segreta del Duce: la vera storia del Carteggio Churchill–Mussolini* (Milan: Rizzoli, 2015).
133. Ferdinando Petacci, 'Clara Petacci spia o tramite fra Churchill e Mussolini?' in Claretta Petacci, *Mussolini segreto*, pp. 11–21.
134. Ferdinando Petacci, 'Claretta: un agente inglese a Palazzo Venezia?' in Claretta Petacci, *Verso il disastro: Mussolini in guerra. Diari 1939–1940* (ed. Mimmo Franzinelli) (Milan: Rizzoli, 2011), pp. 407–19.
135. *Ibid.*, p. 417.

136. The phrase is Pieter Geyl's and springs from his reckoning with his Second World War. For my own background in this regard, see R.J.B. Bosworth, *Explaining Auschwitz and Hiroshima: history writing and the Second World War 1945–1990* (London: Routledge, 1993).

Chapter 1 Sex and the coming dictator

1. One per day: Quinto Navarra, *Memorie del cameriere di Mussolini* (Milan: Longanesi, 1946), p. 200; 5,000: Pier Luigi Bullone, *La psicologia di Mussolini* (Milan: Mondadori, 2007), p. 119, ascribing the figure to 'Farrel' [*sic*]; 400: Franco Bandini, *Claretta*, p. 55; 162: Giordano Bruno Guerri, *Galeazzo Ciano: una vita 1903–1944* (Milan: Bompiani, 1979), p. 69, with a note that Ciano surpassed that number in his seven years as minister of foreign affairs (the number is ascribed to Duilio Susmel); about 20: this low figure was Rachele's and, she stated, it did not infringe her man's eternal love for her and their children: Bruno D'Agostini, *Colloqui con Rachele Mussolini*, p. 27, and Rachele Mussolini, *La mia vita con Benito*, pp. 268–9.
2. Nino D'Aroma, *Mussolini segreto* (Rocca San Casciano: Cappelli, 1958), p. 134.
3. Claretta Petacci, *Mussolini segreto*, pp. 127–8; 319. Number two on the list was Margherita Sarfatti, with whom he elsewhere claimed to have ended sexual congress.
4. *Ibid.*, p. 397. For Sarfatti and Ceccato, see below, and note that, by then, there is quite a bit of evidence that their sexual dealings with Mussolini were over.
5. Quinto Navarra, *Memorie del cameriere*, p. 200.
6. Denis Mack Smith, *Mussolini* (London: Weidenfeld & Nicolson, 1981), p. 115.
7. Indro Montanelli, *L'Italia in camicia nera (1919–3 gennaio 1925)* (Milan: Rizzoli, 1976), p. 17.
8. Roberto Olla, *Il Duce and his women*, p. 3.
9. Carlo Emilio Gadda, *Eros e Priapo (da furore a cenere)* (Milan: Garzanti, 1967), pp. 13; 42.
10. Alexander C.T. Geppert, ' "Dear Adolf!" Locating love in Nazi Germany', in Luisa Passerini, Liliana Ellena and Alexander C.T. Geppert (eds.), *New dangerous liaisons: discourses on Europe and love in the twentieth century* (New York: Berghahn Books, 2010), pp. 169–70.
11. Giorgio Boatti (ed.), *Caro Duce: lettere di donne italiane a Mussolini 1922–1943* (Milan: Rizzoli, 1989), p. 61.
12. For the best account, see Paul Corner, *The Fascist Party and popular opinion in Mussolini's Italy* (Oxford University Press, 2012).
13. For a selection, see Giorgio Boatti (ed.), *Caro Duce*, and Teresa Maria Mazzatosta and Claudio Volpi, *L'Italietta fascista (lettere al potere 1936–1943)* (Bologna: Cappelli, 1980).
14. Annich Cojean, *Gaddafi's harem* (New York: Grove Press, 2013), p. 9.
15. Brian Titley, *Dark Age: the political odyssey of Emperor Bokassa* (Liverpool University Press, 1997), pp. 51; 57.
16. Christopher Hibbert, *Napoleon: his women and wives* (London: HarperCollins, 2002), p. 48.
17. R.J.B. Bosworth, *Mussolini*, pp. 154–7.
18. Claretta Petacci, *Mussolini segreto*, pp. 73; 125; 129; 386.
19. For the English-language version, published in the year of formal accommodation between church and Fascist state, see Benito Mussolini, *The Cardinal's mistress* (London: Cassell, 1929). In Italian, another edition of the work appeared during the era of Berlusconian revisionism. See Benito Mussolini, *L'amante del Cardinale. Claudia Particella. Romanzo storico* (ed. Paolo Orvieto) (Roma: Salerno, 2009).
20. Paul Ginsborg, *Family politics*, p. 142. Patriarchy remained a key Futurist theme. For an early statement, see Filippo Tommaso Marinetti, *Come si seducono le donne* (Rome: R.S. Casciano, 1918).
21. Filippo T. Marinetti, *Let's murder the moonshine: selected writings* (ed. Robert W. Flint) (Los Angeles: Sun and Moon Classics, 1991), p. 84.

22. Lucy Hughes-Hallett, *The pike*.
23. Doris Duranti, *Il romanzo della mia vita* (ed. Gian Franco Venè) (Milan: Mondadori, 1987), p. 9. Among her post-Fascist tally, she listed the dictators Fidel Castro and Rafael Trujillo.
24. Segreteria particolare del Duce, Carteggio Riservato, report of 25 March 1942.
25. Giordano Bruno Guerri, *Italo Balbo* (Milan: Garzanti, 2013), pp. 391; 502.
26. For popular account, see Anon (ed.), *Playdux: storia erotica del Fascismo* (Rome: Tattilo Editore, 1973).
27. For some description, see R.J.B. Bosworth, '*Per necessità famigliare*: hypocrisy and corruption in Fascist Italy', *European History Quarterly*, 30, 2000.
28. Robert Dallek, *John F. Kennedy: an unfinished life 1917–1963* (London: Penguin, 2013), p. 476.
29. Laurence Leamer, *The Kennedy women: the triumph and tragedy of America's first family* (London: Bantam Press, 1994), pp. 332; 583. Leamer adds wisely that Kennedy almost certainly did not have sex with this many women.
30. Robert Dallek, *John F. Kennedy*, p. 480.
31. For an introduction, see http://www.bbc.co.uk/news/world-europe-13405268 (accessed 3 February 2016).
32. For a wry account of the American reading of Berlusconi's character and policies, see Mimmo Franzinelli and Alessandro Giacone, *La Provincia e l'Impero: il giudizio Americano sull'Italia di Berlusconi* (Milan: Feltrinelli, 2011).
33. Lucy Riall, 'The sex life of Italian patriots' in Valeria Babini, Chiara Beccalossi and Lucy Riall (eds), *Italian sexualities uncovered, 1789–1914* (Houndmills: Palgrave Macmillan, 2015), pp. 42–4.
34. Victoria De Grazia, *How Fascism ruled women: Italy, 1922–1945* (Berkeley: University of California Press, 1992), p. 1.
35. Emil Ludwig, *Talks with Mussolini* (London: George Allen and Unwin, 1932), pp. 115; 168.
36. For background, see Carl Ipsen, *Dictating demography: the problem of population in Fascist Italy* (Cambridge University Press, 1996).
37. Paul Ginsborg, *Family politics*, pp. 167; 171; 193.
38. Claretta Petacci, *Mussolini segreto*, p. 236.
39. *Ibid.*, p. 99.
40. Antonio Spinosa, *I figli del Duce: il destino di chiamarsi Mussolini* (Milan: Rizzoli, 1983), p. 10.
41. See, for example, Claretta Petacci, *Mussolini segreto*, p. 141.
42. See R.J.B. Bosworth, *Mussolini*, pp. 56–7.
43. Amedeo La Mattina, *Mai sono stato tranquilla: la vita di Angelica Balabanoff, la donna che ruppe con Mussolini e Lenin* (Turin: Einaudi, 2011), pp. 78–9.
44. Angela Balabanoff, *Il traditore: Mussolini e la conquista del potere* (Rome: Universale Napoleone, 1973), pp. 75; 142.
45. Yvon De Begnac, *Taccuini mussoliniani* (ed. Francesco Perfetti) (Bologna: Il Mulino, 1990), p. 5.
46. Claretta Petacci, *Mussolini segreto*, p. 81.
47. Nicholas Farrell, *Mussolini: a new life*, p. 40.
48. Angelo Colleoni, *Claretta Petacci: rivelazioni sulla vita, gli amori, la morte* (Milan: Tipografia Editoriale Lucchi, 1945), p. 3. In his diary, Joseph Goebbels, no friend of the Cianos, surmised that Edda's own unconfined sexuality showed that, from Balabanoff, she had inherited 'Jewish blood'. See Arrigo Petacco, *La storia ci ha mentito*, pp. 133–4.
49. Maria José Cereghino and Giovanni Fasanella, *Le carte segrete del Duce: tutte le rivelazioni su Mussolini conservate negli archivi inglesi* (Milan: Mondadori, 2014), p. 222.
50. Benito Mussolini, *Opera omnia*, vol. XXXIII, p. 268.

51. He then did contact Rachele, as the woman who should receive such news. See Benito Mussolini, *Giornale di guerra 1915–1917: Alto Isonzo – Carnia – Carso* (ed. Mimmo Franzinelli) (Gorizia: Edizioni Srl, 2016), p. 159.
52. Myriam Petacci, *Chi ama è perduto*, p. 20.
53. For the Roman background, see R.J.B. Bosworth, *Whispering city*.
54. Benito Mussolini, *Opera omnia*, vol. III, p. 190.
55. *Ibid.*, vol. XXXVIII, p. 30. For a more developed account of the affair, see R.J.B. Bosworth, *Mussolini*, pp. 77–80.
56. Benito Mussolini, *Opera omnia*, vol. XXXVIII, p. 40.
57. Leda Rafanelli, *La 'castità' clericale* (Rome: 'La Rivolta', [1946]).
58. Leda Rafanelli, *Una donna e Mussolini* (ed. Pier Carlo Masini) (Milan: Rizzoli, 1975).
59. Philip V. Cannistraro and Brian R. Sullivan, *Il Duce's other woman* (New York: William Morrow, 1993).
60. R.J.B. Bosworth, *Mussolini*, p. 65.
61. Karen Wieland, *Margherita Sarfatti: l'amante del Duce* (Trafarello: UTET, 2010), pp. 97–8.
62. Philip V. Cannistraro and Brian R. Sullivan, *Il Duce's other woman*, p. 61.
63. Simona Urso, *Margherita Sarfatti: dal mito del Dux al mito americano* (Venice: Marsilio, 2003), p. 9.
64. R.J.B. Bosworth, *Mussolini*, p. 57.
65. Rachele Mussolini, *The real Mussolini*, p. 66.
66. Claretta Petacci, *Mussolini segreto*, p. 99.
67. Margherita Grassini Sarfatti, *My fault: Mussolini as I knew him* (ed. Brian A. Sullivan) (New York: Enigma Books, 2014).
68. Paul O'Brien, *Mussolini in the First World War: the journalist, the soldier, the Fascist* (Oxford: Berg, 2005).
69. Georg Zachariae, *Mussolini si confessa* (rev. edn; Milan: BUR, 2004).
70. See R.J.B. Bosworth, *Mussolini*, pp. 328–9; 334. For the bathetic story of the eventual return of Mussolini's purloined parts, see Anita Pensotti, *La restituzione dei resti di Mussolini nel drammatico racconto della vedova* (Rome: Dino Editore, 1972).
71. Pierluigi Baima Bollone, *Le ultime ore di Mussolini* (Milan: Mondadori, 2005), pp. 91–100.
72. *Ibid.*, p. 15.
73. *Ibid.*, p. 46.
74. Mimmo Franzinelli, *Il Duce e le donne: avventure e passioni extraconiugali di Mussolini* (Milan: Mondadori, 2013), pp. 13–14.
75. *Ibid.*, pp. 14–15, using material from Marco Zeni, *La moglie di Mussolini*, photographic additions after p. 160.
76. Alfredo Pieroni, *Il figlio segreto del Duce: la storia di Benito Albino Mussolini e di sua madre Ida Dalser* (Milan: Garzanti, 2006), p. 17.
77. R.J.B. Bosworth, *Mussolini*, pp. 89–90.
78. Marco Zeni, *La moglie di Mussolini* (Trento: Edizioni Effe e Erre, 2005), p. 57.
79. Mimmo Franzinelli, *Il Duce e le donne*, p. 15.
80. See, for example, http://www.rottentomatoes.com/m/vincere (accessed 28 October 2015).
81. Mimmo Franzinelli, *Il Duce e le donne*, p. 30.
82. Claretta Petacci, *Mussolini segreto*, p. 110.
83. Alfredo Pieroni, *Il figlio segreto del Duce*, p. 38.
84. Cesare Rossi, *Mussolini com'era* (Rome: Ruffolo Editore, 1947), pp. 202–3.
85. *Ibid.*, pp. 205–6.
86. Claretta Petacci, *Mussolini segreto*, p. 475.

87. For a favourable account of their dealings, see Marcello Staglieno, *Arnaldo e Benito: due fratelli* (Milan: Mondadori, 2003). See p. 343, for Arnaldo's semi-paternal role in making over 100,000 lire to Benito Albino in 1925 as a patrimony.
88. Alfredo Pieroni, *Il figlio segreto del Duce*, pp. 61–7.
89. See, for example, Daniele Baratieri, '"Wrapped in passionless impartiality?" Italian psychiatry during the Fascist regime' in Daniele Baratieri, Mark Edele and Giuseppe Finaldi (eds), *Totalitarian dictatorship: new histories. Essays in honour of R.J.B. Bosworth* (London: Routledge, 2014), pp. 147–8; 'Sanity from a lunatic asylum: Ida Dalser a threat to Mussolini's image' in Stephen Gundle, Christopher Duggan and Giuliana Pieri (eds), *The cult of the Duce: Mussolini and the Italians* (Manchester University Press, 2013), pp. 57–71.
90. Alfredo Pieroni, *Il figlio segreto del Duce*, pp. 99–103.
91. For a visual history of the place, see https://www.youtube.com/watch?v=-q5nLQAz_9U (accessed 28 October 2015).
92. Alfredo Pieroni, *Il figlio segreto del Duce*, p. 124; Mimmo Franzinelli, *Il Duce e le donne*, pp. 56–64.
93. For the background, see Renzo De Felice, *Mussolini il rivoluzionario 1883–1920* (Turin: Einaudi, 1965), pp. 333–80.
94. R.J.B. Bosworth, *Mussolini*, p. 106.
95. Bianca Veneziana, *Storia italiana d'amore* (Milan: Garzanti, 1977), p. 27.
96. *Ibid.*, pp. 35–6.
97. *Ibid.*, p. 36.
98. *Ibid.*, p. 37.
99. *Ibid.*, pp. 38–9.
100. *Ibid.*, p. 40.
101. *Ibid.*, p. 41.
102. *Ibid.*, pp. 49–50.
103. *Ibid.*, p. 53.
104. *Ibid.*, pp. 82–3.
105. *Ibid.*, p. 138.
106. Claretta Petacci, *Mussolini segreto*, pp. 66; 121–2.
107. Elena Curti, *Il chiodo a tre punte: schegge di memoria della figlia segreta del Duce* (Pavia: Gianni Iuculano Editore, 2003). Some sources put the birthdate in 1923. See, for example, Myriam Petacci, *Chi ama è perduto*, p. 185.
108. Roberto Festorazzi, *Claretta Petacci*, p. 78; Elena Curti, *Il chiodo a tre punte*, p. 8. See also http://cinquantamila.corriere.it/storyTellerThread.php?threadId=CURTI+Elena (accessed 30 October 2015); http://www.liberoquotidiano.it/news/politica/11782561/La-figlia-di-Benito-Mussolini-.html (accessed 30 October 2015); http://www.dagospia.com/rubrica-3/politica/parla-elena-curti-ultima-figlia-duce-classe-1923-ricordo-che-99277.htm (accessed 3 February 2016).
109. Roberto Festorazzi, *Claretta Petacci*, p. 71.
110. Elena Curti, *Il chiodo a tre punte*, p. 20.
111. Segretaria particolare del Duce, Carteggio Riservato, 117, 10 March 1933, Chiavolini to Angela Curti; 28 June 1933, report.
112. *Ibid.*, 22 July 1933, F. Morelli note.
113. Elena Curti, *Il chiodo a tre punte*, pp. 19; 31–2.
114. *Ibid.*, p. 32.
115. Segreteria particolare del Duce, Carteggio Riservato, 117, 15 July 1941, Elena Curti to Mussolini.
116. Elena Curti, *Il chiodo a tre punte*, p. 191.
117. For a recent evocation of this primacy of violence, see Matteo Millan, *Squadrismo e squadristi nella dittatura fascista* (Rome: Viella, 2014).
118. R.J.B. Bosworth, *Mussolini*, p. 170.

NOTES to pp. 56–64

Chapter 2 A dictator's distractions

1. For a biography of the attempted assassin, see Frances Stonor Saunders, *The woman who shot Mussolini* (London: Faber and Faber, 2010).
2. It is still open. See http://www.standrewshealthcare.co.uk/ (accessed 2 November 2015).
3. Francesco Saverio Petacci, 'Prefazione' to Marcello Petacci, *Raccolta di alcuni lavori scientifici* (Rome: Italgraf, 1961), p. 7.
4. *Ibid.*
5. *Ibid.*
6. Roberto Festorazzi, *Claretta Petacci*, p. 5.
7. Enrico Sturani, *Otto milioni di cartoline per il Duce* (Turin: Centro Scientifico Editore, 1995), p. 39.
8. Franco Bandini, *Claretta*, pp. 16–17; Roberto Gervaso, *Claretta, la donna che morì per Mussolini*, pp. 16–17.
9. Claretta Petacci, *Mussolini segreto*, p. 103.
10. Margherita Sarfatti, *The life of Benito Mussolini* (London: Thornton Butterworth, 1925); *Dux* (Milan: Mondadori, 1926).
11. Luisa Passerini, *Mussolini immaginario: storia di una biografia, 1915–1939* (Bari: Laterza, 1991), p. 79.
12. Philip V. Cannistraro and Brian R. Sullivan, *Il Duce's other woman*, p. 301.
13. *Ibid.*, p. 303.
14. *Ibid.*
15. *Ibid.*, p. 306.
16. For an example, see Claretta Petacci, *Mussolini segreto*, p. 96, where Rachele had called her 'that whore'. In her later tract, Sarfatti defined Rachele derisively as 'formed from the same raw elements that made up the power strata of Mussolini's personality'. Margherita Grassini Sarfatti, *My fault*, p. 126.
17. Margherita Sarfatti, *Dux*, p. 103.
18. Philip V. Cannistraro and Brian R. Sullivan, *Il Duce's other woman*, pp. 306–7.
19. Margherita Sarfatti, *Dux*, p. 308.
20. For a recent endorsement of this role, see Françoise Liffran, *Margherita Sarfatti: l'égérie di Duce: biografie* (Paris: Éditions du Seuil, 2009).
21. Margherita Sarfatti, *Dux*, p. 311.
22. Philip V. Cannistraro and Brian R. Sullivan, *Il Duce's other woman*, pp. 265–85.
23. Roberto Festorazzi, *Margherita Sarfatti: la donna che inventò Mussolini* (Vicenza: Angelo Colla Editore, 2010), pp. 110–11.
24. Sergio Marzorati, *Margherita Sarfatti: saggio biografico* (Como: Nodo Libri, 1990), p. 186.
25. For its functioning and the gifts sent there to the Mussolinis – for example, in 1931, a cow donated by peasants from Livorno province – see Segreteria particolare del Duce, Carteggio Riservato, 121, 29 July 1931, note. Cf. 10 August 1928, note, with its record of Mussolini donating beds to peasants who worked on the estate.
26. For background, see R.J.B. Bosworth, *Mussolini*, pp. 194–5.
27. Roberto Festorazzi, *Margherita Sarfatti*, pp. 72–3.
28. For a biography, see Gianni Scipione Rossi, *Cesira e Benito: storia segreta della governante di Mussolini* (Soveria Mannelli: Rubbettino, 2007).
29. See Segreteria particolare del Duce, Carteggio Riservato, 116, 6 June 1944, note; cf. 27 July 1934, Barella to Carocci.
30. Mimmo Franzinelli, *Il Duce e le donne*, pp. 104–13.
31. Ercole Boratto, *A spasso col Duce: le memorie dell'autista di Benito Mussolini* (Rome: Castelvecchi, 2014), p. 69. He makes the unlikely claim that sex between the two began in 1934.
32. For romantic biography, see Anna Volpe, 'La contessa Brambilla', *Ventaglio 90*, 44, 2012.
33. For an account, see http://www.liberoquotidiano.it/news/sfoglio/11690725/Benito-Mussolini-e-quella-notte-bollente.html (accessed 3 November 2015).

34. Gustavo Bocchini Padiglione, *L'harem del Duce* (Milan: Mursia, 2006), p. 172.
35. See, for example, Claretta Petacci, *Mussolini segreto*, p. 170.
36. *Ibid.*, pp. 254–5.
37. Gustavo Bocchini Padiglione, *L'harem del Duce*, p. 172.
38. Claretta Petacci, *Mussolini segreto*, pp. 190–1; 237.
39. *Ibid.*, pp. 242; 249.
40. *Ibid.*, pp. 279; 297; 374.
41. Segreteria particolare del Duce, Carteggio Riservato, 116, 24 December 1944, Mussolini to Brambilla. The Rovigo police also kept Mussolini informed of various charges against Count Brambilla, involving disloyalty in July 1943 and corruption. See letter, June 1944.
42. See http://archiviostorico.corriere.it/1996/novembre/25/ROMA_LIBERATA_Giustizia_all_italiana_co_0_96112510670.shtml (accessed 4 November 2015).
43. Ugo Guspini, *L'orecchio del regime: le intercettazioni telefoniche al tempo del fascismo* (Milan: Mursia, 1973), p. 122; Angelo Colleoni, *Claretta Petacci*, p. 7.
44. Carte Petacci, 9/130, entry for 21 January 1938.
45. Claretta Petacci, *Mussolini segreto*, pp. 129–30.
46. Ugo Guspini, *L'orecchio del regime*, p. 122, noting the 1934 tap where Tanzi had read the auspices from a set of cards to complain that Mussolini was having yet another woman.
47. Claretta Petacci, *Mussolini segreto*, pp. 402–3.
48. Claretta Petacci, *Verso il disastro*, pp. 206–7.
49. Claretta Petacci, *Mussolini segreto*, p. 208
50. Benito Mussolini, *A Clara*, p. 115.
51. Claretta Petacci, *Verso il disastro*, pp. 113–14.
52. *Ibid.*, p. 116.
53. Margherita Grassini Sarfatti, *My fault*, pp. 123; 289.
54. *Ibid.*, p. 253.
55. Claretta Petacci, *Mussolini segreto*, pp. 99–100.
56. For background in English, see Renzo De Felice, *The Jews in Fascist Italy: a history* (New York: Enigma Books, 2001); Aaron Gillette, *Racial theories in Fascist Italy* (London: Routledge, 2002); Michael A. Livingston, *The Fascists and the Jews of Italy: Mussolini's race laws, 1938–1945* (Cambridge University Press, 2014).
57. Claretta Petacci, *Mussolini segreto*, pp. 229; 268.
58. *Ibid.*, pp. 126–7.
59. *Ibid.*, p. 397.
60. *Ibid.*, pp. 402–5.
61. *Ibid.*, p. 405.
62. *Ibid.*, pp. 393; 448.
63. Claretta Petacci, *Verso il disastro*, pp. 280–1.
64. *Ibid.*, pp. 281–2.
65. Philip V. Cannistraro and Brian R. Sullivan, *Il Duce's other woman*, pp. 520–5.
66. *Ibid.*, pp. 528–9.
67. See http://ricerca.repubblica.it/repubblica/archivio/repubblica/1989/09/30/fiammetta-ricordi-la-collezione-sarfatti.html (accessed 6 November 2015).
68. See Ercole Boratto, *A spasso col Duce*, p. 49; Roberto Olla, *Il Duce and his women*, pp. 232–3; 312; Mimmo Franzinelli, *Il Duce e le donne*, pp. 188–97; Brian R. Sullivan, insert in Margherita Grassini Sarfatti, *My fault*, pp. 248–50.
69. Claretta Petacci, *Mussolini segreto*, p. 239.
70. Ercole Boratto, *A spasso col Duce*, pp. 51–2.
71. For popular accounts, see Silvio Bertoldi, *L'ultimo re. L'ultima regina* (Milan: Rizzoli, 1992); Arrigo Petacco, *Regina: la vita e i segreti di Maria José* (Milan: Mondadori, 1997). The claim, noted earlier, that she bedded Balbo in 1935 seems based merely on the allegation that they were on unspecified occasions alone together. See Bertoldi, p. 44.

72. Luciano Regolo, *Così combattevamo il duce: l'impegno antifascista di Maria José di Savoia nell'archivio inedito dell'amica Sofia Jaccarino* (Rome: Kogoi Edizioni, 2013), pp. 90–1.
73. Cristina Siccardi, *Maria José Umberto di Savoia: la fine degli ultimi regnanti* (Milan: Paoline Editoriale, 2004), p. 1.
74. Claretta Petacci, *Mussolini segreto*, pp. 84–8.
75. *Ibid.*, p. 133.
76. *Ibid.*, pp. 285–6.
77. Mimmo Franzinelli, *Il Duce e le donne*, pp. 229–30.
78. The popular literature makes two or three further claims. But the evidence is not too convincing. See, for example, the reckoning of eleven in http://archiviostorico.corriere.it/2005/gennaio/26/Molte_amanti_almeno_figli_avventure_co_9_050126071.shtml (accessed 14 November 2015).
79. Roberto Festorazzi, *La pianista del Duce: vita, passione e misteri di Magda Brard, l'artista francese che stregò Benito Mussolini* (Milan: Simonelli Editore, 2000), pp. 11–13.
80. *Ibid.*, pp. 18–19.
81. *Ibid.*, pp. 29–30.
82. See, generally, Roberto Festorazzi, *La pianista del Duce*.
83. Mimmo Franzinelli, *Il Duce e le donne*, pp. 178–9.
84. Raffaello De Rensis, *Mussolini musicista* (Mantua: Edizioni Paladino, 1927), p. 22.
85. Mimmo Franzinelli, *Il Duce e le donne*, pp. 156–8, and cf. the file under her name in Segreteria particolare del Duce, Carteggio Riservato, 116.
86. Segreteria particolare del Duce, Carteggio Riservato, 116, 17 November 1926, 23 March 1927, reports.
87. *Ibid.*, 13 December 1927, note.
88. *Ibid.*, 5 February 1927, note.
89. *Ibid.*, undated and 1 March 1933, Ricci reports. Cf. also Mimmo Franzinelli, *Il Duce e le donne*, pp. 164–73.
90. Mimmo Franzinelli, *Il Duce e le donne*, pp. 170–1.
91. Segreteria particolare del Duce, Carteggio Riservato, 116, 14 November 1933, note.
92. *Ibid.*, undated notes.
93. Claretta Petacci, *Mussolini segreto*, p. 319.
94. Roberto Festorazzi, *La pianista del Duce*, p. 61.
95. *Ibid.*, pp. 147–8; cf. also Roberto Festorazzi, *Bruno e Gina Mussolini: un amore del ventennio* (Milan: Sperling and Kupfer, 2007), pp. 233–6.
96. See Segreteria particolare del Duce, Carteggio Riservato, 116, letters of 19 August, 12 September, 20 December 1944; 7 January, 10 March, 26 March, 1 April 1945.
97. For description of its atmosphere at that time, see Roberto Festorazzi, *San Donnino, cella 31. La prigionia dei fascisti scampati dal massacro di Dongo nella testimonianza inedita di un protagonista: Alfredo Degasperi. Un documento di straordinario valore sull'altra storia d'Italia* (Milan: Simonelli Editore, 1999).
98. Gianni Scipione Rossi, *Storia di Alice: la Giovanna d'Arco di Mussolini* (Soveria Mannelli: Rubbettino, 2010).
99. *Ibid.*, pp. 17–18.
100. Segreteria particolare del Duce 120, 21 February 1941, report by 'Valente'.
101. Mimmo Franzinelli, *Il Duce e le donne*, pp. 204–5.
102. Gianni Scipione Rossi, *Storia di Alice*, p. 145. Cf. p. 143 for a more youthful image when she was indeed blonde.
103. Claretta Petacci, *Mussolini segreto*, p. 292.
104. See, for example, *ibid.*, p. 437.
105. *Ibid.*, pp. 451–2; 468.
106. Claretta Petacci, *Verso il disastro*, pp. 402–3.

107. Segreteria particolare del Duce, Carteggio Riservato, 120, 21 February 1923, Pallottelli to Mussolini; 26 February 1936, Mussolini to Pallottelli.
108. *Ibid.*, 9 July 1927, anonymous report.
109. Segreteria particolare del Duce, Carteggio Ordinario, 509065, 5 June 1935, Nani note. Franzinelli says that the accident had caused a fatality. M. Franzinelli, *Il Duce e le donne*, p. 213.
110. See *ibid.*, April 1938, Sebastiani to M. Rava; 29 April 1938, Rava to Sebastiani; [9 July 1938], Pallottelli to Sebastiani; December 1938, Pallottelli to Rava; 28 November 1940, Pallottelli note; [1941], Ministero dell'Africa Italiana memorandum.
111. *Ibid.*, December 1942, memorandum.
112. *Ibid.*, 3, 22 March 1943, Alice Pallottelli to De Cesare.
113. *Ibid.*, 18 June 1943, Alice Pallottelli to De Cesare; 24 June 1943, De Cesare to Alice Pallottelli; 14 July 1943, Alice Pallottelli to De Cesare. 545014, 25 October 1942, memorandum. Earlier that year the secretariat received another denunciation of the alleged corruption of the Pallottelli couple. See Segreteria particolare del Duce, Carteggio Riservato, 120, 21 February 1942, 'Valente' note.
114. In the Archivio Centrale, see Segreteria particolare del Duce, Carteggio Riservato, 123, note of a meeting between Ruspi (called 'Signora Minardi) and her son and the dictator on 3 April 1944.
115. Angelo Colleoni, *Claretta Petacci*, pp. 5–6.
116. Claretta Petacci, *Mussolini segreto*, p. 344.
117. Segreteria particolare del Duce, Carteggio Ordinario, 531933, file.
118. Angelo Colleoni, *Claretta Petacci*, p. 6.
119. Claretta Petacci, *Verso il disastro*, p. 26.
120. Ercole Boratto, *A spasso col Duce*, p. 46.
121. Claretta Petacci, *Verso il disastro*, p. 39.
122. See *ibid.*, p. 230.
123. *Ibid.*, pp. 362–3 from Carte Petacci, 8/115.
124. Gustavo Bocchini Padiglione, *L'harem del Duce*.
125. Claretta Petacci, *Verso il disastro*, p. 72.
126. Myriam Petacci, *Chi ama è perduto*, p. 45.
127. Mauro Suttora, 'Questo diario' in Claretta Petacci, *Verso il disastro*, p. 5.

Chapter 3 And so . . . pause . . . to bed

1. Alberto Moravia, *Gli indifferenti* (Milan: Bompiani, 2005). For English version, see *The time of indifference* (Harmondsworth: Penguin, 1970).
2. Alberto Moravia, *Il Conformista* (Milan: Bompiani, 1951). For English version, see *The conformist* (London: Secker and Warburg, 1952). There is irony in the fact that Moravia's publishers, Bompiani, also put out the fake Mussolini diaries.
3. A more extreme advocate of the idea that Fascists were orgasm rejecters was Wilhelm Reich (1897–1957). See especially his *Mass psychology of fascism* (New York: Condor, 1970). The book was first published in 1933 but had avoided any serious analysis of Italian habits and attitudes. Even more drastic in such absence of comparison is Klaus Theweleit, *Male fantasies* (2 vols) (Cambridge: Polity Press, 1987–9).
4. Erich Fromm, *The fear of freedom* (London: Kegan Paul Trench, Trubner and Co., 1942).
5. See https://it.wikipedia.org/wiki/Federici_%28famiglia%29 (accessed 17 November 2015).
6. Myriam Petacci, *Chi ama è perduto*, p. 62.
7. Arrigo Petacco, *Eva e Claretta*, p. 5.
8. Ercole Boratto, *A spasso col Duce*, p. 35.
9. Emil Ludwig, *Talks with Mussolini*, pp. 15; 32; 37.

10. *Ibid.*, pp. 73–4; 217.
11. Claretta Petacci, *Mussolini segreto*, p. 33.
12. For background, see Ray Moseley, *Mussolini's shadow*, pp. 14–15. For the doubtful allegations, see Anne Sebba, *That woman: the life of Wallis Simpson, Duchess of Windsor* (London: Weidenfeld & Nicolson, 2011), pp. 55–6, noting the existence of a story about sex, pregnancy and an abortion. Arrigo Petacco simply assumes the stories are true. Arrigo Petacco, *La storia ci ha mentito*, p. 173.
13. See Niccolò Serri, 'Fascist imperialism and the Italian arms trade to Nationalist China 1929-1937', *Nuova Rivista Storica*, 99, 2015, pp. 438–42.
14. See Renzo De Felice, *Mussolini il duce: gli anni di consenso 1929–1936* (Turin: Einaudi, 1974), pp. 815–17.
15. Myriam Petacci, *Chi ama è perduto*, p. 61.
16. *Ibid.*, pp. 62–4.
17. Angelo Colleoni, *Claretta Petacci*, p. 9.
18. There were many ways to express the pronoun 'you' in Italian and the matter was made more complex by politics during the Fascist years. Claretta, in her talk with her lover, moved, but not seamlessly, from the super formal third person *Ella* on to *Lei*, also third person and formal but derided by Fascism as a Spanish intrusion into Italian. The regime urged the use of *voi*, that is, the second person plural, to replace *Lei* in addressing a more senior person where in the past *Lei* would have been used. The intimate form is *tu* and that is what eventually the lovers both use. It was also possible for *Voi* or *Tu* to be capitalised when Claretta was still signifying Mussolini's high status. In the text such usages will, where relevant, be marked but my translation will always be the simple English 'you'.
19. Myriam Petacci, *Chi ama è perduto*, pp. 64–6.
20. See R.J.B. Bosworth, *Mussolini*, p. 314; Elena Curti, *Il chiodo a tre punte*, pp. 48; 70–2.
21. *Ibid.*, p. 68.
22. Cesare Rossi, *Trentatre vicende mussoliniane* (Milan: Casa Editrice Ceschina, 1958), p. 375.
23. Claretta Petacci, *Mussolini segreto*, pp. 26–8.
24. *Ibid.*, pp. 28–9.
25. Loreto Di Nucci, *Lo stato partito del fascismo: genesi, evoluzione e crisi 1919–1943* (Bologna: il Mulino, 2009), p. 432.
26. For background, see R.J.B. Bosworth, *Mussolini*, pp. 214–18.
27. Paolo Monelli, *Mussolini: an intimate life* (London: Thames and Hudson, 1953), p. 126.
28. For the image and others from around the same time, see Renzo De Felice and Luigi Goglia, *Mussolini il mito* (Bari: Laterza, 1983), p. 192.
29. Elisabetta Cerutti, *Ambassador's wife* (London: George Allen and Unwin, 1952), p. 204.
30. Marco Innocenti, *Le signore del Fascismo: donne in un mondo di uomini* (Milan: Mursia, 2001), p. 54.
31. Claretta Petacci, *Mussolini segreto*, pp. 30–2.
32. *Ibid.*, pp. 31–3.
33. *Ibid.*, pp. 37–8.
34. Carte Petacci, 8/117, entry for 2 February 1933.
35. Claretta Petacci, *Mussolini segreto*, pp. 483–4.
36. *Ibid.*, pp. 38–9; 484–5.
37. For background in Italy, see Martyn Lyons, ' "Questo cor che tuo si rese": the private and public in Italian women's love letters in the long nineteenth century', *Modern Italy*, 19, 2014, pp. 355–68.
38. Claretta Petacci, *Mussolini segreto*, pp. 485–6.
39. Nonetheless a wry local historian has tallied that, during the dictatorship, the regime gave special assistance to 105 of Rachele's relatives and 229 of Benito's. See Vittorio Emiliani, *Il paese dei Mussolini* (Turin: Einaudi, 1984), pp. 48–9.
40. Claretta Petacci, *Mussolini segreto*, pp. 39–45.

41. For background, see R.J.B. Bosworth, *Italian Venice: a history* (London: Yale University Press, 2014), pp. 135–7.
42. See R.J.B. Bosworth, *Mussolini*, p. 228.
43. Myriam Petacci, *Chi ama è perduto*, p. 10.
44. *Ibid.*, p. 85.
45. *Ibid.*, pp. 85–7.
46. *Ibid.*, pp. 87–8.
47. Claretta Petacci, *Mussolini segreto*, pp. 488–90.
48. Claudio M. Mancini, 'Isaia Levi: vita di un Ebreo italiano a cavallo di due secoli', *Annali della Fondazione Ugo La Malfa*, XXIV, 2009, p. 306.
49. Claretta Petacci, *Mussolini segreto*, p. 490.
50. *Ibid.*, pp. 491–2.
51. Myriam Petacci, *Chi ama è perduto*, pp. 92–3.
52. Benito Mussolini, *Opera omnia*, vol. XXVII, pp. 265–6; 268–9.
53. Spartacus [Raffaele Offidani], *Claretta: fiore del mio giardino* (np: Azione Letteraria Italiana, nd [1945]), pp. 8–9. Cf. also Jacky Tronel, 'Magda Fontanges: maîtresse du Duce, écrouée à Mauzac (Dordogne)', *Arkheia*, 17–18, 2007; Giorgio D'Aurora, *La maschera e il volto di Magda Fontanges* (Milan: Cebas, 1946), pp. 11–12.
54. Claretta Petacci, *Mussolini segreto*, p. 102.
55. A wartime source raised the total of sexual meetings to twenty. 'Calipso', *Vita segreta di Mussolini* (Rome: IEDC, 1944), p. 23. The last congress was said to have been on 4 July.
56. Claretta Petacci, *Mussolini segreto*, p. 245. Cf. p. 452 where, on 10 November, he repeated some of the details.
57. Indro Montanelli, *Soltanto un giornalista: testimonianza resa a Tiziana Abate* (Milan: Rizzoli, 2002), pp. 39–40.
58. Claretta Petacci, *Mussolini segreto*, p. 330.
59. Giorgio D'Aurora, *La maschera e il volto di Magda Fontanges*, p. 25.
60. For further details, see Jacky Tronel, 'Magda Fontanges'.
61. Edvige Mussolini, *Mio fratello Benito*, p. 167.
62. Claretta Petacci, *Mussolini segreto*, pp. 492–3.
63. *Ibid.*, p. 493.
64. *Ibid.*, pp. 495–6.
65. *Ibid.*, p. 496.
66. For her biography, see Lorenzo Baratter, *Anna Maria Mussolini: l'ultima figlia del Duce* (Milan: Mursia, 2008) and cf. R.J.B. Bosworth, *Mussolini*, pp. 252–3.
67. Claretta Petacci, *Mussolini segreto*, pp. 494–5.
68. *Ibid.*, p. 496.
69. *Ibid.*, pp. 498–9.
70. Carte Petacci, 9/130, entry for 6 February 1938.
71. Claretta Petacci, *Mussolini segreto*, p. 88.
72. Myriam Petacci, *Chi ama è perduto*, pp. 96–7.
73. Roberto Festorazzi, *Claretta Petacci*, pp. 65–6.
74. Claretta Petacci, *Mussolini segreto*, p. 500.
75. See Myriam Petacci, *Chi ama è perduto*, p. 109; Roberto Festorazzi, *Claretta Petacci*, p. 13; Roberto Olla, *Il Duce and his women*, pp. 374–5; Roberto Gervaso, *Claretta, la donna che morì per Mussolini*, p. 31.
76. Marco Innocenti, *Edda contro Claretta: una storia di odio e di amore* (Milan: Mursia, 2003), p. 43.
77. Arrigo Petacco, *Eva e Claretta*, p. 76.
78. For background, see Lucetta Scaraffia, *La santa degli impossibili: vicende e significati della devozione a S. Rita* (Turin: Rosenberg and Sellier, 1990).
79. Marco Innocenti, *Edda contro Claretta*, p. 43.

80. Franco Rovere, *Vita amorosa di Claretta Petacci* (Milan: Lucchi, 1946), p. 137.
81. For crass statements in this regard, see Brian Sullivan's inserts into Margherita Grassini Sarfatti, *My fault*, pp. 246–7.
82. Claretta Petacci, *Mussolini segreto*, p. 497.
83. *Ibid.*, pp. 497–8.
84. *Ibid.*, pp. 47–8.
85. See Gore Vidal's memory of what he thought was the 'degeneracy' involved in such a habit, Fred Kaplan, *Gore Vidal: a biography* (New York: Doubleday, 1999), p. 96.
86. See R.J.B. Bosworth, *Mussolini*, pp. 224–5.
87. See, for example, Carte Petacci, 8/118, 10 October 1936, an entry that is twenty pages long.
88. For background, see R.J.B. Bosworth, *Whispering city*, pp. 186–93.
89. Claretta Petacci, *Mussolini segreto*, pp. 49–50.
90. Zita Ritossa, 'La mia vita con Claretta Petacci', *Oggi*, 9 April 1975.
91. Zita Ritossa, 'Mia "cognata" Claretta Petacci', *Tempo*, 4 April 1957, pp. 16–17; 21.
92. See, for example, Carte Petacci, 8/118, entry for 21 January 1937.
93. Franco Rovere, *Vita amorosa di Claretta Petacci*, p. 28.
94. Claretta Petacci, *Mussolini segreto*, p. 49.
95. *Ibid.*, p. 50.
96. *Ibid.*
97. *Ibid.*, pp. 50–1.
98. *Ibid.*, pp. 51–2.
99. *Ibid.*, p. 52. For arguments whether she painted them and ironical commentary on their eventual exhibition at the Collegio Romano, see chapter 6.
100. See Pia Toscano, *Imprenditori a Roma nel secondo dopoguerra: industria e terziario avanzato dal 1950 ai nostri giorni* (Rome: Gangemi Editore, 2010).
101. Giuseppe Pardini, 'L'amante di Claretta: Il duce, i confidenti, la gelosia, l'Ovra ...', *Nuova Storia Contemporanea*, 19, 2015, pp. 64–7.
102. Luigi Freddi, *Il cinema: il governo dell'immagine* (Rome: Centro Sperimentale di Cinematografia Gremese Editore, 1994), p. 172.
103. Claretta Petacci, *Mussolini segreto*, pp. 52–3.
104. Giuseppe Pardini, 'L'amante di Claretta', p. 69.
105. For a popular biography of Bocchini, another Fascist fond of sexual escapades, see Domizia Carafoli and Gustavo Bocchini Padiglione, *Il Vice Duce: Arturo Bocchini, capo della polizia fascista* (Milan: Mondadori, 2003).
106. Mimmo Franzinelli, *I tentacoli dell'Ovra: agenti, collaboratori e vittime della polizia politica fascista* (Turin: Bollati Boringhieri, 1999), p. 673.
107. Giuseppe Pardini, 'L'amante di Claretta', pp. 69–76.
108. Claretta Petacci, *Mussolini segreto*, pp. 53–4.

Chapter 4 Sex, love and jealousy

1. Claretta Petacci, *Mussolini segreto:*, pp. 74–6.
2. *I Documenti diplomatici italiani* 8s, VII, 421, 11 October 1937, Grandi to Ciano.
3. Galeazzo Ciano, *Diary 1937–1943*, pp. 15–16.
4. Renzo De Felice, *Mussolini il duce: lo stato totalitario 1936–1940* (Turin: Einaudi, 1981), p. 266.
5. Claretta Petacci, *Mussolini segreto*, p. 55.
6. Anon, *Clara Petacci: la favorita del Littorio: documentazione fotografica di ciò che fu e di ciò che rappresentò la Venere di Palazzo Venezia* (Rome: Stampatrice Novissima, nd [?1945]), p. 4.
7. Marcello Sorgi, *Edda Ciano e il comunista*, p. 73.

8. For a popular account, see Marco Innocenti, *Edda contro Claretta*.
9. For the background of Fascist policy on women and its uneven application, see Victoria De Grazia, *How Fascism ruled women*.
10. Claretta Petacci, *Mussolini segreto*, pp. 71–2.
11. For the secret police report on the trip, see Segreteria particolare del Duce, Carteggio Riservato, 109, September 1937.
12. *Il Popolo d'Italia*, 20 December 1938.
13. Claretta Petacci, *Mussolini segreto*, pp. 304; 307.
14. Claretta Petacci, *Verso il disastro*, p. 76.
15. Claretta Petacci, *Mussolini segreto*, pp. 55–60.
16. *Ibid.*, p. 368.
17. *Ibid.*, pp. 79–80.
18. *Ibid.*, p. 387.
19. *Ibid.*, pp. 380–1.
20. Carte Petacci, 8/127, entry for 31 October 1937.
21. Claretta Petacci, *Mussolini segreto*, p. 252.
22. *Ibid.*, p. 110.
23. *Ibid.*, p. 281. Cf. Claretta Petacci, *Verso il disastro*, p. 145.
24. Claretta Petacci, *Mussolini segreto*, p. 304.
25. Claretta Petacci, *Verso il disastro*, pp. 21–4.
26. Carte Petacci, 8/127, entry for 2 December 1937.
27. *Ibid.*, entry for 6 December 1937. Two days later, his last call was at 1.15 a.m.
28. Carte Petacci, 9/130, entry for 3 January 1938.
29. Claretta Petacci, *Mussolini segreto*, p. 127. Cf. p. 136 when holding his penis again brought Claretta to his mind.
30. *Ibid.*, p. 224.
31. See, for example, Claretta Petacci, *Verso il disastro*, p. 31.
32. Claretta Petacci, *Mussolini segreto*, p. 258.
33. For an introduction to his early 'love' of the lessons of the past, see Paola S. Salvatori, *Mussolini e la storia: dal socialismo al fascismo (1900–1922)* (Rome: Viella, 2016).
34. Claretta Petacci, *Mussolini segreto*, p. 243.
35. Claretta Petacci, *Verso il disastro*, pp. 21–8.
36. Claretta Petacci, *Mussolini segreto*, p. 340.
37. *Ibid.*, p. 294.
38. *Ibid.*, pp. 344–5.
39. Claretta Petacci, *Verso il disastro*, pp. 256–7.
40. Carte Petacci, 8/116, has a list of records bought for the two, including also Respighi and Paganini. They cost almost 4,000 lire.
41. Claretta Petacci, *Mussolini segreto*, p. 128.
42. Claretta Petacci, *Verso il disastro*, pp. 234–5.
43. Claretta Petacci, *Mussolini segreto*, p. 238.
44. *Ibid.*, p. 455.
45. See, for example, Carte Petacci, 9/130, entry for 23 January 1938. Another such occasion was 28 August 1939. Claretta Petacci, *Verso il disastro*, p. 180
46. Claretta Petacci, *Mussolini segreto*, p. 384.
47. Claretta Petacci, *Verso il disastro*, pp. 57–8; 201. Cf. Myriam Petacci, *Chi ama è perduto*, p. 26.
48. See, for example, Claretta Petacci, *Mussolini segreto*, pp. 465–7. That afternoon they instead listened to a radio description of the Italy–France football match. Italy won.
49. Claretta Petacci, *Verso il disastro*, p. 231.
50. Claretta Petacci, *Mussolini segreto*, p. 413.
51. Claretta Petacci, *Verso il disastro*, pp. 102–5.

52. *Ibid.*, pp. 203–5.
53. *Ibid.*, pp. 184–8.
54. *Ibid.*, p. 191.
55. *Ibid.*, p. 111.
56. Roberto Olla, *Il Duce and his women*, p. 47.
57. Claretta Petacci, *Verso il disastro*, pp. 275–6.
58. *Ibid.*, p. 297.
59. *Ibid.*, pp. 308–9.
60. *Ibid.*, pp. 304.
61. *Ibid.*, pp. 322–3.
62. Galeazzo Ciano, *Diary 1937–1943*, p. 362.
63. Claretta Petacci, *Verso il disastro*, p. 327.
64. Ugo Guspini, *L'orecchio del regime*, p. 175.
65. Claretta Petacci, *Verso il disastro*, pp. 329; 332.
66. *Ibid.*, pp. 334–9; 344–5.
67. *Ibid.*, pp. 352–7.
68. *Ibid.*, pp. 366–8.
69. *Ibid.*, pp. 375–8.
70. *Ibid.*, pp. 212–13.
71. *Ibid.*, pp. 385–6; cf. Roberto Festorazzi, *Claretta Petacci*, pp. 59–60.
72. Claretta Petacci, *Verso il disastro*, pp. 387–92.
73. Ugo Guspini, *L'orecchio del regime*, pp. 192–3.
74. Claretta Petacci, *Verso il disastro* pp. 394–7.
75. Roberto Festorazzi, *Claretta Petacci*, p. 63.
76. Claretta Petacci, *Mussolini segreto*, pp. 66–7.
77. *Ibid.*, pp. 78–9.
78. Carte Petacci, 9/130.
79. Claretta Petacci, *Mussolini segreto*, p. 266.
80. *Ibid.*, p. 277.
81. *Ibid.*, p. 354.
82. *Ibid.*, p. 127.
83. Claretta Petacci, *Verso il disastro*, p. 318.
84. Claretta Petacci, *Mussolini segreto*, p. 79.
85. Claretta Petacci, *Verso il disastro*, p. 89.
86. Rachele Mussolini, *La mia vita con Benito*, pp. 250–1.
87. See, for example, Claretta Petacci, *Mussolini segreto*, p. 364.
88. *Ibid.*, p. 98.
89. *Ibid.*, pp. 117–18; 123.
90. Carte Petacci 9/130, entries for 3, 10 January 1938.
91. Claretta Petacci, *Mussolini segreto*, p. 274.
92. *Ibid.*, pp. 268; 272.
93. *Ibid.*, p. 284.
94. *Ibid.*, pp. 336–7.
95. *Ibid.*, p. 451.
96. *Ibid.*, p. 418.
97. Claretta Petacci, *Verso il disastro*, pp. 56–9.
98. *Ibid.*, p. 158.
99. *Ibid.*, p. 195.
100. *Ibid.*, p. 213.
101. *Ibid.*, p. 225.
102. *Ibid.*, pp. 320–1; 325.
103. *Ibid.*, pp. 323; cf. pp. 325–6.
104. *Ibid.*, p. 328.

105. *Ibid.*, pp. 351–2.
106. Claretta Petacci, *Mussolini segreto*, p. 115.
107. *Ibid.*, pp. 125–6.
108. Claretta Petacci, *Verso il disastro*, p. 174.
109. *Ibid.*, p. 193.
110. Claretta Petacci, *Mussolini segreto*, pp. 281–2.
111. *Ibid.*, pp. 422; 425.
112. *Ibid.*, p. 235.
113. *Ibid.*, p. 467.
114. *Ibid.*, p. 386.
115. *Ibid.*, pp. 332–3.
116. Claretta Petacci, *Verso il disastro*, p. 208.
117. *Ibid.*, p. 193; cf. Claretta Petacci, *Mussolini segreto*, p. 152.
118. Claretta Petacci, *Mussolini segreto*, p. 78.
119. *Ibid.*, p. 196.
120. *Ibid.*, pp. 241–6.
121. *Ibid.*, p. 333.
122. *Ibid.*, p. 290.
123. *Ibid.*, pp. 315–16.
124. *Ibid.*, pp. 413–16.
125. Claretta Petacci, *Verso il disastro*, pp. 79–80.
126. *Ibid.*, p. 221.
127. *Ibid.*, pp. 262–3.
128. *Ibid.*, pp. 235–6.
129. *Ibid.*, pp. 319–21.
130. Claretta Petacci, *Mussolini segreto*, p. 73.
131. Claretta Petacci, *Verso il disastro*, pp. 76–7.
132. Claretta Petacci, *Mussolini segreto*, pp. 107–9.
133. *Ibid.*, pp. 113–14. Mussolini shared such stereotypes with the radical Fascist Roberto Farinacci, who was sent off to visit Spain. For his report on Spanish bloodthirstiness, see R.J.B. Bosworth, *Mussolini's Italy: life under the dictatorship 1915–1945* (London: Allen Lane, 2005), p. 402.
134. Claretta Petacci, *Mussolini segreto*, p. 95.
135. *Ibid.*, pp. 93–5.
136. *Ibid.*, pp. 196–7.
137. Claretta Petacci, *Verso il disastro*, p. 122.
138. Claretta Petacci, *Mussolini segreto*, p. 240.
139. Claretta Petacci, *Verso il disastro*, pp. 73–4.
140. Carte Petacci, 8/127, entry for 4 December 1937.
141. Claretta Petacci, *Mussolini segreto*, pp. 299–300.
142. *Ibid.*, p. 404.
143. *Ibid.*, p. 422–3.
144. *Ibid.*, p. 116.
145. *Ibid.*, p. 374.
146. *Ibid.*, p. 421.
147. Ugo Guspini, *L'orecchio del regime*, pp. 158–9.
148. Claretta Petacci, *Mussolini segreto*, p. 285. Cf. Carte Petacci, 8/127, entry for 6 December 1937.
149. Claretta Petacci, *Mussolini segreto*, p. 401.
150. *Ibid.*, pp. 423–6.
151. For brief but telling account, see Simon Levis Sullam, *I carnefici italiani: scene dal genocidio degli ebrei, 1943–1945* (Milan: Feltrinelli, 2015).
152. Claretta Petacci, *Verso il disastro*, p. 228.

153. Claretta Petacci, *Mussolini segreto*, p. 331.
154. See, for example, Carte Petacci, 5/78 [February 1945], Myriam Petacci to Mussolini.
155. Candido, *Mussolini in pantofole* (Rome: Istituto Editoriale di Cultura, 1944), pp. 159–61; cf. Ercole Boratto, *A spasso col Duce*, pp. 63–4.
156. Margherita Grassini Sarfatti, *My fault*, p. 242. Cf., for example, the partially sceptical Mimmo Franzinelli, *Il Duce e le donne*, pp. 235–40.
157. Claretta Petacci, *Mussolini segreto*, p. 333.
158. Claretta Petacci, *Verso il disastro*, pp. 86–7.
159. Claretta Petacci, *Mussolini segreto*, pp. 122–3.
160. Carte Petacci, 8/127, entry for 31 October 1937.
161. Claretta Petacci, *Mussolini segreto*, pp. 104–5.
162. For its history, see Giuseppe Talamo, Il Messaggero: *un giornale durante il fascismo: cento anni di storia vol. II, 1919–1946* (Florence: Le Monnier, 1984).
163. Carte Petacci, 8/127, entry for 31 October 1937.
164. *Il Messaggero*, 9 January, 17 February 1938.
165. Indro Montanelli, *Soltanto un giornalista*, p. 197.
166. Carte Petacci 9/130, entries for 7, 9 January 1938.
167. *Il Messaggero*, 10 March 1938.
168. See, for example, Luigi De Vincentis, *Io son te* (Milan: Cebes, 1946), p. 80.
169. *Il Messaggero*, 18 October 1938.
170. *Ibid.*, 4 April 1939.
171. *Ibid.*, 19, 26 April 1939.
172. *Ibid.*, 31 May 1939.
173. Roberto Festorazzi, *Claretta Petacci*, p. 63.
174. *Il Messaggero*, 15 June, 16 July 1940.
175. *Ibid.*, 30 January 1941.
176. *Ibid.*, 19 March 1943.
177. Francesco Saverio Petacci, *La vita e i suoi nemici* (Rome: Unione Editoriale d'Italia, 1940).
178. Segreteria particolare del Duce, Carteggio Riservato, b. 103, undated memorandum.
179. Francesco Saverio Petacci, *La vita e i suoi nemici*, pp. 3; 7.
180. *Ibid.*, pp. 10–12; 21; 26.
181. *Ibid.*, pp. 57–65; 108–10.

Chapter 5 Warring in public and private life

1. Somewhat paradoxically in a Fascist 'revolution', the viceroy's proper name was – in the royal manner – Amedeo Umberto Isabella Luigi Filippo Maria Giuseppe Giovanni di Savoia-Aosta.
2. For the background, see R.J.B. Bosworth, *Mussolini*, pp. 290–309.
3. Thomas Schlemmer, *Invasori non vittime: la campagna italiana di Russia, 1941–1943* (Rome: Laterza, 2009).
4. For many graphic examples of such *mentalité*, see Mimmo Franzinelli, *Disertori: una storia mai raccontata della seconda guerra mondiale* (Milan: Mondadori, 2016).
5. For such details, see Ian Dear and Michael Foot (eds), *The Oxford companion to World War II* (Oxford University Press, 2001).
6. R.J.B. Bosworth, *Mussolini's Italy*, pp. 492–3.
7. Marco Patricelli, *L'Italia sotto le bombe: guerra aerea e vita civile 1940–1945* (Bari: Laterza, 2009), p. 193.
8. Alan Milward, *War, economy and society 1939–1945* (Harmondsworth: Penguin, 1987), p. 97.
9. Joseph Goebbels, *The Goebbels Diaries 1939–1941* (ed. Fred Taylor) (London: Hamish Hamilton, 1982), p. 429.

10. For background, see Roberto Festorazzi, *Bruno e Gina Mussolini*.
11. See, for example, Segreteria particolare del Duce, Carteggio Riservato, 108, 13, 16 April 1935, reporting firstly an outing of Bruno with Gina and then a forty-minute stop by Bruno in 'a well-known brothel', three days later.
12. For a police file on the wedding and reports on the bride's 'purity', see Segreteria particolare del Duce, Carteggio Riservato, 109, 12 December 1934, 2 September and 7 November 1936.
13. Claretta Petacci, *Mussolini segreto*, pp. 436–9.
14. Segreteria particolare del Duce, Carteggio Riservato, 109, reports of 6 April, 8 July, 12 October 1938, 12 January 1940, 13 February 1941.
15. Roberto Festorazzi, *Bruno e Gina Mussolini*, p. 159.
16. R.J.B. Bosworth, *Mussolini's Italy*, p. 478.
17. Segreteria particolare del Duce, Carteggio Riservato, 110, undated reports [August 1941].
18. *Ibid.*, report, August 1941.
19. Benito Mussolini, *Opera omnia*, vol. XXXIV, pp. 197–200; 255; 269.
20. Carte Petacci, diary entry, 7 August 1941 and note. I owe to Mimmo Franzinelli access to his unpublished selection from the Petacci papers, 1941–5.
21. Carte Petacci, diary entry, 24 December 1941.
22. *Ibid.*, 25 December 1941.
23. *Ibid.*, 28 December 1941.
24. *Ibid.*, 30 December 1941.
25. *Ibid.*, 23 January 1942.
26. *Ibid.*, 5, 6, 7 March 1941.
27. *Ibid.*, 1 March 1941.
28. *Ibid.*, 12 June, 6 August 1941.
29. *Ibid.*, 26 October 1941.
30. *Ibid.*, 8 March 1941.
31. *Ibid.*, 25 March, 7, 13 April 1941.
32. For summaries of these problems, see Segreteria particolare del Duce, Carteggio Riservato, 104, 14 October, 29 November 1942, Frugoni to De Cesare; 5, 24 January, 7 February 1943, Frugoni to Rachele Mussolini.
33. Carte Petacci, diary entry, 17 January 1942.
34. Galeazzo Ciano, *Diary 1937–1943*, p. 429.
35. *Ibid.*, p. 467.
36. Segreteria particolare del Duce, Carteggio Riservato, 114, undated file.
37. Amedeo Luccichenti and Vincenzo Monaco, 'Villa Petacci alla Camilluccia con scale audaci e pronunciate cavità, Roma 1937–9', *Casabella*, 805, October 2011, p. 56.
38. Marco Innocenti, *Edda contro Claretta*, p. 73.
39. 'Calipso', *Vita segreta di Mussolini*, p. 26.
40. Carte Petacci 16. The agreement was dated 9 January 1942.
41. Marco Innocenti, *Edda contro Claretta*, p. 74.
42. *Ibid.*; cf. Fondo Petacci, b. 139.
43. Nino D'Aroma, *Mussolini segreto*, p. 433.
44. See, for example, Spartacus, *Claretta*, p 20.
45. Arrigo Petacco, *Eva e Claretta*, pp. 77–8.
46. Antonio Spinosa, *Edda: una tragedia italiana* (Milan: Mondadori, 1993), p. 251.
47. See Fondo Monelli, b. 139; cf. www.bunkerdiroma.it/index.htm (accessed 23 December 2015).
48. Cesare Rossi, *Mussolini com'era*, p. 280.
49. Doris Duranti, *Il romanzo della mia vita*, pp. 68; 100.
50. *Ibid.*, p. 151.
51. Myriam Petacci, *Chi ama è perduto*, p. 11.

52. Myriam Petacci, 'Questa è la mia storia', *Oggi*, 14 April 1955.
53. Luigi De Vincentis, *Io son te*, p. 79.
54. Stephen Gundle, *Mussolini's dream factory: film stardom in Fascist Italy* (New York: Berghahn, 2013), p. 265.
55. Luigi De Vincentis, *Io son te*, pp. 182–3.
56. Roberto Gervaso, *Claretta, la donna che morì per Mussolini*, p. 83.
57. Luigi Freddi, *Il cinema: il governo dell'immagine* (Rome: Centro Sperimentale di Cinematografia Gremese Editore, 1994), p. 172.
58. *Ibid.*, pp. 171–2.
59. *Il Corriere della Sera*, 13 September 1942.
60. See Aldo Palazzeschi, 'Un cultore della bellezza', *Il Mattino dell'Italia Centrale*, 14 December 1948.
61. For the background, see R.J.B. Bosworth, *Italian Venice*, pp. 164–5.
62. Stephen Gundle, *Mussolini's dream factory*, p. 245.
63. *Il Gazzettino*, 4, 13 September 1942.
64. Giuseppe Bottai, *Diario 1935–1944*, p. 337.
65. Anon., *Cinema*, 25 May 1943.
66. Luigi Freddi, *Il cinema*, p. 173.
67. See http://www.treccani.it/enciclopedia/ferdinando-maria-poggioli_%28Enciclopedia-del-Cinema%29/ (accessed 4 February 2016).
68. For its plot, see http://www.comingsoon.it/film/l-invasore/27944/scheda/ (accessed 4 February 2016).
69. For basic introduction to Fascist film, see Peter Bondanella, *A history of the Italian cinema* (New York: Continuum, 2009); cf. Ruth Ben-Ghiat, *Italian Fascism's empire cinema* (Bloomington: Indiana University Press, 2015).
70. See Natalia and Valerio Emanuele Marino, *L'Ovra a Cinecittà: polizia politica e spie in camicia nera* (Turin: Bollati Boringhieri, 2005).
71. For an example, see Mimmo Franzinelli, *Disertori*, pp. 34–5.
72. Myriam Petacci, *Chi ama è perduto*, p. 188.
73. See http://www.collegio-araldico.it/librodoro.html (accessed 4 February 2016).
74. Doris Duranti, *Il romanzo della mia vita*, p. 86.
75. Zita Ritossa, 'Mia "cognata" Claretta Petacci', *Tempo*, 21 March 1957.
76. The pro-Fascist poet Ezra Pound is perhaps a more powerful ghost from the regime in the town. After his release by the American authorities from the psychiatric hospital where he was confined after the war, he found sanctuary at the Castle Brunnerberg, not so far from the Villa Schildhof but rather more grandiose and 'historic'.
77. Interview with the Villa Schildhof's current owner, Verena Vok, 8 April 2016.
78. Luigi De Vincentis, *Io son te*, p. 186. For the furs, see Zita Ritossa, 'Mia "cognata" Claretta Petacci', *Tempo*, 21 March 1957.
79. Luigi De Vincentis, *Io son te*, pp. 178–80.
80. Zita Ritossa, 'Mia "cognata" Claretta Petacci', *Tempo*, 21 March 1957.
81. For physical description on her passport, see Carte Petacci 10/160/3.
82. For a newsreel image, see https://www.youtube.com/watch?v=6ebm7eMVnKw (accessed 4 February 2016); cf. Carte Petacci 25 for a set of photos of the wedding, as well as some of Myriam's publicity images. The *busta* also has photos of the Villa Camilluccia in construction and some family images of Zita Ritossa and her fair-headed sons.
83. Galeazzo Ciano, *Diary 1937–1943*, p. 535.
84. Myriam Petacci, *Chi ama è perduto*, p. 53.
85. *Ibid.*, pp. 200; 206.
86. Zita Ritossa, 'Mia "cognata" Claretta Petacci', *Tempo*, 21 February 1957.
87. Luigi De Vincentis, *Io son te*, pp. 184–91.
88. 'Calipso', *Vita segreta di Mussolini*, p. 30.

89. Carte Petacci, 10/162.
90. Myriam Petacci, *Chi ama è perduto*, p. 9.
91. Marcello Petacci, *Raccolta di alcuni lavori scientifici*, pp. 47–86; 146–60; 206–13.
92. *Ibid.*, Francesco Saverio Petacci, 'Prefazione', pp. 10–20.
93. *Ibid.*, p. 6.
94. See http://www.treccani.it/enciclopedia/mario-donati_%28Dizionario_Biografico%29/ (accessed 4 February 2016).
95. *Cronache*, 20 October 1945, as preserved in the Fondo Monelli, b. 139.
96. Zita Ritossa, 'La mia vita con Claretta Petacci', *Oggi*, 9 April 1975.
97. The couple did not take the chance to call their son Francesco Saverio, even though at Trieste's central Santa Maria Maggiore, a Petazzi chapel is dedicated to Saint Francis Xavier. See http://www.santuariosantamariamaggiore.it/download_file/depSMM_ita.pdf (accessed 15 April 2016).
98. Zita Ritossa, 'La mia vita con Claretta Petacci', *Oggi*, 9 April 1975.
99. See *ibid*. For his memorial at Campo Verano, see http://www.inmiamemoria.com/scatole_dei_ricordi/Petacci/Benvenuto/Petacci_Benvenuto___556894.php (accessed 4 February 2016).
100. Francesco Saverio Petacci, 'Prefazione', pp. 7–10.
101. Carte Petacci, diary entry, 19 January 1941.
102. Claretta Petacci, *Mussolini segreto*, p. 240.
103. *Ibid.*, p. 275.
104. Claretta Petacci, *Verso il disastro*, p. 41.
105. *Ibid.*, p. 207.
106. Nino D'Aroma, *Mussolini segreto*, pp. 431–2.
107. Luigi De Vincentis, *Io son te*, p. 17.
108. Piero Saporito, *Empty balcony* (London: V. Gollancz, 1945), p. 109 fn. 1.
109. Spartacus, *Claretta*, p. 28.
110. Zita Ritossa, 'Mia "cognata" Claretta Petacci', p. 36.
111. Segreteria particolare del Duce, Carteggio Riservato, 103, 10 May 1938, M. Petacci to Sebastiani; 16 May 1938, M. Petacci to Sebastiani; 2 September 1938, Sebastiani to M. Petacci; 16 January 1939, Sebastiani to Ministry of Education and separate note.
112. *Ibid.*, Ministry of the Navy to Sebastiani.
113. *Ibid.*, note, 14 August 1938.
114. *Ibid.*, 25 August 1938, M. Petacci to Sebastiani; 22 September, 3 October 1938, Goiran reports.
115. *Ibid.*, undated note [1942].
116. Franco Rovere, *Vita amorosa di Claretta Petacci*, p. 125. Rovere claimed that a Hungarian, who wanted to obtain Italian citizenship, sold it for 1 million lire, when it was worth seven. He was pressured to do so by the ubiquitous Buffarini Guidi. For a further summary omitting Buffarini Guidi, see Paolo Valente, *Porto di mare: Frammenti dell'anima multiculturale di una piccola città europea. Italiani (e molti altri) a Merano tra esodi, deportazioni e guerre (1934–1953)* (Trento: Temi 2005), pp. 199–204; Cf. Myriam Petacci, *Chi ama è perduto*, pp. 37, 207.
117. The cadastral record registers the successive sales and the price of 1.625 million lire but neither confirms nor denies rumour of sharp dealing. See Libro fondiario, catasto fondiario e urbano, Ufficio del libro fondiario di Merano (Provincia autonoma di Bolzano – Alto Adige), 837/1654/2016.
118. The villa's architectural history has been recorded by a sometime tenant from Sweden. See Gunvor Björkman, *Schildhof* (Stockholm: Ivar Halggstroms Büktryckeri AB, 1959).
119. *Guardian*, 13 October 2009.
120. Segreteria particolare del Duce, Carteggio Riservato, 103, M. Petacci plan, 21 February 1943.

121. Mimmo Franzinelli, *I tentacoli dell'Ovra*, p. 261; Mauro Canali, *Le spie del regime* (Bologna: Il Mulino, 2004), pp. 245–55.
122. Carte Petacci 5/83, 4 June 1939, Riccardi to [F.S. Petacci]; 5 May 1941, Riccardi to 'Donna Clara'; 20 October 1941, Riccardi to F.S. Petacci; 6 November, 6 December 1942, 12 March, 16 April 1943, Riccardi to 'Donna Clara'.
123. Galeazzo Ciano, *Diary 1937–1943*, p. 467.
124. *Ibid.*, p. 486. For a scandalous report of longstanding corrupt financial dealings between Osio and Riccardi, cf. Segreteria particolare del Duce, Carteggio Riservato, 91, 28 January 1943.
125. Myriam Petacci, *Chi ama è perduto*, p. 247.
126. The memorandum is published in Roberto Festorazzi, *Claretta Petacci*, pp. 293–307. This version includes further detail assembled after July 1943.
127. Galeazzo Ciano, *Diary 1937–1943* (ed. Renzo De Felice) (London: Phoenix Press, 2002), pp. 532–3; cf. Giuseppe Bottai, *Diario 1935–1944*, p. 316.
128. Ugo Guspini, *L'orecchio del regime*, p. 196.
129. Carmine Senise, *Quando ero capo della polizia 1940–1943* (Rome: Ruffolo Editore, 1946), pp. 154–63.
130. Galeazzo Ciano, *Diary 1937–1943*, p. 511.
131. Edda Mussolini Ciano, *My truth*, p. 186.
132. Giuseppe Bottai, *Diario 1935–1944*, pp. 337; 366.
133. *Ibid.*, p. 219.
134. For biographical introduction, see http://www.treccani.it/enciclopedia/guido-buffarini-guidi_%28Dizionario_Biografico%29/ (accessed 4 February 2016).
135. Io' Di Benigno, *Occasioni mancate: Roma in un diario segreto 1943–1944* (Rome: Edizioni SEI, 1945), p. 46.
136. Roberto Festorazzi, *Claretta Petacci*, pp. 88–92.
137. Arrigo Petacco, *Eva e Claretta*, pp. 106–7. For documentation, see Carte Petacci 10/160.
138. Carte Petacci, diary entry, 1 January 1942.
139. *Ibid.*, 17 January 1942.
140. *Ibid.*, 22, 23 January 1942.
141. *Ibid.*, 10, 20 May 1942.
142. *Ibid.*, late May 1942.
143. *Ibid.*, 15, 18, 19 September 1942.
144. *Ibid.*, 30 November 1942.
145. *Ibid.*, 2 December 1942.
146. *Ibid.*, 4 December 1942.
147. *Ibid.*, 12, 14, 16, 18 December 1942.
148. *Ibid.*, 20 December 1942.
149. Fondo Monelli, b. 139, Carboni report.
150. Carte Petacci, diary entry, 20 December 1942.
151. *Ibid.*, February 1943.
152. Spartacus, *Claretta: fiore del mio giardino*, p. 23.
153. Edda Mussolini Ciano, *My truth*, pp. 182–3.
154. Carte Petacci, undated diary entry, [May 1943].
155. Giuseppe Bottai, *Diario 1935–1944*, p. 376.
156. Fondo Monelli, b. 139.
157. Carte Petacci, diary entry, 17 May 1943.
158. *Ibid.*, 17 May 1943.
159. Carte Petacci 4/58, undated letter, Giuseppina Persichetti to Mussolini.
160. Giuseppe Bottai, *Diario 1935–1944*, p. 379. Cf. Edda Mussolini Ciano, *My truth*, p. 187.
161. Renzo De Felice, *Mussolini l'alleato 1940–1945*, vol. 1, *L'Italia in guerra 1940–1943*, part 2, p. 1536.

162. Natalia and Valerio Emanuele Marino, *L'Ovra a Cinecittà*, p. 241.
163. Quirino Armellini, *Diario di guerra: nove mesi al comando supremo* (Cernusco sul Naviglio: Garzanti, 1946), p. 269.
164. Renzo De Felice, *Mussolini l'alleato 1940–1945*, vol. I, *L'Italia in guerra 1940–1943*, part 2, p. 1345.
165. Carte Petacci, diary entry, 17 July 1943.
166. Ugo Guspini, *L'orecchio del regime*, p. 224.
167. Carte Petacci, diary entry, 25 July 1943. For Rachele, see Paolo Monelli, *Mussolini: piccolo borghese* (Milan: Garzanti, 1950), p. 183 as reported in Ray Moseley, *Mussolini's shadow*, pp. 173–4.

Chapter 6 The winter of a patriarch and his *Ducessa*

1. *Il Messaggero*, 6 December 1941.
2. *Ibid.*, 29 August 1943.
3. Fondo Monelli, b. 139.
4. *La Stampa*, 27 August 1943. Copies of both the newspaper pieces are preserved in the Petacci papers. See Carte Petacci, 16.
5. Carte Petacci, 4/60, [August 1943], M. Petacci memorandum.
6. Renzo Montagna, *Mussolini e il processo di Verona* (Milan: Edizioni Omnia, 1949), p. 53.
7. Carte Petacci, 16, 20 October 1943, Sister Margherita Vaccari to the Petaccis.
8. *Ibid.*, undated inventory.
9. Vittorio Mussolini, *Mussolini*, pp. 14–15.
10. Ray Moseley, *Mussolini's shadow*, pp. 176–84.
11. R.J.B. Bosworth, *Mussolini*, pp. 325–8.
12. For a graphic example, see Mimmo Franzinelli, *Disertori*, pp. 158–79.
13. For populist version, see Arrigo Petacco, *Ammazzate quel fascista! Vita intrepida di Ettore Muti*, (Milan: Mondadori, 2003).
14. In her memoirs, Myriam remembered him, despite their different political tracks. Myriam Petacci, *Chi ama è perduto*, pp. 5–6. So did the Resistance hero and eventual socialist president of the republic Sandro Pertini, who recalled that Persichetti fell almost beside him while they tried to oppose the Germans. Gianni Bisiach, *Pertini racconta: gli anni 1915–1945* (Milan: Mondadori, 1983), p. 98.
15. For background, see R.J.B. Bosworth, 'War, totalitarianism and "deep belief" in Fascist Italy 1935–1943', *European History Quarterly*, 34, 2004.
16. Edvige Mussolini, *Mio fratello Benito*, p. 168.
17. Clara Petacci, *Il mio diario* (Cernusco sul Naviglio: Editori Associati, 1946), p. vii. In his unpublished collection of the Petacci papers 1941–5, Franzinelli has prepared a new edition of this section of Claretta's diaries.
18. Clara Petacci, *Il mio diario*, pp. 1–4.
19. Carte Petacci, 16 [August 1943], Giuseppina Persichetti to Questore of Novara.
20. Clara Petacci, *Il mio diario*, p. 4.
21. *Ibid.*, p. 5.
22. *Ibid.*, pp. 5–6.
23. *Ibid.*, pp. 7–11.
24. See Silvio Pellico, *My prisons: le mie prigioni* (London: Oxford University Press, 1963).
25. Clara Petacci, *Il mio diario*, pp. 20, 43.
26. *Ibid.*, pp. 38–40. For background, see Antonio V. Savona and Michele L. Straniero, *Canti dell'Italia fascista (1919–1945)* (Milan: Garzanti, 1979).
27. Clara Petacci, *Il mio diario*, pp. 34–5.
28. *Ibid.*, pp. 48–9.

29. *Ibid.*, pp. 76–80.
30. *Ibid.*, pp. 81–6.
31. *Ibid.*, pp. 95; 100–2.
32. *Ibid.*, pp. 104–7.
33. *Ibid.*, pp. 122–42.
34. *Ibid.*, p. 144.
35. *Ibid.*, p. 144.
36. *Ibid.*, pp. 148–62.
37. Clara Petacci, *Il mio diario*, pp. 163–5.
38. For the speech, see Benito Mussolini, *Opera omnia*, vol. XXXII, pp. 1–5.
39. Clara Petacci, *Il mio diario*, pp. 165–78.
40. Benito Mussolini, *Opera omnia*, vol. XXXII, p. 4. In the following year, Mussolini put together another work entitled *Storia di un anno (tempo del bastone e della carota)*. It went back over the events leading to 25 July, the forty-five days and Mussolini's romantic escape from the Gran Sasso, with a nationalist, as much as a radical Fascist, message. See vol. XXXIV, pp. 301–444. There was no mention of any Petacci in its pages.
41. *Ibid.*, vol. XXXIV, p. 286.
42. *Ibid.*, vol. XXXIV, p. 294.
43. For narration, see Renzo De Felice, *Mussolini l'alleato 1940–1945*, vol. II, *La guerra civile 1943–1945* (Turin: Einaudi, 1997), pp. 3–71.
44. Georg Zachariae, *Mussolini si confessa*. Eventually, Mussolini sent a note of thanks to Hitler's personal – and idiosyncratic – doctor, Theo Morrell, for choosing Zachariae. Segreteria particolare del Duce, Carteggio Riservato, 122, 22 September 1944, Mussolini to Morrell.
45. Renzo De Felice, *Mussolini l'alleato 1940–1945*, vol. II, *La guerra civile 1943–1945*, pp. 345–62.
46. Pasquale Chessa and Barbara Raggi, *L'ultima lettera di Benito Mussolini: amore e politica a Salò 1943–45* (Milan: Mondadori, 2010), p. 53.
47. Benito Mussolini, *A Clara* (Milan: Mondadori, 2011), p. 347.
48. Giovanni Dolfin, *Con Mussolini nella tragedia: diario del capo della segreteria particolare del Duce 1943–1944* (Cernusco sul Naviglio: Garzanti, 1949), pp. 81–2.
49. Segreteria particolare del Duce, Carteggio Riservato, 122, 25 October 1943, pro-memoria for Dolfin.
50. Giovanni Dolfin, *Con Mussolini nella tragedia*, pp. 32; 42.
51. Benito Mussolini, *A Clara*, pp. 152–4; Vincenzo Costa, *L'ultimo federale: memorie della guerra civile 1943–1945* (Bologna: Il Mulino, 1997), pp. 312–13.
52. Carte Petacci, diary entry [4 October 1943].
53. Benito Mussolini, *A Clara*, pp. 73–7. His letter of 10 October followed up the phone call of 4 October and dealt with many of the same issues
54. Zita Ritossa, 'Mia "cognata" Claretta Petacci', *Tempo*, 21 February 1957.
55. *Ibid.*, 11 April 1957.
56. Carte Petacci, diary entry, 28 October 1943.
57. Eugen Dollmann, *Roma Nazista* (Milan: Longanesi, 1951), p. 370.
58. For its current use for dancing and other entertainment, see http://www.classvenues.com/wedding-venue/671/wedding-venues-in-italy/torre-san-marco-e-villa-fiordaliso (accessed 28 January 2016).
59. Carte Petacci, diary entry, 14 April 1944.
60. Fondo Monelli, b. 139.
61. For background, see Reto Hofmann, *The Fascist effect: Japan and Italy, 1915–1952* (Ithaca: Cornell University Press, 2015), pp. 8–37.
62. I owe this information to Dr Reto Hofmann and to a memoir Ono published in 1951–2; it was highly sympathetic to Fascism.

NOTES to pp. 188–196

63. Cf. also Segreteria particolare del Duce, Carteggio Ordinario, 42, Repubblica Sociale Italiana, 43, reports of meetings between Ono and Mussolini. Cf. Benito Mussolini, *A Clara*, pp. 90; 92.
64. Benito Mussolini, *A Clara*, p. 80.
65. *Ibid.*, pp. 80–4.
66. *Ibid.*, pp. 87–8.
67. Segreteria particolare del Duce, Carteggio Riservato, Repubblica Sociale Italiana, 120 [October 1943], A. Pallottelli to Mussolini; 25 November 1943, Dolfin to A. Pallottelli.
68. *Ibid.*, 120, undated letter, A. Pallottelli to Dolfin.
69. *Ibid.*, 123, 30 May 1944, V. Pallottelli to Mussolini.
70. Zita Ritossa, 'Mia "cognata" Claretta Petacci', *Tempo*, 11 April 1957.
71. Pasquale Chessa and Barbara Raggi, *L'ultima lettera di Benito Mussolini*, pp. 61–2.
72. Carte Petacci, letters of 16, 18 January 1944.
73. Benito Mussolini, *A Clara*, p. 115, for another effort on her part to raise Marcello's prominence.
74. Carte Petacci, 4/59, undated letter [?October 1943], Giuseppina Persichetti to Mussolini.
75. *Ibid.*, 3/32, 31 January '1943' [evidently 1944], Giuseppina Persichetti to Mussolini.
76. Myriam Petacci, *Chi ama è perduto*, p. 317.
77. Carte Petacci, 4/61, undated letter, Francesco Saverio Petacci to Mussolini.
78. Carte Petacci, letter of 21 February 1944.
79. *Ibid.*, 3/34, undated letter [1944], Myriam to Mussolini.
80. *Ibid.*, 3/34, undated letter [early 1944], Myriam to Mussolini.
81. *Ibid.*, 3/34, undated letter [1944], Myriam to Mussolini. Her appeal was duly backed up by her sister. Benito Mussolini, *A Clara*, p. 159.
82. Benito Mussolini, *A Clara*, p. 171.
83. Carte Petacci, 3/33, 23 May 1944, Marcello to Mussolini.
84. *Ibid.*, undated letter [1944], Marcello to Mussolini.
85. Benito Mussolini, *A Clara*, pp. 92–105.
86. *Ibid.*, pp. 106–9.
87. *Ibid.*, p. 118.
88. *Ibid.*, p. 115.
89. *Ibid.*, pp. 120–1.
90. Carte Petacci, letter of 23 March 1944.
91. *Ibid.*, letter of 30 March 1944.
92. Benito Mussolini, *A Clara*, pp. 151–4.
93. *Ibid.*, pp. 159–60.
94. *Ibid.*, p. 160.
95. Pasquale Chessa and Barbara Raggi, *L'ultima lettera di Benito Mussolini*, pp. 92–4.
96. Benito Mussolini, *A Clara*, pp. 164–5.
97. Carte Petacci, letter of 23 April 1944.
98. Benito Mussolini, *A Clara*, pp. 167–8.
99. Carte Petacci, 5/79, undated letter, Giuseppina Persichetti to Mussolini, italics in original.
100. *Ibid.*, 3/34, [May 1944], Myriam to Mussolini.
101. See *ibid.*, [June 1944]. Two letters, Myriam to Mussolini; 3/32, [1944], also Myriam to Mussolini. They were not restrained by Mussolini's request to Clara that they cease. Benito Mussolini, *A Clara*, p. 210.
102. See, for example, Benito Mussolini, *A Clara*, pp. 233–4.
103. *Ibid.*, p. 188.
104. Carte Petacci, letters of late May, 6 June 1944, partially reported in Pasquale Chessa and Barbara Raggi, *L'ultima lettera di Benito Mussolini*, pp. 112–13. Cf. Benito Mussolini, *A Clara*, pp. 204–6.

105. Benito Mussolini, *A Clara*, p. 202. Cf. 1 July (p. 228), with his denial that he had seen her again.
106. *Ibid.*, pp. 215; 222; 284; 286–7.
107. Carte Petacci, undated letter [June–July 1944].
108. Pasquale Chessa and Barbara Raggi, *L'ultima lettera di Benito Mussolini*, pp. 121–2.
109. *Ibid.*, pp. 123–4.
110. Benito Mussolini, *A Clara*, pp. 240–3.
111. Carte Petacci, 5/78 [?June 1944], Myriam to Mussolini.
112. *Ibid.* [?June 1944], Myriam to Mussolini.
113. *Ibid.*, 3/34 [?June 1944], Myriam to Mussolini.
114. Ibid., 5/79 [?August 1944], Myriam to Claretta.
115. Myriam Petacci, *Chi ama è perduto*, p. 323. Carte Petacci, 5/84, 16 August 1944, E. Morreale report.
116. Giovanni Tassani, *Diplomatico tra due guerre: vita di Giacomo Paulucci di Calboli Barone* (Florence: Le Lettere, 2012), pp. 427–61.
117. Carte Petacci, 5/84, 16 August 1944, E. Morreale report.
118. Benito Mussolini, *A Clara*, p. 282. Cf. Carte Petacci, 5/84, 13 December 1944, E. Morreale report.
119. Carte Petacci, undated letter [August 1944].
120. Benito Mussolini, *A Clara*, p. 234.
121. *Ibid.*, p. 261.
122. Carte Petacci, undated letter [?August 1944].
123. Benito Mussolini, *A Clara*, pp. 259–61; 285; 290–1.
124. *Ibid.*, pp. 281–2.
125. *Ibid.*, p. 283.
126. *Ibid.*, pp. 291–2.
127. *Ibid.*, pp. 293–4; 296–7.
128. *Ibid.*, pp. 298–9; 332.
129. Roberto Festorazzi, *Claretta Petacci*, pp. 183–7.
130. Antonio Bonino, *Mussolini mi ha detto: memorie del vicesegretario del Partito fascista repubblicano 1944–1945* (ed. Marino Viganò) (Rome: Settimo Sigillo, 1995), p. 60.
131. Eugen Dollmann, *Roma nazista*, pp. 370–2. His later English account somewhat varies from the first Italian one.
132. Roberto Gervaso, *Claretta, la donna che morì per Mussolini*, p. 13.
133. Bruno Spampanato, *Contromemoriale* (Rome: Edizione di 'Illustrato', 1952), vol. 1, p. 234.
134. Eugen Dollmann, *The interpreter: memoirs* (London: Hutchinson, 1967), pp. 327–8.
135. *Ibid.*, p. 326.
136. Benito Mussolini, *A Clara*, p. 301.
137. *Ibid.*, pp. 302–3.
138. Pasquale Chessa and Barbara Raggi, *L'ultima lettera di Benito Mussolini*, p. 141–2.

Chapter 7 Death in the afternoon

1. For background, see Lucy Hughes-Hallett, *The pike*.
2. The Villa Mirabella is now part of the historic site of Il Vittoriale degli Italiani. Most recently it housed an exhibition of the sentimental paintings of the Bolognese artist, Antonio Saliola. They are given sentimental endorsement by the president of the Fondazione Il Vittoriale degli Italiani, Giordano Bruno Guerri, the anti-anti-Fascist historian. The paintings feature young women and the moon. There is, however, no explicit reference to Claretta. See Cristina Baldassari (ed.), *Che fai tu, luna, in ciel nei quadri di Saliola? Dipinti di Antonio Saliola con una lettera di Giordano Bruno Guerri* (Villa Mirabella: Fondazione Il Vittoriale degli Italiani, 2016).

3. An Australian historian might enjoy the information that the boat, commissioned in 1901, cruised around Australian ports from Fremantle to Brisbane on its first major voyage. See further details at http://www.vittoriale.it/nave-puglia (accessed 14 September 2016).
4. Benito Mussolini, *A Clara*, pp. 303–4.
5. *Ibid.*, p. 304.
6. *Ibid.*, pp. 304–5.
7. *Ibid.*
8. *Ibid.*, pp. 306–14; 319; 325–6; 328–9. Cf. Carte Petacci (from unpublished selection by Mimmo Franzinelli), letter of 30 November 1944.
9. Benito Mussolini, *A Clara*, p. 329.
10. Carte Petacci, undated letter [December 1944].
11. *Ibid.*, undated letters [December 1944]. Cf. Fulvio Balisti, *Da Bir el Gobi alla Repubblica Sociale Italiana* (Abano Terme: Piovan Editore, 1986), pp. 167–8; 186, for an erratic stance on the Petaccis.
12. Carte Petacci, undated letters [December 1944].
13. R.J.B. Bosworth, *Mussolini*, pp. 25–6.
14. Benito Mussolini, *A Clara*, p. 332.
15. *Ibid.*, pp. 335–6.
16. *Ibid.*, pp. 337–8.
17. *Ibid.*, p. 348.
18. *Ibid.*, pp. 338–40.
19. *Ibid.*, pp. 353–4.
20. *Ibid.*, pp. 341–2.
21. Carte Petacci, letter of 28 December 1944.
22. Benito Mussolini, *A Clara*, p. 343.
23. Carte Petacci, letters of 6 January 1945.
24. *Ibid.*, 13 September 1944, Enrico and Maria Mancini [*sic*] to 'Rita Colfosco'.
25. Benito Mussolini, *A Clara*, p. 346.
26. *Ibid.*, p. 361.
27. Carte Petacci, letters of 4 February 1945.
28. Benito Mussolini, *A Clara*, p. 359.
29. *Ibid.*, pp. 357; 367–8.
30. In fact, by this time all Mussolini's office documents were redone for him in large type in order to relieve his failing sight. Antonio Bonino, *Mussolini mi ha detto*, p. 135.
31. Benito Mussolini, *A Clara*, pp. 364–5.
32. Pasquale Chessa and Barbara Raggi, *L'ultima lettera di Benito Mussolini*, pp. 163–6.
33. *Ibid.*, pp. 167–8.
34. Carte Petacci, 5/78, letter [February 1945], Myriam to Mussolini.
35. Antonio Bonino, *Mussolini mi ha detto*, p. 63.
36. Carte Petacci, 5/78, letter [February 1945], Myriam to Mussolini.
37. See, for example, Benito Mussolini, *A Clara*, p. 371.
38. *Ibid.*, pp. 374–6.
39. *Ibid.*, pp. 377–8.
40. *Ibid.*, pp. 381–2.
41. *Ibid.*, p. 389.
42. *Ibid.*, pp. 391–3.
43. *Ibid.*, p. 385.
44. *Ibid.*, pp. 387–9.
45. *Ibid.*, pp. 389–90.
46. *Ibid.*, p. 390.
47. *Ibid.*, p. 393.

48. Carte Petacci, undated letter [March or April 1945].
49. Benito Mussolini, *A Clara*, pp. 394–6.
50. *Ibid.*, pp. 396–7.
51. *Ibid.*, pp. 397–8.
52. Pasquale Chessa and Barbara Raggi, *L'ultima lettera di Benito Mussolini*, p. 179.
53. Myriam Petacci, *Chi ama è perduto*, p. 339.
54. For the latter suspicion, see Oreste Del Buono, *Amori neri* (Rome: Edizioni Theoria, 1985), p. 60.
55. Carte Petacci, 5/78, letters, [April 1945], Myriam to Mussolini.
56. *Ibid.*, 5/82, 10 April 1945, 'Giuseppina Petacci' to Mussolini.
57. Franco Rovere, *Vita amorosa di Claretta Petacci*, p. 137.
58. Anon, *L'ultima favorita*, p. 3.
59. Myriam Petacci, *Chi ama è perduto*, pp. 347–9.
60. *Ibid.*, pp. 343–5.
61. Ferdinando Petacci, 'Claretta: un agente inglese a Palazzo Venezia?', in Claretta Petacci, *Verso il disastro*, pp. 410–11.
62. See, for example, Fabio Andriola, *Mussolini–Churchill: carteggio segreto* (Casale Monferrato: Piemme, 1996), p. 252.
63. Zita Ritossa, 'Mia "cognata" Claretta Petacci', *Tempo*, 18 April 1957.
64. For description, see R.J.B. Bosworth, *Mussolini*, pp. 27–31.
65. For Pallottelli's friendship with Curti before and after 1945, see Elena Curti, *Il chiodo a tre punte*, pp. 210–11.
66. Urbano Lazzaro, *L'oro di Dongo: il mistero del tesoro del duce* (Milan: Mondadori, 1995), pp. 30–1.
67. *Ibid.*, pp. 31–2.
68. Walter Audisio, *In nome del popolo italiano* (Milan: Teti Editore, 1975), p. 371.
69. Pierlugi Bellini delle Stelle and Urbano Lazzaro, *Dongo: the last act* (London: Macdonald, 1964), p. 105.
70. Giorgio Cavalleri, Franco Giannantoni and Mario J. Cereghino, *La fine: gli ultimi giorni di Benito Mussolini nei documenti dei servizi segreti americani (1945–1946)* (Milan: Garzanti, 2009), p. 142.
71. Pierlugi Bellini delle Stelle and Urbano Lazzaro, *Dongo*, p. 104.
72. *Ibid.*, pp. 170–8.
73. Vincenzo Costa, *L'ultimo federale*, pp. 125; 312.
74. Pierlugi Bellini delle Stelle and Urbano Lazzaro, *Dongo*, pp. 123–4.
75. Alessandro Zanella, *L'ora di Dongo* (Milan: Rusconi, 2011), p. 387.
76. Pierlugi Bellini delle Stelle and Urbano Lazzaro, *Dongo*, p. 128.
77. *Ibid.*, pp. 128–38.
78. Roberto Festorazzi, *Claretta Petacci*, p. 237.
79. Giorgio Pisanò, *Gli ultimi cinque secondi di Mussolini: un'inchiesta giornalista durata quarant'anni* (Milan: Saggiatore, 2009). The original edition, then thought worthy of republication, had appeared in 1996. Cf. also his *Io, fascista* (Milan: Il Saggiatore, 1997).
80. For one autobiographical account of the decision, see Gianni Bisiach, *Pertini racconta*, pp. 174–8.
81. Walter Audisio, *In nome del popolo italiano*, p. 377.
82. Franco Bandini, *Le ultime 95 ore di Mussolini* (Milan: Mondadori, 1968), p. 315.
83. Walter Audisio, *In nome del popolo italiano*, p. 381.
84. Anon, *L'ultima favorita*, p. 3.
85. Fabrizio Bernini, *Il giustiziere di Dongo: Walter Audisio: il Colonello Valerio. Luci ed ombre sulla fucilazione del secolo, quella del Duce e di Claretta Petacci* (Pavia: Gianni Iuculano Editore, 2004), pp. 163–4.
86. Peter Tompkins, *Dalle carte segrete del Duce* (Milan: Marco Tropea Editore, 2001), p. 319.
87. Walter Audisio, *In nome del popolo italiano*, p. 386.

88. Angelo Colleoni, *La verità sulla fine di Mussolini e della Petacci: come furono catturati e giustiziati Mussolini, la Petacci, il fratello e quindici gerarconi* (Milan: Tipografia Editoriale Lucchi, 1946), p. 23.
89. Pierlugi Bellini delle Stelle and Urbano Lazzaro, *Dongo*, pp. 185–6.
90. Zita Ritossa, 'Mia "cognata" Claretta Petacci', *Tempo*, 9 May 1957.
91. Luciano Garibaldi, *Mussolini: the secrets of his death* (New York: Enigma Books, 2004), p. 205.
92. Ugo Zatterin, *Al Viminale con il morto*, p. 75.
93. Pierlugi Bellini delle Stelle and Urbano Lazzaro, *Dongo*, p. 187.
94. Myriam Petacci, *Chi ama è perduto*, p. 8.
95. Gianni Bisiach, *Pertini racconta*, p. 182. The chief analysis by a historian of these events is Sergio Luzzatto, *Il corpo del duce*. He is severely critical of crowd behaviour. Claudio Pavone, the great historian of the period from 1943 to 1945, agreed that Claretta was 'a faithful woman, worthy of respect'. See Claudio Pavone, *Una guerra civile: saggio storico sulla moralità nella Resistenza* (Turin: Bollati Boringhieri, 1991), p. 512.
96. Sergio Luzzatto, *Il corpo del duce*, p. 64.
97. Rossana Rossanda, *The comrade from Milan* (London: Verso, 2010), p. 84.
98. For the US Arrmy film record of the event, see http://www.dailymotion.com/video/x2ku5ip (accessed 18 January 2016).
99. For visual evidence of the place, see, for example, http://photosecrets.com/cimitero-maggiore-di-milano (accessed 18 January 2016).
100. Giuseppina Persichetti, *La enamoranda di Mussolini* (Mexico City: Editorial Fren, 1954).
101. Myriam's other films were *El Emigrado* (1946), *Lluvia de hijos* and *Doña Maria la Brava* (both 1947), *Confidencia* (1948), *Tempestad en el alma* (1949), and *Vendaval, Flor de lago* and *Torturados* (all 1950).
102. Luigi Cavicchioli, 'Il testamento di Claretta ha commosso il pubblico: al processo di Brescia Clara Petacci è risultata una donna fedele e coraggiosa', *Oggi*, 10 July 1952.
103. Myriam Petacci, 'Questa è la mia storia', *Oggi*, 14, 21, 28 April, 5 May 1955.
104. Myriam Petacci, *Chi ama è perduto*, pp. 395–6.
105. *Ibid.*, p. 54.
106. See http://www.jus.unitn.it/users/pascuzzi/privcomp00-01/topics/3/Cass_1963.htm (accessed 16 January 2016).
107. For an evocation of the background, see Roberto Festorazzi, *San Donnino, cella 31*.
108. Giuseppe Bottai, *Diario 1944–1948* (ed. Giordano Bruno Guerri) (Milan: Rizzoli, 1988), p. 177.
109. Bruno D'Agostini, *Colloqui con Rachele Mussolini*, pp. 8–9.
110. For an excess of such theorising, see Roberto Festorazzi, *Bruno e Gina Mussolini*, pp. 240–66.
111. Renata Broggini, 'La "famiglia Mussolini": colloqui di Edda Ciano con lo psichiatra svizzero Respond 1944–1945', *Italia contemporanea*, 203, 1996, p. 352.
112. Marcello Sorgi, *Edda Ciano e il comunista*.
113. Anita Pensotti, *Le italiane*, p. 34.
114. For an interview, published posthumously, see Edda Ciano, *La mia vita: intervista di Domenico Olivieri* (ed. Nicola Caracciolo) (Milan: Mondadori, 2001). There is also a popular biography, Antonio Spinosa, *Edda*.
115. For her story, see Lorenzo Baratter, *Anna Maria Mussolini*. Cf. more generally, the chatty Antonio Spinosa, *I figli del Duce*.

Conclusion

1. See chapter 2 and Gustavo Bocchini Padiglione, *L'harem del Duce*.
2. Claretta Petacci, *Verso il disastro*, p. 370.
3. Jan Plamper, *The history of emotions* (Oxford University Press, 2015), p. 43.

4. For some example, see Denis Mack Smith, *Mussolini*, p. 3. Cf. the naive Con Coughlin, *Saddam: the secret life* (London: Macmillan, 2002).
5. See https://www.washingtonpost.com/opinions/donald-trump-isnt-todays-wendell-willkie-hes-todays-benito-mussolini/2015/12/08/77c81b0c-9ddc-11e5-a3c5-c77f2cc5a43c_story.html (accessed 1 March 2016). *The Economist*, 5 March 2016, with its own obsessions, deemed Trump rather a 'blond Berlusconi'.
6. Despina Stratigakos, *Hitler at home* (London: Yale University Press, 2015).
7. Volker Ullrich, *Hitler: ascent 1889–1939* (London: Bodley Head, 2016), pp. 270–84; 611–22
8. Adolf Hitler, *Hitler's Table Talk 1941–1944* (ed. Hugh Trevor-Roper) (London: Weidenfeld & Nicolson, 1953).
9. Ranuccio Bianchi Bandinelli, *Dal diario di un borghese* (ed. Marcello Barbanera) (Rome: Riuniti, 1996), p. 124.
10. Sheila Fitzpatrick, *On Stalin's team: the years of living dangerously in Soviet politics* (Princeton University Press, 2015), p. 67.
11. Christopher Duggan, *Fascist voices: an intimate history of Mussolini's Italy* (London: Bodley Head, 2012), p. 218.
12. Giuseppe Finaldi, 'Blueblood and Blacksmith: a comparative view of Churchill's and Mussolini's speeches', in Daniela Baratieri, Mark Edele and Giuseppe Finaldi (eds), *Totalitarian dictatorship*, pp. 103–22.
13. See David Lough, *No more champagne: Churchill and his money* (London: Head of Zeus, 2015). The British leader was a case study in the use of *raccomandazioni*, patron–client networks and what might now draw criticism as insider trading. He demonstrated that, what in Italian history is often called 'corruption', is by no means confined to that nation.
14. Paolo Valente, *Porto di mare*, p. 204.
15. Michael Ebner, *Ordinary violence in Mussolini's Italy* (Cambridge University Press, 2011).
16. See, for example, Emilio Gentile, *La via italiana al totalitarismo: il partito e lo stato nel regime fascista* (Rome: La Nuova Italia Scientifica, 1995).
17. Francis Fukuyama, *The end of history and the last man* (London: Hamish Hamilton, 1992).
18. Roberto Vivarelli, *Fascismo e storia d'Italia* (Bologna: Il Mulino, 2008), pp. 9; 22; 106–7. Cf his autobiographical piece *La fine di una stagione: memoria 1943–1945* (Bologna: Il Mulino, 2000) and his fiercely nationalist reaction to a foreign history of Italy, 'Di una pseudo-storia d'Italia', *Rivista Storica Italiana*, 121, 2009.

BIBLIOGRAPHY

Archivio Centrale dello Stato

Segreteria particolare del Duce, Carteggio Riservato.
Segreteria particolare del Duce, Carteggio Riservato 1943–1945.
Segreteria particolare del Duce, Carteggio Ordinario.
Segreteria particolare del Duce, Carte della cassetta di zinco.
Segreteria particolare del Duce, Carte della valigia.
Carte Petacci, scatole 1, 2, 3, 4, 5, 8, 9, 10, 16 and 25.
Ministero dell'Interno Gabinetto, 1957–60, busta 43.

Ufficio del catasto, Merano/Meran (Provincia autonoma di Bolzano – Alto Adige).
Libro fondiario, catasto fondiario e urbano, Ufficio del libro fondiario di Merano/Meran (Provincia autonoma di Bolzano – Alto Adige).
Fondo Paolo Monelli, Biblioteca Statale Antonio Baldini, Rome, buste 139, 145: Manoscritto, bozze (some in English), articoli e pubblicazioni su Claretta Petacci, appunti, corrispondenza, 1945–1953.

Journals and newspapers

Annuario della nobiltà italiana.
Casabella.
Il Corriere della Sera.
Il Corriere di Brescia.
Critica Fascista.
Il Gazzettino.
Il Messaggero.
Il Popolo d'Italia.
La Provincia di Como.
Oggi.
Storia illustrata.
Tempo.
The Times (London).

BIBLIOGRAPHY

Published books and articles

Agarossi, Elena. *A nation collapses: the Italian surrender of September 1943* (Cambridge University Press, 2000).
Alfieri, Dino. *Dictators face to face* (London: Elek, 1954).
Almirante, Giorgio. *Autobiografia di un 'fucilatore'* (Milan: Edizioni del Borghese, 1974).
Amicucci, Ermanno. *I 600 giorni di Mussolini (dal Gran Sasso a Dongo)* (Rome: Editrice 'Faro', 1948).
Andriola, Fabio. *Mussolini–Churchill: carteggio segreto* (Casale Monferrato: Piemme, 1996).
Anfuso, Filippo. *Da Palazzo Venezia al Lago di Garda (1936–1945)* (Rome: Settimo Sigillo, 1996).
— *Roma-Berlino-Salò 1936–1945* (Cernusco sul Naviglio: Garzanti, 1950).
Anon. *Agonia e morte di Mussolini e del Fascismo nel racconto di chi prese parte alla cattura* (Rome: Tipografici Assistenziario-Chillemi, 1945).
Anon. *Clara Petacci: la favorita del Littorio: documentazione fotografica di ciò che fu e di ciò che rappresentò la Venere di Palazzo Venezia* (Rome: Stampatrice Novissima, nd [?1945]).
Anon. *Come ho giustiziato Mussolini e Clara Petacci: 'Devi morire pure tu': gli ultimi istanti di vita dei criminali fascisti* (Naples: Arti Grafiche Dott. Amodio, nd [1945]).
Anon. *L'ultima favorita: Clara Petacci* (Rome: Editore Francesco Mondini, 1945).
Anon (ed.). *Mussolini giudicato dal mondo* (Milan: Universus, 1946).
Anon (ed.). *Playdux: storia erotica del Fascismo* (Rome: Tattilo Editore, 1973).
Armellini, Quirino. *Diario di guerra: nove mesi al comando supremo* (Cernusco sul Naviglio: Garzanti, 1946).
Arthurs, Joshua. *Excavating modernity: the Roman past in Fascist Italy* (Ithaca: Cornell University Press, 2012).
Audisio, Walter. *In nome del popolo italiano* (Milan: Teti Editore, 1975).
Avvocatura Generale dello Stato. *Ecc.ma Corte di Appello di Roma per il Ministero dell'Interno patrocinato dall'avvocatura generale dello stato (avv. Salorni) contro gli eredi di Clara Petacci, patrocinati dagli avvocati De Pilato, d'Amico e Luciani* (Rome: Tipografia Consorzio Nazionale, 1953).
Babini, Valeria P., Chiara Beccalossi and Lucy Riall (eds). *Italian sexualities uncovered, 1789–1914* (Houndmills: Palgrave Macmillan, 2015).
Bacci, Andrea. *Mussolini: il primo sportivo d'Italia: il duce, lo sport, il fascismo, i grandi campioni degli anni Trenta* (Ivrea: Bradipolibri Editore, 2013).
Badoglio, Pietro. *Italy in the Second World War: memories and documents* (Oxford University Press, 1948).
Bailey, Roderick. *Target Italy: the secret war against Mussolini 1940–1943. The official history of SOE operations in Fascist Italy* (London: Faber and Faber, 2014).
Baima Bollone, Pierluigi. *La psicologia di Mussolini* (Milan: Mondadori, 2007).
— *Il traditore: Mussolini e la conquista del potere* (Rome: Universale Napoleone, 1973).
— *Le ultime ore di Mussolini* (Milan: Mondadori, 2005).
Balabanoff, Angelica. *My life as a rebel* (London: Hamish Hamilton, 1938).
Baldassari, Cristina (ed.). *Che fai tu, luna, in ciel nei quadri di Saliola? Dipinti di Antonio Saliola con una lettera di Giordano Bruno Guerri* (Villa Mirabella: Fondazione Il Vittoriale degli Italiani, 2016).
Baldassini, Cristina. *L'ombra di Mussolini: l'Italia moderata e la memoria del fascismo (1945–1960)* (Soveria Mannelli: Rubbettino, 2008).
Baldoli, Claudia and Marco Fincardi. 'Italian society under Anglo-American bombs: propaganda, experience and legend, 1940–1945', *Historical Journal*, 52, 2009.
Balisti, Fulvio. *Da Bir el Gobi alla Repubblica Sociale Italiana* (Abano Terme: Piovan Editore, 1986).
Bandini, Franco. *Claretta: profilo di Clara Petacci e dei suoi tempi* (Milan: Sugar Editore, 1960).

BIBLIOGRAPHY

— *Le ultime 95 ore di Mussolini* (Milan: Mondadori, 1968).
Baratieri, Daniele, Mark Edele and Giuseppe Finaldi (eds). *Totalitarian dictatorship: new histories. Essays in honour of R.J.B. Bosworth* (London: Routledge, 2014).
Baratter, Lorenzo. *Anna Maria Mussolini: l'ultima figlia del Duce* (Milan: Mursia, 2008).
Barzini, Luigi. *Memories of mistresses: reflections from a life* (New York: Collier Books, 1986).
Bastianini, Giuseppe. *Uomini, cose, fatti: memorie di un ambasciatore* (Milan: Vitagliano, 1959).
— *Volevo fermare Mussolini: memorie di un diplomatico fascista* (Milan: RCS Libri, 2005).
Baxa, Paul. 'Capturing the Fascist moment: Hitler's visit to Italy in 1938 and the radicalization of Fascist Italy', *Journal of Contemporary History*, 42, 2007.
Bedeschi, Sante and Rino Alessi. *Anni giovanili di Mussolini* (Milan: Mondadori, 1939).
Bellini delle Stelle, Pierluigi and Urbano Lazzaro. *Dongo: the last act* (London: Macdonald, 1964).
Benedetti, Virginia. *Rosa Maltoni Mussolini* (Brescia: Vittorio Gatti Editore, 1928).
Ben-Ghiat, Ruth. *Fascist modernities: Italy 1922–1945* (Berkeley: University of California Press, 2001).
Benito Mussolini: lo stato sociale nel centennio: pagine di storia dimenticata (Rome: ilibridelBorghese, 2016).
Berezin, Mabel. *Making the Fascist self: the political culture of interwar Italy* (Ithaca: Cornell University Press, 1997).
Berneri, Camillo. *Mussolini: psicologia di un dittatore* (ed. Pier Carlo Masini) (Milan: Edizioni Azione Comune, 1966).
Bernini, Fabrizio. *Il giustiziere di Dongo: Walter Audisio: il Colonello Valerio. Luci ed ombre sulla fucilazione del secolo, quella del Duce e di Claretta Petacci* (Pavia: Gianni Iuculano Editore, 2004).
Bertoldi, Silvio. *Gli arricchiti all'ombra di Palazzo Venezia* (ed. Filippo Maria Battaglia and Beppe Benvenuto) (Milan: Mursia, 2009).
— *Piazzale Loreto* (Milan: Rizzoli, 2001).
Best, Nicholas. *Five days that shook the world: eyewitness accounts from Europe at the end of World War II* (Oxford: Osprey Publishing, 2012).
Bianchi Bandinelli, Ranuccio. *Dal diario di un borghese* (ed. Marcello Barbanera) (Rome: Riuniti, 1996).
Bianchini Braglia, Elena. *Donna Rachele: con il Duce, oltre il Duce* (Milan: Mursia, 2007).
Bini, Martina. *'Sull'ondivaga prora'. Margherita Sarfatti: arte, passione e politica* (Florence: Centro Editoriale Toscano, 2009).
Bisiach, Gianni. *Pertini racconta: gli anni 1915–1945* (Milan: Mondadori, 1983).
Björkman, Gunvor. *Schildhof* (Stockholm: Ivar Halggstroms Büktryckeri A.B., 1959).
Blasetti, Alessandro. *Scritti sul cinema* (ed. Adriano Aprà) (Venice: Marsilio, 1982).
Boatti, Giorgio (ed.). *Caro Duce: lettere di donne italiane a Mussolini 1922–1943* (Milan: Rizzoli, 1989).
Bocca, Giorgio. *La repubblica di Mussolini* (Bari: Laterza, 1977).
Bocchini Padiglione, Gustavo. *L'harem del Duce* (Milan: Mursia, 2006).
Boddice, Rob (ed.). *Pain and emotion in modern history* (Houndmills: Palgrave Macmillan, 2014).
Bojano, Filippo. *In the wake of the goose-step* (London: Cassell, 1944).
Bolla, Luigi. *Perché a Salò: diario della Repubblica Sociale Italiana* (ed. Giordano Bruno Guerri) (Milan: Bompiani, 1982).
— *Il segreto di due re* (Milan: Rizzoli, 1951).
Bonino, Antonio. *Mussolini mi ha detto: memorie del vicesegretario del Partito fascista repubblicano 1944–1945* (ed. Marino Viganò) (Rome: Settimo Sigillo, 1995).
Boratto, Ercole. *A spasso col Duce: le memorie dell'autista di Benito Mussolini* (Rome: Castelvecchi, 2014).
Bordeux, Vahdah Jeanne. *Benito Mussolini: the man* (London: Hutchinson, 1927).

BIBLIOGRAPHY

Borghese, Junio Valerio. *Decima Flottiglia Mas: dalle origini all'armistizio* (Rome: Garzanti, 1950).
Bosworth, R.J.B. *The Italian dictatorship: problems and perspectives in the interpretation of Mussolini and Fascism* (London: Arnold, 1998).
— *Italian Venice: a history* (London: Yale University Press, 2014).
— *Mussolini* (rev. ed.; London: Bloomsbury, 2010).
— *Mussolini's Italy: life under the dictatorship 1915–1945* (London: Allen Lane, 2005).
— (ed.) *The Oxford handbook of Fascism* (Oxford University Press, 2009).
— 'Victimhood asserted: Italian memories of the Second World War', in Manuel Bragança and Peter Tame (eds), *The long aftermath: cultural legacies of Europe at war, 1936–2016* (New York: Berghahn, 2016).
— 'War, totalitarianism and "deep belief" in Fascist Italy 1935–1943', *European History Quarterly*, 34, 2004.
— *Whispering city: Rome and its histories* (London: Yale University Press, 2011).
Bottai, Bruno. *Fascismo famigliare* (Casale Monferrato: Piemme, 1997).
Bottai, Giuseppe. *Diario 1935–1944* (ed. Giordano Bruno Guerri) (Milan: Rizzoli, 1982).
— *Diario 1944–1948* (ed. Giordano Bruno Guerri) (Milan: Rizzoli, 1988).
— *Vent'anni e un giorno (24 luglio 1943)* (Milan: BUR, 2008).
Boyd, Rich. *La verità sulla morte di Mussolini (vista da un bambino)* (Rome: ilibridelBorghese, 2011).
Bravo, Anna and Anna Maria Bruzzone. *In guerra senza armi: storie di donne 1940–1945* (Bari: Laterza, 1995).
Broggini, Renata. 'La "famiglia Mussolini": colloqui di Edda Ciano con lo psichiatra svizzero Respond 1944–1945', *Italia contemporanea*, 203, 1996.
Brunetta, Gian Piero. *Storia del cinema italiano 1895–1945* (Rome: Riuniti, 1979).
Bruni, Pierfranco. *Claretta e Ben: il mio amore è con te* (Cosenza: Pellegrini Editore, 1996).
Buckley, Réka. 'The emergence of film fandom in postwar Italy: reading Claudia Cardinale's fan mail', *Historical Journal of Film, Radio and Television*, 29, 2009.
Buffarini Guidi, Glauco. *La vera verità* (Milan: Sugar, 1970).
Calcagno, Tullio. *Guerra di giustizia* (Milan: Mondadori, 1944).
'Calipso'. *Vita segreta di Mussolini* (Rome: IEDC, 1944).
Cambria, Adele. *Maria José* (Milan: Longanesi, 1966).
Camnasio, Aldo. *Storia di un fatto di cronaca: la vicenda Carteggio Mussolini* (Milan: Paneuropa, 1956).
Campi, Alessandro. *Mussolini* (Bologna: Il Mulino, 2001).
Campini, Dino. *Mussolini Churchill: i carteggi* (Milan: Editrice Italpress, 1952).
— *Piazzale Loreto* (Milan: Edizioni del Conciliatore, 1972).
— *Strano gioco di Mussolini* (Milan: PG, 1952).
Canali, Mauro. *Le spie del regime* (Bologna: Il Mulino, 2004).
'Candido'. *Mussolini in pantofole* (Rome: Istituto Editoriale di Cultura, 1944).
Cannistraro, Philip V. and Brian R. Sullivan. *Il Duce's other woman* (New York: William Morrow, 1993).
Cantoni, Guglielmo. 'Ho visto chi ha ucciso Mussolini', *Oggi*, 1 March 1958.
Carafoli, Domizia and Gustavo Bocchini Padiglione. *Il vice Duce: Arturo Bocchini, capo della polizia fascista* (Milan: Mondadori, 2003).
Carteggio Arnaldo-Benito Mussolini (ed. Duilio Susmel) (Florence: La Fenice, 1954).
Castelli, Francesca Romana and Piero Ostilio Rossi. 'Una villa per la "banda Petacci"', *Capitolium*, III, 1999.
Castellini, Fabrizio. *Il ribelle di Predappio: amori e giovinezza di Mussolini* (Milan: Mursia, 1996).
Catholic Truth Society. *Saint Rita of Cascia* (London: CTS, 2009).
Caudana, Mino. *Processo a Mussolini* (3 vols) (Rome: Centro Editoriale Nazionale, 1965).

BIBLIOGRAPHY

Cavalleri, Giorgio. *Ombre sul lago: dal carteggio Churchill–Mussolini all'oro del PCI* (Casale Monferrato: Piemme, 1995).

Cavalleri, Giorgio and Franco Giannantoni. *'Gianna' e 'Neri' fra speculazioni e silenzi: la verità è nella sentenza degli anni '70: fu il Pci e non la Resistenza a volere la morte dei due partigiani 'garibaldini'* (Varese: Edizioni Arterigere, 2002).

Cavalleri, Giorgio, Franco Giannantoni and Mario J. Cereghino. *La fine: gli ultimi giorni di Benito Mussolini nei documenti dei servizi segreti americani (1945–1946)* (Milan: Garzanti, 2009).

Cavallero, Ugo. *Comando supremo: diario 1940–43 del capo di S.M.G.* (Bologna: Cappelli, 1948).

Cavalli, Luciano. 'Considerations on charisma and the cult of charismatic leadership', *Modern Italy*, 3, 1998.

Cavallo, Pietro. *Italiani in guerra: sentimenti e immagini dal 1940 al 1943* (Bologna: Il Mulino, 1997).

Cavicchioli, Luigi. 'Il testamento di Claretta ha commosso il pubblico: al processo di Brescia Clara Petacci è risultata una donna fedele e coraggiosa', *Oggi*, 10 July 1952.

Centini, Massimo. *Ottanta ore per vivere o morire: i luoghi degli ultimi giorni di Mussolini* (Varese: Macchione Editore, 2007).

Cerasi, Laura. 'Empires ancient and modern: strength, modernity and power in imperial ideology from the Liberal period to Fascism', *Modern Italy*, 19, 2014.

Cereghino, Mario José and Giovanni Fasanella. *Le carte segrete del Duce: tutte le rivelazioni su Mussolini conservate negli archivi inglesi* (Milan: Mondadori, 2014).

Cersosimo, Vincenzo. *Dall'istruttoria alla fucilazione: storia del processo di Verona* (Milan: Garzanti, 1961).

Cerruti, Elisabetta. *Ambassador's wife* (London: George Allen and Unwin, 1952).

Cetti, Carlo. *Come fu arrestato e soppresso Mussolini* (Como: Edizioni 'Il Ginepro', 1945).

— *Cronaca dei fatti di Dongo (27 e 28 aprile 1945)* (Como: a cura del Autore, 1959).

Chessa, Pasquale and Barbara Raggi. *L'ultima lettera di Benito Mussolini: amore e politica a Salò 1943–45* (Milan: Mondadori, 2010).

Chiarini, Roberto. *25 aprile: la competizione politica sulla memoria* (Venice: Marsilio, 2005).

— (ed.). *Mussolini ultimo atto: i luoghi della Repubblica di Salò* (Salò: CSDRSI, 2004).

Chiesa, Eugenio. *La mano nel sacco e altri scritti editi e inediti* (ed. Mary Tibaldi Chiesa) (Milan: Tarantola Editore, 1946).

Chiocci, Francobaldo. *Donna Rachele* (Rome: Ciarrapico Editore, 1983).

Cianetti, Tullio. *Memorie dal carcere di Verona* (ed. Renzo De Felice) (Milan: Rizzoli, 1983).

Ciano, Edda. *La mia vita: intervista di Domenico Olivieri* (ed. Nicola Caracciolo) (Milan: Mondadori, 2001).

Ciano, Edda Mussolini. *My truth: as told to Albert Zarca* (London: Weidenfeld & Nicolson, 1977).

Ciano, Fabrizio. *Quando il nonno fece fucilare papà* (ed. Dino Cimagalli) (Milan: Mondadori, 1991).

Ciano, Galeazzo *Diario 1937–1943* (ed. Renzo De Felice) (Milan: Rizzoli, 1980).

— *Diary 1937–1943* (ed. Renzo De Felice) (London: Phoenix Press, 2002).

Ciccolo, Nicola and Elena Manetti. *Mussolini e il suo doppio: i diari svelati* (Rome: Pioda Editore, 2012).

Cipriani, Giuseppe. *Questi sono gli inglesi* (Rome: Società Editrice del Libro Italiano, 1941).

Colarizi, Simona. *L'opinione degli italiani sotto il regime 1929–1943* (Bari: Laterza, 1991).

Colleoni, Angelo. *Claretta Petacci: rivelazioni sulla vita, gli amori, la morte* (Milan: Tipografia Editoriale Lucchi, 1945).

— *La verità sulla fine di Mussolin e della Petacci: come furono catturati e giustiziati Mussolini, la Petacci, il fratello e quindici gerarconi* (Milan: Tipografia Editoriale Lucchi, 1946).

BIBLIOGRAPHY

Colombo, Paolo. *Il processo a Benito Mussolini* (Cesena: Tipografia A. Bettini, 1951).
Consonni, Manuela. *L'eclisse dell'antifascismo: Resistenza, questione ebraica e cultura politica in Italia dal 1943 al 1989* (Bari: Laterza, 2015).
Conti, Giuseppe. *Una guerra segreta: il Sim nel secondo conflitto mondiale* (Bologna: Il Mulino, 2009).
Contini, Gaetano. *La valigia di Mussolini: i documenti segreti dell'ultima fuga del duce* (Milan: Mondadori, 1982).
Contini, Mila. *Maria José: la regina sconosciuta* (Milan: Eli, 1955).
Corner, Paul. *The Fascist Party and popular opinion in Mussolini's Italy* (Oxford University Press, 2012).
Corradini, Giorgio. *Storia degli amori Mussolini–Petacci* ([?Rome]: np, 1945).
Corvaja, Santi. *Hitler and Mussolini: the secret meetings* (New York: Enigma Books, 2001).
Costa, Vincenzo. *L'ultimo federale: memorie della guerra civile 1943–1945* (Bologna: Il Mulino, 1997).
Curami, Andrea. 'Miti e realtà dell'industria bellica della RSI', *Rivista di storia contemporanea*, 22, 1993.
Curti, Elena. *Il Chiodo a tre punte: schegge di memoria della figlia segreta del Duce* (Pavia: Gianni Iuculano Editore, 2003).
D'Agostini, Bruno. *Colloqui con Rachele Mussolini* (Rome: OET, 1946).
D'Aroma, Nino. *Mussolini segreto* (Rocca San Casciano: Cappelli, 1958).
— *Vent'anni insieme: Vittorio Emanuele e Mussolini* (Rocca San Casciano: Cappelli, 1957).
D'Aurora, Giorgio. *La maschera e il volto di Magda Fontanges* (Milan: Cebas, 1946).
Dallek, Robert. *John F. Kennedy: an unfinished life 1917–1963* (London: Penguin, 2013).
Deakin, Frederick W. *The Brutal Friendship* (London: Weidenfeld & Nicolson, 1962).
De Begnac, Yvon. *Intervista sul fascismo* (ed. Michael Ledeen) (Bari: Laterza, 1975).
— *The Jews in Fascist Italy: a history* (New York: Enigma books, 2001).
— *Mussolini* (8 vols) (Turin: Einaudi, 1965–1997).
— *Palazzo Venezia: storia di un regime* (Rome: Editrice la Rocca, 1950).
— *Rosso e Nero* (ed. Pasquale Chessa) (Milan: Baldini e Castoldi, 1995).
— *Taccuini mussoliniani* (ed. Francesco Perfetti) (Bologna: Il Mulino, 1990).
De Felice, Renzo (ed.). *Benito Mussolini: quattro testimonianze – Alceste De Ambris, Luigi Campolonghi, Mario Girardon, Maria Rygier* (Florence: La Nuova Italia, 1976).
— 'Dalle "memorie" di Fulvio Balisti: un dannunziano di fronte alla crisi del 1943 e alla Repubblica Sociale Italiana', *Storia contemporanea*, 17, 1986.
— 'Due diari del 1943 1. Dino Grandi, "Pagine del diario del 1943". II. Egidio Ortona, "Il 1943 da Palazzo Chigi. Note di diario"', *Storia contemporanea*, 14, 1983.
De Felice, Renzo and Luigi Goglia. *Mussolini il mito* (Bari: Laterza, 1983).
De Grazia, Victoria. *How Fascism ruled women: Italy 1922–1945* (Berkeley: University of California Press, 1992).
Del Buono, Oreste. *Amori neri* (Rome: Edizioni Theoria, 1985).
De Rensis, Raffaello. *Mussolini musicista* (Mantua: Edizioni Paladino, 1927).
De' Rossi dell'Arno, Giulio. *Pio XI e Mussolini* (Rome: Corso Editore, 1954).
De Vecchi, Cesare Maria. *Il Quadrumviro scomodo: il vero Mussolini nelle memorie del più monarchico dei fascisti* (ed. Luigi Romersa) (Milan: Mursia, 1983).
De Vincentis, Luigi. *Io son te* (Milan: Cebes, 1946).
'De Wyss, M.' *Rome under the terror* (London: Robert Hale, 1945).
Di Benigno, Jo'. *Occasioni mancate: Roma in un diario segreto 1943–1944* (Rome: Edizioni SEI, 1945).
Di Michele, Vincenzo. *Mussolini, finto prigioniero al Gran Sasso* (Florence: Curiosando Editrice, 2011).
Di Nucci, Loreto. *Lo stato partito del fascismo: genesi, evoluzione e crisi 1919–1943* (Bologna: Il Mulino, 2009).

Di Rienzo, Eugenio. *Storia d'Italia e identità nazionale dalla Grande Guerra alla repubblica* (Florence: Le Lettere, 2006).

Di Rienzo, Eugenio and Emilio Gin. 'Quella mattina del 25 luglio 1943. Mussolini, Shinrokuro Hidaka e il progetto di pace separate con l'Urss', *Nuova Rivista Storica*, 95, 2011.

Dinale, Ottavio. *Quarant'anni di colloqui con lui* (Milan: Ciarrocca, 1953).

Dolcetti, Giovanni. *Le origini storiche della famiglia Mussolini* (Venice: Casa Editrice Pietro Brasolin, 1928).

Dolfin, Giovanni. *Con Mussolini nella tragedia: diario del capo della segreteria particolare del Duce 1943–1944* (Cernusco sul Naviglio: Garzanti, 1949).

Dollmann, Eugen. *The interpreter: memoirs* (London: Hutchinson, 1967).

— *Roma Nazista* (Milan: Longanesi, 1951).

Dombrowski, Roman *Mussolini: twilight and fall* (London: Heinemann, 1956).

Duggan, Christopher. *Fascist voices: an intimate history of Mussolini's Italy* (London: Bodley Head, 2012).

Dunnage, Jonathan. 'Ideology, clientalism and the "Fascistization" of the Italian state: Fascists in the Interior Ministry police', *Journal of Modern Italian Studies,* 14, 2009.

— *Mussolini's policemen: behaviour, ideology and institutional culture in representation and practice* (Manchester University Press, 2012).

Duranti, Doris. *Il romanzo della mia vita* (ed. Gian Franco Venè) (Milan: Mondadori, 1987).

Ebner, Michael. *Ordinary violence in Mussolini's Italy* (Cambridge University Press, 2011).

Emiliani, Vittorio. *Il fabbro di Predappio: vita di Alessandro Mussolini* (Bologna: Il Mulino, 2010).

— *Il paese di Mussolini* (Turin: Einaudi, 1984).

— *I tre Mussolini: Luigi, Alessandro, Benito* (Milan: Baldini e Castoldi, 1997).

Ercolani, Antonella. *Gli ultimi giorni di Mussolini nei documenti inglesi e francesi* (Rome: Editrice Apes, 1989).

Fabre, Giorgio. *Il contratto: Mussolini editore di Hitler* (Bari: Edizioni Dedalo, 2004).

— 'Mussolini, Claretta e la questione della razza 1937–38', *Annali della Fondazione Ugo La Malfa,* XXIV, 2009.

— *Mussolini razzista: dal socialismo al fascismo la formazione di un antisemita* (Milan: Garzanti, 2005).

Falasca-Zamponi, Simonetta. *Fascist spectacle: the aesthetics of power in Mussolini's Italy* (Berkeley: University of California Press, 1997).

Farrell, Nicholas. *Mussolini: a new life* (London: Weidenfeld & Nicolson, 2003).

Fattorini, Emma. *Hitler, Mussolini, and the Vatican: Pope Pius XI and the speech that was never made* (Cambridge: Polity, 2011).

Favagrossa, Carlo. *Perché perdemmo la guerra: Mussolini e la produzione bellica* (Milan: Rizzoli, 1946).

Federzoni, Luigi. *Italia di ieri per la storia di domani* (Milan: Mondadori, 1967).

Ferrandi, Maurizio. *Mussolini e l'Alto Adige: fantasmi e stelle alpini* (Trento: Curcu e Genovese Editore, 2016).

Festorazzi, Roberto. *Bruno e Gina Mussolini* (Milan: Sperling and Kupfer, 2007).

— *Churchill–Mussolini le carte segrete: la straordinaria vicenda dell'uomo che ha salvato l'epistolario più scottante del ventesimo secolo* (Rome: DATAEWS Editrice, 1998).

— *Claretta Petacci: la donna che morì per amore di Mussolini* (Bologna: Minerva Edizioni, 2012).

— *Margherita Sarfatti: la donna che inventò Mussolini* (Vicenza: Angelo Colla Editore, 2010).

— *Mistero Churchill: settembre 1945 che cosa cercava sul Lario lo statista inglese? Perchè si celava dietro l'identità del colonnello Warden?* (Varese: Pietro Macchione Editore, 2013).

— *Mussolini e le sue donne* (Varese: Pietro Macchione Editore, 2013).

— *Il nonno in camicia nera* (Como: Il Silicio, 2004).

— *La pianista del Duce: vita, passione e misteri di Magda Brard, l'artista francese che stregò Benito Mussolini* (Milan: Simonelli Editore, 2000).
— *San Donnino, cella 31. La prigionia dei fascisti scampati dal massacro di Dongo nella testimonianza inedita di un protagonista: Alfredo Degasperi. Un documento di straordinario valore sull'altra storia d'Italia* (Milan: Simonelli Editore, 1999).
— *Starace: il mastino della rivoluzione fascista* (Milan: Mursia, 2002).
— 'Tutti i segreti del carteggio fantasma con una testimonianza di Luigi Carissimi-Priori sul carteggio Churchill–Mussolini', *Nuova Storia Contemporanea*, 4, 2000.
— *I veleni di Dongo* (Milan: Il Minotauro, 1997).
Fincardi, Marco. 'Gli italiani e l'attesa di un bombardamento della capitale 1940–1943', *Italia contemporanea*, 263, 2011.
Fitzpatrick, Sheila. *On Stalin's team: the years of living dangerously in Soviet politics* (Princeton University Press, 2015).
Focardi, Filippo. *Il cattivo tedesco e il buon italiano: la rimozione delle colpe della seconda guerra mondiale* (Bari: Laterza, 2013).
Foley, Susan K. and Charles Sowerwine. *A political romance: Léon Gambetta, Léonie Léon and the making of the French Republic 1872–82* (Houndmills: Palgrave Macmillan, 2012).
Foppiani, Oreste. *The Allies and the Italian Social Republic (1943–1945): Anglo-American relations with, perceptions of, and judgments on the RSI during the Italian Civil War* (Oxford: P. Lang, 2011).
— *L'arma segreta del Duce: la vera storia del Carteggio Churchill–Mussolini* (Milan: Rizzoli, 2015).
Franzinelli, Mimmo. *Autopsia di un falso: i diari di Mussolini e la manipolazione della storia* (Turin: Bollati Boringhieri, 2011).
— *Delatori: spie e confidenti anonimi: l'arma segreta del regime fascista* (Milan: Mondadori, 2001).
— *Disertori: una storia mai raccontata della seconda guerra mondiale* (Milan: Mondadori, 2016).
— *Il Duce e le donne: avventure e passioni extraconiugali di Mussolini* (Milan: Mondadori, 2014).
— *Guerra di spie: i servizi segreti fascisti, nazisti e alleati 1939–1943* (Milan: Mondadori, 2004).
— *RSI: la repubblica del Duce 1943–1945* (Milan: Mondadori, 2007).
— *I tentacoli dell'Ovra: agenti, collaboratori e vittime della polizia politica fascista* (Turin: Bollati Boringhieri, 1999).
Franzinelli, Mimmo and Emanuele Valerio Marino. *Il Duce proibito: le fotografie di Mussolini che gli italiani non hanno mai visto* (Milan: Mondadori, 2003).
Frassati, Luciana. *Il destino passa per Varsavia* (Bologna: Capelli, 1949; rev. edn Milan: Bompiani, 1985).
Freddi, Luigi. *Il cinema: il governo dell'immagine* (Rome: Centro Sperimentale di Cinematografia Gremese Editore, 1994).
Fusco, Gian Carlo. *Mussolini e le donne* (Palermo: Sellerio, 2006).
Gadda, Carlo Emilio. *Eros e Priapo (da furore a cenere)* (Milan: Garzanti, 1967).
Gagliani, Dianella. *Brigate nere: Mussolini e la militarizzazione del Partito fascista repubblicano* (Turin: Bollati Boringhieri, 1999).
Galbiati, Enzo. *Il 25 luglio e la MVSN* (Milan: Edizioni Bernabò, 1950).
Ganapini, Luigi. *La repubblica delle camicie nere* (Milan: Garzanti, 1999).
Garibaldi, Luciano. *Mussolini: the secrets of his death* (New York: Enigma books, 2004).
— (ed.) *Mussolini e il professore: vita e diari di Carlo Alberto Biggini* (Milan: Mursia, 1983).
— *La pista inglese: Chi uccise Mussolini e la Petacci* (Milan: Edizioni Ares, 2002).
Gentile, Emilio. *Il culto del littorio: la sacralizzazione della politica nell'Italia fascista* (Bari: Laterza, 1993).
— *Fascismo di pietra* (Bari: Laterza, 2007).
— 'Mussolini's charisma', *Modern Italy*, 3, 1998.

— *La via italiana al totalitarismo: il partito e lo stato nel regime fascista* (Rome: La Nuova Italia Scientifica, 1995).
Gervaso, Roberto. *Claretta, la donna che morì per Mussolini* (Milan: Rizzoli, 1982).
Giannantoni, Franco. *'Gianna' e 'Neri': vita e morte di due partigiani comunisti. Storia di un 'tradimento' tra la fucilazione di Mussolini e l'oro di Dongo* (Milan: Mursia, 1992).
Giannini, Filippo. *Benito Mussolini nell'Italia dei miracoli* (Chieti: Solfanelli, 2010).
Gibson, Stephen. 'Clara Petacci's handkerchief', *New Orleans Review*, 21, 1995.
Gillette, Aaron. *Racial theories in Fascist Italy* (London: Routledge, 2002).
Gin, Emilio. 'Speak of war and prepare for peace, 10 June 1940', *Nuova Rivista Storica*, 98, 2014.
Ginsborg, Paul. *Family politics: domestic life, devastation and survival 1900–1950* (New Haven: Yale University Press, 2014).
Giuliani-Balestrino, Ubaldo. *Il carteggio Churchill–Mussolini alla luce del processo Guareschi* (Rome: Edizioni Settimo Sigillo, 2010).
Goebbels, Joseph. *The Goebbels Diaries 1939–1941* (ed. Fred Taylor) (London: Hamish Hamilton, 1982).
Gori, Gigliola. 'Model of masculinity: Mussolini, the new Italian of the Fascist era', in James A. Mangan (ed.), *Superman supreme: Fascist body as political icon – global fascism* (London: Frank Cass, 2000).
Grandi, Aldo. *I giovani di Mussolini: Fascisti convinti, fascisti pentiti, antifascisti* (Milan: Baldini e Castoldi, 2001).
— *Gli eroi di Mussolini: Niccolò Giani e la Scuola di Mistica Fascista* (Milan: Rizzoli, 2004) .
Grandi, Dino. *Il mio paese: ricordi autobiografici* (ed. Renzo De Felice) (Bologna: Il Mulino, 1985).
— 'Tutta la verità sul 25 luglio. Memorandum dei rapporti tra Dino Grandi e la Corona prima del 25 luglio 1943' (ed. Francesco Perfetti), *Nuova Storia Contemporanea*, 17, 2013.
Grassini Sarfatti, Margherita. *My fault: Mussolini as I knew him* (ed. Brian A. Sullivan), (New York: Enigma books, 2014).
Gravelli, Asvero. *Mussolini aneddotico* (Rome: Casa Editrice Latinità, 1951).
Graziani, Rodolfo. *Ho difeso la patria* (Cernusco sul Naviglio: Garzanti, 1947).
Grazzi, Emanuele. *Il principio della fine (l'impresa di Grecia)* (Rome: Editrice, Faro, 1945).
Guerri, Giordano Bruno. *Galeazzo Ciano: una vita 1903–1944* (Milan: Bompiani, 1979).
— *Giuseppe Bottai: un fascista critico: ideologia e azione del gerarca che avrebbe voluto portare intelligenza nel fascismo e il fascismo alla liberalizzazione* (Milan: Feltrinelli, 1976).
— *Italo Balbo* (Milan: Garzanti, 2013).
Guidi, Guido. *Pio XI* (Milan: Tipografia Editoriale Lucchi, 1938).
Gundle, Stephen. 'Laughter and Fascism: humour and ridicule in Italy 1922–1943', *History Workshop*, 79, 2015.
— *Mussolini's dream factory: film stardom in Fascist Italy* (New York: Berghahn, 2013).
Gundle, Stephen, Christopher Duggan and Giuliana Pieri (eds). *The cult of the Duce: Mussolini and the Italians* (Manchester University Press, 2013).
Guspini, Ugo. *L'orecchio del regime: le intercettazioni telefoniche al tempo del fascismo* (Milan: Mursia, 1973).
Härmänmaa, Marja. *Un patriota che sfidò la decadenza: F.T. Marinetti e l'idea dell'Uomo Nuovo Fascista 1929–1944* (Helsinki: Academia Scientarium Fennica, 2000).
Hitler, Adolf. *Hitler's Table Talk 1941–1944* (ed. Hugh Trevor-Roper) (London: Weidenfeld & Nicolson, 1953).
Hofmann, Reto. *The Fascist effect: Japan and Italy, 1915–1952* (Ithaca: Cornell University Press, 2015).
Hruska, Artur. *Memorie segrete del dentista dei papi e dei re* (Milan: Edizioni Bietti, 2002).
Hughes-Hallett, Lucy. *The pike: Gabriele D'Annunzio, poet, seducer and preacher of war* (London: Fourth Estate, 2013).

BIBLIOGRAPHY

Ignazi, Piero. *Postfascisti? Dal Movimento sociale italiano ad Alleanza nazionale* (Bologna: Il Mulino, 1994).
Imbriani, Angelo Michele. *Gli italiani e il Duce: il mito e l'immagine di Mussolini negli ultimi anni del fascismo (1938–1943)* (Naples: Liguori Editore, 1992).
Innocenti, Marco. *Edda contro Claretta: una storia di odio e di amore* (Milan: Mursia, 2003).
— *I gerarchi del Fascismo: storia del ventennio attraverso gli uomini del Duce* (Milan: Mursia, 1992).
— *Le signore del Fascismo: donne in un mondo di uomini* (Milan: Mursia, 2001).
Ipsen, Carl. *Dictating demography: the problem of population in Fascist Italy* (Cambridge University Press, 1996).
Israel, Giorgio and Pietro Nastasi. *Scienza e razza nell'Italia fascista* (Bologna: Il Mulino, 1998).
'Iuvenalis'. *Mussolini alla luce infrarossa* (Rome: Edizioni Lazzaro, nd [1944]).
Kallis, Aristotle A. *The third Rome, 1922–1943: the making of the Fascist capital* (Houndmills: Palgrave Macmillan, 2014).
Kertzer, David I. *The pope and Mussolini: the secret history of Pius XI and the rise of fascism in Europe* (Oxford University Press, 2014).
Klinkhammer, Lutz. *L'occupazione tedesca in Italia 1943–1945* (Turin: Bollati Boringhieri, 1993).
Knox, Macgregor. *Hitler's Italian allies: royal armed forces, Fascist regime and the war of 1940–1943* (Cambridge University Press, 2000).
La Mattina, Amedeo. *Mai sono stato tranquilla: la vita di Angelica Balabanoff, la donna che ruppe con Mussolini e Lenin* (Turin: Einaudi, 2011).
Lamb, Richard. *Mussolini and the British* (London: John Murray, 1997).
— *War in Italy: a brutal story* (London: John Murray, 1993).
Lanoue, Guy. *Rome eternal: the city as fatherland* (London: Legenda, 2015).
Lazzaro, Urbano. *Il compagno Bill: diario dell'uomo che catturò Mussolini* (Turin: Società Editrice Internazionale, 1989).
— *Dongo: mezzo secolo di menzogne* (Milan: Mondadori, 1993) .
— *L'oro di Dongo: il mistero del tesoro del duce* (Milan: Mondadori, 1995).
Lazzero, Ricciotti. *Il sacco d'Italia: razzie e stragi tedesche nella Repubblica di Salò* (Milan: Mondadori, 1994).
Leamer, Laurence. *The Kennedy women: the triumph and tragedy of America's first family* (London: Bantam Press, 1994).
Leccisi, Domenico. *Con Mussolini prima e dopo Piazzale Loreto* (Rome: Edizioni settimo sigillo, 1991).
Legnani, Massimo. 'Guerra e governo delle risorse: strategie economiche e soggetti sociali nell'Italia 1940–1943', *Italia contemporanea*, 179, 1990.
Lessona, Alessandro. *Un ministro di Mussolini racconta* (Milan: Edizioni Nazionali, 1973).
Leto, Guido. *Ovra: fascismo-antifascismo* (Rocca San Casciano: Cappelli Editore, 1952).
Levis Sullam, Simon. *I carnefici italiani: scene dal genocidio degli ebrei, 1943–1945* (Milan: Feltrinelli, 2015).
Liffran, Françoise. *Margherita Sarfatti: l'égérie di Duce: biografie* (Paris: Éditions du Seuil, 2009).
Liucci, Raffaele. *Spettatori di un naufragio: l'intellettuale italiano nella seconda guerra mondiale* (Turin: Einaudi, 2011).
Livingston, Michael A. *The Fascists and the Jews of Italy: Mussolini's race laws, 1938–1945* (Cambridge University Press, 2014).
Lolli, Mario. *Ebrei, chiesa e Fascismo* (Tivoli: Officine Grafiche Mantero, 1938).
Lonati, Bruno Giovanni. *Quel 28 aprile: Mussolini e Claretta: la verità* (Milan: Mursia, 1994).
Lough, David. *No more champagne: Churchill and his money* (London: Head of Zeus, 2015).
Loy, Rosetta. *First words: a childhood in Fascist Italy* (New York: Henry Holt and Company, 2000).

BIBLIOGRAPHY

Luccichenti, Amedeo and Vincenzo Monaco. 'Villa Petacci alla Camilluccia con scale audaci e pronunciate cavità, Roma 1937–9', *Casabella*, 805, October 2011.

Ludwig, Emil. *Talks with Mussolini* (London: George Allen and Unwin, 1932).

Lumbroso, Alberto. *Elena di Montenegro: regina d'Italia* (Florence: Edizione di "Fiamma Fedele" e di "Fiamme Gialle d'Italia", 1935).

Lupo, Salvatore. *Il Fascismo: la politica in un regime totalitario* (Rome: Donzelli, 2000).

Luzzatto, Sergio. *Il corpo del duce: un cadavere tra immaginazione, storia e memoria* (Turin: Einaudi, 1998).

— *L'immagine del duce: Mussolini nelle fotografie dell'Istituto Luce* (Rome: Riuniti, 2001).

— *Partigia: una storia della Resistenza* (Milan: Mondadori, 2013).

Lyons, Martyn. ' "Questo cor che tuo si rese": the private and public in Italian women's love letters in the long nineteenth century', *Modern Italy*, 19, 2014.

MacDonald, Robert David. *Summit conference* (London: Amber Lane Press, 1982).

Mack Smith, Denis. *Mussolini* (London: Weidenfeld & Nicolson, 1981).

— *Mussolini's Roman Empire* (London: Longmans, 1976).

Malaparte, Curzio. *Muss: il grande imbecille* (Milan: Luni Editore, 1999).

Mammone, Andrea. *Transnational neofascism in France and Italy* (Cambridge University Press, 2015).

Mancini, Claudio M. 'Isaia Levi: vita di un ebreo italiano a cavallo di due secoli', *Annali della Fondazione Ugo La Malfa*, XXIV, 2009.

Mariani, M. *Il romanzo di Claretta Petacci* (Rome: Francesco Mondini Editore, 1946).

Marinetti, Filippo Tommaso. *Come si seducono le donne* (Rome: R.S. Casciano, 1918).

— *Let's murder the moonshine: selected writings* (ed. Robert W. Flint) (Los Angeles: Sun and Moon Classics, 1991).

— *Taccuini 1915–1921* (ed. Alberto Bertoni) (Bologna: Il Mulino, 1987).

Marino, Natalia and Emanuele Valerio. *L'Ovra a Cinecittà: polizia politica e spie in camicia nera* (Turin: Bollati Boringhieri, 2005).

Martinelli, Franco. *Mussolini ai raggi X* (Milan: Giovanni De Vecchi Editore, 1964).

Marzorati, Sergio. *Margherita Sarfatti: saggio biografico* (Como: Nodo Libri, 1990).

Matt, Susan and Peter N. Stearns. *Doing emotions history* (Ann Arbor: University of Illinois Press, 2013).

Maugeri, Franco. *From the ashes of disgrace* (New York: Reynal and Hitchcock, 1948).

Mawdsley, Evan (ed.). *The Cambridge history of the Second World War* (3 vols) (Cambridge University Press, 2015).

Mazzantini, Carlo. *I balilla andarono a Salò* (Venice: Marsilio, 1997).

Mazzatosta, Teresa Maria and Claudio Volpi. *L'Italietta fascista (lettere al potere 1936–1943)* (Bologna, Cappelli, 1980).

Mazzini, Gianluca. *Montanelli mi ha detto: avventure, aneddoti, ricordi del più grande giornalista italiano* (Rimini: Il Cerchio, 2002).

McBirnie, William S. *What the bible says about Mussolini* (Norfolk, Va.: McBirnie Publications, 1944).

Medeghini, Cesare. *Il processo di Mussolini* (Milan: Gastaldi, 1948).

Meldini, Piero. *Sposa e madre esemplare: ideologia e politica della donna e della famiglia durante il fascismo* (Florence: Guaraldi, 1975).

Melis, Paolo. 'Un limpido volume di travertino dorato e di cristallo con scale audaci e pronunciate cavità', *Casabella*, 805, 2011 (in section entitled 'Amedeo Luccichenti e Vincenzo Monaco: Villa Petacci alla Camiluccia').

Melli, Giorgio. *Le donne di Mussolini* (Milan: Casa Editrice Astoria, nd [1960]).

Miccoli, Giovanni. 'L'enciclica mancata di Pio XI sul razzismo e l'antisemitismo', *Passato e Presente*, 40, 1997.

Milward, Alan. *War, economy and society 1939–1945* (Harmondsworth: Penguin, 1987).

Milza, Pierre. *Gli ultimi giorni di Mussolini* (Milan: Longanesi, 2011).

— *Mussolini* (Paris: Fayard, 1999).
Moellhausen, Eitel F. *La carta perdente: memorie diplomatiche 25 luglio 1943–2 maggio 1945* (ed. Virginio Rusca) (Rome: Sestante, 1948).
Mollier, Madeleine. *Pensieri e previsioni di Mussolini al tramonto* (Milan: Tipografia G. Colombi, nd [1948]).
Monelli, Paolo. *Da Milano a Dongo: l'ultimo viaggio di Mussolini* (ed. Beppe Benvenuti) (Milan: Mursia, 2009).
— *Mussolini: an intimate life* (London: Thames and Hudson, 1953).
— *Mussolini, piccolo borghese* (Milan: Garzanti, 1950).
— *Roma 1943* (Milan: Mondadori, 1948).
Montagna, Renzo. *Mussolini e il processo di Verona* (Milan: Edizioni Omnia, 1949).
Montanelli, Indro. *Il buonuomo Mussolini* (Milan: Edizioni Riunite, 1947).
— *Controcorrente 1974–1986* (Milan: Mondadori, 1987).
— *Facce di bronzo (incontri)* (Milan: Longanesi, 1955).
— *L'Italia in camicia nera (1919–3 gennaio 1925)* (Milan: Rizzoli, 1976).
— *Soltanto un giornalista: testimonianza resa a Tiziana Abate* (Milan: Rizzoli, 2002).
— *Il testimone* (ed. Manlio Cancogni and Piero Malvolti) (Milan: Longanesi, 1992).
Moravia, Alberto. *The time of indifference* (Harmondsworth: Penguin, 1970).
Morgan, Philip. *The fall of Mussolini: Italy, the Italians and the Second World War* (Oxford University Press, 2007).
Morgan, Thomas B. *Spurs on the boot: Italy under her masters* (London: Harrap, 1942).
Moseley, Ray. *Mussolini's shadow: the double life of Count Galeazzo Ciano* (New Haven: Yale University Press, 1999).
— *Mussolini: the last 600 days of Il Duce* (Dallas: Taylor Trade Publishing, 2004).
Murialdi, Paolo. *La stampa italiana del dopoguerra 1943–1972* (Bari: Laterza, 1973).
Musiedlak, Didier. *Mussolini* (Paris: Presses de Sciences Po, 2005).
— *Lo stato fascista e la sua classe politica 1922–1943* (Bologna, il Mulino, 2003).
[Mussolini, Benito] *I diari del mistero: piccola antologia di manoscritti attribuiti a Mussolini a presa del potere all'entrata in guerra* (Milan: Mondadori, 1994).
— *I diari di Mussolini [veri e presunti]* (4 vols) (Milan: Bompiani, 2010–2012).
Mussolini, Benito. *A Clara: tutte le lettere a Clara Petacci 1943–1945* (ed. Luisa Montevecchi) (Milan: Mondadori, 2011).
— *Corrispondenza inedita* (ed. Duilio Susmel) (Milan: Edizioni del Borghese, 1972).
— *Giornale di guerra 1915–1917: Alto Isonzo – Carnia – Carso* (ed. Mimmo Franzinelli) (Gorizia: Edizioni Srl, 2016).
— *Memoirs 1942–1943 with documents relating to the period* (London: George Weidenfeld & Nicolson, 1949).
— *My rise and fall* (ed. Richard Lamb) (New York: Da Capo Press, 1998).
— *Opera omnia* (ed. E. and D. Susmel) (36 vols) (Florence: La Fenice, 1951–62).
— *Opera omnia* (ed. Edoardo and Duilio Susmel) *Appendici I–VIII* (vols 37–44) (Florence: Giovanni Volpe Editore, 1978–80).
— *Testamento spirituale con uno studio di Duilio Susmel* (Milan: Comitato Repubblica Sociale Italiana, 1956).
Mussolini, Edvige. *Mio fratello Benito: memorie raccolte e trascritte da Rosetta Ricci Crisolini* (Florence: La Fenice, 1957).
Mussolini, Rachele. *La mia vita con Benito* (Milan: Mondadori, 1948).
— *My life with Mussolini* (London: R. Hale, 1959).
— *The real Mussolini (as told to A. Zarca)* (Farnborough: Saxon House, 1973).
— 'La verità sulla salma la dico qui: dodici anni di angoscia nel drammatico racconto di Rachele Mussolini', *Oggi*, 19 September 1957.
Mussolini, Romano. *Benito Mussolini: apologia di mio padre* (Bologna: Rivista Romana, 1969).

— *My father Il Duce: a memoir by Mussolini's son* (New York: Kales Press, 2006).
Mussolini, Vittorio. *Anno XIII: ludi iuvenalis* (Rome: Tipografia Luzzatti, 1935).
— *Mussolini: the tragic women in his life* (London: NEL, 1973).
— *Vita con il mio padre* (Milan: Mondadori, 1957).
— *Voli sulle Ambe* (Florence: Sansoni, 1937).
Navarra, Quinto. *Memorie del cameriere di Mussolini* (Milan: Longanesi, 1946).
Nello, Paolo. *Dino Grandi* (Bologna: Il Mulino, 2003).
Novero, Giuseppe. *Mussolini e il generale Pietro Gazzera, ministro della guerra lungo le tragedie del Novecento* (Soveria Mannelli: Rubbettino Editore, 2009).
Oatley, Keith. *Emotions: a brief history* (Oxford: Blackwell Publishing, 2004).
O'Brien, Paul. 'Al capezzale di Mussolini: ferite e malattia 1917–1945', *Italia contemporanea*, 226, 2002.
— *Mussolini in the First World War: the journalist, the soldier, the Fascist* (Oxford: Berg, 2005).
Oliva, Gianni. *L'Alibi della Resistenza ovvero come abbiamo vinto la Seconda guerra mondiale* (Milan: Mondadori, 2003).
— *Piazzale Loreto: la resa dei conti (aprile–maggio 1945)* (Florence: Giunti, 2000).
Olla, Roberto. *Il Duce and his women* (Richmond: Aline Books, 2011).
Ortona, Egidio. *Diplomazia di guerra: diari 1937–1943* (Bologna: Il Mulino, 1993).
Pace, Alfredo. *Benito Mussolini Claretta Petacci: chi ha ucciso, come, dove, quando. Diverse ipotesi, qualche certezza* (Milan: Greco e Greco Editore, 2008).
Packard, Reynolds and Eleanor Packard. *Balcony empire: Fascist Italy at war* (London: Chatto and Windus, 1943).
Pallottelli, Virgilio. 'Le memorie del pilota del Duce', *Storia illustrata*, 332, July 1985.
Palma, Giuseppe. *L'altro Duce: Benito Mussolini e Fascismo: le verità nascoste* (Avellino: Il Cerchio, 2012).
Palma, Paolo. *Il telefonista che spiava il Quirinale: 25 luglio 1943* (Soveria Mannelli: Rubbettino, 2006).
Pansa, Giampaolo. *Bella ciao: controstoria della Resistenza* (Milan: Rizzoli, 2014).
— *La grande bugia* (Milan: Sperling and Kupfer, 2006).
— *La guerra sporca dei partigiani e dei fascisti* (Milan: Rizzoli, 2012).
— *Il sangue dei vinti* (Milan: Sperling and Kupfer, 2003).
Pansini, Anthony J. *The Duce's dilemma: an analysis of the tragic events associated with Italy's part in World War II* (Waco, Tx: Greenvale Press, 1997).
Pantaleo, Nino. *A Bruno Mussolini* (Turin: C. Ranotti, 1941).
Panunzio, Vito. *Il 'secondo fascismo' 1936–1943: la reazione della nuova generazione alla crisi del movimento e del regime* (Milan: Mursia, 1988).
Pardini, Giuseppe. 'L'amante di Claretta: Il duce, i confidenti, la gelosia, l'Ovra . . .', *Nuova Storia Contemporanea*, 19, 2015.
— *Roberto Farinacci, ovvero della Rivoluzione Fascista* (Florence: Le Lettere, 2007).
Passerini, Luisa. *Mussolini immaginario: storia di una biografia, 1915–1939* (Bari: Laterza, 1991).
Passerini, Luisa, Liliana Ellena and Alexander C.T. Geppert (eds). *New dangerous liaisons: discourses on Europe and love in the twentieth century* (New York: Berghahn Books, 2010).
Patricelli, Marco. *L'Italia sotto le bombe: guerra aerea e vita civile 1940–1945* (Bari: Laterza, 2009).
Paulicelli, Eugenia. *Fashion under Fascism beyond the black shirt* (Oxford: Berg, 2004).
Pavone, Claudio. *Una guerra civile: saggio storico sulla moralità nella Resistenza* (Turin: Bollati Boringhieri, 1991).
Paxton, Robert. *The anatomy of fascism* (London: Allen Lane, 2004).
Pellegrinotti, Mario. *Sono stato il carceriere di Ciano* (Milan: Editrice Cavour, 1975).
Pensotti, Anita. *Le italiane* (Milan: Simonelli Editore, 1999).

BIBLIOGRAPHY

— *Rachele: sessant'anni con Mussolini nel bene e nel male* (Milan: Bompiani, 1983).
— *Rachele e Benito: biografia di Rachele Mussolini* (Milan: Mondadori, 1993).
— *La restituzione dei resti di Mussolini nel drammatico racconto della vedova* (Rome: Dino Editore, 1972)
Perfetti, Francesco (ed.). *La mia vita col puzzone: diario di Tobia, il gatto di Mussolini* (Florence: Le Lettere, 2005) .
— *Parola di Re: il diario segreto di Vittorio Emanuele* (Florence: Le Lettere, 2006).
Perretta, Giusto. *Dongo, 25 aprile 1945: la verità* (Como: Editrice Lariologo, 2011).
Persichetti, Giuseppina. *La enamoranda di Mussolini* (Mexico City: Editorial Fren, 1954).
Petacci, Clara. *Il mio diario* (Cernusco sul Naviglio: Editori Associati, 1946).
Petacci, Claretta. *Mussolini segreto: diari 1932–1938* (ed. Mauro Suttora) (Milan: Rizzoli, 2009).
— *Verso il disastro: Mussolini in guerra. Diari 1939–1940* (ed. Mimmo Franzinelli) (Milan: Rizzoli, 2011).
Petacci, Francesco Saverio. *La vita e i suoi nemici* (Rome: Unione Editoriale d'Italia, 1940).
Petacci, Marcello. *Raccolta di alcuni lavori scientifici* (Rome: Italgraf, 1961).
Petacci, Myriam *Chi ama è perduto: mia sorella Claretta* (ed. Santi Corvaja) (Gardolo di Trento: Luigi Reverdito Editore, 1988).
— 'Questa è la mia storia', *Oggi*, 14, 21, 28 April, 5 May 1955.
Petacco, Arrigo. *Ammazzate quel fascista! Vita intrepida di Ettore Muti* (Milan: Mondadori, 2002).
— *L'archivio segreto di Mussolini* (Milan: Mondadori, 1997).
— *Dear Benito, Caro Winston: verità e misteri del carteggio Churchill–Mussolini* (Milan: Mondadori, 1985).
— *Eva e Claretta: le amanti del diavolo* (Milan: Mondadori, 2012).
— *Regina: la vita e i segreti di Maria José* (Milan: Mondadori, 1997).
— *La storia ci ha mentito: dai misteri della borsa scomparsa di Mussolini alle 'armi segrete' di Hitler: le grandi menzogne del Novecento* (Milan: Mondadori, 2014).
— *Il superfascista: vita e morte di Alessandro Pavolini* (Milan: Mondadori, 1998).
— *A tragedy revealed: the story of the Italian population of Istria, Dalmatia, and Venezia Giulia, 1943–1956* (University of Toronto Press, 2005).
Phillips, William. *Ventures in diplomacy* (London: John Murray, 1955).
Pieroni, Alfredo. *Il figlio segreto del Duce: la storia di Benito Albino Mussolini e di sua madre Ida Dalser* (Milan: Garzanti, 2006).
'Pierson, Lucia' [Ellen Forest]. *Mussolini visto da una scrittrice olandese* (Rome: Anonimo Tipo Editoriale Libraria, 1933).
Pighin, Bruno Fabio (ed.). *Vatican Cardinal: Celso Costantini's wartime diaries* (Montreal: McGill-Queen's University Press, 2014).
Pini, Giorgio. *Filo diretto con Palazzo Venezia* (Milan: Edizioni FPE, 1967).
— *Itinerario tragico (1943–1945)* (Milan: Edizioni Omnia, 1950).
— *The official life of Benito Mussolini* (London: Hutchinson, 1939).
Pini, Giorgio and Duilio Susmel. *Mussolini: l'uomo e l'opera* (4 vols) (Florence: La Fenice, 1953–5).
Pinkus, Karen. *Bodily regimes: Italian advertising under Fascism* (Minneapolis: University of Minnesota Press, 1995).
Pirelli, Alberto. *Taccuini 1922–1943* (ed. Donato Barbone) (Bologna: Il Mulino, 1984).
Pirjevec, Jože. *Foibe: una storia d'Italia* (Turin: Einaudi, 2009).
Pisanò, Giorgio. *Gli ultimi cinque secondi di Mussolini: un'inchiesta giornalistica durata quarant'anni* (Milan: Saggiatore, 2009).
— *Io, fascista* (Milan: Il Saggiatore, 1997).
— *Mussolini e gli ebrei* (Milan: Edizioni FPE, 1967).
Pisanò, Giorgio and Paolo Pisanò. *Il triangolo della morte: la politica della strage in Emilia durante e dopo la guerra civile* (Milan: Mursia, 1992).

BIBLIOGRAPHY

Piscitelli, Marika. 'Carteggio Mussolini–Petacci: l'intera vicenda. Consultazione dei documenti conservati negli archivi di Stato alla luce della nuova disciplina – Segretezza della corrispondenza e diritto alla riservatezza', *Rassegna Avvocatura dello Stato*, LVII, 2005.

Pisenti, Piero. *Una repubblica necessaria (RSI)* (Rome: G. Volpe Editore, 1977).

Pizzetti, Silvia. *I rotocalchi e la storia: la divulgazione storica nei periodici illustrati (1950–1975)* (Rome: Bulzoni Editore, 1982).

Plamper, Jan. *The history of emotions* (Oxford University Press, 2015).

Pollard, John. *Money and the rise of the modern papacy: financing the Vatican, 1850–1950* (Cambridge University Press, 2005).

— *The papacy in the age of totalitarianism, 1914–1958* (Oxford University Press, 2014).

— 'Pius XI's promotion of the Italian model of Catholic Action in the World-Wide Church', *Journal of Ecclesiastical History*, 63, 2012.

Potocki, Wladislaw. 'Clara Petacci: "io sono la Petacci, voglio morire col Duce"', *Plush*, 1964.

Pound, Ezra. *Jefferson and/or Mussolini: l'idea statale. Fascism as I have seen it* (London: S. Nott, 1935).

— *The Pisan cantos* (London: Faber and Faber, 1949).

Pozzi, Arnaldo. *Come li ho visto io: dal diario di un medico* (Milan: Mondadori, 1947).

Preziosi, Giovanni. *Giudaismo–bolscevismo–plutocrazia–massoneria* (Milan: Mondadori, 1941).

Pricolo, Francesco. *Ignavia contro eroismo: l'avventura italo-greca: ottobre 1940–aprile 1941* (Rome: Nicola Ruffolo Editore, 1946).

Quartermaine, Luisa. *Mussolini's last republic: propaganda and politics in the Italian Social Republic (RSI) 1943–45* (Exeter: Elm Book Publications, 2000).

Querèl, Vittore. *Constanzo Ciano* (Rome: Edizioni M. Tupini, 1940).

— *Il paese di Benito: cronache di Predappio e dintorni* (Rome: Corso Editore, 1954).

Rafanelli, Leda. *Una donna e Mussolini* (ed. Pier Carlo Masini) (Milan: Rizzoli, 1975).

Rahn, Rudolf. *Ambasciatore di Hitler a Vichy e a Salò* (Milan: Garzanti, 1950).

Ramperti, Marco. *Benito I Imperatore* (Rome: Scirè, 1950).

Re, Emilio. *Storia di un archivio: le carte di Mussolini* (Milan: Edizioni del Milione, 1946).

Reay, Barry, Nina Attwood and Claire Gooder. *Sex addiction: a cultural history* (Cambridge: Polity, 2015).

Redman, Tim. *Ezra Pound and Italian Fascism* (Cambridge University Press, 1991).

Regolo, Luciano. *Così combattevamo il duce: l'impegno antifascista di Maria José di Savoia nell'archivio inedito dell'amica Sofia Jaccarino* (Rome: Kogoi Edizioni, 2013).

Revelli, Nuto. *Mussolini's death march: eyewitness accounts of Italian soldiers on the Eastern Front* (Lawrence: Kansas University Press, 2013).

Riccardi, Raffaello. *La collaborazione economica europea* (Rome: Edizioni italiane, 1943).

— *Economia fascista: sanzioni, commercio estero, autarchia* (Rome: Unione Editoriale d'Italia, 1939).

— *Pagine squadristiche* (Rome: Unione Editoriale d'Italia, 1939).

Ridolfi, Maurizio and Franco Moschi (eds). *Il Giovane Mussolini 1883–1914: la Romagna, la formazione, l'ascesa politica* (Forlì: Neri Wolff, 2013).

Ritossa, Zita. 'Mia "cognata" Claretta Petacci', *Tempo*, 7, 14, 21, 28 February, 7, 14, 21, 28 March, 4, 11, 18, 24 April, 2, 9 May 1957.

— 'La mia vita con Claretta Petacci', *Oggi*, 9 April 1975.

Roatta, Mario. *Otto milioni di baionette: l'esercito italiano in guerra dal 1940 al 1944* (Milan: Mondadori, 1946).

Roberts, David D. *The totalitarian experiment in twentieth-century Europe: understanding the poverty of great politics* (New York: Routledge, 2006).

Robbe, Federico. 'Il neofascismo delle origini e l'ossessione antibritannica', *Nuova Storia Contemporanea*, 19, 2015.

Rodogno, Davide. *Il nuovo ordine mediterraneo: le politiche di occupazione dell'Italia fascista in Europa (1940–1943)* (Turin: Bollati Boringhieri, 2003).

BIBLIOGRAPHY

Romualdi, Pino. *Fascismo repubblicano* (ed. Marino Viganò) (Varese: SugarCo, 1992).
Ronchi, Vittorio. *Guerra e crisi alimentare in Italia: 1940–1950 ricordi ed esperienze* (Rome: Vittorio Ronchi, 1977).
Rossi, Cesare. *Mussolini com'era* (Rome: Ruffolo Editore, 1947).
— *Trentatre vicende mussoliniane* (Milan: Casa Editrice Ceschina, 1958).
Rossi, Ernesto (ed.). *Una spia del regime: documenti e note* (Milan: Feltrinelli, 1955).
Rossi, Gianni Scipione. *Cesira e Benito: storia segreta della governante di Mussolini* (Soveria Mannelli, Rubbettino, 2007).
— *Mussolini e il diplomatico: la vita e i diari di Serafino Mazzolini, un monarchico a Salò* (Soveria Mannelli, Rubbettino, 2005).
— *Storia di Alice: La Giovanna d'Arco di Mussolini* (Soveria Mannelli: Rubbettino, 2010).
Rovere, Franco. *Vita amorosa di Claretta Petacci* (Milan: Lucchi, 1946).
Saini, Ezio. *La notte di Dongo* (Rome: Casa Editrice Libreria Corso, 1950).
Salotti, Guglielmo. *Nicola Bombacci da Mosca a Salò* (Rome: Bonacci, 1986).
Salvadori, Massimo. *The labour and the wounds: a personal chronicle of one man's fight for freedom* (London: Pall Mall Press, 1958).
Salvadori, Max. 'La fine di Mussolini', *Nuova Storia Contemporanea*, 8, 2004.
— 'Servizi segreti alleati e Resistenza' (ed. Giorgio Vaccarino) *Italia contemporanea*, 206, 1997.
Salvatori, Paolo S. *Mussolini e la storia: dal socialismo al fascismo (1900–1922)* (Rome: Viella, 2016).
Salvati, Mariuccia. *Il regime e gli impiegati: la nazionalizzazione piccolo-borghese nel ventennio fascista* (Bari: Laterza, 1992).
Sapio, Michaela. 'Gli ultimi giorni di Mussolini tra storia e verità: il rapporto del colonnello Lada Mocarski per conto dell'Oss', *Nuova Storia Contemporanea*, 13, 2009.
— 'Ma davvero è stata scritta la parola Fine? Considerazioni e documenti negli ultimi giorni di Mussolini', *Nuova Storia Contemporanea*, 13, 2009.
Saporito, Piero. *Empty balcony* (London: V. Gollancz, 1945).
Sarfatti, Margherita. *Acqua passata* (Rocca San Casciano, 1955).
— *Dux* (Milan: Mondadori, 1982; first published, 1926).
Sarfatti, Margherita G. *L'amore svalutato* (Rome: ERS, 1958).
— *The life of Benito Mussolini* (London: T. Butterworth, 1934).
Saunders, Frances Stonor. *The woman who shot Mussolini* (London: Faber and Faber, 2010).
Savona, Antonio V. and Michele L. Straniero. *Canti dell'Italia fascista (1919–1945)* (Milan: Garzanti, 1979).
Scaraffia, Lucetta. *La santa degli impossibili: vicende e significati della devozione a S. Rita* (Turin: Rosenberg and Sellier, 1990).
Schlemmer, Thomas. *Invasori non vittime: la campagna italiana di Russia, 1941–1943* (Rome: Laterza, 2009).
Schuster, Ildefonso. *Gli ultimi tempi di un regime* (Milan: La Via, 1945).
Scorza, Carlo. *La notte del Gran Consiglio* (Milan: Palazzi Editore, 1968).
'Scrivener, Jane' [Jessie Lynch]. *Inside Rome with the Germans* (New York: Macmillan, 1945).
Sebastian, Peter. *I servizi segreti speciali britannici e l'Italia (1940–1945)* (Rome: Bonacci, 1986).
Sebba, Anne. *That woman: the life of Wallis Simpson, duchess of Windsor* (London: Weidenfeld & Nicolson, 2011).
Senise, Carmine. *Quando ero capo della polizia 1940–1943* (Rome: Ruffolo Editore, 1946).
Serri, Mirella. *Un amore partigiano: storia di Gianni e Neri, eroi scomodi della Resistanza* (Milan: Longanesi, 2014).
Serri, Niccolò. 'Fascist imperialism and the Italian arms trade to Nationalist China 1929–1937', *Nuova Rivista Storica*, 99, 2015.
Servello, Franco and Luciano Garibaldi. *Perché uccisero Mussolini e Claretta: la verità negli archivi del PCI* (Soveria Mannelli: Rubbettino, 2012).

BIBLIOGRAPHY

Settimelli, Emilio. *Edda contro Benito: indagine sulla personalità del Duce attraverso un memoriale autografo di Edda Ciano Mussolini, qui riprodotto* (Rome: Casa Editrice Libreria Corso, 1952).
Siccardi, Cristina. *Maria José Umberto di Savoia: la fine degli ultimi regnanti* (Milan: Paoline Editoriale, 2004).
Sinopoli, Nicola. *Vito Casalinuovo e il diario di Clara* (Naples: G. Greco Editore, 1992).
Slaughter, Jane. *Women and the Italian Resistance 1943–1945* (Denver: Arden Press, 1997).
Soffici, Ardengo and Giuseppe Prezzolini. *Diari 1939–1945* (Milan: Edizioni del Borghese, 1962).
Somma, Luigi. *Mussolini morto e vivo* (Naples: Vito Bianco Editore, 1960).
Sorgi, Marcello. *Edda Ciano e il comunista: l'inconfessabile passione della figlia del Duce* (Milan: Rizzoli, 2009).
Spampanato, Bruno. *A Roma si vive così* (Milan: Mondadori, 1944).
— *Contromemoriale* (3 vols) (Rome: Edizione di "Illustrato", 1952).
— *L'Italia 'liberata' dopo la capitolazione* (Naples: Edizioni Illustrato, 1958).
'Spartacus' [Raffaele Offidani]. *Claretta: fiore del mio giardino* (np: Azione Lettaria Italiana, nd [1945]).
Spinosa, Antonio. *Edda: una tragedia italiana* (Milan: Mondadori, 1993).
— *I figli del Duce: il destino di chiamarsi Mussolini* (Milan: Rizzoli, 1989).
Staderini, Alessandra. *Fascisti a Roma: il partito nazionale fascista nella capitale (1921–1943)* (Rome: Carocci, 2014).
Staglieno, Marcello. *Arnaldo e Benito: due fratelli* (Milan: Mondadori, 2003).
Stafford, David. *Mission accomplished: SOE and Italy 1943–45* (London: Bodley Head, 2011).
Steyn, Mark. 'He made the refrains run on time: Romano Mussolini (1927–2006)', *Atlantic Monthly*, May 2006.
Strabolgi, Lord [Joseph Montague Kenworthy]. *The conquest of Italy* (London: Hutchinson, 1944).
Stratigakos, Despina. *Hitler at home* (London: Yale University Press, 2015).
Sturani, Enrico. *Otto milioni di cartoline per il Duce* (Turin: Centro Scientifico Editore, 1995).
Susmel, Duilio. *Mussolini e il suo tempo* (Cernusco sul Naviglio: Garzanti, 1950).
— *Vita sbagliata di Galeazzo Ciano* (Milan: Aldo Palazzi Editore, 1962).
Talamo, Giuseppe. *Il 'Messagero': un giornale durante il fascismo: cento anni di storia: vol. II, 1919–1946* (Florence: Le Monnier, 1984).
Talbot, George. 'Alberto Moravia and Italian Fascism: censorship, racism and *le ambizioni sbagliate*', *Modern Italy*, 11, 2006.
Taliani, Filippo Maria. *Vita del Cardinale Gasparri: segretario di stato e povero prete* (Milan: Mondadori, 1938).
Tarchi, Angelo. *Teste dure* (Milan: Editrice SELC, 1967).
Tarchi, Marco. *Cinquant'anni di nostalgia: intervista di Antonio Carioti* (Milan: Rizzoli, 1995).
Tassani, Giovanni. *Diplomatico tra due guerre: vita di Giacomo Paulucci di Calboli Barone* (Florence: Le Lettere, 2012).
Toeplitz, Ludovico. *Ciak a chi tocca* (Milan: Edizioni Milano Nuovo, 1964).
Tompkins, Peter. *L'altra resistenza* (Milan: Rizzoli, 1995).
— *Dalle carte segrete del Duce* (Milan: Marco Tropea Editore, 2001) .
Toscano, Pia. *Imprenditori a Roma nel secondo dopoguerra: industria e terziario avanzato dal 1950 ai nostri giorni* (Rome: Gangemi editore, 2010).
Tranfaglia, Nicola. *Un passato scomodo: Fascismo e postfascismo* (Bari: Laterza, 1996).
Trevelyan, Raleigh. *Rome '44: the battle for the Eternal City* (London: Pimlico, 2004).
Treves, Paolo. *What Mussolini did to us* (London: V. Gollancz, 1940).
Tripodi, Nino. *Il Fascismo secondo Mussolini* (Milan: Edizioni del Borghese, 1971).
Trizzino, Antonio. *Mussolini ultimo* (Milan: Casa Editrice Bietti, 1968).
Tronel, Jacky. 'Magda Fontanges: maîtresse du Duce, écrouée à Mauzac (Dordogne)', *Arkheia*, 17–8, 2007.

BIBLIOGRAPHY

Ullrich, Volker. *Hitler: ascent 1889–1939* (London: Bodley Head, 2016).
Ungari, Andrea. *Un conservatore scomodo: Leo Longanesi dal fascismo alla repubblica* (Florence: Le Lettere, 2007).
Urso, Simona. *Margherita Sarfatti: dal mito del Dux al mito americano* (Venice: Marsilio, 2003).
Vacca, Alberto. *Duce truce: insulti, barzellette, caricature: l'opposizione popolare al Fascismo nei rapporti segreti dei prefetti (1930–1945)* (Rome: Castelvecchi, 2011).
Valente, Paolo. *Porto di mare: Frammenti dell'anima multiculturale di una piccola città europea. Italiani (e molti altri) a Merano tra esodi, deportazioni e guerre (1934–1953)* (Trento: Temi 2005).
Veneziana, Bianca. *Storia italiana d'amore* (Milan: Garzanti, 1977).
Viganò, Marino. 'Il carteggio Mussolini–Churchill: una precisazione e una testimonianza', *Nuova Storia Contemporanea*, 8, 2004.
Visconti Prasca, Sebastiano. *Io ho aggredito la Grecia* (Milan: Rizzoli, 1946).
Vivarelli, Roberto. 'Di una pseudo-storia d'Italia', *Rivista Storica Italiana*, 121, 2009.
— *Fascismo e storia d'Italia* (Bologna: Il Mulino, 2008).
— *La fine di una stagione: memoria 1943–1945* (Bologna: Il Mulino, 2000).
— 'Le leggi razziali nella storia del fascismo italiano', *Rivista Storica Italiana*, 121, 2009.
Volpe, Anna. 'La contessa Brambilla', *Ventaglio 90*, 44, 2012.
Von Hassell, Ulrich. *The Von Hassell diaries 1938–1944* (London: Hamish Hamilton, 1948).
Weber, Max. *On charisma and institution building: selected papers* (ed. Shmuel N. Eisenstadt) (University of Chicago Press, 1968).
Welles, Sumner. *The time for decision* (London: Hamish Hamilton, 1944).
Whittle, Peter. *One afternoon at Mezzegra* (London: W.H. Allen, 1969).
Wieland, Karin. *Margherita Sarfatti: l'amante del Duce* (Trafarello: UTET, 2010).
Wildvang, Franke. 'The enemy next door: Italian collaboration in deporting Jews during the German occupation of Rome', *Modern Italy*, 12, 2007.
Zachiariae, Georg. *Mussolini si confessa* (rev. edn; Milan: BUR, 2004).
Zagheni, Guido. *La Croce e il Fascio: i cattolici italiani e la dittatura* (Cinisello Balsamo: Edizioni San Paolo, 2006).
Zamboni, Armando. *Personalità di Mussolini* (Pisa: Nistri-Lischi Editore, 1941).
Zanella, Alessandro. *L'ora di Dongo* (Milan: Rusconi, 2011).
Zangrandi, Ruggero. *Il lungo viaggio attraverso il fascismo: contributo alla storia di una generazione* (Milan: Feltrinelli, 1964).
Zatterin, Ugo. *Al Viminale con il morto: tra lotte e botte l'Italia di ieri* (Milan: Baldini e Castoldi, 1996).
Zeni, Marco. *La moglie di Mussolini* (Trento: Edizioni Effe e Erre, 2005).
Zimmerman, Joshua. *Jews in Italy under Fascist and Nazi rule, 1922–1945* (Cambridge University Press, 2005).
Zuccotti, Susan. *Under his very windows: the Vatican and the Holocaust in Italy* (New Haven: Yale University Press, 2002).

Films

L'amico delle donne (directed by Ferdinando Maria Poggioli, 1942).
Claretta (directed by Pasquale Squitieri, 1984).
Hotel Meina (directed by Carlo Lizzani, 2007).
L'invasore (directed by Nino Giannini, 1943).
Mussolini: ultimo atto (directed by Carlo Lizzani, 1975).
Quattro donne nella notte (directed by Henri Decoin, 1954).
Sogno d'amore (directed by Ferdinando Maria Poggioli, 1943).
Le vie del cuore (directed by Camillo Mastrocinque, 1942).
Vincere (directed by Marco Bellocchio, 2009).

INDEX

Abbazia (Opatija) 159
Abwehr 109
Accademia della musica (Turin) 75
Adami, Laura 33
Addis Ababa 99, 102
Adriatic 11, 62, 173
Adua (Adowa) 78
Africa Orientale Italiana (Italian East Africa) 98, 132, 141
Afrika Korps 141
Alban hills 88
Albania 124, 146–7
Albergo Nettuno 145
Albergo Parco 182
Alexandria 38, 97, 109
Alfa Romeo 4, 86, 222
Algeria 80, 164, 232
Alliata di Monreale, Giulia, principessa di Gangi 63
All Souls College, Oxford 20
Alto Adige/Süd Tirol 187, 199, 208, 211
Amba Alagi 101
Amedeo, duke of Aosta 141
Anarchism 39–40
Annales 238
Anschluss 100, 118, 130
anti-anti-Fascism 21, 52, 229
anti-Comintern Pact 70
anti-Communism 227
anti-Fascism 15, 21, 151
anti-Semitism 26, 43, 67, 119, 134, 137, 191, 245

Antonetti, Luciano 109
Apennines 175
Apollonio, Eugenio 213
Arabs 39–40, 115, 132–3, 163
Archivio Centrale dello Stato 24–5, 31, 247
Arenzano 166
Argentina 69, 233
Arizona 24
Armellini, Quirino 171
Assad family 244
Associazione di promozione sociale Casa Pound 21
Associazione National Ghost Uncover 4
Associazione Nazionalista Italiana (ANI; Italian Nationalist Association) 57
Athens 97, 141, 147
Audisio, Walter 223–4, 227
Augustus, emperor 39
Aurelian, emperor 62
Australia 5, 126, 139, 162
Austria 35, 37, 44, 49, 91, 96, 100, 130–1, 158, 178
Avanti! 37, 39, 44
Axis 17, 81, 111, 141–2, 166, 185, 224

Badoglio, Pietro 104, 141, 156, 169, 171, 173, 175, 192–3, 216
Balabanoff, Angelica 35–7, 72, 241
Balbo, Italo 33, 240
Balilla 157, 182
Balkans 141
Banca Nazionale del Lavoro 139, 149, 163

INDEX

Barcelona 132, 198, 220, 231
Barzini, Luigi vi
BBC (British Broadcasting Corporation) 2
Beauharnais, Josephine 32
Bedouins 31
Beethoven, Ludwig van 119, 147–8, 167, 235
Befana fascista 211
Belgium 98
Bellini delle Stelle, Pier Luigi 225–6, 229
Bellocchio, Marco 45
Belpietro, Mario 21
Benedict XV, pope 97
Berbers 163
Bergamo 182
Berlusconi, Silvio 4
Bernardi, Giulio 47
Bertolucci, Bernardo 85
Bianchi, Michele 33
Bianchi, Riccardo 79
Biennale (Venetian) 3, 152
Bigazzi Capanni, Emilio 200–1
Birkenhead, Frederick Smith, second earl of 2
Bismarck, Otto von 132
Blitz, the 176
Blum, Léon 129
Boccaccio, Giovanni 118
Bocchini, Arturo 33, 79, 109, 135
Boggiano, Armando 61, 153–6, 166, 171, 173, 176, 181–2, 190
Bokassa, Jean-Bédel 31–2
Bologna 42, 111
Bolshevism 150, 192, 209, 239
Bombacci, Nicolò 224, 228, 246
Bompiani 21–3
Bonaparte, Napoleon 129, 235
Bondanini, Colombo 54
Boniface VIII, pope 61
Bonzanigo 226, 231
Boothby, Robert 33
Boratto, Ercole 63, 70, 86
Borghese gardens 84
Borgo, Edmondo Michele 73–4
Borgo, Reginaldo 73
Borgo, Vanna 73
Bottai, Bruno 18
Bottai, Giuseppe 148, 153, 164, 169–70, 232, 240
Botturi-Polenghi family 5
Brard, Alfred 73
Brard, Magda 72–7
Brard, Roger 73
Braun, Eva 2, 239

Brazil 29
Brescia 66
Bressanone/Brixen 84
Brindisi 176
Britain 4, 26, 33, 45, 80, 111, 116, 129–31, 138–9, 141–3, 162–3, 166, 221, 227, 233, 241
Brittany 73
Brussels 57, 157
Budapest 155, 165, 188
Buenos Aires 233
Buffarini Guidi, Guido 76, 165, 169, 174, 190–1, 194, 201–2, 208, 213–14, 232
Burton, Richard 3

Caesar, Julius 2, 80, 110, 130, 142
Caligula, emperor 31, 154–6
Calle de Lagasca 231
Cameron, David 4
Campidoglio 56
Campo Imperatore 175
Campo Verano 7–9, 229
Campus Martius 173
Canada 162
Cannistraro, Philip 41–2, 61
Capitol 39
Caporetto 48
Cappa, Benedetta 32
Cappella del Sacro Cuore 51
Caprera 175
Capri 151, 233
Caproni factory 123
Carabinieri 150
Carboni, Giacomo 15
Cardinale, Claudia 3, 5
Carminati di Brambilla, Giulia (Giulia Matavelli), countess 63–5, 68, 73, 77, 93, 200
Carocci, Cesira 62–3, 183
Carol II, king 130
Carrà, Carlo 41
Casa del Fascio (Predappio) 11
Casella, Alfredo 119
Cassazione, court of 13, 162
Castello Visconteo-Sforzesco 174
Castelporziano 70, 86, 108, 112, 179
Catholicism 7, 26, 28, 34, 38, 46, 51, 58, 61, 83–4, 86, 91, 97, 104–5, 109, 115, 120, 133–4, 138, 145, 147, 150–1, 171, 177–8, 181, 205, 233, 236, 246

302

INDEX

Ceccato, Bianca 29, 48–9, 51–2, 72–4, 82, 89, 104, 237
Central African Republic 31
Centro Studi Romano Mussolini 11
Cerio, Ferruccio 231
Cervia 11
Cervis, Caterina 23, 25, 204
Chamberlain, Neville 111, 116, 131
Chambrun, Charles de 101
Charlemagne 32
Charles of Austria-Este, emperor 158
Cherubini, Luigi 151
Chiang Kai Shek (Jiǎng Jièshí) 87, 162
Chicago 54
China 87, 162
Chopin, Frédéric 118
Christian Democracy (Democrazia Cristiana) 14, 41
Churchill, Winston S. 19, 25–6, 53, 196, 221, 225, 241
Ciampino 104
Ciano, Costanzo 62
Ciano, Edda Mussolini 11, 17–18, 36–7, 39, 54, 87, 89, 103, 106, 112, 114, 123, 135, 148, 164, 167, 169–70, 175, 185–6, 190, 233, 240
Ciano, Fabrizio 11
Ciano, Galeazzo, count of Cortelazzo 4, 11, 17–18, 26, 33, 62, 84, 87, 102–3, 111, 114, 121, 135, 148, 154, 163–5, 169–71, 175, 185–7, 190, 210, 240
Ciminata, Antonio 157
Cinecittà 150–1, 153, 170
cinema 3, 13, 21, 32, 45, 96, 113, 144, 150–4, 197–8, 231
Coca-Cola 87
cocaine 150
Codreanu, Corneliu Zelea 10
Collegio Romano 173
Comitato di Liberazione Nazionale Alta Italia (CLNAI; Upper Italy Committee for National Liberation) 227
communism 10, 85, 113, 132, 142, 180, 209, 223, 227–8, 233, 244
Como 9, 42, 64, 69, 76–7, 200, 221–2, 233–4, 246
Compagnia italiana scambi estero ed Europa (the 'Italian exchange company with Europe and abroad') 164
Constantinople 38, 109
'continuation' 122, 237–9

Corriere della Sera, Il 19, 23
Corso Vittorio Emanuele 86, 105–6
Cortina 151, 154
Corvaja, Santi 13
Croatia 157, 220
Cuba 127
Curti, Angela Cucciati 53–4, 82, 140, 147
Curti, Bruno 53
Curti, Elena 52–4, 89–90, 140, 189, 197, 200, 207, 210, 212, 215, 222, 228, 237
Cyrenaica 39, 141
Czechoslovakia 130–1

D'Agostini, Rita 24–5
Daily Telegraph 2
Daladier, Édouard 131
Dallas 5
Dalmatia 84, 166
Dalser, Ida 37, 43–7, 49, 57, 60, 64, 72–3, 151, 237
D'Annunzio, Gabriele 5, 19, 23, 32, 42, 78, 151, 204
Dante Alighieri 57
D'Aroma, Nino 160
Darwinism 192, 236
De Felice, Renzo 14–15, 19–20, 27, 88
De Filippo, Eduardo 8
De Filippo, Peppino 8
De Grazia, Victoria 34
Dell'Utri, Marcello 20–3
De Maria family 226
De Marsanich, Augusto 84
Depression, Great 87
De Pilato, Ugo 7
De Spuches, Ines 66, 72–3, 210, 237
Diocletian, emperor 155
Di Rienzo, Eugenio 21
Di Salle, Giuseppe 51
Di Salle, Glauco 48, 51–2
Disraeli, Benjamin 129
Dolfin, Giovanni 184–5, 189
Dollfuss, Engelbert 91, 96, 130
Dollfuss family 96
Dollmann, Eugen 202
Donati, Mario 137, 157, 168
Donati, Pio 157
Dongo 13, 158, 223–5, 227–31
Donizetti, Gaetano 50
Dopolavoro 139
Duggan, Christopher 241
Dumas, Alexandre 152, 156

INDEX

Duranti, Doris 32, 150, 154
Duse, Eleonora 151
Dutch East Indies (Indonesia) 162

Ebner, Michael 243
Eden, Anthony 134
Egypt 38, 41
Erdödy, Rodolfo 154, 161
Ethiopia 47, 78–80, 98, 100, 103, 132, 134, 138, 141, 144, 148, 157, 175, 243
Esposizione Universale Romana (EUR) 24

Fabriano 77, 80, 148
Fallmayer, Hans 222
familism 52, 105, 156, 217, 237
Farinacci, Roberto 33, 197, 228, 232, 240
Farrell, Nicholas 3, 20
Fascio Parlamentare di Difesa Nazionale (Parliamentary Union for National Defence) 48
Fasci di combattimento (Fascist fighting leagues) 48
Fascism 1–2, 7–8, 11, 15, 17, 21, 79
  after 1945 9–10, 14–6, 49, 227
  French fascism 244
  as ideology 2, 6, 34, 42, 48, 67, 85, 101, 109, 138, 145, 156, 159–60, 165, 168, 170, 181, 183, 208, 215, 217, 236, 243–5
  as regime 9, 11, 32, 40, 54, 67, 109, 142, 169, 179, 244
Fascist Grand Council 15, 143, 171
Febvre, Lucien 238
Federazione Italiana del Cricket 18
Federici, Riccardo 83, 86, 88, 92–9, 103–5, 108, 165, 199
feminism 16, 42, 60, 68
Ferraris, Attilio 8
Festorazzi, Roberto 16, 53, 73, 76, 145
Fiat 182, 201, 227
Finaldi, Giuseppe 241
First World War 40, 162, 217, 244
Fitzpatrick, Sheila 239
Florence 10, 30, 77, 196
Foligno 4
Fonda, Henry 3
Fonseca, Edoardo 77
Fontanges, Magda (Madeleine Coraboeuf) 100–1
Forlì 11, 36, 40, 62, 207, 233
Formia 196
Forni, Cesare 64

Foro Italico (Foro Mussolini) 66
Forte Boccea 174
Forza Italia 20
Four-Power Pact (*Patto Mussolini*) 166
France 76, 81, 84, 112, 122, 131, 163, 166
France Soir 170
Francis of Assisi, saint 38, 57
Franco, Francisco 13, 103, 111, 132, 162–3, 168, 198, 214–15, 218, 220, 223, 231, 246
Franzinelli, Mimmo v, 19, 22, 25, 45, 77
Frascati 80
Freddi, Luigi 151, 153
Freemasonry 73, 171
French Revolution 67
Freud, Sigmund 115, 150, 181
Fromm, Erich 85
Fukuyama, Francis 244
Funk, Walther 143
Futurism 32, 38, 41, 207

Gadda, Carlo Emilio 30, 90, 236
Gaddafi, Muammar 31
Gaeta 196
Gaetani d'Aragona, Livio 61–2
Galicia 44
Gallarati Scotti, Tommaso 198
Galli, Giuseppe 157
Gardone 187, 205, 209
Gare du Nord 101
Gargnano 76, 184, 210
Garibaldi, Giuseppe 33–4, 102, 175
Gasparri, Pietro, cardinal 97, 105
Gastoni, Lisa 3
Gazzetta dello Sport, La 179
Gazzettinoi, Il 152
Genoa 78, 233
Genoa, Ferdinando, duke of 161
Gente 12
Gentile, Emilio 20, 21, 243
Geppert, Alexander 30–1
Gerarchia 61, 68
Germany 5–6, 10, 16–18, 22, 30, 65, 69–70, 76, 86–7, 91, 93, 96, 100–1, 104, 111, 114, 118, 120–1, 124, 129–131, 133–5, 141–2, 146, 162–3, 166, 169, 174–6, 180–7, 190, 194, 196, 200, 202, 204, 206, 208, 211–14, 221–4, 239, 245
Germasino 223, 225–6
Gervaso, Roberto 5
Giannini, Nino 153

INDEX

Gibson, Violet 56–9, 88, 97
Giraudoux, Jean 2
Giulino di Mezzegra 9, 226, 228
Giunta, Francesco 64
Goebbels, Joseph 130, 143, 152, 191
Goiran, Ildebrando 161
Gondar 141
Grand Hotel 155
Grandi, Dino 111, 169, 171, 240
Greece 124, 138, 141
Grottaferrata 88
Guadalajara 111
Guarda di Finanza 225
Guarda Nazionale Repubblicana (GNR; National Republican Guard) 66
Guardian 3
Guerri, Giordano Bruno 20–1
Guidi, Anna 36

Habsburg Empire 44, 158, 235
Hardouin di Gallese, Maria, principessa di Montenevoso 23, 204
Herriot, Édouard 129
Himmler, Heinrich 131, 194
Hindenburg, Paul von 91
Hitler, Adolf 2, 10, 16, 22, 30, 68, 86–7, 91, 93, 96, 113, 116, 121, 130–1, 134, 142, 175–6, 181, 183, 190, 192, 194, 196–7, 208, 238–9, 241, 245–6
Hoare, Samuel 162
Hochhuth, Rolf 2
Hollywood 113, 231
Holocaust 2, 26, 129, 238, 243
Hormovin 121, 140, 150, 167
Horthy, Miklós 168
Hotel Danieli 97
Hotel Dongo 228–9
Hotel Ritz (Barcelona) 198, 220, 231

Ibárruri, Dolores 132
India 162–3
Innsbruck 44
Iraq 7, 244
Ischia 18, 233
Isonzo river 37
Istanbul 97
Istituto cattolico di Sant'Apollinare 57
Istituto del Santissimo Crocefisso 7
Istituto Luce 121
Istria 157–8, 161, 242

Jackson, Glenda 2

Japan 5, 70, 103–4, 131, 142, 162, 188, 194, 199, 214
Jerusalem 97
Jesuits 61
John Paul II, pope 12

Kazakhstan 5
Kennedy, John F. 33
Kennedy, Joseph 4
Klessheim 194

La Fenice 10–11
Lago di Garda 4, 23, 78, 174, 184, 197, 199, 207, 216, 221
Lake Como 9, 42, 69, 77, 200, 221, 234, 246
Lake Lugano 222
L'Aquila 109
La Scala 51, 74
La Spezia 47, 161
Lateran Pacts 97
Lebanon 21
Le Corbusier (Charles-Édouard Jeanneret-Gris) 7
Legion of the Archangel Michael 10
Legione Autonoma Ettore Muti 229
Leonardo da Vinci airport 149
Leto, Guido 148
Libero 21, 23
Liberté 100
Libya 33, 39, 56, 66, 132, 141–2, 243
Lido, Roman 70, 81, 173, 175
Liguria 154
Lizzani, Carlo 3
Lodi 53
Lombardo, Ester 68
Lombardy 4–5, 47, 173
London 2, 111, 212
Lotta di Classe, La 36
Ludwig, Emil 34, 87
Lungotevere de' Cenci 59
Lupescu, Magda 130
Luxembourg 163

MacDonald, Robert 2
Machiavelli, Niccolò 2, 132–3, 162, 213, 245
Mack Smith, Denis 20, 30
Macmillan, Harold 33
Maddalena 175
Madonna of Pompeii (*la Beata Vergine del Santo Rosario di Pompei*) 105, 181–2
Madrid 162–3, 198, 206, 215, 231–2
Mafia 20, 237

305

INDEX

Maginot Line 120
Mainichi Nichinichi 188
Malcesine 187
Malpensa 220
Maltoni, Rosa 35, 52, 60
Mancini, Enrico 191, 197–8, 206, 214–15, 218–20
March on Rome 48, 52
Marche 77
Maremma 98
Maria Beatrice, princess 70
Maria Gabriella, princess 70
Maria José, crown princess 33, 70–2
Maria Pia, princess 70
Marinetti, Filippo Tommaso 32, 38, 42, 207
Marxism 35, 239, 244
Mastrocinque, Camillo 151–2
Matin, Le 100
Matteotti, Giacomo 54, 60, 137
Mazzini, Giuseppe 37
Medici del Vascello, Carla 228
Meina 173–4
Merano/Meran 6, 154, 182, 186, 190, 200, 205, 242
Merendi, Massimo 4
Messaggero, Il 8, 137–9, 155, 161, 172–3, 179
Mezzasoma, Fernando 191
Middle East 163
Midway, Battle of 142
Milan 1, 3, 10, 23, 37, 39–41, 44–5, 48–9, 53–4, 56, 61–3, 107, 137, 147, 150, 157–8, 166, 173, 189, 191, 200, 207–11, 214–18, 220–2, 227, 229, 231–2
Miller, Henry 242
Minardi, Giovanni 81, 103
Minardi, Massimo 81
Mirren, Helen 2
Missiroli, Mario 137
modernism 6, 61, 83, 107, 119, 149–50, 162
Molotov, Vyacheslav 121, 131
Monbello 47
Mondadori 10, 12, 19, 48
Monelli, Paolo 170, 173
Montagna, Renzo 174
Montanelli, Indro 30, 100
Monte Mario 6, 140
Montecassino 193
Monteverde 38, 57
Montevideo 69
Monti, Mario 22
Monza 157, 189, 222

Moravia, Alberto 84–5, 105
Moro, Aldo 14
Morocco 162
Moschi, Franco 11
Mostra della Rivoluzione Fascista 79
Movimento Sociale Italiano (MSI; Italian Social Movement – neo-fascists) 10–11, 24, 84
Munich 6, 175, 197
Munich conference 119, 130, 138
Musocco cemetery 231–2
Musso 223
Mussolini, Alessandra 11, 234
Mussolini, Alessandro 36, 87
Mussolini, Anna Maria 10, 55, 102, 113–14, 184, 206, 221, 233–4
Mussolini, Arnaldo 46, 54, 56, 82, 87, 147, 184–5, 240
'Mussolini', Benito Albino (Benittino) 43, 45–7, 237
Mussolini, Benito 14, 24–5, 30, 32, 85,
  and Claretta 1, 3, 5–10, 13–14, 16–18, 22–4, 26, 29, 32, 34, 38–9, 46, 52, 54, 57–9, 63–73, 76–8, 80–3, 87–130, 132–7, 141, 144–52, 154–5, 159, 164–71, 173, 176–232, 235–43, 245–6
  and the Devil 120
  'diaries' 19–23, 25, 27, 53
  as dictator 17, 26–7, 31, 33, 48, 54, 56–7, 59–62, 67, 82–3, 86–7, 90–1, 95–7, 99, 101–3, 106–7, 111–12, 115, 118–22, 124, 129–35, 137, 139, 141–3, 145–6, 148, 159–60, 162, 164–6, 169–71, 175–6, 183–5, 189–90, 195–7, 204, 207–10, 221, 223, 238–41, 243–5
  as ideologist 9–10, 16, 32, 34, 36–7, 39–40, 42–3, 67–9, 82, 87, 90–1, 93, 119, 129–35, 137, 141, 150, 159, 176, 183–4, 192, 213, 235, 238–9, 243–5
  and (legitimate) family 10–14, 16–18, 20, 22, 24–5, 35–9, 45–6, 51–2, 54, 57, 60, 62, 64, 72, 75–7, 87, 91, 101–3, 105, 107, 112, 123, 125–6, 143–6, 148–9, 153–4, 164–5, 167, 169–71, 175, 183–5, 187–8, 190, 193–4, 200–8, 212, 214, 217–19, 221–3, 225, 232–4, 236–7
  and lovers 4, 10, 29–31, 33–54, 59–83, 89, 99–101, 125–9, 140, 146–9,

306

INDEX

165–6, 171, 176, 189, 196, 199, 210, 215–16, 222, 236–7, 241
   as post-war myth 3, 6, 8–13, 15, 226
Mussolini, Bruno 14, 18, 37, 48, 53–4, 57, 62, 76, 103, 143–7, 167, 185, 233, 240
Mussolini, Edvige 10, 62, 101, 164
Mussolini, Marina 184, 211
Mussolini, Rachele Guidi 6, 11–12, 14, 16–19, 22–3, 29, 36–8, 41–2, 45–6, 48, 51–2, 54–5, 59–60, 62–4, 72, 77, 82–3, 102, 105, 114, 123, 125–6, 144–5, 147–8, 169–71, 180, 183–6, 192, 195, 197, 200–2, 204–5, 207, 212, 214–15, 218, 221, 232–3, 236–7
Mussolini, Romano 11, 20, 54, 72, 108, 184, 221, 233–4
Mussolini, Vito 184, 193
Mussolini, Vittorio 10, 37, 45, 54, 57, 62, 103, 113, 144, 153, 184, 188, 194, 207, 214, 224, 233
Muti, Ettore 33, 143, 175

Naifweg 162
Naples 50, 97, 176
NATO 104
Navarra, Quinto 30
Nazism 16–17, 43, 66, 70, 86, 96, 104, 130–1, 133, 140–3, 149, 157, 162, 181–4, 194, 211, 223, 237, 239, 245
neofascism 10, 19
neoliberalism 15, 244
Nero, emperor 31, 154
Nerone-Caligola (a cat) 154–5
New South Wales 79
New York 36, 73, 113
New Zealand 2, 5
Nice 74, 77
Nietzsche, Friedrich 40, 175
North Africa 39, 162–3
Northampton 56
Norton, Clifford 221
Novara 172, 174, 176–7, 181, 190
Novecento italiano 61
Nuova Rivista Storica 21

Obermais/Maia Alta 6, 154, 162
Oggi 12–3, 23
Olivier, Laurence 5
Olla, Roberto 30
Ono Shichiro 194

Orbetello 97
Orsini, Luigi 117
Osio, Arturo 163
Oss Facchinelli, Fernanda 35, 72–3
Ostia 81, 86, 88–9
Ostiense station 176
Ottoman Empire 38–9
OVRA (secret police) 148, 163

Pacific Ocean 142
Pachmann, Vladimir de 79
Palazzeschi, Aldo 152
Palazzi restaurant 7
Palazzo Venezia 30, 89, 93–4, 97, 104, 106, 108–10, 116–18, 121, 123, 167, 170, 209
Pálffy, Francesco Paolo 154, 161
Palladio, Andrea 7
Pallottelli, Adua 78
Pallottelli, Alice Corinaldesi de Fonseca 72, 77–80, 82, 85, 107, 125, 127–8, 140, 144, 146–8, 165, 171, 176, 180, 189, 200, 210, 237
Pallottelli, Duilio 78
Pallottelli, Francesco Corinaldesi, count 77–80, 176
Pallottelli, Virgilio 77, 80, 189, 222, 228
Panorama 49
Panvini Rosati, Amalia 19–20
Panvini Rosati, Giulio 19
Paolucci di Calboli, Giacomo 79
Parenzo (Poreč) 157–8
Paris 4, 44, 61, 69, 73, 76–7, 81, 92, 100–1, 129, 158
Parisi, Donatella 161
Partito Comunista Italiano (PCI; Italian Communist Party) 84–5, 227
Partito Fascista Repubblicano (PFR; Republican Fascist Party) 32–3
Partito Nazionale Fascista (PNF; National Fascist Party) 48, 57, 75, 90, 111, 133, 175
Partito Socialista Italiano (PSI; Italian Socialist Party) 37
Pavolini, Alessandro 32–3, 150, 152, 193, 224, 246
Pearl Harbor 142
Pellico, Silvio 178
Pensotti, Anita 14
Pergine 44, 46–7
Perón, Juan 233
Perrone, Mario 137

INDEX

Perrone, Pio 137
Persichetti, Augusto 38
Persichetti, Giuseppina *see* Petacci, Giuseppina
Persichetti, Guglielmo 109
Persichetti, Raffaele 176
Pertini, Sandro 230
Pesaro 80
Petacci, Benvenuto Edgardo ('Benghi') 13, 158–9, 219, 229, 232
Petacci, Claretta 33, 35–6, 43, 53, 77, 184, 189, 200–2, 235–6
   approaching sex 57–9, 86–102
   and her family
      brother 4, 6–7, 13, 24, 38–9, 94, 107, 112–13, 137, 140, 156, 159–60, 164, 168–9, 175, 181–2, 188, 191–3, 198, 219, 222, 224–5, 228–9, 231, 246
      father 7–8, 24, 38–9, 86, 88, 97, 99, 105, 107, 109–10, 136–8, 148, 154, 168, 172–4, 177–82, 190–1, 199, 220
      mother 7–8, 24, 38–9, 86, 88–9, 103–5, 107–10, 119, 148, 154, 156, 168, 173–4, 177–82, 199, 219, 231
      sister 3, 7–8, 13, 24, 39, 86, 89, 99, 108, 119, 135–6, 140, 150–4, 156, 160, 164, 168, 172–4, 177–83, 191, 194–5, 198, 211, 213–14, 218, 220, 231, 242
   as lover 6, 10, 17–18, 27–9, 32, 34, 43, 46, 52, 54, 63–73, 76–83, 102–10, 112–29, 144–50, 164–8, 170–3, 177–83, 186–8, 191–200, 202–7, 210–17, 219–23, 225–30, 234, 236–7, 239, 240–2
   as political adviser, audience and commentator 16, 28, 32, 111, 117, 119, 129–35, 141, 168–71, 176, 183–8, 190–200, 207–9, 212–15, 232, 241, 245–6
   post-war myth 1–17, 22–7, 232
Petacci, Edoardo (jun.) 109
Petacci, Edoardo (sen.) 38
Petacci, Ferdinando 9, 13, 24–6, 158, 221, 232
Petacci, Francesco Saverio 7–8, 24, 26, 38, 88, 97, 105, 109–10, 120–1, 124, 133, 136–40, 147, 149, 155, 157–8, 166, 168, 171–3, 177–8, 180, 190, 220, 222, 242
Petacci, Giuseppe 38
Petacci, Giuseppina Persichetti 7, 23–4, 38–9, 86, 89, 104–5, 107–10, 123, 149, 151, 155–6, 158, 166, 168, 170–3, 177–8, 180, 186, 190, 195, 205, 219, 231, 242
Petacci, Marcello 4, 6–7, 13, 24, 38–9, 55, 57–8, 85, 94, 98, 104, 107–8, 112–13, 137, 140, 143, 148, 151–2, 154–66, 168–9, 171, 174–5, 178, 181–2, 186, 188, 190–5, 198–200, 205, 215–16, 218–24, 228–9, 231–2, 242, 246
Petacci, Myriam 3, 7–8, 13, 24–5, 38–9, 61, 86, 89, 97, 99, 103–4, 108, 119, 135–6, 138, 140, 150–6, 160–1, 164, 166, 168, 170, 173–5, 177–9, 181, 183, 186, 191, 195, 197–9, 206, 211, 213–15, 218–20, 229, 231–2, 235, 242–3
Petazzi family 151, 158
Piazzale Loreto 1–2, 7, 229, 246
Piedmont 47, 173
Piovene, Guido 152
Pisa 2, 57, 143, 145, 157
Pius XI, pope 56, 97, 134
Pius XII, pope 2, 105, 134, 193
Plamper, Jan 238
Poggioli, Ferdinando Maria 152–3
Poland 2, 69, 87, 130–1
Ponte Chiasso 221
Pontine Marshes 139
Ponza 175, 183
Popolo d'Italia, Il 37, 44, 48–9, 62, 82, 113, 162
Portugal 69, 164, 218
Potocki, Wladislaw, 'count' 2
Pound, Ezra 2
Predappio 3, 11, 60, 123, 233
Prelli, Rosetta 19–20
Prezzolini, Giuseppe 42
Prussia 106, 114
Puccini, Giacomo 118

Quirinal 62
Quran 40

racism 139, 216, 237
Rafanelli, Leda 37, 39–43, 241
Ranke, Leopold von 14, 27
Rapallo 151
Rastenburg 183
Re, Emilio 23–4
Red Brigade 14
Reggio Emilia 37

INDEX

Regina Coeli prison 174
Repubblica Sociale Italiana (RSI; Italian Social Republic) 4, 10, 16–17, 19, 28, 52, 66, 76, 80, 104, 156, 188–91, 194, 198, 201, 209, 213, 221, 231, 241, 245
Riall, Lucy 34
Ribbentrop, Joachim von 121, 131
Riccardi, Arturo 163
Riccardi, Raffaello 163–5, 174
Riccardi, Roberto 163
Ricci, Umberto 75
Riccione 62, 91, 96, 109
Rimini 151
Risorgimento 33, 159, 178
Rita, saint (of Cascia) 1, 105, 182, 187, 194, 197, 211, 223, 242
Ritossa, Zita 13, 24, 107, 157–8, 160–2, 182, 186, 190, 221, 223, 232, 242
Rocca della Caminate 62, 121, 126, 181, 186, 193, 195, 199
Romagna 11, 23, 58, 60, 62, 100, 117, 200–1
Romania 10, 130
romanità 38–9, 54, 85, 213, 236
Romano, Ruggero 223–4
Rome 4, 6–9, 12, 21, 24, 37, 39, 44, 48, 51–4, 56–7, 61–2, 65, 74–5, 77–9, 81, 84–6, 88, 93, 97–100, 104, 106–7, 109, 111–12, 115, 119, 128, 130, 137, 139–40, 148–9, 153, 157–8, 161, 165–7, 173–6, 178–9, 189, 195–6, 212, 229, 232–3, 243
Rome Olympics 149
Rome University 20
Rommel, Erwin 141
Roosevelt, Franklin D. 134, 196, 216
Rosselli, Carlo 84, 112
Rosselli, Nello 84, 112
Rossellini, Roberto 153
Rossi, Cesare 46
Rossini, Gioachino 118
Rovigo 63
Ruberti, Gina 76, 143, 184, 202, 208, 212, 233
Ruspi, Renata 81
Ruspi, Romilda Minardi 72–3, 80–2, 85, 103, 107–8, 125–8, 136, 140, 144–8, 165–6, 171, 176, 180, 189, 196, 199–200, 207, 210–12, 214, 217, 222, 237
Russia 35, 72, 79, 131, 142, 180

Sacra Romana Rota 74
Saddam Hussein 244
St Moritz 156
St Peter's 58
Sala del Mappamondo 104, 106
Sala dello Zodiaco 106, 116–8, 121, 144, 147, 171, 180
Salò 4, 20, 150, 184, 186, 240
Salone Orientale d'Igiene e Bellezza Mademoiselle Ida 44
San Cassiano 233
San Clemente 47, 151
San Donnino 76, 232
San Giuseppe (Via Nomentana) 144
San Lorenzo 7
San Marco (Rome) 97
San Servolo 150–1
Sant'Apollinare 57
Santa Chiara 38, 169, 192
Santa Maria degli Angeli 155
Santo Spirito 99
San Vittore prison 229
Saolini, Luigi 13
Sardinia 166, 175, 183
Sarfatti, Amedeo 61, 69
Sarfatti, Cesare 41–2, 44, 59
Sarfatti, Fiammetta (Gaetani) 61, 69–70
Sarfatti, Margherita Grassini 29, 37, 41–4, 46, 55, 59–63, 66–70, 72–3, 75, 84, 107, 133, 136, 149, 181, 241
Sarfatti, Roberto 42
Sartoria Ventura 158
Saudi Arabia 244
Savoy dynasty 70, 86
Schuster, Alfredo Idelfonso 3, 221, 230
Schwarzkopf, Norman 5
Scorza, Carlo 143, 169, 171
Scuola di Mistica Fascista 149–50
Sebastiani, Osvaldo 112
Second World War II 48, 69–70, 73, 76, 121, 128, 142, 231, 238
Segal, Eric 49
Senise, Camillo 164
Serena, Adelchi 143
Serrano Suñer, Ramón 198, 218
Settimelli, Emilio 11
Shanghai 11, 87
Shimoi Harukichi 188
Shinrokuro Hidaka 194
Sicily 142
Simpson, Wallis 87
Snow White and the Seven Dwarfs 144

INDEX

socialism 35–9, 41–2, 44–5, 53–4, 157, 207, 209, 221, 224, 240, 244
Sondrio 49
Sopramonte 44
Sordi, Alberto 8
Sotheby's 20
Sotis, Gino 165
Spain 13, 17, 23, 52, 69, 111, 132, 144, 162–4, 168, 197–200, 206, 211, 213–16, 219, 223, 231–3
Spallanzani, Lazzaro 107
Spanish Civil War 103, 231
Spectator 3
Spögler, Franz 187, 206, 218
Squitieri, Pasquale 3, 21
SS (Schutzstaffel) 5, 131, 184–5, 187–8, 204, 216, 218
Stalin, Joseph 46, 142, 162, 239–41, 243, 245
Stalingrad 142
Starace, Achille 90–1, 112, 143, 230, 246
Stauffenberg, Klaus von 196
Steiger, Rod 3
Strauss-Kahn, Dominique 33
Stresa 151
Suetonius (Gaius Suetonius Tranquillus) 31
Sullivan, Brian 41–3, 61
Sunday Times, The 19
Suore di Carità Figlie di Nostra Signora al Monte Calvario 98
Suttora, Mauro 23, 25
Sweden 130
Switzerland 18, 22, 35–6, 72, 157, 163, 185, 188, 214, 221, 223, 225
syphilis 43, 67, 129, 156

Tacchi Venturi, Pietro 61
Tacitus (Publius Cornelius Tacitus) 31
Tanzi, Cornelia 65–6, 73, 134
Taranto 174
Tasso liceo, Torquato 62
Taylor, Liz 3
Teatro Lirico (Milan) 50, 208
Tel Aviv 113
Tempe 24
Tempo 13–14
Terminillo 107, 160, 175
Terni 233
Terracina 196
Teruzzi, Attilio 174
Texas 244
Tiber 54, 58

Tiberius, Emperor 31
Time-Life 19
Tokyo 103–4, 165, 188
Tolmezzo 35, 120
Torlonia, Giovanni 81
Torlonia, Maria in Sforza Cesarini 81
Torlonia family 63
Torre San Marco 5, 187
Tosetti, Max 5
totalitarianism 15, 27, 48, 112, 128, 133, 175, 185, 236, 243–6
Totò (Antonio De Curtis) 152
Tower of London 212
Trentino 6, 35, 47,
Trento 35, 44, 46–7
Treviso 49
Trieste 151, 158, 182, 217
Tripartite Alliance 104, 131
Tripoli 141
Tripolitania 39
Trump, Donald 238
Turin 73, 75, 143
Turkey 162
Tyrrhenian Sea 86

Umberto I, king 157
Umberto II, king 33, 70
Umbria 1
United Kingdom *see* Britain
Uruguay 69, 127
USA 9, 24, 36, 69, 77, 79, 113, 142, 162, 232, 244
USSR 46, 121, 142, 146, 162

Val Padana (Po Valley) 22, 244
Valori, Corrado 125
Valtellina 214, 233
Varese 199
Vassalli *gelateria* 4
Vatican 26, 38, 54, 82–3, 86, 88, 93, 97, 133, 162, 168–9, 232
Venice 3, 49, 51, 96–7, 149, 152, 159, 161, 166, 184, 191
Vercelli 19, 22
Verdi, Giuseppe 118–19
Verona 17, 176, 185, 210
Vezzari, Santorre 163–4
Via dei Villini 61
Via degli Astalli 106
Via della Camilluccia 6
Via delle Terme di Diocleziano 161
Via del Mare 88

INDEX

Via Margutta 65
Via Nazionale 38, 155, 172, 174
Via Nomentana 62, 77, 106, 144
Via Rasella 62–3, 75–6, 78, 180
Via Saffi 98
Via Spallanzani 106–7, 109, 127, 173
Via Tuscolana 150
Viale Adolf Hitler 176
Victor Emmanuel III, king (Vittorio Emanuele) 99, 104, 134, 153, 169, 175
Victor Emmanuel monument (Vittoriano) 39, 58
Victoria, queen 129
Vidussoni, Aldo 143
Villa Belmonte 9, 227
Villa Camilluccia 6–7, 15, 24, 114, 123–4, 147–50, 156, 166, 171, 173–4, 186, 188
Villa Carpena 11, 62, 118, 125–6, 233–4
Villa Crivelli Pusterla 47
Villa del Sole 98
Villa Feltrinelli 6, 184, 187, 193–5, 200–2, 204–5, 212, 233
Villa Fiordaliso 5, 187–8, 190, 194, 200–1, 204–5
Villa Gloria 77
Villa Mirabella 23, 204, 206–7, 217
Villa Roccabruna 76
Villa Schildhof 6, 154, 161–2, 182, 199, 205, 242
Villa Torlonia 12, 61–3, 74, 77–8, 80–1, 84, 87, 106, 114, 116, 121, 124–7, 149, 173
Villa Virgilio 77
Vittoriale degli Italiani 5, 23, 78, 204, 248
Vittorio Emanuele, prince 70
Vittorio Veneto 206
Vivaldi, Antonio 118, 167
Vivarelli, Roberto 245
Voce, La 42

Wagner, Richard 118
Washington, DC 2
Wild, Enrico 74
Wild, Micaela 74
World Cup 8

Yugoslavia 242

Zachariae, Georg 43, 184
Zerbino, Paolo 214, 224
Zionism 42
Zita, empress 158

ILLUSTRATION CREDITS

1 Ullstein bild via Getty Images. 3 Photo by Frieda Riess/Ullstein bild via Getty Images. 6 and 35 Ullstein/Lebrecht. 7 Alinari/Lebrecht. 13 Photo by Mondadori Portfolio via Getty Images. 20 Photo by © CORBIS/Corbis via Getty Images. 21 Permission granted by the Ministero per i Beni e le attività culturali, Central State Archive. 29 Luxardo. 33 Historical Archive – Istituto Luce Cinecittà.